Gift of Mr. Ca...

THE GREAT WORKS OF THE MEN WHO MADE AMERICA FREE

"Tyranny in every form, shape, and appearance was their disdain and abhorrence; no fear of punishment, nor even of death itself in exquisite tortures, had been sufficient to conquer that steady, manly, pertinacious spirit with which they had opposed the tyrants of those days in church and state. They were very far from being enemies to monarchy; and they knew as well as any men, the just regard and honor that is due to the character of a dispenser of the mysteries of the gospel of grace. But they saw clearly, that popular powers must be placed as a guard, a control, a balance, to the powers of the monarch and the priest, in every government, or else it would soon become the man of sin, the whore of Babylon, the mystery of iniquity, a great and detestable system of fraud, violence, and usurpation."

John Adams

ESSENTIAL WORKS OF THE FOUNDING FATHERS

The Editor:

Leonard Kriegel, assistant professor of English at City College of New York, earned his Ph.D. in American Civilization at New York University. The author of many articles on nineteenth-century American literature, he is also the author of an autobiography, THE LONG WALK HOME, and editor of THE LIFE AND REMARKABLE ADVENTURES OF ISRAEL POTTER, the book on which Melville based his famous novel.

BANTAM MATRIX EDITIONS

is a series of original and reprint works in the fields of mathematics, history, education, biology, philosophy, literary criticism and the other major disciplines. They are selected for the enduring insights they offer into the nature of the conditions which shape the life of man.

Matrix Editions in the field of History: AMERICAN FOREIGN POLICY TODAY / ESSENTIAL WORKS OF THE FOUNDING FATHERS / THE AMERICAN SCENE: 1600-1860 / FREEDOM IN THE ANCIENT WORLD / THE CONQUEST OF MEXICO.

BANTAM MATRIX EDITIONS

essential works of the founding fathers

•

Edited by
Leonard Kriegel
City College of New York

•

BANTAM BOOKS
NEW YORK/TORONTO/LONDON

ESSENTIAL WORKS OF THE FOUNDING FATHERS
Bantam Matrix Edition published November 1964

ACKNOWLEDGMENTS

Princeton University Press for the permission to reprint "A Summary View of the Rights of British America" and "The Declaration of Independence" from The Papers of Thomas Jefferson, *edited by Julian P. Boyd, 1950.*

Wesleyan University Press for permission to reprint selected papers from The Federalist, *edited by Jacob E. Cooke, 1961.*

Library of Congress Catalog Card Number: 64-25019

Bantam Books are published by Bantam Books, Inc. Its trade-mark, consisting of the words "Bantam Books" and the portrayal of a bantam, is registered in the United States Patent Office and in other countries. Marca Registrada. Printed in the United States of America. Bantam Books, Inc., 271 Madison Ave., New York 16, N. Y.

For my brother

CONTENTS

PART I

THE ORIGINS OF THE AMERICAN REVOLUTION

Perhaps no period in American history has been as victimized by the blending of history with popular mythology as has the period of the American Revolution. Not only have the Founding Fathers themselves been placed into a dehumanized political pantheon, but their ideas have frequently been embalmed with a scriptural authority that borders on religious dogma. Where they approached the problems of government in the spirit of rational and pragmatic inquiry, where they felt far too much respect for ideas to view their purveyors as sacrosanct, we often approach their ideas as necessarily applicable to our own time and situation. Criticism of present American foreign policy based upon Washington's *Farewell Address,* in which he warned the nation against entangling foreign alliances, is the most obvious example of this. But the Founding Fathers would probably be the first to assert that Washington's arguments are inapplicable today. We are no longer, as we were then, a relatively weak nation separated from Europe by weeks of ocean travel. There may be valid reasons for criticizing our foreign policy, but they are not the reasons cited by Washington in his *Farewell Address.*

But "the generation which commences a revolution rarely completes it," as Jefferson wrote to John Adams in 1823. Nor does it have the opportunity to see what posterity has made of its efforts. One wonders what Jefferson would think of the nation he helped to create, with its huge industrial working class, its political and religious conservatism, its sprawling cities, its factories, its massive military machine, its racial problems. And what would Jefferson, that child of eighteenth-century rationalism, say to the numerous political parties and groups which claim him as their own, a claim usually pressed with the vehement intolerance and religious fervor so characteristic of all he fought against?

Like Jefferson himself, the American Revolution was the product of the eighteenth-century Enlightenment. Its intellectual foundations were rational and empirical; its leaders men of culture and learning, convinced of the feasibility of applying such knowledge to the affairs of men; its optimism nourished by a belief in the natural rights philosophy and an idea of human progress based upon faith in man's rational potential. If the ideas which helped generate the Revolution antedate the Enlightenment (some of them are to be found in the Old Testament and in the works of Plato and Aristotle), it was the Enlightenment which produced those thinkers who directly fed the Founding Fathers.

The philosophers and politicians who influenced the colonists—Locke, Harrington, Hume, Cromwell—were predominantly English, and, since the colonists considered themselves Englishmen, the Revolution itself was, on the level of political heritage at least, a war to maintain those rights which were looked upon as the natural rights of Englishmen. Though now seen as an inevitable conflict, the colonists entered the Revolution with the utmost hesitation and a great deal of moral apprehension. To hope that reason and law would produce a sensible retreat on the part of parliament may seem to us a vain hope, but the writings of the Fathers indicate that this was their hope. John Dickinson was so opposed to the use of force, so fearful of a break in the traditional allegiance of colonies to crown, that he could not bring himself to vote for independence. For even if the Declaration of Independence were based upon reason and the doctrine of natural rights, even if it were an almost perfect reflection of the Enlightenment mind, it nonetheless threatened to turn the world upside down by destroying the relationship of subject to sovereign. And Dickinson feared, as a number of his colleagues feared, that such a course could only result in anarchy—that most dreaded disease of the body politic.

From the end of the French and Indian Wars in 1763 to the adoption of the Declaration of Independence in 1776, the struggle between parliament and colonies grew in intensity and scope. The fundamental question upon which they could not agree was that of equality: were the colonies to continue as subordinate to the interests of England, or was the relationship between colonies and mother country to be transformed into a relationship of equals? The Treaty of Paris of 1763 ended what Edmund Burke called parliament's "salutary neglect" of the colonies. England emerged as the most powerful empire in the world, endowed with a huge post-war debt, heavy taxation at home, and the necessity of supporting troops throughout the empire. Not to have chosen to alleviate the financial burden at home by raising revenue in the colonies would have required farsighted statesmanship, but the ministries which ruled England from 1763 to the outbreak of the Revolution were not particularly farsighted. The temptation of gaining popularity at home by raising revenue elsewhere could be defended on any number of grounds, not the least of which was the pragmatic justification of the politician for anything that served to increase his popularity.

By 1763, the colonies had achieved a degree of material prosperity that brought with it not merely self-assurance but an as yet unformulated belief that the relations of men to each other and to the state were finding a new definition in America. Given the kind of frontier existence which characterized life in the colonies, it was almost inevitable that the hereditary class distinctions of England and Europe would not mean very much in an environment which demanded that an individual prove himself solely on his merits as an individual. Jefferson's natural aristocracy had much in common with Rousseau—but it should be remembered that Jefferson had seen his theories tested and re-tested on the American frontier. When Jefferson wrote in his *Autobiography* that his mother's family, the Randolphs, "trace their pedigree far back in England and Scotland," he was quick to follow it with the laconic "to which let every one ascribe the faith and merit he chooses." For Jefferson, and for the majority of his colleagues, "that all men are created equal, that they are endowed by their Creator with certain unalienable rights" were, indeed, "self-evident" truths. The equality of men, while undoubtedly a manifestation of the foremost desires of the Enlightenment, was also a product of the American environment, where natural talent was far more important than birth as far as a man's ability to survive and prosper were concerned.

It would be inaccurate to claim that the Fathers were all exponents of democracy. With a few notable exceptions, they were members of the upper segments of colonial society, were well educated, and viewed the general populace from spectrums that ranged from charitable suspicion to forthright scorn. But the sources of American democracy are to be found in what they wrote and said. From the idea of natural aristocracy to the glorification of that undefined creature, the common man, one finds a consistent and logical development. Once hereditary aristocracy had been dismissed, it was but a short step to where natural aristocracy was conceived of as embracing all men. Just as the Revolution was planted in the natural rights philosophy of John Locke and other English constitutionalists, so the triumph of Jacksonian democracy had its origins in the Declaration of Independence. The "self-evident" equality of birth evolved into the manifest equality of the ballot, and the humanitarianism of Paine and Jefferson found a fuller expression in the reign of "King Andrew."

The inherent democracy of the Revolution is basic to an understanding of it, since so much recent historical scholarship has attempted to prove its fundamentally conservative character. Focusing almost exclusively on the conservative, constitutional heritage, many scholars have ignored the vigorous radicalism of the Founding Fathers. But the Revolution, if looked upon exclusively as the product of English constitutionalism, becomes far more conservative than it actually was. Without attempting to interpret it as a social and political millennium, one does find in the American Revolution a basically radical expression of human needs and human rights. The Declaration of Independence remains as important to an understanding of the Revolution as the Constitution.

Until the Declaration of Independence, most of the writings of the Fathers were simply vindications of the colonial position. Their immediate occasion was parliament's attempt to raise revenue by taxing the colonists. But the argument which began over taxation soon turned into a general investigation of what the rights of the colonists were. The "rights of Englishmen" needed further defining. "No taxation without representation" really meant no taxation—by parliament or any other non-colonial body. When the colonists were told that they had "virtual" representation in parliament, they were quick to point out that since their interests were not the same as those of England, there could be no such thing as virtual representation. Nor did the great majority of colonists want actual representation in a legislative body where their interests were bound to be in a small minority. The Stamp Act Congress of 1765, in its *Declaration of Rights and Grievances,* after rejecting taxation without the consent of the taxed as a violation of the basic rights of the colonists, went on to reject representation in parliament when it declared, "That the People of these Colonies are not, and from their local Circumstances cannot be, Represented in the House of Commons in Great-Britain."

The heart of the argument over taxation was whether or not the colonies were to be controlled by parliament. Possessing the natural right to exercise authority over themselves, the colonists soon became convinced that they shared with parliament only a common heritage of individual liberty and a common allegiance to the king. Once parliament's right to tax had been questioned, then parliament's right to govern had been questioned. From the passage of the Sugar Act in 1764 to the outbreak of actual hostilities at Lexington and Concord in 1775, the relationship between England and the colonies remained undefined. And, while they were reluctant to admit it even to themselves, the colonists were actually arguing that no such relationship really existed, that they, and they alone, had the right to legislate where their own self-interests were concerned.

Thus, what began as a constitutional argument was soon to embrace far more than constitutionalism. James Otis' *The Rights of the British Colonies Asserted and Proved,* published in the summer of 1764, is almost exclusively concerned with parliament's power over the colonies, particularly its power to tax. But a year later, the young John Adams, in *A Dissertation on the Canon and the Feudal Law,* has already broadened the controversy into a discussion of the very nature of freedom and liberty. Otis' pamphlet had a greater immediate effect upon the colonies, but if we wish to understand the spirit of the times, it is Adams' essay to which we must turn. Adams attempted to analyze what the nature of American liberty was; in his essay, he offered an American (or, more exactly, a New England) tradition, which was distinct from, although it drew upon, the English tradition. An emergent American nationalism is to be found in Adams' celebration of the Puritan heritage, his praise of American literacy and independence, his anti-papal prejudices. In a letter written more than thirty years after the successful culmination of the Revolution, Adams said, "The revolution was effected before the war commenced. The revolution was in the minds and hearts of the people." The American Revolution was not alone the product of a constitutional opposition to taxation; it was rather a recognition that the rights of Englishmen were the rights of all men.

Note: The numbered footnotes in the text are the editor's.

JOHN ADAMS Adams' first major contribution to American political writing was originally published in the *Boston Gazette*. Although he himself was later to dismiss it as a "lamentable bagatelle," it remains of great interest to any student of the Revolution. Arguing from a decisively American vantage point, Adams embraces the concept of America as a chosen land, a legacy from New England Puritanism. Adams, who was to grow more conservative after independence became a reality, was at this time emerging as one of the leaders of the radical faction among the colonists. And *A Dissertation* is as radical a document as any he penned, coming close to the "romantic idealism" Vernon Louis Parrington claimed he scorned. The work of an incisive political mind, the essay is rooted in a knowledge of history and a passionate belief in the necessity of liberty.

Text: Charles Francis Adams, ed., *The Works of John Adams*. Boston, 1851.

A Dissertation on the Canon and the Feudal Law (1765)

"Ignorance and inconsideration are the two great causes of the ruin of mankind." This is an observation of Dr. Tillotson, with relation to the interest of his fellow men in a future and immortal state.[1] But it is of equal truth and importance if applied to the happiness of men in society, on this side the grave. In the earliest ages of the world, absolute monarchy seems to have been the universal form of government. Kings, and a few of their great counsellors and captains, exercised a cruel tyranny over the people, who held a rank in the scale of intelligence, in those days, but little higher than the camels and elephants that carried them and their engines to war.

By what causes it was brought to pass, that the people in the middle ages became more intelligent in general, would not, perhaps, be possible in these days to discover. But the fact is certain; and wherever a general knowledge and sensibility have prevailed among the people, arbitrary government and every kind of oppression have lessened and disappeared in

[1] John Tillotson (1630–1694) was a prominent religious writer and preacher who became Archbishop of Canterbury in 1691.

proportion. Man has certainly an exalted soul; and the same principle in human nature,—that aspiring, noble principle founded in benevolence, and cherished by knowledge; I mean the love of power, which has been so often the cause of slavery,—has, whenever freedom has existed, been the cause of freedom. If it is this principle that has always prompted the princes and nobles of the earth, by every species of fraud and violence to shake off all the limitations of their power, it is the same that has always stimulated the common people to aspire at independency, and to endeavor at confining the power of the great within the limits of equity and reason.

The poor people, it is true, have been much less successful than the great. They have seldom found either leisure or opportunity to form a union and exert their strength; ignorant as they were of arts and letters, they have seldom been able to frame and support a regular opposition. This, however, has been known by the great to be the temper of mankind; and they have accordingly labored, in all ages, to wrest from the populace, as they are contemptuously called, the knowledge of their rights and wrongs, and the power to assert the former or redress the latter. I say RIGHTS, for such they have, undoubtedly, antecedent to all earthly government,—*Rights*, that cannot be repealed or restrained by human laws—*Rights*, derived from the great Legislator of the universe.

Since the promulgation of Christianity, the two greatest systems of tyranny that have sprung from this original, are the canon and the feudal law. The desire of dominion, that great principle by which we have attempted to account for so much good and so much evil, is, when properly restrained, a very useful and noble movement in the human mind. But when such restraints are taken off, it becomes an encroaching, grasping, restless, and ungovernable power. Numberless have been the systems of iniquity contrived by the great for the gratification of this passion in themselves; but in none of them were they ever more successful than in the invention and establishment of the canon and the feudal law.

By the former of these, the most refined, sublime, extensive, and astonishing constitution of policy that ever was conceived by the mind of man was framed by the Romish clergy for the aggrandisement of their own order.* All the epithets I have here given to the Romish policy are just, and will be allowed to be so when it is considered, that they even persuaded man-

* Robertson's History of Charles V. ch. v. pp. 54, 141, 315.

kind to believe, faithfully and undoubtingly, that God Almighty had entrusted them with the keys of heaven, whose gates they might open and close at pleasure; with a power of dispensation over all the rules and obligations of morality; with authority to license all sorts of sins and crimes; with a power of deposing princes and absolving subjects from allegiance; with a power of procuring or withholding the rain of heaven and the beams of the sun; with the management of earthquakes, pestilence, and famine; nay, with the mysterious, awful, incomprehensible power of creating out of bread and wine the flesh and blood of God himself. All these opinions they were enabled to spread and rivet among the people by reducing their minds to a state of sordid ignorance and staring timidity, and by infusing into them a religious horror of letters and knowledge. Thus was human nature chained fast for ages in a cruel, shameful, and deplorable servitude to him, and his subordinate tyrants, who, it was foretold, would exalt himself above all that was called God, and that was worshipped.

In the latter we find another system, similar in many respects to the former;* which, although it was originally formed, perhaps, for the necessary defence of a barbarous people against the inroads and invasions of her neighboring nations, yet for the same purposes of tyranny, cruelty, and lust, which had dictated the canon law, it was soon adopted by almost all the princes of Europe, and wrought into the constitutions of their government. It was originally a code of laws for a vast army in a perpetual encampment. The general was invested with the sovereign propriety of all the lands within the territory. Of him, as his servants and vassals, the first rank of his great officers held the lands; and in the same manner the other subordinate officers held of them; and all ranks and degrees held their lands by a variety of duties and services, all tending to bind the chains the faster on every order of mankind. In this manner the common people were held together in herds and clans in a state of servile dependence on their lords, bound, even by the tenure of their lands, to follow them, whenever they commanded, to their wars, and in a state of total ignorance of every thing divine and human, excepting the use of arms and the culture of their lands.

But another event still more calamitous to human liberty, was a wicked confederacy between the two systems of tyranny

* Rob. Hist. ch. v. pp. 178–9, &c.

above described. It seems to have been even stipulated between them, that the temporal grandees should contribute every thing in their power to maintain the ascendency of the priesthood, and that the spiritual grandees in their turn, should employ their ascendency over the consciences of the people, in impressing on their minds a blind, implicit obedience to civil magistracy.

Thus, as long as this confederacy lasted, and the people were held in ignorance, liberty, and with her, knowledge and virtue too, seem to have deserted the earth, and one age of darkness succeeded another, till God in his benign providence raised up the champions who began and conducted the Reformation. From the time of the Reformation to the first settlement of America, knowledge gradually spread in Europe, but especially in England; and in proportion as that increased and spread among the people, ecclesiastical and civil tyranny, which I use as synonymous expressions for the canon and feudal laws, seem to have lost their strength and weight. The people grew more and more sensible of the wrong that was done them by these systems, more and more impatient under it, and determined at all hazards to rid themselves of it; till at last, under the execrable race of the Stuarts, the struggle between the people and the confederacy aforesaid of temporal and spiritual tyranny, became formidable, violent, and bloody.

It was this great struggle that peopled America. It was not religion alone, as is commonly supposed; but it was a love of universal liberty, and a hatred, a dread, a horror, of the infernal confederacy before described, that projected, conducted, and accomplished the settlement of America.

It was a resolution formed by a sensible people,—I mean the Puritans,—almost in despair. They had become intelligent in general, and many of them learned. For this fact, I have the testimony of Archbishop King himself, who observed of that people, that they were more intelligent and better read than even the members of the church, whom he censures warmly for that reason.[2] This people had been so vexed and tortured by the powers of those days, for no other crime than their knowledge and their freedom of inquiry and examination, and they had so much reason to despair of deliverance from those miseries on that side the ocean, that they at last resolved to fly to the wilderness for refuge from the temporal

[2] John King (1559?–1621) was an Anglican clergyman who served as Bishop of London from 1611 until his death.

and spiritual principalities and powers, and plagues and scourges of their native country.

After their arrival here, they began their settlement, and formed their plan, both of ecclesiastical and civil government, in direct opposition to the canon and the feudal systems. The leading men among them, both of the clergy and the laity, were men of sense and learning. To many of them the historians, orators, poets, and philosophers of Greece and Rome were quite familiar; and some of them have left libraries that are still in being, consisting chiefly of volumes in which the wisdom of the most enlightened ages and nations is deposited,—written, however, in languages which their great-grandsons, though educated in European universities, can scarcely read.*

Thus accomplished were many of the first planters in these colonies. It may be thought polite and fashionable by many modern fine gentlemen, perhaps, to deride the characters of these persons, as enthusiastical, superstitious, and republican. But such ridicule is founded in nothing but foppery and affectation, and is grossly injurious and false. Religious to some degree of enthusiasm it may be admitted they were; but this can be no peculiar derogation from their character; because it was at that time almost the universal character not only of England, but of Christendom. Had this, however, been otherwise, their enthusiasm, considering the principles on which it was founded and the ends to which it was directed, far from being a reproach to them, was greatly to their honor; for I believe it will be found universally true, that no great enterprise for the honor or happiness of mankind was ever achieved without a large mixture of that noble infirmity. Whatever imperfections may be justly ascribed to them, which, however, are as few as any mortals have discovered, their judgment in framing their policy was founded in wise, humane, and benevolent principles. It was founded in revelation and in reason too. It was consistent with the principles of the best and greatest and wisest legislators of antiquity. Tyranny in every form, shape, and appearance was their disdain and abhorrence; no fear of punishment, nor even of death itself in exquisite tortures, had been sufficient to conquer that steady, manly, pertinacious spirit with which they had opposed the

* "I always consider the settlement of America with reverence and wonder, as the opening of a grand scene and design in Providence for the illumination of the ignorant, and the emancipation of the slavish part of mankind all over the earth."

tyrants of those days in church and state. They were very far from being enemies to monarchy; and they knew as well as any men, the just regard and honor that is due to the character of a dispenser of the mysteries of the gospel of grace. But they saw clearly, that popular powers must be placed as a guard, a control, a balance, to the powers of the monarch and the priest, in every government, or else it would soon become the man of sin, the whore of Babylon, the mystery of iniquity, a great and detestable system of fraud, violence, and usurpation. Their greatest concern seems to have been to establish a government of the church more consistent with the Scriptures, and a government of the state more agreeable to the dignity of human nature, than any they had seen in Europe, and to transmit such a government down to their posterity, with the means of securing and preserving it forever. To render the popular power in their new government as great and wise as their principles of theory, that is, as human nature and the Christian religion require it should be, they endeavored to remove from it as many of the feudal inequalities and dependencies as could be spared, consistently with the preservation of a mild limited monarchy. And in this they discovered the depth of their wisdom and the warmth of their friendship to human nature. But the first place is due to religion. They saw clearly, that of all the nonsense and delusion which had ever passed through the mind of man, none had ever been more extravagant than the notions of absolutions, indelible characters, uninterrupted successions, and the rest of those fantastical ideas, derived from the canon law, which had thrown such a glare of mystery, sanctity, reverence, and right reverend eminence and holiness, around the idea of a priest, as no mortal could deserve, and as always must, from the constitution of human nature, be dangerous in society. For this reason, they demolished the whole system of diocesan episcopacy; and, deriding, as all reasonable and impartial men must do, the ridiculous fancies of sanctified effluvia from episcopal fingers, they established sacerdotal ordination on the foundation of the Bible and common sense. This conduct at once imposed an obligation on the whole body of the clergy to industry, virtue, piety, and learning, and rendered that whole body infinitely more independent on the civil powers, in all respects, than they could be where they were formed into a scale of subordination, from a pope down to priests and friars and confessors,—necessarily and essentially a sordid, stupid, and wretched herd,—or than they could be in any other country, where an archbishop held the place of a universal bishop, and the vicars and curates that of the ignorant, dependent, miserable rabble aforesaid,—and infinitely more sensible and learned than they could be in either. This subject has been seen in the same light by many illustrious patriots, who have lived in America since the days of our forefathers, and who have adored their memory for the same reason. And methinks there has not appeared in New England a stronger veneration for their memory, a more penetrating insight into the grounds and principles and spirit of their policy, nor a more earnest desire of perpetuating the blessings of it to posterity, than that fine institution of the late Chief Justice Dudley, of a lecture against popery, and on the validity of presbyterian ordination.[3] This was certainly intended by that wise and excellent man, as an eternal memento of the wisdom and goodness of the very principles that settled America. But I must again return to the feudal law. The adventurers so often mentioned, had an utter contempt of all that dark ribaldry of hereditary, indefeasible right,—the Lord's anointed, —and the divine, miraculous original government, with which the priesthood had enveloped the feudal monarch in clouds and mysteries, and from whence they had deduced the most mischievous of all doctrines, that of passive obedience and non-resistance. They knew that government was a plain, simple, intelligible thing, founded in nature and reason, and quite comprehensible by common sense. They detested all the base services and servile dependencies of the feudal system. They knew that no such unworthy dependencies took place in the ancient seats of liberty, the republics of Greece and Rome; and they thought all such slavish subordinations were equally inconsistent with the constitution of human nature and that religious liberty with which Jesus had made them free. This was certainly the opinion they had formed; and they were far from being singular or extravagant in thinking so. Many celebrated modern writers in Europe have espoused the same sentiments. Lord Kames, a Scottish writer of great reputation, whose authority in this case ought to have the more weight as his countrymen have not the most worthy ideas of liberty, speaking of the feudal law, says,—"A constitution so contradictory to all the principles which govern mankind can never be brought about, one should imagine, but by

[3] Paul Dudley (1675–1751) was Chief Justice of Massachusetts Bay from 1745 until his death.

foreign conquest or native usurpations."*[4] Rousseau, speaking of the same system, calls it,—"That most iniquitous and absurd form of government by which human nature was so shamefully degraded."† It would be easy to multiply authorities, but it must be needless; because, as the original of this form of government was among savages, as the spirit of it is military and despotic, every writer who would allow the people to have any right to life or property or freedom more than the beasts of the field, and who was not hired or enlisted under arbitrary, lawless power, has been always willing to admit the feudal system to be inconsistent with liberty and the rights of mankind.

To have holden their lands allodially, or for every man to have been the sovereign lord and proprietor of the ground he occupied, would have constituted a government too nearly like a commonwealth. They were contented, therefore, to hold their lands of their king, as their sovereign lord; and to him they were willing to render homage, but to no mesne or subordinate lords; nor were they willing to submit to any of the baser services. In all this they were so strenuous, that they have even transmitted to their posterity a very general contempt and detestation of holdings by quitrents, as they have also a hereditary ardor for liberty and thirst for knowledge.

They were convinced, by their knowledge of human nature, derived from history and their own experience, that nothing could preserve their posterity from the encroachments of the two systems of tyranny, in opposition to which, as has been observed already, they erected their government in church and state, but knowledge diffused generally through the whole body of the people. Their civil and religious principles, therefore, conspired to prompt them to use every measure and take every precaution in their power to propagate and perpetuate knowledge. For this purpose they laid very early the foundations of colleges, and invested them with ample privileges and emoluments; and it is remarkable that they have left among their posterity so universal an affection and veneration for those seminaries, and for liberal education, that the meanest of the people contribute cheerfully to the support and maintenance of them every year, and that nothing is more generally popular than projections for the honor, reputation, and advantage of those seats of learning. But the

* Brit. Ant. p. 2.
[4] Henry Home (1696–1782), Lord Kames, was a Scottish jurist and author.
† Social Compact, page 164.

wisdom and benevolence of our fathers rested not here. They made an early provision by law, that every town consisting of so many families, should be always furnished with a grammar school. They made it a crime for such a town to be destitute of a grammar schoolmaster for a few months, and subjected it to a heavy penalty. So that the education of all ranks of people was made the care and expense of the public, in a manner that I believe has been unknown to any other people ancient or modern.

The consequences of these establishments we see and feel every day. A native of America who cannot read and write is as rare an appearance as a Jacobite or a Roman Catholic, that is, as rare as a comet or an earthquake. It has been observed, that we are all of us lawyers, divines, politicians, and philosophers. And I have good authorities to say, that all candid foreigners who have passed through this country, and conversed freely with all sorts of people here, will allow, that they have never seen so much knowledge and civility among the common people in any part of the world. It is true, there has been among us a party for some years, consisting chiefly not of the descendants of the first settlers of this country, but of high churchmen and high statesmen imported since, who affect to censure this provision for the education of our youth as a needless expense, and an imposition upon the rich in favor of the poor, and as an institution productive of idleness and vain speculation among the people, whose time and attention, it is said, ought to be devoted to labor, and not to public affairs, or to examination into the conduct of their superiors. And certain officers of the crown, and certain other missionaries of ignorance, foppery, servility, and slavery, have been most inclined to countenance and increase the same party. Be it remembered, however, that liberty must at all hazards be supported. We have a right to it, derived from our Maker. But if we had not, our fathers have earned and bought it for us, at the expense of their ease, their estates, their pleasure, and their blood. And liberty cannot be preserved without a general knowledge among the people, who have a right, from the frame of their nature, to knowledge, as their great Creator, who does nothing in vain, has given them understandings, and a desire to know; but besides this, they have a right, an indisputable, unalienable, indefeasible, divine right to that most dreaded and envied kind of knowledge, I mean, of the characters and conduct of their rulers. Rulers are no more than attorneys, agents, and trustees, for the people; and if the cause, the interest and trust, is insidiously betrayed, or wantonly trifled away, the people have a right to revoke the authority that they themselves deputed, and to constitute abler and better agents, attorneys, and trustees. And the preservation of the means of knowledge among the lowest ranks, is of more importance to the public than all the property of all the rich men in the country. It is even of more consequence to the rich themselves, and to their posterity. The only question is, whether it is a public emolument; and if it is, the rich ought undoubtedly to contribute, in the same proportion as to all other public burdens,—that is, in proportion to their wealth, which is secured by public expenses. But none of the means of information are more sacred, or have been cherished with more tenderness and care by the settlers of America, than the press. Care has been taken that the art of printing should be encouraged, and that it should be easy and cheap and safe for any person to communicate his thoughts to the public. And you, Messieurs printers,* whatever the tyrants of the earth may say of your paper, have done important service to your country by your readiness and freedom in publishing the speculations of the curious. The stale, impudent insinuations of slander and sedition, with which the gormandizers of power have endeavored to discredit your paper, are so much the more to your honor; for the jaws of power are always opened to devour, and her arm is always stretched out, if possible, to destroy the freedom of thinking, speaking, and writing. And if the public interest, liberty, and happiness have been in danger from the ambition or avarice of any great man, whatever may be his politeness, address, learning, ingenuity, and, in other respects, integrity and humanity, you have done yourselves honor and your country service by publishing and pointing out that avarice and ambition. These vices are so much the more dangerous and pernicious for the virtues with which they may be accompanied in the same character, and with so much the more watchful jealousy to be guarded against.

> "Curse on such virtues, they've undone their country."

Be not intimidated, therefore, by any terrors, from publishing with the utmost freedom, whatever can be warranted by the laws of your country; nor suffer yourselves to be wheedled out of your liberty by any pretences of politeness, delicacy, or

* Edes and Gill, printers of the Boston Gazette.

decency. These, as they are often used, are but three different names for hypocrisy, chicanery, and cowardice. Much less, I presume, will you be discouraged by any pretences that malignants on this side the water will represent your paper as factious and seditious, or that the great on the other side the water will take offence at them. This dread of representation has had for a long time, in this province, effects very similar to what the physicians call a hydropho, or dread of water. It has made us delirious; and we have rushed headlong into the water, till we are almost drowned, out of simple or phrensical fear of it. Believe me, the character of this country has suffered more in Britain by the pusillanimity with which we have borne many insults and indignities from the creatures of power at home and the creatures of those creatures here, than it ever did or ever will by the freedom and spirit that has been or will be discovered in writing or action. Believe me, my countrymen, they have imbibed an opinion on the other side the water, that we are an ignorant, a timid, and a stupid people; nay, their tools on this side have often the impudence to dispute your bravery. But I hope in God the time is near at hand when they will be fully convinced of your understanding, integrity, and courage. But can any thing be more ridiculous, were it not too provoking to be laughed at, than to pretend that offence should be taken at home for writings here? Pray, let them look at home. Is not the human understanding exhausted there? Are not reason, imagination, wit, passion, senses, and all, tortured to find out satire and invective against the characters of the vile and futile fellows who sometimes get into place and power? The most exceptionable paper that ever I saw here is perfect prudence and modesty in comparison of multitudes of their applauded writings. Yet the high regard they have for the freedom of the press, indulges all. I must and will repeat it, your paper deserves the patronage of every friend to his country. And whether the defamers of it are arrayed in robes of scarlet or sable, whether they lurk and skulk in an insurance office, whether they assume the venerable character of a priest, the sly one of a scrivener, or the dirty, infamous, abandoned one of an informer, they are all the creatures and tools of the lust of domination.

The true source of our sufferings has been our timidity.

We have been afraid to think. We have felt a reluctance to examining into the grounds of our privileges, and the extent in which we have an indisputable right to demand them, against all the power and authority on earth. And many who have not scrupled to examine for themselves, have yet for certain prudent reasons been cautious and diffident of declaring the result of their inquiries.

The cause of this timidity is perhaps hereditary, and to be traced back in history as far as the cruel treatment of the first settlers of this country received, before their embarkation for America, from the government at home. Everybody knows how dangerous it was to speak or write in favor of any thing, in those days, but the triumphant system of religion and politics. And our fathers were particularly the objects of the persecutions and proscriptions of the times. It is not unlikely, therefore, that although they were inflexibly steady in refusing their positive assent to any thing against their principles, they might have contracted habits of reserve, and a cautious diffidence of asserting their opinions publicly. These habits they probably brought with them to America, and have transmitted down to us. Or we may possibly account for this appearance by the great affection and veneration Americans have always entertained for the country from whence they sprang; or by the quiet temper of which they have been remarkable, no country having been less disposed to discontent than this; or by a sense they have that it is their duty to acquiesce under the administration of government, even when in many smaller matters grievous to them, and until the essentials of the great compact are destroyed or invaded. These peculiar causes might operate upon them; but without these, we all know that human nature itself, from indolence, modesty, humanity, or fear, has always too much reluctance to a manly assertion of its rights. Hence, perhaps, it has happened, that nine tenths of the species are groaning and gasping in misery and servitude.

But whatever the cause has been, the fact is certain, we have been excessively cautious of giving offence by complaining of grievances. And it is as certain, that American governors, and their friends, and all the crown officers, have availed themselves of this disposition in the people. They have prevailed on us to consent to many things which were grossly injurious to us, and to surrender many others, with voluntary tameness, to which we had the clearest right. Have we not been treated, formerly, with abominable insolence, by officers of the navy? I mean no insinuation against any gentleman now on this station, having heard no complaint of any one of them to his dishonor. Have not some generals from England treated us like servants, nay, more like slaves than like Britons? Have we not been under the most ignominious contribution, the most abject submission, the most supercilious insults, of some custom-house officers? Have we not been trifled with, browbeaten, and trampled on, by former governors, in a manner which no king of England since James the Second has dared to indulge towards his subjects? Have we not raised up one family, in them placed an unlimited confidence, and been soothed and flattered and intimidated by their influence, into a great part of this infamous tameness and submission? "These are serious and alarming questions, and deserve a dispassionate consideration."

This disposition has been the great wheel and the mainspring in the American machine of court politics. We have been told that "the word *rights* is an offensive expression;" "that the king, his ministry, and parliament, will not endure to hear Americans talk of their *rights;*" "that Britain is the mother and we the children, that a filial duty and submission is due from us to her," and that "we ought to doubt our own judgment, and presume that she is right, even when she seems to us to shake the foundations of government;" that "Britain is immensely rich and great and powerful, has fleets and armies at her command which have been the dread and terror of the universe, and that she will force her own judgment into execution, right or wrong." But let me entreat you, sir, to pause. Do you consider yourself as a missionary of loyalty or of rebellion? Are you not representing your king, his ministry, and parliament, as tyrants,—imperious, unrelenting tyrants,—by such reasoning as this? Is not this representing your most gracious sovereign as endeavoring to destroy the foundations of his own throne? Are you not representing every member of parliament as renouncing the transactions at Runing Mede, (the meadow, near Windsor, where Magna Charta was signed;) and as repealing in effect the bill of rights, when the Lords and Commons asserted and vindicated the rights of the people and their own rights, and insisted on the king's assent to that assertion and vindication? Do you not represent them as forgetting that the prince of Orange was created King William, by the people, on purpose that their rights might be eternal and inviolable? Is there not something extremely fallacious in the common-place images of mother country and children colonies? Are we the children of Great Britain any more than the cities of London, Exeter, and Bath? Are we not brethren and fellow subjects with those in Britain, only under a somewhat different method of legislation, and a totally different method of taxation? But admitting we are children, have not children a right to complain when their parents are attempting to break their limbs, to administer poison, or to sell them to enemies for slaves? Let me entreat you to consider, will the mother be pleased when you represent her as deaf to the cries of her children,—when you compare her to the infamous miscreant who lately stood on the gallows for starving her child,—when you resemble her to Lady Macbeth in Shakspeare, (I cannot think of it without horror,) who

> "Had given suck, and knew
> How tender 't was to love the babe that milked her,"

but yet, who could

> "Even while 't was smiling in her face,
> Have plucked her nipple from the boneless gums,
> And dashed the brains out."

Let us banish for ever from our minds, my countrymen, all such unworthy ideas of the king, his ministry, and parliament. Let us not suppose that all are become luxurious, effeminate, and unreasonable, on the other side the water, as many designing persons would insinuate. Let us presume, what is in fact true, that the spirit of liberty is as ardent as ever among the body of the nation, though a few individuals may be corrupted. Let us take it for granted, that the same great spirit which once gave Cæsar so warm a reception, which denounced hostilities against John till Magna Charta was signed, which severed the head of Charles the First from his body, and drove James the Second from his kingdom, the same great spirit (may heaven preserve it till the earth shall be no more) which first seated the great grandfather of his present most gracious majesty on the throne of Britain,—is still alive and active and warm in England; and that the same spirit in America, instead of provoking the inhabitants of that country, will endear us to them for ever, and secure their good-will.

This spirit, however, without knowledge, would be little better than a brutal rage. Let us tenderly and kindly cherish, therefore, the means of knowledge. Let us dare to read, think, speak, and write. Let every order and degree among the people rouse their attention and animate their resolution. Let them all become attentive to the grounds and principles of government, ecclesiastical and civil. Let us study the law of nature; search into the spirit of the British constitution; read the histories of ancient ages; contemplate the great examples of Greece and Rome; set before us the conduct of our own British ancestors, who have defended for us the inherent rights of mankind against foreign and domestic tyrants and usurpers, against arbitrary kings and cruel priests, in short, against the gates of earth and hell. Let us read and recollect and impress upon our souls the views and ends of our own more immediate forefathers, in exchanging their native country for a dreary, inhospitable wilderness. Let us examine into the nature of that power, and the cruelty of that oppression, which drove them from their homes. Recollect their amazing fortitude, their bitter sufferings,—the hunger, the nakedness, the cold, which they patiently endured,—the severe labors of clearing their grounds, building their houses, raising their provisions, amidst dangers from wild beasts and savage men, before they had time or money or materials for commerce. Recollect the civil and religious principles and hopes and expectations which constantly supported and carried them through all hardships with patience and resignation. Let us recollect it was liberty, the hope of liberty for themselves and us and ours, which conquered all discouragements, dangers, and trials. In such researches as these, let us all in our several departments cheerfully engage,—but especially the proper patrons and supporters of law, learning, and religion!

Let the pulpit resound with the doctrines and sentiments of religious liberty. Let us hear the danger of thraldom to our consciences from ignorance, extreme poverty, and dependence, in short, from civil and political slavery. Let us see delineated before us the true map of man. Let us hear the dignity of his nature, and the noble rank he holds among the works of God,—that consenting to slavery is a sacrilegious breach of trust, as offensive in the sight of God as it is derogatory from our own honor or interest or happiness,—and that God Almighty has promulgated from heaven, liberty, peace, and good-will to man!

Let the bar proclaim, "the laws, the rights, the generous plan of power" delivered down from remote antiquity,—inform the world of the mighty struggles and numberless sacrifices made by our ancestors in defence of freedom. Let it be known, that British liberties are not the grants of princes or parliaments, but original rights, conditions of original contracts, coequal with prerogative, and coeval with government; that many of our rights are inherent and essential, agreed on as maxims, and established as preliminaries, even before a parliament existed. Let them search for the foundations of British laws and government in the frame of human nature, in the constitution of the intellectual and moral world. There let us see that truth, liberty, justice, and benevolence, are its everlasting basis; and if these could be removed, the superstructure is overthrown of course.

Let the colleges join their harmony in the same delightful concert. Let every declamation turn upon the beauty of liberty and virtue, and the deformity, turpitude, and malignity, of slavery and vice. Let the public disputations become researches into the grounds and nature and ends of government, and the means of preserving the good and demolishing the evil. Let the dialogues, and all the exercises, become the instruments of impressing on the tender mind, and of spreading and distributing far and wide, the ideas of right and the sensations of freedom.

In a word, let every sluice of knowledge be opened and set a-flowing. The encroachments upon liberty in the reigns of the first James and the first Charles, by turning the general attention of learned men to government, are said to have produced the greatest number of consummate statesmen which has ever been seen in any age or nation. The Brookes, Hampdens, Vanes, Seldens, Miltons, Nedhams, Harringtons, Nevilles, Sidneys, Lockes, are all said to have owed their eminence in political knowledge to the tyrannies of those reigns.[5] The prospect now before us in America, ought in the same manner to engage the attention of every man of learning, to matters of power and of right, that we may be neither led nor driven blindfolded to irretrievable destruction. Nothing less than this seems to have been meditated for us, by somebody or other in Great Britain. There seems to be a direct and formal design on foot, to enslave all America. This, however, must be done by degrees. The first step that is intended, seems to be an entire subversion of the whole system of our fathers, by the introduction of the canon and feudal law into America. The canon and feudal systems, though greatly mutilated in England, are not yet destroyed. Like the temples and palaces in which the great contrivers of them once wor-

[5] The Brookes, Hampdens, *et al.* were all English political writers and statesmen noted for their passionate belief in liberty and their suspicion of any potential tyranny. The implication of this last paragraph is that George III is like the Stuarts.

shipped and inhabited, they exist in ruins; and much of the domineering spirit of them still remains. The designs and labors of a certain society, to introduce the former of them into America, have been well exposed to the public by a writer of great abilities;* and the further attempts to the same purpose, that may be made by that society, or by the ministry or parliament, I leave to the conjectures of the thoughtful. But it seems very manifest from the Stamp Act itself, that a design is formed to strip us in a great measure of the means of knowledge, by loading the press, the colleges, and even an almanack and a newspaper, with restraints and duties; and to introduce the inequalities and dependencies of the feudal system, by taking from the poorer sort of people all their little subsistence, and conferring it on a set of stamp officers, distributors, and their deputies. But I must proceed no further at present. The sequel, whenever I shall find health and leisure to pursue it, will be a "disquisition of the policy of the stamp act." In the mean time, however, let me add,—These are not the vapors of a melancholy mind, nor the effusions of envy, disappointed ambition, nor of a spirit of opposition to government, but the emanations of a heart that burns for its country's welfare. No one of any feeling, born and educated in this once happy country, can consider the numerous distresses, the gross indignities, the barbarous ignorance, the haughty usurpations, that we have reason to fear are meditating for ourselves, our children, our neighbors, in short, for all our countrymen and all their posterity, without the utmost agonies of heart and many tears.

* The late Rev. Dr. Mayhew.

JOHN DICKINSON As the man chiefly responsible for the *Declaration of Rights and Grievances* issued by the Stamp Act Congress, John Dickinson was the ideal colonial writer to refute the arguments advanced in support of the Townshend Acts of 1767. In these *Letters,* which were originally published as newspaper articles between December 2, 1767, and February 15, 1768, Dickinson effectively questioned the distinction between internal and external taxes. The distinction was artificial, as both the colonists and the English ministry knew. Quoting the Resolves of the Stamp Act Congress in support of his argument, Dickinson admits only parliament's right to levy duties for the regulation of trade, but denies its right to levy duties for raising revenue. The denial of parliament's right to tax was a constitutional argument which proved enormously popular with the colonists and which placed Dickinson in the forefront of colonial opposition to England. His inherent political conservatism, however, is evident even in these *Letters.* Once the American situation became so intolerable as to demand the use of force, Dickinson lost much of his popularity. A believer in moderation and in conciliation, he functioned effectively only when such recourses were open to him. His is essentially the mind of the lawyer, arguing from tradition and precedent, only partially aware of the turbulent nature of the times.

Text: Paul Leicester Ford, ed., *The Writings of John Dickinson.* Philadelphia, 1895.

Letters from a Farmer in Pennsylvania (1768)

LETTER I.

My dear Countrymen,

I am a *Farmer,* settled, after a variety of fortunes, near the banks of the river *Delaware,* in the province of *Pennsylvania.* I received a liberal education, and have been engaged in the busy scenes of life; but am now convinced, that a man may be as happy without bustle, as with it. My farm is small; my servants are few, and good; I have a little money at interest; I wish for no more; my employment in my own affairs is easy; and with a contented grateful mind, (undisturbed by worldly hopes or fears, relating to myself,) I am completing the number of days allotted to me by divine goodness.

Being generally master of my time, I spend a good deal of it in a library, which I think the most valuable part of my small estate; and being acquainted with two or three gentlemen of abilities and learning, who honour me with their friendship, I have acquired, I believe, a greater knowledge in history, and the laws and constitution of my country, than is generally attained by men of my class, many of them not being so fortunate as I have been in the opportunities of getting information.

From my infancy I was taught to love *humanity* and *liberty*. Enquiry and experience have since confirmed my reverence for the lessons then given me, by convincing me more fully of their truth and excellence. Benevolence towards mankind, excites wishes for their welfare, and such wishes endear the means of fulfilling them. *These* can be found in liberty only, and therefore her sacred cause ought to be espoused by every man, on every occasion, to the utmost of his power. As a charitable, but poor person does not withhold his *mite*, because he cannot relieve *all* the distresses of the miserable, so should not any honest man suppress his sentiments concerning freedom, however small their influence is likely to be. Perhaps he "may touch some wheel,"* that will have an effect greater than he could reasonably expect.

These being my sentiments, I am encouraged to offer to you, my countrymen, my thoughts on some late transactions, that appear to me to be of the utmost importance to you. Conscious of my own defects, I have waited some time, in expectation of seeing the subject treated by persons much better qualified for the task; but being therein disappointed, and apprehensive that longer delays will be injurious, I venture at length to request the attention of the public, praying, that these lines may be *read* with the same zeal for the happiness of *British America*, with which they were *wrote*.

With a good deal of surprize I have observed, that little notice has been taken of an act of parliament, as injurious in its principle to the liberties of these colonies, as the *Stamp-Act* was: I mean the act for suspending the legislation of *New-York*.[1]

* Pope.

[1] Because it had refused to supply General Gage's troops in accordance with the provisions of the Quartering Act, parliament suspended the New York Assembly's legislative powers as of October 1, 1767.

The assembly of that government complied with a former act of parliament, requiring certain provisions to be made for the troops in *America,* in every particular, I think, except the articles of salt, pepper and vinegar. In my opinion they acted imprudently, considering all circumstances, in not complying so far as would have given satisfaction, as several colonies did: But my dislike of their conduct in that instance, has not blinded me so much, that I cannot plainly perceive, that they have been punished in a manner pernicious to *American* freedom, and justly alarming to all the colonies.

If the *British* parliament has a legal authority to issue an order, that we shall furnish a single article for the troops here, and to compel obedience to *that* order, they have the same right to issue an order for us to supply those troops with arms, cloths, and every necessary; and to compel obedience to *that* order also; in short, to lay *any burthens* they please upon us. What is this but *taxing* us at a *certain sum,* and leaving to us only the *manner* of raising it? How is this mode more tolerable than the *Stamp Act?* Would that act have appeared more pleasing to *Americans,* if being ordered thereby to raise the sum total of the taxes, the mighty privilege had been left to them, of saying how much should be paid for an instrument of writing on paper, and how much for another on parchment?

An act of parliament, commanding us to do a certain thing, if it has any validity, is a *tax* upon us for the expence that accrues in complying with it; and for this reason, I believe, every colony on the continent, that chose to give a mark of their respect for *Great-Britain,* in complying with the act relating to the troops, cautiously avoided the mention of that act, lest their conduct should be attributed to its supposed obligation.

The matter being thus stated, the assembly of *New-York* either had, or had not, a right to refuse submission to that act. If they had, and I imagine no *American* will say they had not, then the parliament had *no right* to compel them to execute it. If they had not *that right,* they had *no right* to punish them for not executing it; and therefore *no right* to suspend their legislation, which is a punishment. In fact, if the people of *New-York* cannot be legally taxed but by their own representatives, they cannot be legally deprived of the privilege of legislation, only for insisting on that exclusive privilege of taxation. If they may be legally deprived in such a case, of the privilege of legislation, why may they not, with equal reason, be deprived of every other privilege? Or why may not every colony be treated in the same manner, when any of them shall dare to deny their assent to any impositions, that shall be directed? Or what signifies the repeal of the *Stamp-Act,* if these colonies are to lose their *other* privileges, by not tamely surrendering *that* of taxation?

There is one consideration arising from this suspension, which is not generally attended to, but shews its importance very clearly. It was not *necessary* that this suspension should be caused by an act of parliament. The crown might have restrained the governor of *New-York,* even from calling the assembly together, by its prerogative in the royal governments. This step, I suppose, would have been taken, if the conduct of the assembly of *New-York* had been regarded as an act of disobedience *to the crown alone;* but it is regarded as an act of* "disobedience to the authority" "of the BRITISH LEGISLATURE." This gives the suspension a consequence vastly more affecting. It is a parliamentary assertion of the *supreme authority* of the *British* legislature over these colonies, in *the point of taxation,* and is intended to COMPEL *New-York* into a submission to that authority. It seems therefore to me as much a violation of the liberty of the people of that province, and consequently of all these colonies, as if the parliament had sent a number of regiments to be quartered upon them till they should comply. For it is evident, that the suspension is meant as a *compulsion;* and the *method* of compelling is totally indifferent. It is indeed probable, that the sight of red coats, and the hearing of drums, would have been most alarming; because people are generally more influenced by their eyes and ears, than by their reason. But whoever seriously considers the matter, must perceive that a dreadful stroke is aimed at the liberty of these colonies. I say, of these colonies; for the cause of *one* is the cause of *all.* If the parliament may lawfully deprive *New-York* of any of *her* rights, it may deprive any, or all the other colonies of *their* rights; and nothing can possibly so much encourage such attempts, as a mutual inattention to the interests of each other. *To divide, and thus to destroy,* is the first political maxim in attacking those, who are powerful by their union. He certainly is not a wise man, who folds his arms, and reposes himself at home, viewing, with unconcern, the flames that have invaded his neighbour's house, without using any endeavours to

* See the act of suspension.

extinguish them. When Mr. *Hampden's* ship money cause,[2] for *Three Shillings* and *Four-pence*, was tried, all the people of *England*, with anxious expectations, interested themselves in the important decision; and when the slightest point, touching the freedom of *one* colony, is agitated, I earnestly wish, that *all the rest* may, with equal ardour, support their sister. Very much may be said on this subject; but I hope, more at present is unnecessary.

With concern I have observed, that *two* assemblies of this province have sat and adjourned, without taking any notice of this act. It may perhaps be asked, what would have been proper for them to do? I am by no means fond of inflammatory measures; I detest them. I should be sorry that any thing should be done, which might justly displease our sovereign, or our mother country: But a firm, modest exertion of a free spirit, should never be wanting on public occasions. It appears to me, that it would have been sufficient for the assembly, to have ordered our agents to represent to the King's ministers, their sense of the suspending act, and to pray for its repeal. Thus we should have borne our testimony against it; and might therefore reasonably expect that, on a like occasion, we might receive the same assistance from the other colonies.

Concordia res parvae crescunt.
Small things grow great by concord.

A FARMER.

**Nov. 5.*

LETTER II.

My dear Countrymen,

There is another late act of parliament, which appears to me to be unconstitutional, and as destructive to the liberty of these colonies, as that mentioned in my last letter; that is, the act for granting the duties on paper, glass, etc.[3]

The parliament unquestionably possesses a legal authority to *regulate* the trade of *Great-Britain*, and all her colonies.

[2] John Hampden (1594–1643), English statesman and soldier, owes his fame to his opposition to ship-money, an estate tax which he resisted on the principle that it was an infringement on personal liberty. As a result of his trial, Hampden became a focal point for the resistance to Charles I.

* The day of King WILLIAM the Third's landing.

[3] The Townshend Acts of 1767. Duties leveled by this act actually conformed to the American position of 1765–66, since the taxes were external. Dickinson, however, denies parliament the power to tax, although he concedes its right to regulate trade.

Such an authority is essential to the relation between a mother country and her colonies; and necessary for the common good of all. He, who considers these provinces as states distinct from the *British Empire,* has very slender notions of *justice,* or of their *interests.* We are but parts of a *whole;* and therefore there must exist a power somewhere to preside, and preserve the connection in due order. This power is lodged in the parliament; and we are as much dependent on *Great-Britain,* as a perfectly free people can be on another.

I have looked over *every statute* relating to these colonies, from their first settlement to this time; and I find every one of them founded on this principle, till the *Stamp-Act* administration.* *All before,* are calculated to regulate trade, and

* For the satisfaction of the reader, recitals from the former acts of parliament relating to these colonies are added. By comparing these with the modern acts, he will perceive their great difference in *expression* and *intention.*

The 12th *Cha.,* Chap. 18, which forms the foundation of the laws relating to *our* trade, by enacting that certain productions of the colonies should be carried to *England* only, and that no goods shall be imported from the plantations but in ships belonging to *England, Ireland, Wales, Berwick,* or the *Plantations,* etc., begins thus: *For the increase of shipping, and encouragement of the navigation of this nation,* wherein, under the good providence and protection of *GOD,* the wealth, *safety,* and strength of this kingdom is so much concerned," *&c.*

The 15th *Cha.* II., Chap. 7, enforcing the same regulation, assigns these reasons for it. "In regard his Majesty's plantations, beyond the seas, are inhabited and peopled by his subjects of this his kingdom of *England, for the maintaining a greater correspondence and kindness between them,* and keeping them in a firmer dependence upon it, and rendering them yet more beneficial and advantageous unto it, *in the further employment and increase of* English *shipping and seamen,* vent of *English* woollen, and other manufactures and commodities, *rendering the navigation to and from the same more safe and cheap,* and making this kingdom a *staple,* not only of the commodities of those plantations, but also of the commodities of other countries and places *for the supplying of them;* and it being the *usage* of other nations to keep their plantations trade to themselves," *&c.*

The 25th *Cha.* II., Chap. 7, made expressly *"for the better securing the plantation trade,"* which imposes duties on certain commodities exported from one colony to another, mentions this cause for imposing them: "Whereas by one act, passed in the 12th year of your Majesty's reign, intituled, An act for *encouragement of shipping and navigation,* and by several other laws, passed since that time, it is permitted to ship, *&c.* sugars, tobacco, *&c.* of the growth, *&c.* of any of your Majesty's plantations in *America, &c.* from the places of their growth, *&c.* to any other of your Majesty's plantations in those parts, *&c.* and that *without paying custom for the same,* either at the lading or unlading the said commodities, by means whereof the trade and navigation in those commodities, from one plantation to another, is greatly increased, and the inhabitants of divers of those colonies, *not contenting themselves with being supplied with those commodities for their own use, free from all customs* (while the subjects of this your kingdom of *England* have paid great customs and impositions for what of them hath been spent here) *but, contrary to the express letter of the aforesaid laws, have brought into divers parts of* Europe great quantities thereof, and do also vend great quantities thereof to the shipping of other nations, who bring them into divers parts of *Europe,* to the great hurt and diminution of your Majesty's customs, and of the *trade* and *navigation* of this your kingdom; For the Prevention thereof, *&c.*

The 7th and 8th *Will.* III., Chap. 22, intituled, "An act for preventing

preserve or promote a mutually beneficial intercourse between the several constituent parts of the empire; and though many of them imposed duties on trade, yet those duties were always imposed *with design* to restrain the commerce of one part, that was injurious to another, and thus to promote the general welfare. The raising a revenue thereby was never intended. Thus the King, by his judges in his courts of justice, imposes fines which all together amount to a very considerable sum, and contribute to the support of government: But this is merely a consequence arising from restrictions, that only meant to keep peace, and prevent confusion; and surely a man would argue very loosely, who should conclude from hence, that the King has a right to levy money in general upon his subjects. Never did the *British* parliament, till the period

---

frauds, and regulating abuses in the plantation trade," recites that, "notwithstanding divers acts, *&c.* great abuses are daily committed *to the prejudice of the* English *navigation, and the loss of a great part of the plantation trade* to this kingdom, by the *artifice* and *cunning* of ill disposed persons; FOR REMEDY WHEREOF, *&c.* And whereas in some of his Majesty's *American* plantations, a doubt or misconstruction has arisen upon the before mentioned act, made in the 25th year of the reign of King *Charles* II. whereby certain duties are laid upon the commodities therein enumerated (which by law may be transported from one plantation to another, for the supply of each others wants) *as if* the same were, by the payment of those duties in one plantation, discharged from giving the securities intended by the aforesaid acts, made in the 12th, 22d and 23d years of the reign of King *Charles* the II. and consequently be at liberty to go to any foreign market in *Europe,*" *&c.*

The 6th *Anne,* Chap. 37, reciting the advancement of trade, and encouragement of ships of war, *&c.* grants to the captors of the property of all prizes carried into *America,* subject to such customs and duties, as if the same had been first imported into any part of *Great-Britain,* and from thence exported, *&c.*

This was a *gift to persons acting under commissions from the crown,* and therefore it was reasonable that the *terms* prescribed in that gift, should be complied with—more especially as the payment of such duties was intended to give a preference to the productions of *British* colonies, over those of other colonies. However, being found inconvenient to the colonies, about four years afterwards, this act was, for that reason, so far repealed, that by another act "all prize goods, imported into any part of *Great-Britain,* from any of the plantations, were made liable to such duties only in *Great-Britain,* as in case they had been of the growth and produce of the plantations."

The 6th *Geo.* II. Chap. 13, which imposes duties on foreign rum, sugar and molasses, imported into the colonies, shews the reasons thus—"Whereas, the welfare and prosperity of your Majesty's sugar colonies in *America,* are of the greatest consequence and importance to the *trade, navigation* and *strength* of this kingdom; and whereas the planters of the said sugar colonies, have of late years *fallen into such great discouragements,* that they are unable to improve or carry on the sugar trade, *upon an equal footing* with the foreign sugar colonies, *without some advantage and relief be given to them from* Great-Britain: FOR REMEDY WHEREOF, AND FOR THE GOOD AND WELFARE OF YOUR MAJESTY'S SUBJECTS," *&c.*

The 29th *Geo.* II. Chap. 26, and the 1st *Geo.* III. Chap. 9, which continue the 6th *Geo.* II. Chap. 13, declare, that the said act hath, by experience, been found *useful* and *beneficial, &c.* These are all the most considerable statutes relating to the commerce of the colonies; and it is thought to be utterly unnecessary to add any observations to these extracts, to prove that they were all intended *solely as regulations of trade.*

above mentioned, think of imposing duties in *America,* FOR THE PURPOSE OF RAISING A REVENUE. Mr. *Grenville* first introduced this language, in the preamble to the 4th *Geo.* III., Chap. 15, which has these words "And whereas it is just and necessary that A REVENUE BE RAISED IN YOUR MAJESTY'S SAID DOMINIONS IN AMERICA, *for defraying the expences of defending, protecting, and securing the same:* We your Majesty's most dutiful and loyal subjects, THE COMMONS OF GREAT-BRITAIN, in parliament assembled, being desirous to make some provision in this present session of parliament, TOWARDS RAISING THE SAID REVENUE IN AMERICA, have resolved to GIVE and GRANT unto your Majesty the several rates and duties herein after mentioned," *&c.*

A few months after came the *Stamp-Act,* which reciting this, proceeds in the same strange mode of expression, thus—"And whereas it is just and necessary, that provision be made FOR RAISING A FURTHER REVENUE WITHIN YOUR MAJESTY'S DOMINIONS IN AMERICA, *towards defraying the said expences,* we your Majesty's most dutiful and loyal subjects, the COMMONS OF GREAT-BRITAIN, &c. GIVE and GRANT," &c. as before.

The last act, granting duties upon paper, &c. carefully pursues these modern precedents. The preamble is, "Whereas it is expedient THAT A REVENUE SHOULD BE RAISED IN YOUR MAJESTY'S DOMINIONS IN AMERICA, *for making a more certain and adequate provision for defraying the charge of the administration of justice, and the support of civil government in such provinces, where it shall be found necessary; and towards the further defraying the expences of defending, protecting and securing the said dominions,* we your Majesty's most dutiful and loyal subjects, the COMMONS OF GREAT-BRITAIN, *&c.* GIVE and GRANT," *&c.* as before.

Here we may observe an authority *expressly* claimed and exerted to impose duties on these colonies; not for the regulation of trade; not for the preservation or promotion of a mutually beneficial intercourse between the several constituent parts of the empire, heretofore the *sole objects* of parliamentary institutions; *but for the single purpose of levying money upon us.*

This I call an* innovation; and a most dangerous innova-

* "It is worthy observation how quietly subsidies, granted in forms *usual* and *accustomable* (though heavy) are borne; such a power hath use and custom. On the other side, what discontentments and disturbances subsidies *framed in a new mould* do raise (SUCH AN INBRED HATRED NOVELTY DOTH HATCH) is evident by examples of former times."

Lord *Coke's* 2d Institute, p. 33.

tion. It may perhaps be objected, that *Great-Britain* has a right to lay what duties she pleases upon her* exports, and it makes no difference to us, whether they are paid here or there.

To this I answer. These colonies require many things for their use, which the laws of *Great-Britain* prohibit them from getting any where but from her. Such are paper and glass.

That we may legally be bound to pay any *general* duties on these commodities relative to the regulation of trade, is granted; but we being *obliged by the laws* to take from *Great-Britain,* any *special* duties imposed on their exportation *to us only, with intention to raise a revenue from us only,* are as much *taxes,* upon us, as those imposed by the *Stamp-Act.*

What is the difference in *substance* and *right* whether the same sum is raised upon us by the rates mentioned in the *Stamp-Act,* on the *use* of paper, or by these duties, on the *importation* of it. It is only the edition of a former book, shifting a sentence from the *end* to the *beginning.*

Suppose the duties were made payable in *Great-Britain.*

It signifies nothing to us, whether they are to be paid here or there. Had the *Stamp-Act* directed, that all the paper should be landed at *Florida,* and the duties paid there, before it was brought to the *British* colonies, would the act have raised less money upon us, or have been less destructive of our rights? By no means: For as we were under a necessity of using the paper, we should have been under the necessity of paying the duties. Thus, in the present case, a like *necessity* will subject us, if this act continues in force, to the payment of the duties now imposed.

Why was the *Stamp-Act* then so pernicious to freedom? It did not enact, that every man in the colonies *should* buy a certain quantity of paper—No: It only directed, that no instrument of writing should be valid in law, if not made on stamped paper, *&c.*

The makers of that act knew full well that the confusions that would arise from the disuse of writings, would COMPEL the colonies to use the stamped paper, and therefore to pay

* Some people think that *Great-Britain* has the same right to impose duties on the exports to these colonies, as on the exports to *Spain* and *Portugal,* &c. Such persons attend so much to the idea of exportation, that they entirely drop *that of the connection between the mother country and her colonies.* If *Great-Britain* had always claimed, and exercised an authority to compel *Spain* and *Portugal* to import manufactures from her only, the cases would be parallel: But as she never pretended to such a right, they are at liberty to get them where they please; and if they chuse to take them from her, rather than from other nations, they voluntarily consent to pay the duties imposed on them.

the taxes imposed. For this reason the *Stamp-Act* was said to be a law THAT WOULD EXECUTE ITSELF. For the very same reason, the last act of parliament, if it is granted to have any force here, WILL EXECUTE ITSELF, and will be attended with the very same consequences to *American* liberty.

Some persons perhaps may say, that this act lays us under no necessity to pay the duties imposed, because we may ourselves manufacture the articles on which they are laid; whereas by the *Stamp-Act* no instrument of writing could be good, unless made on *British* paper, and that too stamped.

Such an objection amounts to no more than this, that the injury resulting to these colonies, from the total disuse of *British* paper and glass, will not be *so afflicting* as that which would have resulted from the total disuse of writing among them; for by that means even the *Stamp-Act* might have been eluded. Why then was it universally detested by them as slavery itself? Because it presented to these devoted provinces nothing but a* choice of calamities, imbittered by indignities, each of which it was unworthy of freemen to bear. But is no injury a violation of right but the *greatest* injury? If the eluding the payment of the taxes imposed by the *Stamp-Act*, would have subjected us to a more dreadful inconvenience, than the eluding the payment of those imposed by the late act; does it therefore follow, that the last is *no violation* of our rights, tho' it is calculated for the same purpose the other was, that is, *to raise money upon us*, WITHOUT OUR CONSENT.

This would be making *right* to consist, not in an exemption from *injury*, but from a certain *degree of injury*.

But the objectors may further say, that we shall suffer no injury at all by the disuse of *British* paper and glass. We might not, if we could make as much as we want. But can any man, acquainted with *America*, believe this possible? I am told there are but two or three *Glass-Houses* on this continent, and but very few *Paper-Mills;* and suppose more should be erected, a long course of years must elapse, before they can be brought to perfection. This continent is a country of planters, farmers, and fishermen; not of manufacturers. The difficulty of establishing particular manufactures in such a country, is almost insuperable. For one manufacture is connected with others in such a manner, that it may be said to be impossible to establish one or two, without establishing several others.

* Either the *disuse* of writing, or the payment of *taxes* imposed by others *without our consent*.

The experience of many nations may convince us of this truth.

Inexpressible therefore must be our distresses in evading the late acts, by the disuse of *British* paper and glass. Nor will this be the extent of our misfortune, if we admit the legality of that act.

Great-Britain has prohibited the manufacturing *iron* and *steel* in these colonies, without any objection being made to her *right* of doing it. The *like* right she must have to prohibit any other manufacture among us. Thus she is possessed of an undisputed *precedent* on that point. This authority, she will say, is founded on the *original intention* of settling these colonies; that is, that we should manufacture for them, and that they should supply her with materials. The *equity* of this policy, she will also say, has been universally acknowledged by the colonies, who never have made the least objections to statutes for that purpose; and will further appear by the *mutual benefits* flowing from this usage ever since the settlement of these colonies.

Our great advocate, Mr. *Pitt,*[4] in his speeches on the debate concerning the repeal of the *Stamp-Act,* acknowledged, that *Great-Britain* could restrain our manufactures. His words are these—"This kingdom, as the supreme governing and legislative power, has ALWAYS bound the colonies by her regulations and RESTRICTIONS in trade, in navigation, in MANUFACTURES—in every thing, *except that of taking their money out of their pockets,* WITHOUT THEIR CONSENT." Again he says, "We may bind their trade, CONFINE THEIR MANUFACTURES, and exercise every power whatever, *except that of taking their money out of their pockets,* WITHOUT THEIR CONSENT.

Here then, my dear countrymen, ROUSE yourselves, and behold the ruin hanging over your heads. If you ONCE admit, that *Great-Britain* may lay duties upon her exportations to us, *for the purpose of levying money on us only,* she then will have nothing to do, but to lay those duties on the articles which she prohibits us to manufacture—and the tragedy of *American* liberty is finished. We have been prohibited from procuring manufactures, in all cases, any where but from *Great-Britain* (excepting linens, which we are permitted to import directly from *Ireland*). We have been prohibited, in some cases, from manufacturing for ourselves; and may be

4 William Pitt (1708–1778), first Earl of Chatham, supported the repeal of the Stamp Act and was a consistent advocate of the rights of the American colonies short of independence.

prohibited in others. We are therefore exactly in the situation of a city besieged, which is surrounded by the works of the besiegers in every part *but one*. If *that* is closed up, no step can be taken, *but to surrender at discretion*. If *Great-Britain* can order us to come to her for necessaries we want, and can order us to pay what taxes she pleases before we take them away, or when we land them here, we are as abject slaves as *France* and *Poland* can shew in wooden shoes, and with uncombed hair.*

Perhaps the nature of the *necessities* of dependent states, caused by the policy of a governing one, for her own benefit, may be elucidated by a fact mentioned in history. When the Carthaginians were possessed of the island of *Sardinia*, they made a decree, that the *Sardinians* should not raise *corn*, nor get it any other way than from the *Carthaginians*. Then, by imposing any duties they would upon it, they drained from the miserable *Sardinians* any sums they pleased; and whenever that oppressed people made the least movement to assert their liberty, their tyrants starved them to death or submission. This may be called the most perfect kind of political necessity.

From what has been said, I think this uncontrovertible conclusion may be deduced, that when a ruling state obliges a dependent state to take certain commodities from her alone, it is implied in the nature of that obligation; is essentially requisite to give it the least degree of justice; and is inseparably united with it, in order to preserve any share of freedom to the dependent state; *that those commodities should never be loaded with duties,* FOR THE SOLE PURPOSE OF LEVYING MONEY ON THE DEPENDENT STATE.

Upon the whole, the single question is, whether the parliament can legally impose duties to be paid *by the people of these colonies only,* FOR THE SOLE PURPOSE OF RAISING A REVENUE, *on commodities which she obliges us to take from her alone,* or, in other words, whether the parliament can legally take money out of our pockets, without our consent. If they can, our boasted liberty is but

Vox et prœterea nihil.
A sound and nothing else.

A FARMER.

* The peasants of *France* wear wooden shoes; and the vassals of *Poland* are remarkable for matted hair, which never can be combed.

LETTER III.

My dear Countrymen,

I rejoice to find that my two former letters to you, have been generally received with so much favour by such of you, whose sentiments I have had an opportunity of knowing. Could you look into my heart, you would instantly perceive a zealous attachment to your interests, and a lively resentment of every insult and injury offered to you, to be the motives that have engaged me to address you.

I am no further concerned in any thing affecting *America*, than any one of you; and when liberty leaves it, I can quit it much more conveniently than most of you: But while Divine Providence, that gave me existence in a land of freedom, permits my head to think, my lips to speak, and my hand to move, I shall so highly and gratefully value the blessing received, as to take care, that my silence and inactivity shall not give my implied assent to any act, degrading my brethren and myself from the birthright, wherewith heaven itself *"hath made us free."*

Sorry I am to learn, that there are some few persons, who shake their heads with solemn motion, and pretend to wonder, what can be the meaning of these letters. *"Great-Britain,"* they say, "is too powerful to contend with; she is determined to oppress us; it is in vain to speak of right on one side, when there is power on the other; when we are strong enough to resist, we shall attempt it; but now we are not strong enough, and therefore we had better be quiet; it signifies nothing to convince us that our rights are invaded, when we cannot defend them; and if we should get into riots and tumults about the late act, it will only draw down heavier displeasure upon us."

What can such men design? What do their grave observations amount to, but this—"that these colonies, totally regardless of their liberties, should commit them, with humble resignation, to *chance, time,* and the tender mercies of *ministers.*"

Are these men ignorant, that usurpations, which might have been successfully opposed at first, acquire strength by continuance, and thus become irresistible? Do they condemn the conduct of these colonies, concerning the *Stamp-Act?* Or have they forgot its successful issue? Ought the colonies at that time, instead of acting as they did, to have trusted for relief to the fortuitous events of futurity? If it is needless "to speak of rights" now, it was as needless then. If the behavior of the colonies was prudent and glorious then, and successful too; it will be equally prudent and glorious to act in the same manner now, if our rights are equally invaded, and may be as successful. Therefore it becomes necessary to enquire, whether "our rights *are* invaded." To talk of "defending" them, as if they could be no otherwise "defended" than by arms, is as much out of the way, as if a man having a choice of several roads to reach his journey's end, should prefer the worst, for no other reason, but because it *is* the worst.

As to "riots and tumults," the gentlemen who are so apprehensive of them, are much mistaken, if they think that grievances cannot be redressed without such assistance.

I will now tell the gentlemen, what is, "the meaning of these letters." The meaning of them is, to convince the people of these colonies, that they are at this moment exposed to the most imminent dangers; and to persuade them immediately, vigorously, and unanimously, to exert themselves, in the most firm, but most peaceable manner, for obtaining relief.

The cause of *liberty* is a cause of too much dignity to be sullied by turbulence and tumult. It ought to be maintained in a manner suitable to her nature. Those who engage in it, should breathe a sedate, yet fervent spirit, animating them to actions of prudence, justice, modesty, bravery, humanity and magnanimity.

To such a wonderful degree were the ancient *Spartans*, as brave and free a people as ever existed, inspired by this happy temperature of soul, that rejecting even in their battles the use of trumpets, and other instruments for exciting heat and rage, they marched up to scenes of havoc, and horror,* with the sound of flutes, to the tunes of which their steps kept pace—"exhibiting," as *Plutarch* says, "at once a terrible and delightful sight, and proceeding with a deliberate valor, full of hope and good assurance, as if some divinity had sensibly assisted them."

I hope, my dear countrymen, that you will, in every colony, be upon your guard against those, who may at any time endeavour to stir you up, under pretences of patriotism, to any measures disrespectful to our Sovereign and our mother country. Hot, rash, disorderly proceedings, injure the reputation of a people, as to wisdom, valor and virtue, without procur-

* *Plutarch* in the life of *Lycurgus*. Archbishop *Potter's* Archaeologia Graeca.

ing them the least benefit. I pray GOD, that he may be pleased to inspire you and your posterity, to the latest ages, with a spirit of which I have an idea, that I find a difficulty to express. To express it in the best manner I can, I mean a spirit, that shall so guide you, that it will be impossible to determine whether an *American's* character is most distinguishable, for his loyalty to his Sovereign, his duty to his mother country, his love of freedom, or his affection for his native soil.

Every government at some time or other falls into wrong measures. These may proceed from mistake or passion. But every such measure does not dissolve the obligation between the governors and the governed. The mistake may be corrected; the passion may subside. It is the duty of the governed to endeavour to rectify the mistake, and to appease the passion. They have not at first any other right, than to represent their grievances, and to pray for redress, unless an emergence is so pressing, as not to allow time for receiving an answer to their applications, which rarely happens. If their applications are disregarded, then that kind of *opposition* becomes justifiable, which can be made without breaking the laws, or disturbing the public peace.

This consists in the *prevention of the oppressors reaping advantage from their oppressions,* and not in their punishment. For experience may teach them, what reason did not; and harsh methods cannot be proper, till milder ones have failed.

If at length it become UNDOUBTED, that an inveterate resolution is formed to annihilate the liberties of the governed, the *English* history affords frequent examples of resistance by force. What particular circumstances will in any future case justify such resistance, can never be ascertained, till they happen. Perhaps it may be allowable to say generally, that it never can be justifiable, until the people are FULLY CONVINCED, that any further submission will be destructive to their happiness.

When the appeal is made to the sword, highly probable is it, that the punishment will exceed the offence; and the calamities attending on war out-weigh those preceding it. These considerations of justice and prudence, will always have great influence with good and wise men.

To these reflections on this subject, it remains to be added, and ought for ever to be remembered, that resistance, in the case of colonies against their mother country, is extremely different from the resistance of a people against their prince. A nation may change their king, or race of kings, and, retaining their antient form of government, be gainers by changing. Thus *Great-Britain,* under the illustrious house of *Brunswick,* a house that seems to flourish for the happiness of mankind, has found a felicity, unknown in the reigns of the *Stewarts.* But if once *we* are separated from our mother country, what new form of government shall we adopt, or where shall we find another *Britain,* to supply our loss? Torn from the body, to which we are united by religion, liberty, laws, affections, relation, language and commerce, we must bleed at every vein.

In truth—the prosperity of these provinces is founded in their dependence on *Great-Britain;* and when she returns to her "old good humour, and her old good nature," as Lord *Clarendon* expresses it, I hope they will always think it their duty and interest, as it most certainly will be, to promote her welfare by all the means in their power.

We cannot act with too much caution in our disputes. Anger produces anger; and differences, that might be accommodated by kind and respectful behavior, may, by imprudence, be enlarged to an incurable rage. In quarrels between countries, as well as in those between individuals, when they have risen to a certain height, the first cause of dissension is no longer remembered, the minds of the parties being wholly engaged in recollecting and resenting the mutual expressions of their dislike. When feuds have reached that fatal point, all considerations of reason and equity vanish; and a blind fury governs, or rather confounds all things. A people no longer regards their interest, but the gratification of their wrath. The sway of the *Cleon's* and *Clodius's,** the designing and detestable flatterers of the *prevailing passion,* becomes confirmed. Wise and good men in vain oppose the storm, and may think themselves fortunate, if, in attempting to preserve their ungrateful fellow citizens, they do not ruin themselves. Their *prudence* will be called *baseness;* their *moderation* will be called *guilt;* and if their virtue does not lead them to destruction, as that of many other great and excellent persons has done, they may survive to receive from their expiring country the mournful glory of her acknowledgment, that their counsels, if regarded, would have saved her.

The constitutional modes of obtaining relief, are those

* *Cleon* was a popular firebrand of *Athens,* and *Clodius* of *Rome;* each of whom plunged his country into the deepest calamities.

which I wish to see pursued on the present occasion; that is, by petitions of our assemblies, or where they are not permitted to meet, of the people, to the powers that can afford us relief.

We have an excellent prince, in whose good dispositions towards us we may confide. We have a generous, sensible and humane nation, to whom we may apply. They may be deceived. They may, by artful men, be provoked to anger against us. I cannot believe they will be cruel or unjust; or that their anger will be implacable. Let us behave like dutiful children, who have received unmerited blows from a beloved parent. Let us complain to our parent; but let our complaints speak at the same time the language of affliction and veneration.

If, however, it shall happen, by an unfortunate course of affairs, that our applications to his Majesty and the parliament for redress, prove ineffectual, let us THEN take *another step*, by withholding from *Great-Britain* all the advantages she has been used to receive from us. THEN let us try, if our ingenuity, industry, and frugality, will not give weight to our remonstrances. Let us all be united with one spirit, in one cause. Let us invent—let us work—let us save—let us, continually, keep up our claim, and incessantly repeat our complaints—But, above all, let us implore the protection of that infinitely good and gracious being,* "by whom kings reign, and princes decree justice."

Nil desperandum.
Nothing is to be despaired of.

A FARMER.

* PRO. viii. 15.

LETTER IV.

My dear Countrymen,

An objection, I hear, has been made against my second letter, which I would willingly clear up before I proceed. "There is," say these objectors, "a material difference between the *Stamp-Act* and the *late Act* for laying a duty on paper, *&c.* that justifies the conduct of those who opposed the former, and yet are willing to submit to the latter. The duties imposed by the *Stamp-Act* were *internal* taxes; but the present are *external,* and therefore the parliament may have a right to impose them."

To this I answer, with a total denial of the power of parliament to lay upon these colonies any "tax" whatever.

This point, being so important to this, and to succeeding generations, I wish to be clearly understood.

To the word *"tax,"* I annex that meaning which the constitution and history of *England* require to be annexed to it; that is—that it is *an imposition on the subject, for the sole purpose of levying money.*

In the early ages of our monarchy, certain services were rendered to the crown *for the general good.* These were personal:* But in process of time, such institutions being found inconvenient, *gifts* and *grants* of their own property were made by the people, under the several names of aids, tallages, tasks, taxes and subsidies, *&c.* These were made, as may be collected even from the names, *for public service* upon "need and necessity."† All these sums were levied upon the people by virtue of their voluntary gift.‡ Their design was to support the *national honor and interest.* Some of those grants com-

* It is very worthy of remark, how watchful our wise ancestors were, lest their *services* should be encreased beyond what the law allowed. No man was bound to go out of the realm to serve the King. Therefore, even in the conquering reign of *Henry* the *Fifth,* when the martial spirit of the nation was highly enflamed by the heroic courage of their Prince, and by his great success, they still carefully guarded against the establishment of illegal services. "When this point (says Lord Chief Justice *Coke*) concerning maintenance of wars out of *England,* came in question, the COMMONS did make their *continual claim* of their *ancient freedom* and *birthright,* as in the first of *Henry the Fifth,* and in the seventh of *Henry the Fifth,* &c. the COMMONS made a PROTEST, that they were not bound to the maintenance of war in *Scotland, Ireland, Calice, France, Normandy,* or other *foreign* parts, and caused their PROTESTS to be entered into the parliament rolls, where they yet remain; which, in effect, agreeth with that which, upon like occasion, was made in the parliament of 25th *Edward* I." 2d Inst. p. 528.

† 4th Inst. p. 28.

‡ *Reges* Angliae, *nihil tale, nisi convocatis primis ordinibus, et assenti-ente populo suscipiunt.* Phil. Comines, 2d *Inst.*

These gifts entirely depending on the pleasure of the donors, were proportioned to the abilities of the several ranks of people who gave, and were regu-

prehended duties arising from trade; being imposts on merchandizes. These Lord Chief Justice *Coke* classes under "subsidies," and "parliamentary aids." They are also called "customs." But whatever the *name* was, they were always considered as *gifts of the people to the crown, to be employed for public uses.*

Commerce was at a low ebb, and surprizing instances might be produced how little it was attended to for a succession of ages. The terms that have been mentioned, and, among the rest, that of *"tax,"* had obtained a national, parliamentary meaning, drawn from the principles of the constitution, long before any *Englishman* thought of *imposition of duties, for the regulation of trade.*

Whenever we speak of "taxes" among *Englishmen,* let us therefore speak of them with reference to the *principles* on which, and the *intentions* with which they have been established. This will give certainty to our expression, and safety to our conduct: But if, when we have in view the liberty of these colonies, we proceed in any other course, we pursue a *Juno** indeed, but shall only catch a cloud.

In the national, parliamentary sense insisted on, the word "tax"† was certainly understood by the congress at *New-York,* whose resolves may be said to form the *American* "bill of rights."[5]

---

lated by *their* opinion of the public necessities. Thus *Edward* I. had in his 11th year a *thirtieth* from the *laity,* a *twentieth* from the *clergy;* in his 22d year, a *tenth* from the *laity,* a *sixth* from *London,* and other corporate towns, *half of their benefices* from the *clergy;* in his 23d year an *eleventh* from the *barons* and others, a *tenth* from the *clergy,* a *seventh* from the *burgesses, &c. Hume's Hist. of England.*

The same difference in the grants of the several ranks is observable in other reigns.

In the famous statute *de tallagio non concedendo,* the king enumerates the several *classes,* without whose consent, he and his heirs never should set or levy any tax . . . *"nullum tallagium, vel auxilium per nos, vel hoeredes nostros in regno nostro ponatur seu levetur, sine voluntate et assensu archiepiscoporum, episcoporum, comitum, baronum, militum, burgensium, et alienum liberorum com. de regno nostro."* 34th *Edward* I.

Lord Chief Justice *Coke,* in his comment on these words, says . . . "for the quieting of the *commons,* and for a *perpetual and constant law for ever after,* both in this AND OTHER LIKE CASES, this act was made. These words are *plain,* WITHOUT ANY SCRUPLE, *absolute,* WITHOUT ANY SAVING." 2d *Coke's* Inst. p. 532, 533. Little did the venerable judge imagine, that *"other* LIKE *cases"* would happen, in which the spirit of this law would be despised by *Englishmen,* the posterity of those who made it.

* The Goddess of *Empire,* in the Heathen Mythology; according to an antient fable, *Ixion* pursued her, but she escaped in a cloud.

† In this sense *Montisquieu* uses the word "tax," in his 13th book of *Spirit of Laws.*

[5] A reference to the Stamp Act Congress which met in New York from October 7, 1765 to October 25, 1765. The "bill of rights" which Dickinson mentions was the *Declaration of Rights and Grievances,* a series of resolutions adopted by the Congress which were chiefly Dickinson's work.

The third, fourth, fifth, and sixth resolves, are thus expressed.

III. "That it is *inseparably essential to the freedom of a people,* and the *undoubted right of Englishmen,* that* NO TAX be imposed on them, *but with their own consent,* given personally, or by their representatives."

IV. "That the people of the colonies are not, and from their local circumstances, cannot be represented in the house of commons in *Great-Britain.*"

V. "That the only representatives of the people of the colonies, are the persons chosen therein by themselves; and that NO TAXES ever have been, or can be constitutionally imposed on them, but by their respective legislatures."

VI. "That all *supplies to the crown,* being free gifts of the people, it is *unreasonable, and inconsistent with the principles and spirit of the* British *constitution,* for the people of *Great-Britain to* grant to his Majesty *the property of the colonies.*"

Here is no distinction made between *internal* and *external* taxes. It is evident from the short reasoning thrown into these resolves, that every imposition "to grant to his Majesty *the property of the colonies,*" was thought a "tax;" and that every such imposition, if laid any other way than "with their consent, given personally, or by their representatives," was not only "unreasonable, and inconsistent with the principles and spirit of the *British* constitution," but destructive "to the freedom of a people."

This language is clear and important. A "TAX" means an imposition to raise money. Such persons therefore as speak of *internal* and *external* "TAXES," I pray may pardon me, if I object to that expression, as applied to the privileges and interests of these colonies. There may be *internal* and *external* IMPOSITIONS, founded on *different principles,* and having *different tendencies,* every "tax" being an imposition, tho' every imposition is not a "tax." But *all taxes* are founded on the *same principles;* and have the *same tendency.*

External impositions, for the regulation of our trade, do not "grant to his Majesty *the property of the colonies.*" They only *prevent the colonies acquiring property,* in things not necessary, in a manner judged to be injurious to the welfare of the whole empire. But the last statute respecting us, "grants to

* The rough draught of the resolves of the congress at *New-York* are now in my hands, and from some notes on that draught, and other particular reasons, I am satisfied that the congress understood the word "tax" in the sense here contended for.

his Majesty *the property of the colonies,*" by laying duties on the manufactures of *Great-Britain* which they MUST take, and which she settled on them, on purpose that they SHOULD take.

What* *tax* can be more *internal* than this? Here is money drawn, *without their consent,* from a society, who have constantly enjoyed a constitutional mode of raising all money among themselves. The payment of their *tax* they have no possible method of avoiding; as they cannot do without the commodities on which it is laid, and they cannot manufacture these commodities themselves. Besides, if this unhappy country should be so lucky as to elude this act, by getting parchment enough, in the place of paper, or by reviving the antient method of writing on wax and bark, and by inventing some-

* It seems to be evident, that Mr. *Pitt* in his defence of *America,* during the debate concerning the repeal of the *Stamp Act,* by "*internal* taxes," meant any duties "for the purpose of raising a revenue;" and by "*external* taxes," meant duties imposed "for the regulation of trade." His expressions are these . . . "If the gentleman does not understand the difference between *internal* and *external* taxes, I cannot help it; but there is a plain distinction between taxes levied FOR THE PURPOSES OF RAISING A REVENUE, and duties imposed FOR THE REGULATION OF TRADE, for the accommodation of the subject; although, in the consequences, some revenue might incidentally arise from the latter."

These words were in Mr. *Pitt's* reply to Mr. *Grenville,* who said he could not understand the difference between external and internal taxes.

In every other part of his speeches on that occasion, his words confirm this construction of his expressions. The following extracts will shew how positive and general were his assertions of our right.

"It is my opinion that this kingdom has NO RIGHT to lay A TAX upon the colonies." . . . "The *Americans* are the SONS, not the BASTARDS of *England.* TAXATION is NO PART of the *governing* and *legislative* power." . . . "The *taxes* are a voluntary *gift* and *grant* of the *commons* ALONE. In LEGISLATION the THREE estates of the realm are ALIKE concerned, but the concurrence of the PEERS and the CROWN to a TAX, is only necessary to close with the FORM of a law. The GIFT *and* GRANT is of the COMMONS ALONE." . . . "*The distinction between* LEGISLATION *and* TAXATION *is essentially necessary to liberty.*" . . . "THE COMMONS of *America,* represented in their several assemblies, have ever been in possession of the exercise of this their constitutional right, of GIVING and GRANTING their own MONEY. *They would have been SLAVES, if they had not enjoyed it.*" "The idea of a *virtual* representation of *America* in this house, is the most contemptible idea that ever entered into the head of man . . . It does not deserve a serious refutation."

He afterwards shews the unreasonableness of *Great-Britain* taxing *America,* thus . . . "When I had the honor of serving his Majesty, I availed myself of the means of information, which I derived from my office. I SPEAK THEREFORE FROM KNOWLEDGE. My materials were good. I was at pains to *collect,* to *digest,* to *consider* them: and *I will be bold to affirm,* that the profit to *Great-Britain* from the trade of the colonies, through all its branches, is TWO MILLIONS A YEAR. *This* is the fund that carried you triumphantly through the last war. The estates that were rented at two thousand pounds a year, threescore years ago, are three thousand pounds at present. Those estates sold then from fifteen to eighteen years purchase; the same may now be sold for thirty. YOU OWE THIS TO AMERICA. THIS IS THE PRICE THAT AMERICA PAYS YOU FOR HER PROTECTION." "I dare not say how much higher these profits may be augmented." . . . "Upon the whole, I will beg leave to tell the house what is really my opinion: it is, that the *Stamp Act* be repealed absolutely, totally, and immediately. That the reason for the repeal be assigned, because it was founded on an ERRONEOUS PRINCIPLE."

thing to serve instead of glass, her ingenuity would stand her in little stead; for then the parliament would have nothing to do but to prohibit such manufactures, or to lay a tax on *hats* and *woollen cloths,* which they have already prohibited the colonies *from supplying each other with;* or on instruments, and tools of *steel* and *iron,* which they have prohibited the provincials *from manufacturing at all:** And then, what little gold and silver they have, must be torn from their hands, or they will not be able, in a short time, to get an ax,† for cutting their firewood, nor a plough, for raising their food. In what respect, therefore, I beg leave to ask, is the late act preferable to the *Stamp-Act,* or more consistent with the liberties of the colonies? For my own part, I regard them both with equal apprehensions; and think they ought to be in the same manner opposed.

Habemus quidem senatus consultum,—tanquam gladium in vagina repositum.

We have a statute, laid up for future use, like a sword in the scabbard.

A FARMER.

LETTER V.

My dear Countrymen,

Perhaps the objection to the late act, imposing duties upon paper, *&c.* might have been safely rested on the argument drawn from the universal conduct of parliaments and ministers, from the first existence of these colonies, to the administration of Mr. *Greenville.*

What but the indisputable, the acknowledged exclusive right of the colonies to tax themselves, could be the reason, that in this long period of more than one hundred and fifty years, no statute was ever passed for the sole purpose of raising a revenue on the colonies? And how clear, how cogent must that reason be, to which every parliament, and every

* "And that *pig* and *bar iron,* made in his Majesty's colonies in *America,* may be FURTHER MANUFACTURED IN THIS KINGDOM, be it further enacted by the authority aforesaid, that from and after the twenty-fourth day of *June,* 1750, no *mill,* or *other engine,* for *fitting* or *rolling* of *iron,* or any *plating forge,* to work with a *tilt hammer,* or any *furnace* for *making steel,* shall be erected, or, after such erection, continued IN ANY OF HIS MAJESTY'S COLONIES IN AMERICA." 23d George II., Chap. 29, Sect. 9.

† Tho' these particulars are mentioned as being absolutely necessary, yet perhaps they are not more so than glass in our severe winters, to keep out the cold from our houses; or than paper, without which such inexpressible confusions must ensue.

minister, for so long a time submitted, without a single attempt to innovate?

England, in part of that course of years, and *Great-Britain,* in other parts, was engaged in several fierce expensive wars; troubled with some tumultuous and bold parliaments; governed by many daring and wicked ministers; yet none of them ever ventured to touch the *Palladium* of *American* liberty. Ambition, avarice, faction, tyranny, all revered it. Whenever it was necessary to raise money on the colonies, the requisitions of the crown were made, and dutifully complied with. The parliament, from time to time, regulated their trade, and that of the rest of the empire, to preserve their dependence, and the connection of the whole in good order.

The people of *Great-Britain,* in support of their privileges, boast much of their antiquity. It is true they are antient; yet it may well be questioned, if there is a single privilege of a *British* subject, supported by longer, more solemn, or more uninterrupted testimony, than the exclusive right of taxation in these colonies. The people of *Great-Britain* consider that kingdom as the sovereign of these colonies, and would now annex to that sovereignty a prerogative never heard of before. How would they bear this, was the case their own? What would they think of a *new* prerogative claimed by the crown? We may guess what their conduct would be from the transports of passion into which they fell about the late embargo, tho' laid to relieve the most emergent necessities of state, admitting of no delay; and for which there were numerous precedents. Let our liberties be treated with the same tenderness, and it is all we desire.

Explicit as the conduct of parliaments, for so many ages, is, to prove that no money can be levied on these colonies by parliament, for the purpose of raising a revenue, yet it is not the only evidence in our favour.

Every one of the most material arguments against the legality of the *Stamp-Act,* operates with equal force against the act now objected to; but as they are well known, it seems unnecessary to repeat them here.

This general one only shall be considered at present: That tho' these colonies are dependent on *Great-Britain;* and tho' she has a legal power to make laws for preserving that dependence; yet it is not necessary for this purpose, nor essential to the relation between a mother country and her colonies, as was eagerly contended by the advocates for the *Stamp-Act,* that she should raise money on them without their consent.

Colonies were formerly planted by warlike nations to keep their enemies in awe; to relieve their country, overburthened with inhabitants; or to discharge a number of discontented and troublesome citizens. But in more modern ages, the spirit of violence being in some measure, if the expression may be allowed, sheathed in commerce, colonies have been settled by the nations of *Europe* for the purposes of trade. These purposes were to be attained, by the colonies raising for their mother country those things which she did not produce herself; and by supplying themselves from her with things they wanted. These were the *national objects,* in the commencement of our colonies, and have been uniformly so in their promotion.

To answer these grand purposes, perfect liberty was known to be necessary; all history proving, that trade and freedom are nearly related to each other. By a due regard to this wise and just plan, the infant colonies, exposed in the unknown climates and unexplored wildernesses of this new world, lived, grew and flourished.

The parent country, with undeviating prudence and virtue, attentive to the first principles of colonization, drew to herself the benefits she might reasonably expect, and preserved to her children the blessings, on which those benefits were founded. She made laws, obliging her colonies to carry to her all those products which she wanted for her own use; and all those raw materials which she chose herself to work up. Besides this restriction, she forbad them to procure *manufactures* from any other part of the globe, or even the *products* of *European* countries, which alone could rival her, without being first brought to her. In short, by a variety of laws, she regulated their trade in such a manner as she thought most conducive to their mutual advantage, and her own welfare. A power was reserved to the crown of *repealing* any laws that should be enacted: The *executive* authority of government was also lodged in the crown, and its representatives; and an *appeal* was secured to the crown from all judgments in the administration of justice.

For all these powers, established by the mother country over the colonies; for all these immense emoluments derived by her from them; for all their difficulties and distresses in fixing themselves, what was the recompence made them? A communication of her rights in general, and particularly of that great one, the foundation of all the rest—that their property, acquired with so much pain and hazard, should be disposed of by none but* themselves—or to use the beautiful and emphatic language of the sacred scriptures, "that they should sit *every man* under his vine, and under his fig-tree, and NONE SHOULD MAKE THEM AFRAID."

Can any man of candor and knowledge deny, that these institutions form an affinity between *Great-Britain* and her colonies, that sufficiently secures their dependence upon her? Or that for her to levy taxes upon them, is to reverse the nature of things? Or that she can pursue such a measure, without reducing them to a state of vassallage?

If any person cannot conceive the supremacy of *Great-Britain* to exist, without the power of laying taxes to levy money upon us, the history of the colonies, and of *Great-Britain,* since their settlement, will prove the contrary. He will there find the amazing advantages arising to her from them—the constant exercise of her supremacy—and their filial submission to it, without a single rebellion, or even the thought of one, from their first emigration to this moment—And all these things have happened, without one instance of *Great-Britain's* laying taxes to levy money upon them.

How many† *British authors* have demonstrated, that the

* "The power of *taxing themselves,* was the privilege of which the *English* were, WITH REASON, *particularly jealous.*" *Hume's Hist. of England.*

† It has been said in the House of Commons, when complaints have been made of the decay of trade to any part of *Europe,* "That such things were not worth regard, as *Great-Britain* was possessed of colonies that could consume more of her manufactures than she was able to supply them with."

"As the case now stands, we shall shew that the *plantations* are a spring of *wealth* to this nation, that they *work* for us, that their TREASURE CENTERS ALL HERE, and that the laws have tied them fast enough to us; so that it must be through our own fault and mismanagement, if they become independent of *England.*" DAVENANT *on the Plantation Trade.*

"It is better that the islands should be supplied from the Northern Colonies than from *England;* for this reason, the provisions we might send to *Barbados, Jamaica, &c.* would be *unimproved* product of the earth, as grain of all kinds, or such product where there is little got by the improvement, as malt, salt beef and pork; indeed the exportation of salt fish thither would be more advantageous; but the goods which we send to the *Northern Colonies,* are such whose *improvement* may be justly laid, one with another, to be near *four-fifths* of the value of the *whole commodity,* as apparel, household furniture, and many other things." *Idem.*

"*New-England* is the most prejudicial plantation to the kingdom of *England;* and yet to do right to that most industrious *English* colony, I must confess, that though we lose by their unlimited trade with other foreign plantations, yet we are very great gainers by their direct trade from *Old England.* Our yearly exportation of *English* manufactures, malt and other goods, from hence thither, amounting in my opinion, to *ten times* the value of what is imported from thence; which calculation I do not make at random, but upon *mature consideration,* and, peradventure, upon *as much experience in this very trade,* as any other person will pretend to; and therefore, whenever reformation of our correspondency in trade with that people shall be thought on, it will, in my poor judgment, require GREAT TENDERNESS, and VERY SERIOUS CIRCUMSPECTION." *Sir* JOSIAH CHILD'S *Discourse on Trade.*

"Our plantations spend mostly our *English* manufactures, and those *of all sorts almost imaginable,* in *egregious quantities,* and employ near

present wealth, power and glory of their country, are founded upon these colonies? As constantly as streams tend to the ocean, have they been pouring the fruits of all their labors into their mother's lap. Good heaven! and shall a total oblivion of former tenderness and blessings, be spread over the minds of a good and wise nation, by the sordid arts of in-

---

two thirds of all our English *shipping;* so that we have *more people* in *England,* by reason of our plantations in *America.*" *Idem.*

Sir JOSIAH CHILD says, in another part of his work, "That not more than fifty families are maintained in *England* by the refining of sugar." From whence, and from what *Davenant* says, it is plain, that the advantages here said to be derived from the plantations by *England* must be meant chiefly of the continental colonies.

"I shall sum up my whole remarks on our *American* colonies, with this observation, that as they are a certain annual revenue of SEVERAL MILLIONS STERLING to their mother country, they ought carefully to be protected, duly encouraged, and every opportunity that presents, improved for their increment and advantage, as every one they can possibly reap, must at last return to us with interest." BEAWES's *Lex Merc. Red.*

"We may safely advance, that our trade and navigation are greatly increased by our colonies, and that they really are a source of treasure and naval power to this kingdom, since THEY WORK FOR US, & THEIR TREASURE CENTERS HERE. Before their settlement, our manufactures were few, and those but indifferent; the number of *English* merchants very small, and the whole shipping of the nation much inferior to what now belongs to the Northern Colonies only. *These are certain facts.* But since their establishment, our condition has altered for the better, almost of a degree beyond credibility. . . . Our MANUFACTURES are prodigiously increased, chiefly by the demand for them in the plantations, where they AT LEAST TAKE OFF ONE HALF, and supply us with many valuable commodities for exportation, which is as great an emolument to the mother kingdom, as to the plantations themselves."

POSTLETHWAYT'*s Univ. Dict. of Trade and Commerce.*

"Most of the nations of *Europe* have interfered with us, more or less, in divers of our staple manufactures, within half a century, not only in our woollen, but in our lead and tin manufactures, as well as our fisheries."

POSTLETHWAYT, *ibid.*

"The inhabitants of our colonies, by carrying on a trade with their *foreign neighbours,* do not only occasion *a greater quantity of the goods and merchandize of* Europe *being sent from hence to them,* and a greater quantity of the product of *America* to be sent from them hither, *which would otherwise be carried from and brought to* Europe *by foreigners,* but an increase of the seamen and navigation in those parts, which is of great strength and security, as well as of great advantage to our plantations in general. And though *some of our colonies* are not only for preventing the *importation of all goods of of the same species they produce,* but suffer particular planters *to keep great runs of land in their possession uncultivated,* with design to prevent new settlements, whereby they imagine the prices of their commodities may be affected; yet if it be considered, that the markets of *Great-Britain* depend on the markets of ALL *Europe in general,* and that the *European* markets *in general* depend on the proportion between the *annual consumption* and the *whole quantity* of each species *annually produced* by ALL *nations;* it must follow, that whether we or foreigners are the producers, *carriers,* importers and exporters of *American* produce, yet their respective prices in *each colony* (the difference of freight, customs and importations considered) will always bear proportion to the *general consumption* of the *whole quantity* of each sort, *produced in all colonies,* and *in all parts,* allowing only for the usual contingencies that trade and commerce, agriculture and manufactures, are liable to in all countries." POSTLETHWAYT, *ibid.*

"It is certain, that from the very time Sir *William Raleigh,* the father of our *English* colonies, and his associates, first projected these establishments, there have been persons who have found an interest, in *misrepresenting,* or lessening the value of them. . . . The attempts were called chimerical and dangerous. Afterwards many malignant suggestions were made about sacri-

triguing men, who, covering their selfish projects under pretences of public good, first enrage their countrymen into a frenzy of passion, and then advance their own influence and interest, by gratifying the passion, which they themselves have basely excited.

Hitherto *Great-Britain* has been contented with her pros-

---

ficing so many *Englishmen* to the obstinate desire of settling colonies in countries which then produced very little advantage. But as these difficulties were gradually surmounted, those complaints vanished. No sooner were *these lamentations* over, but *others* arose in their stead; when it could be no longer said, that the colonies were *useless*, it was alledged that they were not *useful enough* to their mother country; that while we were loaded with taxes, they were absolutely free; that the *planters* lived like *princes*, while he inhabitants of *England* laboured hard for a tolerable subsistence."

POSTLETHWAYT, *ibid.*

"Before the settlement of these colonies," says *Postlethwayt*, "our manufactures were few, and those but indifferent. In those days we had not only our naval stores, but our ships from our neighbours. *Germany* furnished us with all things made of metal, even to nails. Wine, paper, linens, and a thousand other things, came from *France*. *Portugal* supplied us with sugar; all the products of *America* were poured into us from *Spain;* and the *Venetians* and *Genoese* retailed to us the commodities of the *East-Indies*, at their own price."

"If it be asked, whether foreigners, for what goods they take of us, do not pay on *that consumption* a great portion of our taxes? It is admitted they do." POSTLETHWAYT'S *Great-Britain's True System*.

"If we are afraid that one day or other the colonies will revolt, and set up for themselves, as some seem to apprehend, let us not *drive* them to a *necessity* to *feel* themselves independent of us; as they *will* do, the moment they perceive that *THEY CAN BE SUPPLIED WITH ALL THINGS FROM WITHIN THEMSELVES*, and do not need our assistance. If we would keep them still dependent upon their mother country, and in some respects, *subservient* to her *views* and welfare; let us make it their INTEREST always to be so." TUCKER *on Trade*.

"Our colonies, while they have *English* blood in their veins, and have relations in *England*, and WHILE THEY CAN GET BY TRADING WITH US, the *stronger* and *greater they* grow, the *more* this *crown* and *kingdom* will *get* by them: and nothing but such an arbitrary power as shall make them desperate, can bring them to rebel." DAVENANT *on the Plantation Trade*.

"The Northern colonies are not upon the same footing as those of the South; and having a worse soil to improve, they must find the recompence some other way, which only can be in property and dominion: Upon which score, any INNOVATIONS in the form of government there, should be cautiously examined, for fear of entering upon measures, by which the industry of the inhabitants be quite discouraged. 'TIS ALWAYS UNFORTUNATE for a people, either by CONSENT, or upon COMPULSION, to depart from their PRIMITIVE INSTITUTIONS, and THOSE FUNDAMENTALS, by which they were FIRST UNITED TOGETHER." *Idem.*

"The most effectual way of *uniting* the colonies, is to make it their common interest to oppose the designs and attempts of *Great-Britain*.

"All wise states will well consider how to preserve the advantages arising from colonies, and avoid the evils. And I conceive that there can be but TWO ways in nature to hinder them from throwing off their dependence; *one* to keep it out of their *power*, and the *other*, out of their *will*. The first must be by *force*, and the *latter* by *using them well*, and keeping them employed in such productions, and making such manufactures, as will support themselves and families comfortably, *and procure them wealth too,* and at least not prejudice their mother country.

"*Force* can never be used effectually to answer the end, *without destroying the colonies themselves*. Liberty and encouragement are necessary to carry people thither, and to keep them together when they are there; and violence will hinder both. Any body of troops, considerable enough to awe them, and keep them in subjection, under the direction too of a needy governor, often

perity. Moderation has been the rule of her conduct. But now, a generous humane people, that so often has protected the liberty of *strangers,* is enflamed into an attempt to tear a privilege from her own children, which, if executed, must, in their opinion, sink them into slaves: AND FOR WHAT? For a pernicious power, not necessary to her, as her own experience may convince her; but horribly dreadful and detestable to them.

It seems extremely probable, that when cool, dispassionate posterity, shall consider the affectionate intercourse, the reciprocal benefits, and the unsuspecting confidence, that have subsisted between these colonies and their parent country, for such a length of time, they will execrate, with the bitterest curses the infamous memory of those men, whose pestilential ambition unnecessarily, wantonly, cruelly, first opened the sources of civil discord between them; first turned their love into jealousy; and first taught these provinces, filled with grief and anxiety, to enquire—

Mens ubi materna est?
Where is maternal affection?

A FARMER.

LETTER VI.

My dear COUNTRYMEN,

It may perhaps be objected against the arguments that have been offered to the public, concerning the legal power of the parliament, "that it has always exercised the power of im-

---

sent thither to make his fortune, and at such a distance from any application for redress, will soon put an end to all planting, and leave the country to the soldiers alone, and if it did not, *would eat up all the profit of the colony.* For this reason, arbitrary countries have not been equally successful in planting colonies with free ones; and what they have done in that kind, has either been by force, or at a vast expence, or *by departing from the nature of their government,* and *giving such privileges to planters* as were *denied to their other subjects.* And I dare say, that a few prudent laws and a little prudent conduct, would soon give us far the greatest share of the riches of all *America,* perhaps drive many of other nations out of it, or into other colonies for shelter.

"There are *so many exigencies* in all states, *so many foreign wars,* and *domestic disturbances,* that these colonies CAN NEVER WANT OPPORTUNITIES, if they watch for them, *to do what they shall find their interest to do;* and therefore we ought to take all the precautions in our power, that it shall never be *their interests* to act against that of their native country; an evil which can no otherwise be averted, than by keeping them *fully employed* in such trades *as will increase their own,* as well as our wealth; for it is much to be feared, if we do not find employment for *them,* they may find it for *us;* the interest of the mother country, is always to keep them dependent, and so employed; and it requires all her address to do it; and it is certainly more *easily* and *effectually* done by *gentle* and *insensible* methods, than by *power* alone." CATO'S *Letters.*

posing duties, for the purposes of raising a revenue on the productions of these colonies carried to *Great-Britain,* which may be called a tax on them." To this objection I answer, that this is no violation of the rights of the colonies, it being implied in the relation between them and *Gerat-Britain,* that they should not carry such commodities to other nations, as should enable them to interfere with the mother country. The imposition of duties on these commodities, when brought to her, is only a consequence of her parental right; and if the point is thoroughly examined, the duties will be found to be laid on the people of the mother country. Whatever they are, they must proportionately raise the price of the goods, and conseqently must be paid by the consumers. In this light they were considered by the parliament in the 25th *Charles* II. Chap. 7, Sect. 2, which says, that the productions of the plantations were carried from one to another free from all customs, "while the subjects of this your kingdom of *England* have paid *great customs and impositions for what of them have been* SPENT HERE," *&c.*

Besides, if *Great-Britain* exports these commodities again, the duties will injure her own trade, so that she cannot hurt us, without plainly and immediately hurting herself; and this is our check against her acting arbitrarily in this respect.

* It may be perhaps further objected, "that it being granted

* If any one should observe that no opposition has been made to the legality of the 4th *Geo.* III. Chap. 15, which is the FIRST act of parliament that ever imposed duties on the importations into *America,* for the *expressed* purpose of raising a revenue there; I answer, First, That tho' the act expressly mentions the raising a revenue in *America,* yet it seems that it had as much in view the "improving and securing the trade between the same and *Great-Britain,*" which words are part of its title: And the preamble says, "Whereas it is expedient that new provisions and regulations should be established for improving the revenue of this kingdom, and *for extending and securing the navigation and commerce between* Great-Britain, *and your Majesty's dominions in* America, which by the peace have been so happily extended and enlarged," *&c.* Secondly, *All* the duties mentioned in that act are imposed solely on the *productions and manufactures of foreign countries,* and not a single duty laid on any production or manufacture of our mother country. Thirdly, the authority of the provincial assemblies is not therein so plainly *attacked* as by the last act, which makes provision for defraying the charges of the "administration of justice," and "the support of civil government." Fourthly, That it being *doubtful,* whether the intention of the 4th *Geo.* III. Chap. 15, was not as much *to regulate trade,* as *to raise a revenue,* the minds of the people here were wholly engrossed by the terror of the *Stamp-Act,* then impending over them, about the intention of which there could be no *doubt.*

These reasons so far distinguish the 4th *Geo.* III. Chap. 15, from the last act, that it is not to be wondered at, that the first should have been submitted to, tho' the *last* should excite the most universal and spirited opposition. For *this* will be found, on the strictest examination, to be, in the *principle* on which it is founded, and in the *consequences* that must attend it, if possible, more destructive than the *Stamp-Act.* It is, to speak plainly, a *prodigy* in our laws; not having one *British* feature.

that statutes made for regulating trade, are binding upon us, it will be difficult for any person, but the makers of the laws, to determine, which of them are made for the regulating of trade, and which for raising a revenue; and that from hence may arise confusion."

To this I answer, that the objection is of no force in the present case, or such as resemble it; because the act now in question, is formed *expressly* FOR THE SOLE PURPOSE OF RAISING A REVENUE.

However, supposing the design of parliament had not been *expressed,* the objection seems to me of no weight, with regard to the influence which those who may make it, might expect it ought to have on the conduct of these colonies.

It is true, that *impositions for raising a revenue,* may be hereafter called *regulations of trade:* But names will not change the nature of things. Indeed we ought firmly to believe, what is an undoubted truth, confirmed by the unhappy experience of many states heretofore free, that UNLESS THE MOST WATCHFUL ATTENTION BE EXERTED, A NEW SERVITUDE MAY BE SLIPPED UPON US, UNDER THE SANCTION OF USUAL AND RESPECTABLE TERMS.

Thus the *Cæsars* ruined the *Roman* liberty, under the titles of *tribunical* and *dictatorial* authorities, old and venerable dignities, known in the most flourishing times of freedom. In imitation of the same policy, *James* II. when he *meant* to establish popery, *talked* of liberty of conscience, the most sacred of all liberties; and had thereby almost deceived the Dissenters into destruction.

All artful rulers, who strive to extend their power beyond its just limits, endeavor to give to their attempts as much semblance of legality as possible. Those who succeed them may venture to go a little further; for each new encroachment will be strengthened by a former. "* That which is now supported by examples, growing old, will become an example itself," and thus support fresh usurpations.

A free people therefore can never be too quick in observing, nor too firm in opposing the beginnings of *alteration* either in *form* or *reality,* respecting institutions formed for their security. The first kind of alteration leads to the last: Yet, on the other hand, nothing is more certain, than that the *forms* of liberty may be retained, when the *substance* is

* TACITUS.

gone. In government, as well as in religion, "The *letter* killeth, but the *spirit* giveth life."*

I will beg leave to enforce this remark by a few instances. The crown, by the constitution, has the prerogative of creating peers. The existence of that order, in due number and dignity, is essential to the constitution; and if the crown did not exercise that prerogative, the peerage must have long since decreased so much as to have lost its proper influence. Suppose a prince, for some unjust purposes, should, from time to time, advance so many needy, profligate wretches to that rank, that all the independence of the house of lords should be destroyed; there would then be a manifest violation of the constitution, *under the appearance of using legal prerogative.*

The house of commons claim the privilege of forming all money bills, and will not suffer either of the other branches of the legislature to add to, or alter them; contending that their power simply extends to an acceptance or rejection of them. This privilege appears to be just: but under pretence of this just privilege, the house of commons has claimed a licence of tacking to money bills, clauses relating to things of a totally different kind, and thus forcing them in a manner on the king and lords. This seems to be an abuse of that privilege, and it may be vastly more abused. Suppose a future house, influenced by some displaced, discontented demagogues—in a time of danger, should tack to a money bill, something so injurious to the king and peers, that they would not assent to it, and yet the commons should obstinately insist on it; the whole kingdom would be exposed to ruin by them, *under the appearance of maintaining a valuable privilege.*

In these cases it might be difficult for a while to determine, whether the king intended to exercise his prerogative in a constitutional manner or not; or whether the commons insisted on their demand factiously, or for the public good: But surely the conduct of the crown or of the house, would in time sufficiently explain itself.

Ought not the PEOPLE therefore to watch? to observe facts? to search into causes? to investigate designs? And have they not a right of JUDGING from the evidence before them, on no slighter points than their *liberty* and *happiness?* It would be less than trifling, wherever a *British* government is established, to make use of any arguments to prove such a right. It is

* 2 COR. iii. 6.

sufficient to remind the reader of the day, on the anniversary of which the first of these letters is dated.[6]

I will now apply what has been said to the present question.

The *nature* of any impositions laid by parliament on these colonies, must determine the *design* in laying them. It may not be easy in every instance to discover that design. Wherever it is doubtful, I think submission cannot be dangerous; nay, it must be right; for, in my opinion, there is no privilege these colonies claim, which they ought in *duty* and *prudence* more earnestly to maintain and defend, than the authority of the *British* parliament to regulate the trade of all her dominions. Without this authority, the benefits she enjoys from our commerce, must be lost to her: The blessings we enjoy from our dependence upon her, must be lost to us. Her strength must decay; her glory vanish; and she cannot suffer without our partaking in her misfortune. *Let us therefore cherish her interests as our own, and give her every thing, that it becomes* FREEMEN *to give or to receive.*

The *nature* of any impositions she may lay upon us may, in general, be known, by considering how far they relate to the preserving, in due order, the connection between the several parts of the *British* empire. One thing we may be assured of, which is this—Whenever she imposes duties on commodities, to be paid only upon their exportation from *Great-Britain* to these colonies, it is not a regulation of trade, but a design to raise a revenue upon us. Other instances may happen, which it may not be necessary at present to dwell on. I hope these colonies will never, to their latest existence, want understanding sufficient to discover the intentions of those who rule over them, nor the resolution necessary for asserting their interests. They will always have the same rights, that all free states have, of judging when their privileges are invaded, and of using all prudent measures for preserving them.

Quocirca vivite fortes,
Fortiaque adversis opponite pectora rebus.
Wherefore keep up your spirits, and gallantly oppose this adverse course of affairs.

A FARMER.

[6] William III landed at Torbay on November 5, 1688, where he accepted the crown under a parliamentary Declaration of Right. With James II's flight from England and with William's acceptance of the throne, parliament asserted its governmental supremacy over the monarchy.

LETTER VII.

My dear COUNTRYMEN,

This letter is intended more particularly for such of you, whose employments in life may have prevented your attending to the consideration of some points that are of great and public importance: For many such persons there must be even in these colonies, where the inhabitants in general are more intelligent than any other people whatever, as has been remarked by strangers, and it seems with reason.

Some of you, perhaps, filled, as I know your breasts are, with loyalty to our most excellent Prince, and with love to our dear mother country, may feel yourselves inclined, by the affections of your hearts, to approve every action of those whom you so much venerate and esteem. A prejudice thus flowing from goodness of disposition, is amiable indeed. I wish it could be indulged without danger. Did I think this possible, the error should have been adopted, and not opposed by me. But in truth, all men are subject to the frailties of nature; and therefore whatever regard we entertain for the *persons* of those who govern us, we should always remember that their conduct, as *rulers*, may be influenced by human infirmities.

When any laws, injurious to these colonies, are passed, we cannot suppose, that any injury was intended us by his Majesty, or the Lords. For the assent of the crown and peers to laws, seems, as far as I am able to judge, to have been vested in them, more for their own security, than for any other purpose. On the other hand, it is the particular business of the people, to enquire and discover what regulations are useful for themselves, and to digest and present them in the form of bills, to the other orders, to have them enacted into laws. Where these laws are to bind *themselves*, it may be expected, that the house of commons will very carefully consider them: But when they are making laws that are not designed to bind *themselves*, we cannot imagine that their deliberations will be as* cautious and scrupulous, as in their own case.

* Many remarkable instances might be produced of the extraordinary inattention with which bills of great importance, concerning these colonies, have passed in parliament; which is owing, as it is supposed, to the bills being brought in by the persons who have points to carry, so artfully framed, that it is not easy for the members in general, in the haste of business, to discover their tendency.

The following instances shew the truth of this remark. When Mr. *Greenville*,

I am told, that there is a wonderful address frequently used in carrying points in the house of commons, by persons experienced in these affairs.—That opportunities are watched—and sometimes votes are passed, that if all the members had been present, would have been rejected by a great majority. Certain it is, that when a powerful and artful man has determined on any measure against these colonies, he has always succeeded in his attempt. Perhaps therefore it will be proper for us, whenever any oppressive act affecting us is passed, to attribute it to the inattention of the members of the house of commons, and to the malevolence or ambition of some factious great man, rather than to any other cause.

Now I do verily believe, that the late act of parliament, imposing duties on paper, *&c.* was formed by Mr. *Greenville,* and his party, because it is evidently a part of that plan, by which he endeavoured to render himself POPULAR at home; and I do also believe, that not one half of the members of the house of commons, even of those who heard it read, did perceive how destructive it was to *American* freedom. For this reason, as it is usual in *Great-Britain,* to consider the King's speech as the speech of the ministry, it may be right here to consider this act as the act of a *party*—per-

---

in the violence of reformation, formed the 4th *Geo.* III. Chap. 15th, for regulating the *American* trade, the word *"Ireland"* was dropt in the clause relating to our iron and lumber, so that we could send these articles to no part of *Europe,* but to *Great-Britain.* This was so unreasonable a restriction, and so contrary to the sentiments of the legislature for many years before, that it is surprizing it should not have been taken notice of in the house. However the bill passed into a law. But when the matter was explained, this restriction was taken off by a subsequent act. I cannot positively say how long after the taking off this restriction, as I have not the act, but I think, in less than 18 months, another act of parliament passed, in which the word *"Ireland"* was left out, just as it had been before. The matter being a second time explained, was a second time regulated.

Now if it be considered, that the omission mentioned struck off with ONE word SO VERY GREAT A PART OF OUR TRADE, it must appear *remarkable*; and equally so is the method by which *Rice* became an enumerated commodity.

"The enumeration was obtained (says Mr. [*a*] *Gee*) by one *Cole,* a Captain of a ship, employed by a company then trading to *Carolina,* for several ships going from *England* thither, and purchasing rice for *Portugal* prevented *the aforesaid Captain* of a loading. Upon his coming home, he possessed one Mr. *Lowndes,* a member of parliament (*who was very frequently employed to prepare bills*) with an opinion, that carrying rice directly to *Portugal,* was a prejudice to the trade of *England,* and PRIVATELY got a clause into an act, to make it an enumerated commodity; *by which means he secured a freight to himself.* BUT THE CONSEQUENCE PROVED A VAST LOSS TO THE NATION."

I find that this clause, "PRIVATELY got into an act," FOR THE BENEFIT OF CAPTAIN COLE, to the "VAST LOSS OF THE NATION," is foisted into the 3d and 4th *Ann,* Chap. 5th, intituled, "An act for granting to her Majesty a further subsidy on wines and merchandizes imported," with which it has no more connection, than with 34th *Edward* I. the 34th and 35th of *Henry* VIII. and the 25th of *Charles* II. WHICH PROVIDE, THAT NO PERSON SHALL BE TAXED BUT BY HIMSELF OR HIS REPRESENTATIVE.

[*a*] *Gee* on Trade, p. 32.

haps I should speak more properly, if I was to use another term.

There are two ways of laying taxes. One is, by imposing a certain sum on particular kinds of property, to be paid by the *user* or *consumer*, or by rating the *person* at a certain sum. The other is, by imposing a certain sum on particular kinds of property, to be paid by the *seller*.

When a man pays the first sort of tax, he *knows with certainty* that he pays so much money *for a tax*. The *consideration* for which he pays it, is remote, and, it may be, does not occur to him. He is sensible too, that he is *commanded and obliged* to pay it *as a tax;* and therefore people are apt to be displeased with this sort of tax.

The other sort of tax is submitted to in a very different manner. The purchaser of an article, very seldom reflects that the seller raises his price, so as to indemnify himself for the tax *he* has paid. He knows that the prices of things are continually fluctuating, and if he thinks about the tax, he thinks at the same time, in all probability, that he *might* have paid as much, if the article he buys had not been taxed. He gets something *visible* and *agreeable* for his money; and tax and price are so confounded together, that he cannot separate, or does not chuse to take the trouble of separating them.

This mode of taxation therefore is the mode suited to arbitrary and oppressive governments. The love of liberty is so natural to the human heart, that unfeeling tyrants think themselves obliged to accommodate their schemes as much as they can to the appearance of justice and reason, and to deceive those whom they resolve to destroy, or oppress, by presenting to them a miserable picture of freedom, when the inestimable original is lost.

This policy did not escape the cruel and rapacious *NERO*. That monster, apprehensive that his crimes might endanger his authority and life, thought proper to do some popular acts, to secure the obedience of his subjects. Among other things, says *Tacitus,* "he remitted the twenty-fifth part of the price on the sale of slaves, but rather in *shew* than *reality;* for the *seller* being ordered to pay it, it became part of the price to the *buyer.*"*

This is the reflection of the judicious *Historian;* but the deluded *people* gave their infamous Emperor full credit for

* *Tacitus's Ann.,* Book 13, § 31.

his false generosity. Other nations have been treated in the same manner the *Romans* were. The honest, industrious *Germans*, who are settled in different parts of this continent, can inform us, that it was this sort of tax that drove them from their native land to our woods, at that time the seats of perfect and undisturbed freedom.

Their Princes, enflamed by the lust of power, and the lust of avarice, two furies that the more they are gorged, the more hungry they grow, transgressed the bounds they ought, in regard to themselves, to have observed. To keep up the deception in the minds of subjects, "there must be," says* a very learned author, "some proportion between the impost and the value of the commodity; wherefore there ought not to be an excessive duty upon merchandizes of little value. There are countries in which the duty exceeds seventeen or eighteen times the value of the commodity. In this case the Prince removes the illusion. His subjects plainly see they are dealt with in an unreasonable manner, which renders them most exquisitely sensible of their slavish situation." From hence it appears, that subjects may be ground down into misery by this sort of taxation, as well as by the former. They will be as much impoverished, if their money is taken from them in this way as in the other; and that it will be taken, may be more evident, by attending to a few more considerations.

The merchant or importer, who pays the duty at first, will not consent to be so much money out of pocket. He therefore proportionably raises the price of his goods. It may then be said to be a contest between him and the person offering to buy, who shall lose the duty. This must be decided by the nature of the commodities, and the purchaser's demand for them. If they are mere luxuries, he is at liberty to do as he pleases, and if he buys, he does it voluntarily: But if they are absolute *necessaries* or *conveniences*, which use and custom have made requisite for the comfort of life, and which he is not permitted, by the power imposing the duty, *to get elsewhere*, there the seller has a plain advantage, and the buyer *must* pay the duty. In fact, the seller is nothing less than a collector of the tax for the power that imposed it. If these duties then are extended to the necessaries and conveniences of life in general, and enormously encreased, the people must at length become indeed "most exquisitely sensible of their slavish situation." Their happiness therefore entirely depends

* *Montesquieu's Spirit of Laws*, Book 13, Chap. 8.

on the moderation of those who have authority to impose the duties.

I shall now apply these observations to the late act of parliament. Certain duties are thereby imposed on paper and glass, imported into these colonies. By the laws of *Great-Britain* we are prohibited to get these articles from any other part of the world. We cannot at present, nor for many years to come, tho' we should apply ourselves to these manufactures with the utmost industry, make enough ourselves for our own use. That paper and glass are not only convenient, but absolutely necessary for us, I imagine very few will contend. Some perhaps, who think mankind grew wicked and luxurious, as soon as they found out another way of communicating their sentiments than by speech, and another way of dwelling than in caves, may advance so whimsical an opinion. But I presume no body will take the unnecessary trouble of refuting them.

From these remarks I think it evident, that we *must* use paper and glass; that what we use *must* be *British;* and that we *must* pay the duties imposed, unless those who sell these articles, are so generous as to make us presents of the duties they pay.

Some persons may think this act of no consequence, because the duties are so *small.* A fatal error. *That* is the very circumstance most alarming to me. For I am convinced, that the authors of this law would never have obtained an act to raise so trifling a sum as it must do, had they not intended by *it* to establish a *precedent* for future use. To console ourselves with the *smallness* of the duties, is to walk deliberately into the snare that is set for us, praising the *neatness* of the workmanship. Suppose the duties imposed by the late act could be paid by these distressed colonies with the utmost ease, and that the purposes to which they are to be applied, were the most reasonable and equitable that can be conceived, the contrary of which I hope to demonstrate before these letters are concluded; yet even in such a supposed case, these colonies ought to regard the act with abhorrence. For WHO ARE A FREE PEOPLE? Not *those,* over whom government is reasonably and equitably exercised, but *those,* who live under a government so *constitutionally checked* and *controuled,* that proper provision is made against its being otherwise exercised.

The late act is founded on the destruction of this constitutional security. If the parliament have a right to lay a duty of Four Shillings and Eight-pence on a hundred weight of glass, or a ream of paper, they have a right to lay a duty of any other sum on either. They may raise the duty, as the author before quoted says has been done in some countries, till it "exceeds seventeen or eighteen times the value of the commodity." In short, if they have a right *to* levy a tax of *one penny* upon us, they have a right to levy a *million* upon us: For where does their right stop? At any given number of Pence, Shillings or Pounds? To attempt to limit their right, after granting it to exist at all, is as contrary to reason—as granting it to exist at all, is contrary to justice. If *they* have any right to tax *us*—then, whether *our own money* shall continue in *our own pockets* or not, depends no longer on *us*, but on *them*. *"There is nothing which" we can call our own; or, to use the words of Mr. *Locke*[7]—"WHAT PROPERTY HAVE WE IN THAT, WHICH ANOTHER MAY, BY RIGHT, TAKE, WHEN HE PLEASES, TO HIMSELF?"

These duties, which will inevitably be levied upon us—which are now levying upon us—are *expressly* laid FOR THE SOLE PURPOSES OF TAKING MONEY. This is the true definition of *"taxes."* They are therefore *taxes*. This money is to be taken from *us*. *We* are therefore *taxed*. *Those* who are *taxed* without their own consent, expressed by themselves or their representatives, are *slaves*. *We are taxed* without our own consent, expressed by ourselves or our representatives. *We* are therefore—†*SLAVES*.

Miserable vulgus
A miserable tribe.

A FARMER.

* Lord *Cambden's* speech.

[7] John Locke (1632–1704), an English political philosopher whose ideas on constitutional government were probably the strongest single intellectual influence on colonial political thinkers.

† "It is my opinion, that this kingdom has no right to lay a TAX upon the colonies."—"The *Americans* are the SONS, not the BASTARDS of *England*."—"The distinction between LEGISLATION and TAXATION is essentially necessary to liberty."—"The COMMONS of *America*, represented in their several assemblies, have ever been in possession of this their constitutional right, of GIVING AND GRANTING THEIR OWN MONEY. They would have been *SLAVES*, if they had not enjoyed it." "The idea of a *virtual representation* of *America* in this house, is the most contemptible idea, that ever entered into the head of man.—It does not deserve a serious refutation." *Mr.* Pitt's *speech on the* Stamp-Act.

That great and excellent man Lord *Cambden*, maintains the same opinion. His speech in the house of peers, on the declaratory bill of the sovereignty of *Great-Britain* over the colonies, has lately appeared in our papers. The following extracts so perfectly agree with, and confirm the sentiments avowed in these letters, that it is hoped the inserting them in this note will be excused.

"As the Affair is of the *utmost importance*, and in its consequences may involve the *fate of kingdoms*, I took the strictest review of my arguments; I re-examined all my authorities; fully determined if I found myself mistaken, publickly to own my mistake, and give up my opinion; But my searches have more and more convinced me, that the *British* parliament have *NO*

LETTER VIII.

My dear COUNTRYMEN,

IN my opinion, a dangerous example is set in the last act relating to these colonies. The power of parliament to levy money upon us for raising a revenue, is therein *avowed* and *exerted*. Regarding the act on this single principle, I must again repeat, and I think it my duty to repeat, that to me it appears to be *unconstitutional*.

No man, who considers the conduct of the parliament since the repeal of the *Stamp-Act*, and the disposition of many people at home, can doubt, that the chief object of attention there, is, to use Mr. *Greenville's* expression, "providing that the DEPENDENCE and OBEDIENCE of the colonies be asserted and maintained."

Under the influence of this notion, instantly on repealing the *Stamp-Act*, an act passed, declaring the power of parliament to bind these colonies *in all cases whatever*.[8] This however was only planting a barren tree, that cast a *shade* indeed

---

RIGHT TO TAX the *Americans*."—"Nor is the doctrine new; it is as old as the constitution; it grew up with it; indeed it is its support."—"TAXATION and REPRESENTATION are inseparably united. *GOD* hath joined them: No *British* parliament can separate them: To endeavour to do it, is to stab our vitals."

"My position is this—I repeat it—I will maintain it to my last hour—TAXATION and REPRESENTATION are inseparable—this position is founded on the laws of nature; it is more, it is itself AN ETERNAL LAW OF NATURE; for whatever is a man's own, is absolutely his own; NO MAN HATH A RIGHT TO TAKE IT FROM HIM WITHOUT HIS CONSENT, either expressed by himself or representative; *whoever attempts to do it, attempts an injury*; WHOEVER DOES IT, *COMMITS A ROBBERY;* HE THROWS DOWN THE DISTINCTION BETWEEN LIBERTY AND SLAVERY."—"There is not a *blade of grass*, in the most obscure corner of the kingdom, which is not, which was not ever *represented*, since the constitution began: There is not a *blade of grass*, which, when taxed, *was not taxed by the consent of the proprietor*." "The forefathers of the *Americans* did not leave their native country, and subject themselves to every danger and distress, TO BE REDUCED TO A STATE OF SLAVERY. They did not give up their rights: They looked for protection, and *not for* CHAINS, from their mother country. By her they expected to be defended in the possession of their property, and not to be deprived of it: For should the present power continue, THERE IS NOTHING WHICH THEY CAN CALL THEIR OWN; or, to use the words of Mr. *Locke*, *"WHAT PROPERTY HAVE THEY IN THAT, WHICH ANOTHER MAY, BY RIGHT, TAKE, WHEN HE PLEASES, TO HIMSELF?"*

It is impossible to read this speech, and Mr. *Pitt*'s, and not be charmed with the generous zeal for the rights of mankind that glows in every sentence. These great and good men, animated by the subject they speak upon, seem to rise above all the former glorious exertions of their abilities. A foreigner might be tempted to think they are *Americans*, asserting with all the ardor of patriotism, and all the anxiety of apprehension, the cause of their native land—and not *Britons*, striving to stop their mistaken countrymen from oppressing others. Their reasoning is not only just—it is, as Mr. *Hume* says of the eloquence of *Demosthenes*, "vehement." It is disdain, anger, boldness, freedom, involved in a continual stream of argument.

[8] The Declaratory Act.

over the colonies, but yield no *fruit*. It being determined to enforce the authority on which the *Stamp-Act* was founded, the parliament having never renounced the right, as Mr. *Pitt* advised them to do; and it being thought proper to disguise that authority in such a manner, as not again to alarm the colonies: some little time was required to find a method, by which both these points should be united. At last the ingenuity of Mr. *Greenville* and his party accomplished the matter, as it was thought, in "an act for granting certain duties in the *British* colonies and plantations in *America*, for allowing drawbacks," *&c.* which is the title of the act laying duties on paper, *&c.*

The parliament having several times before imposed duties to be paid in *America*, IT WAS EXPECTED, NO DOUBT, THAT THE REPETITION OF SUCH A MEASURE WOULD BE PASSED OVER, AS AN USUAL THING. But to have done this, without expressly "asserting and maintaining" the power of parliament to take our money without our consent, and to apply it as they please, would not have been, in Mr. *Greenville's* opinion, sufficiently declarative of its supremacy, nor sufficiently depressive of *American* freedom.

Therefore it is, that in this memorable act we find it *expressly* "provided," that money shall be levied upon us without our consent, for PURPOSES, that render it *if possible*, more dreadful than the *Stamp-Act*.

That act, alarming as it was, declared, the money thereby to be raised, should be applied "towards defraying the expences of defending, protecting and securing the *British* colonies and plantations in *America*." And it is evident from the whole act, that by the word "*British*," were intended colonies and plantations *settled by* British *people*, and not generally, *those subject to the* British *crown*. That act therefore seemed to have something gentle and kind in its intention, and to aim only at *our own welfare*: But the act now objected to, impose duties upon *British* colonies, "to defray the expences of defending, protecting and securing *his Majesty's* DOMINIONS *in* America."

What a *change* of words! What an *incomputable addition* to the expences intended by the *Stamp-Act*! "*His Majesty's* DOMINIONS" comprehended not only *the* British *colonies*, but also *the conquered provinces of* Canada *and* Florida, *and the* British *garrisons of* Nova-Scotia; for *these* do not deserve the name of *colonies*.

What justice is there in making US pay for "defending,

protecting and securing" THESE PLACES? What benefit *can* WE, or have WE ever derived *from them?* None of them was conquered *for* US; nor will "be defended, protected or secured" *for* US.

In fact, however advantageous the subduing or keeping any of these countries may be to *Great Britain,* the acquisition is greatly injurious to these colonies. Our chief property consists in *lands.* These would have been of much greater value, if such prodigious additions had not been made to the *British* territories on this continent. The natural increase of our own people, if confined within the colonies, would have raised the value still higher and higher every fifteen or twenty years: Besides we should have lived more compactly together, and have been therefore more able to resist any enemy. But now the inhabitants will be thinly scattered over an immense region, as those who want settlements, will chuse to make new ones, rather than pay great prices for old ones.

These are the consequences to the colonies, of the hearty assistance they gave to *Great-Britain* in the late war—a war *undertaken solely for her own benefit.* The objects of it were, the securing to herself the rich tracts of land on the back of these colonies, with the *Indian* trade; and *Nova-Scotia,* with the fishery.[9] *These and much more, has that kingdom gained;* but the *inferior animals,* that hunted with the *lion,* have been amply rewarded for all the sweat and blood their loyalty cost them, by the honor of having sweated and bled in such company.

I will not go so far as to say, that *Canada* and *Nova-Scotia* are curbs on *New-England;* the *chain of forts* through the back woods, on the *Middle Provinces;* and *Florida,* on the *rest:* But I will venture to say, that if the products of *Canada, Nova-Scotia,* and *Florida,* deserve any consideration, the two first of them are only rivals of our Northern Colonies, and the other of our Southern.

It has been said, that without the conquest of these countries, the colonies could not have been "protected, defended, and secured." If that is true, it may with as much propriety be said, that *Great-Britain* could not have been "defended, protected, and secured," without that conquest: For the colonies are parts of her empire, which it *as much* concerns

[9] That the colonies expected to benefit from the victory in the French and Indian Wars must have been evident to Dickinson. The Treaty of Paris of 1763 opened up the western lands for settlement and gave considerable impetus to land speculation and trading.

her as *them* to keep out of the hands of any other power.

But these colonies, when they were much weaker, defended themselves, before this Conquest was made; and could again do it, against any that might properly be called *their* Enemies. If *France* and *Spain* indeed should attack them, *as members of the* British *empire,* perhaps they might be distressed; but it would be in a *British* quarrel.

The largest account I have seen of the number of people in *Canada,* does not make them exceed 90,000. *Florida* can hardly be said to have any inhabitants. It is computed that there are in our colonies 3,000,000. *Our* force therefore must increase with a disproportion to the growth of *their* strength, that would render us very safe.

This being the state of the case, I cannot think it just that these colonies, labouring under so many misfortunes, should be loaded with *taxes,* to maintain countries, not only not useful, but hurtful to them. The support of *Canada* and *Florida* cost yearly, it is said, half a million sterling. From hence, we may make some guess of the load that is to be laid *upon* US; for we are not only to "defend, protect and secure" *them,* but also to make "an adequate provision for defraying the charge of the administration of justice, and the support of civil government, in such provinces where it shall be found necessary."

Not one of the provinces of *Canada, Nova-Scotia,* or *Florida,* has ever defrayed *these expences within itself:* And if the duties imposed by the last statute are collected, *all of them together,* according to the best information I can get, will not pay *one quarter as much as* Pennsylvania *alone.* So that the *British colonies* are to be drained of the rewards of their labor, to cherish the scorching sands of *Florida,* and the icy rocks of *Canada* and *Nova-Scotia,* which never will return to us one farthing that we send to them.

Great-Britain—I mean the ministry in *Great-Britain,* has cantoned *Canada* and *Florida* out into *five* or *six* governments, and may form *as many more.* There now are *fourteen* or *fifteen* regiments on this continent; and there soon may be as *many more.* To make "an adequate provision" FOR ALL THESE EXPENCES, is, no doubt, to be the *inheritance* of the colonies.

Can any man believe that the duties upon paper, *&c.,* are the *last* that will be laid for these purposes? It is in vain to hope, that because it is imprudent to lay duties on the exportation of manufactures from a mother country to colonies, as it may promote manufactures among them, that this consideration will prevent such a measure.

Ambitious, artful men have made it popular, and whatever injustice or destruction will attend it in the opinion of the colonists, at home it will be thought just and salutary.*

The people of *Great-Britain* will be told, and have been told, that *they* are sinking under an immense debt—that great part of this debt has been contracted in defending the colonies—that *these* are so ungrateful and undutiful, that they will not contribute one mite to its payment—nor even to the support of the army now kept up for their "defence and security,"—that they are rolling in wealth, and are of so bold and republican a spirit, that they are aiming at independence—that the only way to retain them in "obedience," is to keep a strict watch over them, and to draw off part of their riches in *taxes*—and that every burden laid upon *them,* is taking off so much from *Great-Britain*—These assertions will be generally believed, and the people will be persuaded that they cannot be too angry with their colonies, as that anger will be profitable to themselves.

In truth, *Great-Britain* alone receives any benefit from *Canada, Nova-Scotia* and *Florida;* and therefore she alone ought to maintain them. The old maxim of the law is drawn from reason and justice, and never could be more properly applied, than in this case.

Qui sentit commodum, sentire debet et onus.
They who feel the benefit, ought to feel the burden.

A FARMER.

LETTER IX.

My dear COUNTRYMEN,

I have made some observations on the PURPOSES for which money is to be levied upon us by the late act of parliament. I shall now offer to your consideration some further reflections on that subject: And, unless I am greatly mistaken, if these purposes are accomplished according to the *expressed* intention of the act, they will be found effectually to *supersede* that authority in our respective assemblies, which is essential to liberty. The question is not, whether some branches shall be

* So *credulous,* as well as *obstinate,* are the people in believing *every thing,* which flatters their *prevailing passion.* *Hume's Hist. of England.*

lopt off—The ax is laid to the root of the tree; and the whole body must infallibly perish, if we remain idle spectators of the work.

No free people ever existed, or can ever exist, without keeping, to use a common, but strong expression, "the purse strings," in their own hands. Where this is the case, *they* have a *constitutional check* upon the administration, which may thereby be brought into order *without violence:* But where such a power is not lodged in the *people,* oppression proceeds uncontrouled in its career, till the governed, transported into rage, seek redress in the midst of blood and confusion.

The elegant and ingenious Mr. *Hume,*[10] speaking of the *Anglo Norman* government, says—"Princes and Ministers were too ignorant, to be themselves sensible of the advantage attending an equitable administration, and there was no established council or *assembly,* WHICH COULD PROTECT THE PEOPLE, and BY WITHDRAWING SUPPLIES, regularly and PEACEABLY admonish the king of his duty, and ENSURE THE EXECUTION OF THE LAWS."

Thus this great man, whose political reflections are so much admired, makes *this power* one of the foundations of liberty.

The *English* history abounds with instances, proving that *this* is the proper and successful way to obtain redress of grievances. How often have kings and ministers endeavoured to throw off this legal curb upon them, by attempting to raise money by a variety of inventions, under pretence of law, without having recourse to parliament? And how often have they been brought to reason, and peaceably obliged to do justice, by the exertion of this constitutional authority of the people, vested in their representatives?

The inhabitants of these colonies have, on numberless occasions, reaped the benefit of this authority lodged *in their assemblies.*

It has been for a long time, and now is, a constant instruction to all governors, *to obtain a* PERMANENT *support for the offices of government.* But as the author of "the administration of the colonies" says, "this order of the crown is generally, if not universally, rejected by the legislatures of the colonies."

They perfectly know *how much* their grievances would be

[10] David Hume (1711–1776), Scottish philosopher and historian.

regarded, if they had *no other* method of engaging attention than by *complaining*. Those who rule, are extremely apt to think well of the constructions made by themselves in support of their own power. *These* are frequently erroneous, and pernicious to those they govern. Dry remonstrances, to shew that such constructions are wrong and oppressive, carry very little weight with them, in the opinions of persons who gratify their own inclinations in making these constructions. *They* CANNOT understand the reasoning that opposes *their* power and desires. But let it be made *their interest* to understand such reasoning—and a *wonderful light* is instantly thrown upon the matter; and then, rejected remonstrances become as clear as* "proofs of holy writ."

The three most important articles that our assemblies, or any legislatures can provide for, are, First—the defence of the society: Secondly—the administration of justice: And Thirdly—the support of civil government.

Nothing can properly regulate the expence of making provision for these occasions, but the *necessities* of the society; its *abilities;* the *conveniency* of the modes of levying money in it; the *manner* in which the laws have been executed: and the conduct of the officers of governments. *All which* are circumstances, that *cannot* possibly be properly *known,* but by the society itself; or if they should be known, *will not* probably be properly *considered* but by that society.

If money be raised upon us by *others,* without our consent, for our "defence," those who are the judges in *levying* it, must also be the judges in *applying* it. Of consequence the money *said* to be taken from us for our defence, *may be employed* to our injury. We may be chained in by a line of fortifications—obliged to pay for the building and maintaining them—and be told, that they are for our defence. With what face can we dispute the fact, after having granted that those who *apply* the money, had a right to *levy* it? For surely, it is much easier for their wisdom to understand how to apply it in the best manner, than how to levy it in the best manner. Besides, the *right of levying* is of infinitely more consequence, that *that of applying*. The people of *England*, who would burst out into fury, if the crown should attempt to *levy* money by its own authority, have always assigned to the crown the *application* of money.

As to "the administration of justice"— the judges ought,

* SHAKESPEARE.

in a well regulated state, to be equally independent of the executive and legislative powers. Thus in *England*, judges hold their commissions from the crown *"during good behaviour,"* and have salaries, suitable to their dignity, *settled* on them by parliament. The purity of the courts of law since this establishment, is a proof of the wisdom with which it was made.

But in these colonies, how fruitless has been every attempt to have judges appointed *"during good behaviour?"* Yet whoever considers the matter will soon perceive, that *such commissions* are beyond all comparison more necessary in these colonies, than they were in *England*.

The chief danger to the subject *there*, arose from the arbitrary *designs of the crown;* but *here*, the time may come, when we may have to contend with the *designs of the crown, and of a mighty kingdom*. What then must be our chance, when the laws of life and death are to be spoken by judges totally dependent on *that crown*, and *that kingdom*—sent over perhaps *from thence*—filled with *British prejudices*—and *backed by a* STANDING *army*—supported out of OUR OWN pockets, to "assert and maintain" OUR OWN "dependence and obedience."

But supposing that through the extreme lenity that will prevail in the government *through all future ages*, these colonies will never behold any thing like the campaign of chief justice *Jeffereys*, yet what innumerable acts of injustice may be committed, and how fatally may the principles of liberty be sapped, by a succession of judges *utterly independent of the people?* Before such judges the supple wretches, who cheerfully join in avowing sentiments inconsistent with freedom, will always meet with smiles; while the honest and brave men, who disdain to sacrifice their native land to their own advantage, but on every occasion boldly vindicate her cause, will constantly be regarded with frowns.

There are two other considerations relating to this head, that deserve the most serious attention.

By the late act, the officers of the customs are "impowered to enter into any HOUSE, warehouse, shop, cellar, or other place, in the *British* colonies or plantations in *America*, to search for or seize prohibited or unaccustomed goods," *&c.*, on "writs granted by the superior or supreme court of justice, having jurisdiction within such colony or plantation respectively."

If we only reflect that the judges of these courts are to be *during pleasure*—that they are to have "*adequate provision*" made for them, which is to continue *during their complaisant behaviour*—that they may be *strangers* to these colonies—what an engine of oppression may this authority be in such hands?

I am well aware, that writs of this kind may be granted at home, under the seal of the court of exchequer: But I know also, that the greatest asserters of the rights of *Englishmen* have always strenuously contended, that *such a power* was dangerous to freedom, and expressly contrary to the common law, which ever regarded a man's *house* as his castle, or a place of perfect security.

If such power was in the least degree dangerous *there*, it must be utterly destructive to liberty *here*. For the people there have two securities against the undue exercise of this power by the crown, which are wanting with us, if the late act takes place. In the first place, if any injustice is done *there*, the person injured may bring his action against the offender, and have it tried before INDEPENDENT JUDGES, who are* NO PARTIES IN COMMITTING THE INJURY. *Here* he must have it tried before DEPENDENT JUDGES, being the men WHO GRANTED THE WRIT.

To say, that the cause is to be tried by a jury, can never reconcile men who have any idea of freedom, to *such a power*. For we know that sheriffs in almost every colony on this continent, are totally dependent on the crown; and packing of the juries has been frequently practised even in the capital of the *British* empire. Even if juries are well inclined, we have too many instances of the influence of overbearing unjust judges upon them. The brave and wise men who accomplished the revolution, thought the *independency of judges* essential to freedom.

The other security which the people have at home, but which we shall want here, is this.

If this power is abused *there*, the parliament, the grand resource of the oppressed people, is ready to afford relief. Redress of grievances must precede grants of money. But what regard can *we* expect to have paid to our assemblies, when they will not hold even the puny privilege of *French* parliaments—that of registering, before they are put in execution, edicts that take away our money.

* The writs for searching houses in *England*, are to be granted "under the seal of the court of exchequer," according to the statute—and that seal is kept by the chancellor of the exchequer. *4th Inst., p.* 104.

The second consideration above hinted at, is this. There is a *confusion* in our laws, that is quite unknown in *Great-Britain.* As this cannot be described in a more clear or exact manner, than has been done by the ingenious author of the history of *New-York,* I beg leave to use his words. "The state of our laws opens a door to much controversy. The *uncertainty,* with respect to them, RENDERS PROPERTY PRECARIOUS, and GREATLY EXPOSES US TO THE ARBITRARY DECISION OF BAD JUDGES. The common law of *England* is generally received, together with such statutes as were enacted before we had a legislature of our own, but our courts EXERCISE A SOVEREIGN AUTHORITY, in determining *what parts of the common and statute law* ought to be extended: For it must be admitted that the *difference of circumstances* necessarily requires us, in some cases *to* REJECT *the determination of both.* In many instances, they have also extended even acts of parliament, passed since we had a distinct legislature, *which is greatly adding to our confusion.* The practice of our courts is no less *uncertain* than the law. Some of the *English* rules are adopted, others rejected. Two things therefore seem to be ABSOLUTELY NECESSARY for the PUBLIC SECURITY. First, the passing an act for settling the extent of the *English* laws. Secondly, that the courts ordain a general sett of rules for the regulation of the practice."

How easy it will be, under this "state of our laws," for an artful judge, to act in the most arbitrary manner, and yet cover his conduct under specious pretences; and how difficult it will be for the injured people to obtain relief, may be readily perceived. We may take a voyage of 3000 miles to complain; and after the trouble and hazard we have undergone, we may be told, that the collection of the revenue, and maintenance of the prerogative, must not be discouraged —and if the misbehavior is so gross as to admit of no justification, it may be said, that it was an error in judgment only, arising from the confusion of our laws, and the zeal of the King's servants to do their duty.

If the commissions of judges are *during the pleasure of the crown,* yet if their salaries are *during the pleasure of the people,* there will be *some check* upon their conduct. Few men will consent to draw on themselves the hatred and contempt of those among whom they live, for the empty honor of being judges. It is sordid love of gain, that tempts men to turn their backs on virtue, and pay their homage where they ought not.

As to the third particular, "the support of civil government,"—few words will be sufficient. Every man of the least understanding must know, that the *executive* power may be exercised in a manner so disagreeable and harassing to the people, that it is absolutely requisite, that *they* should be enabled by the gentlest method which human policy has yet been ingenious enough to invent, that is, *by shutting their hands,* to "ADMONISH" (as Mr. *Hume* says) certain persons "OF THEIR DUTY."

What shall we now think when, upon looking into the late act, we find the assemblies of these provinces thereby stript of their authority *on these several heads?* The *declared* intention of the act is, "that a revenue should be raised IN HIS MAJESTY'S DOMINIONS IN AMERICA, for making a more certain and adequate provision *for defraying the charge of* THE ADMINISTRATION OF JUSTICE, and *the support of* CIVIL GOVERNMENT in such provinces where it shall be found necessary, and *towards further defraying the expences of* DEFENDING, PROTECTING AND SECURING THE SAID DOMINIONS."

Let the reader pause here one moment—and reflect—whether the colony in which *he* lives, has not made such "certain and adequate provision" *for these purposes,* as is *by the colony judged suitable to its abilities, and all other circumstances.* Then let him reflect—whether if this act takes place, money is not to be raised on *that* colony *without its consent,* to make "provision" *for these purposes,* which *it does not judge to be suitable to its abilities, and all other circumstances.* Lastly, let him reflect—whether the people of that country are not in a state of the most abject slavery, *whose property may be taken from them* under the notion of right, *when they have refused to give it.*

For my part, I think I have good reason for vindicating the honor of the assemblies on this continent, by publicly asserting, that THEY *have made as "certain and adequate provision" for the purposes abovementioned, as they ought to have made,* and that it should not be presumed, that they will not do it hereafter. Why then should *these most important trusts* be wrested out of their hands? Why should they not now be permitted to enjoy that authority, which they have exercised from the first settlement of these colonies? Why should they be scandalized by this innovation, when their respective provinces are now, and will be, for several years, labouring under loads of debt, imposed on them for the very purpose now spoken of? Why should all the inhabitants of these colonies be, with the utmost indignity, treated as a herd of despicable stupid wretches, so utterly void of common sense, that they will not even make "adequate provision" for "the administration of justice, and the support of civil government" among them, or for their own "defence"—though without such "provision" every people must inevitably be overwhelmed with anarchy and destruction? Is it possible to form an idea of a slavery more *compleat,* more *miserable,* more *disgraceful,* than that of a people, where *justice is administered, government exercised,* and a *standing army maintained,* AT THE EXPENCE OF THE PEOPLE, and yet WITHOUT THE LEAST DEPENDENCE UPON THEM? If we can find no relief from this infamous situation, it will be fortunate for us, if Mr. *Greenville,* setting his fertile fancy again at work, can, as by one exertion of it he has stript us of our *property* and *liberty,* by another deprive us of so much of our *understanding;* that, unconscious of what we *have been* or *are,* and ungoaded by tormenting reflections, we may bow down our necks, with all the stupid serenity of servitude, to any drudgery, which our lords and masters shall please to command.

When the charges of the "administration of justice," the "support of civil government," and the expences of defending, protecting and securing" us, are provided for, I should be glad to know, upon *what occasions* the crown will ever call our assemblies together. Some few of them may meet of their own accord, by virtue of their charters. But what will they have to do, when they are met? To what shadows will they be reduced? The men, whose deliberations heretofore had an influence on every matter relating to the *liberty* and *happiness* of themselves and their constituents, and whose authority in domestic affairs at least, might well be compared to that of *Roman* senators, will *now* find their deliberations of no more consequence, than those of *constables.* They may *perhaps* be allowed to make laws *for the yoking of hogs,* or *the pounding of stray cattle.* Their influence will hardly be permitted to extend *so high,* as the *keeping roads in repair,* as *that business* may more properly be executed by those who receive the public cash.

One most memorable example in history is so applicable to the point now insisted on, that it will form a just conclusion of the observations that have been made.

Spain was once *free.* Their *Cortes* resembled our parliaments. No *money* could be raised on the subject, *without their consent*. One of their Kings having received a grant from them, to maintain a war against the *Moors*, desired, that if the sum which they had given, should not be sufficient, he might be allowed, *for that emergency only*, to raise more money *without assembling the Cortes*. The request was violently opposed by the best and wisest men in the assembly. It was, however, complied with by the votes of a majority; and this single concession was a PRECEDENT for other concessions of the like kind, until at last the crown obtained a general power of raising money, in cases of necessity. From that period the *Cortes* ceased to be *useful*,—the *people* ceased to be *free*.

Venienti occurite morbo.
Oppose a disease at its beginning.

A FARMER.

LETTER X.

My dear COUNTRYMEN,

The consequences, mentioned in the last letter, will not be the utmost limits of our *misery* and *infamy*, if the late act is acknowledged to be binding upon us. We feel too sensibly, that *any ministerial measures** relating to these colonies, are soon carried successfully through the parliament. Certain prejudices operate there so strong against us, that it may be justly questioned, whether *all* the provinces united, will ever be able effectually to call to an account before the parliament, any minister who shall abuse the power by the late act given to the crown in *America*. He may divide the spoils torn from us in what manner he pleases, *and we shall have no way of making him responsible*. If he should order, that every *governor* shall have a yearly salary of 5000 l. sterling; every *chief justice* of 3000 l.; every inferior officer in proportion; and should then reward the most profligate, ignorant, or needy dependents on himself or his friends, with places of the greatest trust, because they were of the greatest

* "The gentleman must not wonder he was not contradicted, when, as *minister*, he asserted the right of parliament to tax *America*. I know not how it is, but there is a MODESTY in this house, *which does not chuse to contradict a minister*. I wish gentlemen would get the better of this *modesty*. IF THEY DO NOT, PERHAPS THE COLLECTIVE BODY MAY BEGIN TO ABATE OF ITS RESPECT FOR THE REPRESENTATIVE." *Mr.* Pitt's *Speech*.

profit, this would be called an arrangement in consequence of the "adequate provision for defraying the charge of the administration of justice, and the support of the civil government:" And if the taxes should prove at any time insufficient to answer all the expences of the numberless offices, which ministers may please to create, surely the members of the house of commons will be so *"modest,"* as not to "contradict a minister" who shall tell them, it is become necessary to lay a new tax upon the colonies, for the laudable purposes of defraying the charges of the "administration of justice, and support of civil government," among them. Thus, in fact, we shall be* taxed by ministers. In short, it will be in their power to settle upon us any CIVIL, ECCLESIASTICAL, or MILITARY establishment, which they choose.

We may perceive, by the example of *Ireland,* how eager ministers are to seize upon any settled revenue, and apply it in supporting their own power. Happy are the men, and *happy the people, who grow wise by the misfortunes of others.* Earnestly, my dear countrymen, do I beseech the author of all good gifts, that you may grow wise in this manner; and if I may be allowed to take such a liberty, I beg leave to recommend to you in general, as the best method of attaining this wisdom, diligently to study the histories of other countries. You will there find all the arts, that can possibly be practiced by cunning rulers, or false patriots among yourselves, so fully delineated, that, changing names, the account would serve for your own times.

It is pretty well known on this continent, that *Ireland* has, with a regular consistency of injustice, been cruelly treated by ministers in the article of *pensions;* but there are some alarming circumstances relating to that subject, which I wish to have better known among us.

† The revenue of the crown there arises principally from

* "Within this act (*statute de tallagio non concedendo*) are all *new* offices erected, with *new* fees, or *old* offices, with *new* fees, for that is a tallage put upon the subject, which cannot be done without common assent by act of parliament. And this doth notably appear by a petition to parliament in anno 13 *H.* IV. where the commons complain, that an office was erected for measurage of cloths and canvas, with a new fee for the same, by colour of the king's letter patents, and pray that these letters patents may be revoked, for that the king could erect no offices with new fees to be taken of the people, who may not so be charged but by parliament."

2d. Inst. p. 533.

† An enquiry into the legality of pensions on the *Irish* establishment, by *Alexander M'Aulay,* Esq; one of the King's council, *&c.*

Mr. *M'Aulay* concludes his piece in the following beautiful manner. "If any *pensions* have been obtained on that establishment, to SERVE THE CORRUPT PURPOSES OF AMBITIOUS MEN.—If his Majesty's revenues of *Ireland* the Excise granted *"for pay of the army and defraying other* PUBLIC *charges, in defence and preservation of the kingdom"* —from the tonnage and additional poundage granted *"for protecting the trade of the kingdom at sea, and augmenting the* PUBLIC *revenue"*—from the hearth money granted—as a "PUBLIC *revenue, for a* PUBLIC *charge and expences."* There are some other branches of the revenue, concerning which there is not any *express* appropriation of them for PUBLIC *service,* but which were plainly *so intended.*

Of *these* branches of the revenue the crown is only *trustee* for the public. They are unalienable. They are inapplicable to any other purposes, but those for which they were established; and therefore are not *legally* chargeable with pensions.

There is another kind of revenue, which is a private revenue. This is not limited to any public uses; but the crown has the same property in it, that any person has in his estate. This does not amount, at the most, to *Fifteen Thousand Pounds* a year, probably not to *Seven,* and is the only revenue, that can be *legally* charged with pensions.

If ministers were accustomed to regard the rights or happiness of the people, the pensions in *Ireland* would not exceed the sum just mentioned: But long since have they exceeded that limit; and in *December* 1765, a motion was made in the house of commons in that kingdom, to address his Majesty on the great increase of pensions on the *Irish* establishment, amounting to the sum of 158,685 l.—in the last two years.

Attempts have been made to gloss over these gross encroachments, by this specious argument—"That expending

---

have been employed in pensions, TO DEBAUCH HIS MAJESTY'S SUBJECTS of both kingdoms.—If the treasure of *Ireland* has been expended in pensions, FOR CORRUPTING MEN OF THAT KINGDOM TO BETRAY THEIR COUNTRY; and men of the neighboring kingdom to betray both.—If *Irish* pensions have been procured, TO SUPPORT GAMESTERS AND GAMING-HOUSES; promoting a vice which threatens national ruin.—If pensions have been purloined out of the national treasure of *Ireland,* under the MASK OF SALARIES ANNEXED TO PUBLIC OFFICES, USELESS TO THE NATION; newly invented, FOR THE PURPOSES OF CORRUPTION.—If *Ireland,* just beginning to recover from the devastations of massacre and rebellion, be obstructed in the progress of her cure, BY SWARMS OF PENSIONARY VULTURES PREYING ON HER VITALS.—If, by squandering the national substance of *Ireland,* in a LICENTIOUS, UNBOUNDED PROFUSION OF PENSIONS, instead of employing it in nourishing and improving her infant *agriculture, trade* and *manufactures,* or in *enlightening* and *reforming* her *poor, ignorant, deluded, miserable natives* (by nature most amiable, most valuable, most worthy of public attention)—If *by such abuse of the national substance, sloth* and *nastiness, cold* and *hunger, nakedness* and *wretchedness, popery, depopulation* and *barbarism,* still maintain their ground; *still deform a country abounding with all the riches of nature,* yet hitherto destined to beggary.—If SUCH PENSIONS be found on the *Irish* establishment; let such be cut off: And let the perfidious advisers be branded with indelible characters of public infamy; adequate, if possible, to the dishonor of their crime."

a competent part of the PUBLIC REVENUE in pensions, from a principle of charity or generosity, adds to the dignity of the crown; and is *therefore* useful to the PUBLIC." To give this argument any weight, it must appear, that the pensions proceed from *charity* or *generosity* only"—and that it "adds to the dignity of the crown," *to act directly contrary to law.*—

From this conduct towards *Ireland* in open violation of law, we may easily foresee what *we* may expect, when a minister will have the *whole revenue* of *America* in his own hands, to be disposed of at his own pleasure: For *all* the monies raised by the late act are to be "*applied* by virtue of warrants under the sign manual, countersigned by the high treasurer, or any three of the commissioners of the treasury." The "RESIDUE" indeed is to be "paid into the receipt of the exchequer, and to be disposed of by parliament." So that a minister will have nothing to do, but to take care, that there shall be no "residue," and he is superior to all controul.

Besides the burden of *pensions* in *Ireland,* which have enormously encreased within these few years, almost all the *offices* in that poor kingdom, have been, since the commencement of the present century, and now are bestowed upon *strangers.* For tho' the merit of persons born there, justly raises them to places of high trust when they go abroad, as all *Europe* can witness, yet he is an uncommonly lucky *Irishman,* who can get a good post *in his* NATIVE *country.*

When I consider the* manner in which that island has been

* In *Charles* the Second's time, the house of commons, influenced by some factious demagogues, were resolved to prohibit the importation of *Irish* cattle into *England.* Among other arguments in favour of *Ireland* it was insisted . . . "That by cutting off almost entirely the trade between the kingdoms, ALL THE NATURAL BANDS OF UNION WERE DISSOLVED, and nothing remained to keep the *Irish* in their duty, but *force* and *violence.*"

"The king (says Mr. *Hume,* in his history of *England*) was so convinced of the justness of these reasons, that he used all his interest to oppose the bill, and he openly declared, that he could not give his assent to it with a safe conscience. But the commons were resolute in their purpose." . . . "And the spirit of *TYRANNY, of which* NATIONS *are as susceptible as* INDIVIDUALS, had animated the *English* extremely TO EXERT THEIR SUPERIORITY *over their dependent state.* No affair could be conducted with greater violence, than this by the commons. They even went so far in the preamble of the bill, as to declare the importation of *Irish* cattle to be a NUISANCE. By this expression they gave scope to their *passion,* and at the same time *barred the king's prerogative,* by which he might think himself intituled to dispense with a law, SO FULL OF INJUSTICE AND BAD POLICY. The lords expunged the word, but as the king was sensible that no supply would be given by the commons, unless they were gratified in all their PREJUDICES, he was obliged both to employ his interest with the peers, to make the bill pass, and to give the royal assent to it. He could not however, forbear expressing his displeasure, at the jealousy entertained against him, and at the intention which the commons discovered, of retrenching his prerogative.

THIS LAW BROUGHT GREAT DISTRESS FOR SOME TIME UPON IRELAND, BUT IT HAS

uniformly depressed for so many years past, with this pernicious particularity *of their* parliament continuing as long as the crown pleases,* I am astonished to observe *such a love of liberty* still animating that LOYAL and GENEROUS nation; and nothing can rise higher my idea of the INTEGRITY and †PUBLIC SPIRIT of a people, who have preserved the sacred fire of freedom from being extinguished, tho' the altar on which it burnt, has been overturned.

In the same manner shall we unquestionably be treated, as soon as the late taxes laid upon us, shall make posts in the "government," and the "administration of justice" *here,* worth the attention of persons of influence in *Great-Britain.* We know enough already to satisfy us of this truth. But this will not be the worst part of our case.

OCCASIONED THEIR APPLYING WITH GREATER INDUSTRY TO MANUFACTURES, AND HAS PROVED IN THE ISSUE BENEFICIAL TO THAT KINGDOM."

Perhaps the *same reason* occasioned the "barring the king's prerogative" in the late act suspending the legislation of *New York.*

This we may be assured of, that WE are as dear to his *Majesty,* as the people of *Great-Britain* are. WE are his *subjects* as well as they, and *as faithful subjects;* and his Majesty has given too many, too constant proofs of his piety and virtue, for any man to think it possible, that *such a prince* can make any unjust distinction between *such subjects.* It makes no difference to his Majesty, whether supplies are raised in *Great-Britain,* or *America;* but it makes *some* difference to the commons of that kingdom.

To speak plainly as becomes an honest man on such important occasions, all our misfortunes are owing to a LUST OF POWER in men of *abilities* and *influence.* This prompts them to seek POPULARITY by *expedients* profitable to themselves, though ever so destructive to their country.

Such is the accursed nature of lawless ambition, and yet . . . What heart but melts at the thought! . . . Such false, detestable PATRIOTS, in *every state,* have led their blind, confiding country, shouting their applauses, into the jaws of *shame* and *ruin.* May the wisdom and goodness of the people of *Great-Britain,* save them from the usual fate of nations.

". . . . . . MENTUM MORTALIA TANGUNT."

* The last *Irish* parliament continued 33 years, during all the late King's reign. The present parliament there has continued from the beginning of this reign; and probably will continue till this reign ends.

† I am informed, that within these few years, a petition was presented to the house of commons, setting forth, "that herrings were imported into *Ireland* from some foreign parts of the north so cheap, as to discourage the *British* herring fishery, and therefore praying that some remedy might be applied in that behalf by parliament."

That upon this petition, the house came to a resolution, to impose a duty of Two Shillings sterling on every barrel of foreign herrings imported into *Ireland;* but afterwards dropt the affair, FOR FEAR OF ENGAGING IN A DISPUTE WITH IRELAND ABOUT THE RIGHT OF TAXING HER.

So much higher was the opinion, which the house entertained of the spirit of *Ireland;* than of that of these colonies.

I find, in the last *English* papers, that the resolution and firmness with which the people of *Ireland* have lately asserted their freedom, have been so alarming in *Great-Britain,* that the Lord Lieutenant, in his speech on the 20th of last *October,* "recommended to that parliament, that such provision may be made for securing the judges in the enjoyment of their *offices* and *appointments,* DURING THEIR GOOD BEHAVIOR, as shall be thought most expedient."

What an important concession is thus obtained, by making demands becoming freemen, with a courage and perseverance becoming Freemen!

The *principals*, in all great offices, will reside in *England*, making some paltry allowance to deputies for doing the business *here*. Let any man consider what an exhausting drain this must be upon us, when ministers are possessed of the power of creating what posts they please, and of affixing to such posts what salaries they please, and he must be convinced how destructive the late act will be. The injured kingdom lately mentioned, can tell us the mischiefs of ABSENTEES; and we may perceive already the same disposition taking place with us. The government of *New-York* has been exercised by a deputy. That of *Virginia* is now held so; and we know of a number of secretary-ships, collector-ships, and other offices, held in the same manner.

True it is, that if the people of *Great-Britain* were not too much blinded by the passions, that have been artfully excited in their breasts, against their dutiful children the colonists, these considerations would be nearly as alarming to them as to us. The influence of the crown was thought by wise men, many years ago, too great by reason of the multitude of pensions and places bestowed by it. These have been vastly encreased since,* and perhaps it would be no difficult matter to prove that the people have decreased.

Surely therefore, those who wish the welfare of their country, ought seriously to reflect, what may be the consequence of such a new creation of offices, in the disposal of the crown. The *army*, the *administration of justice*, and the *civil government* here, with such salaries as the crown shall please to annex, will extend *ministerial influence* as much

* One of the reasons urged by that great and honest statesman, Sir *William Temple* to *Charles* the Second, in his famous remonstrance, to dissuade him from aiming at arbitrary power, was, that the King "had few offices to bestow." *Humes Hist.* of *England*.

"Tho' the wings of prerogative have been clipt, the influence of the crown is greater than ever it was in any period of our history. For when we consider in how many boroughs the government has the votes at command; when we consider the vast body of persons employed in the collection of the revenue, in every part of the kingdom, the inconceivable number of placemen, and candidates for places in the customs, in the excise, in the post-office, in the dock-yards, in the ordinance, in the salt-office, in the stamps, in the navy and victualling offices, and in a variety of other departments; when we consider again the extensive influence of the money corporations, subscription jobbers and contractors, the endless dependencies created by the obligations conferred on the bulk of the gentlemen's families throughout the kingdom, who have relations preferred in our navy and numerous standing army; when I say, we consider how wide, how binding a dependence on the crown is created by the above enumerated particulars, and the great, the enormous weight and influence which the crown derives from this extensive dependence upon its favor and power, any lord in waiting, any lord of the bed-chamber, any man may be appointed minister."

A doctrine to this effect is said to have been the device of L—— H——.
Late News Paper.

beyond its former bounds, as the late war did the *British* dominions.

But whatever the people of *Great-Britain* may think on this occasion, I hope the people of these colonies will unanimously join in this sentiment, that the late act of parliament is injurious to their liberty, and that this sentiment will unite them in a firm opposition to it, in the same manner as the dread of the *Stamp-Act* did.

Some persons may imagine the sums to be raised by it, are but small, and therefore may be inclined to acquiesce under it. A conduct more dangerous to freedom, as before has been observed, can never be adopted. Nothing is wanted at home but a* PRECEDENT, the force of which shall be established, by the tacit submission of the colonies. With what zeal was the statute erecting the post-office, and another relating to the recovery of debts in *America,* urged and tortured, as *precedents* in support of the *Stamp-Act*, tho' wholly inapplicable. If the parliament succeeds in this attempt, other statutes will impose other duties. Instead of taxing ourselves, as we have been accustomed to do, from the first settlement of these provinces, all our usual taxes will be converted into parliamentary taxes on our importations; and thus the parliament will levy upon us such sums of money as they chuse to take, *without any other* LIMITATION, *than their* PLEASURE.

We know how much labor and care have been bestowed by these colonies, in laying taxes in such a manner, that they should be most *easy* to the people, by being laid on the proper articles; most *equal,* by being proportioned to every man's circumstances; and *cheapest,* by the method directed for collecting them.

But *parliamentary* taxes will be laid on us, without any consideration, whether there is any *easier* mode. The *only point* regarded will be, the *certainty of levying the taxes,* and not the *convenience* of the people on whom they are to be levied; and therefore all statutes on this head will be such as will be most likely, according to the favorite phrase, "*to execute themselves.*"

* "Here may be observed, that when any ancient law or custom of parliament is broken, and the crown *possessed* of a *precedent,* how *difficult a thing it is to restore the subject again to his* FORMER FREEDOM *and* SAFETY."
2d. Coke's Inst. p. 529.

"It is not almost credible to *foresee,* when any maxim or *fundamental law* of this realm is altered (as elsewhere hath been observed) what *dangerous inconvenience* do follow." *4th Coke's Inst. p.* 41.

Taxes in every free state have been, and ought to be, as exactly *proportioned as is possible to the abilities of those who are to pay them.* They cannot otherwise be *just.* Even a *Hottentot* would comprehend the *unreasonableness* of making a poor man pay as much for "defending" the property of a rich man, as the rich man pays himself.

Let any person look into the late act of parliament, and he will immediately perceive, that the immense estates of Lord *Fairfax,* Lord* *Baltimore,* and our *Proprietaries,*[11] which are amongst his Majesty's other "DOMINIONS" to be "defended, protected and secured" by the act, will not pay a *single farthing* for the duties thereby imposed, except Lord *Fairfax* wants some of his windows glazed; Lord *Baltimore* and our *Proprietaries* are quite secure, as they live in *England.*

I mention these particular cases, as striking instances how far the late act is a deviation from *that principle of justice,* which has so constantly distinguished our own laws on this continent, and ought to be regarded in all laws.

The third consideration with our continental assemblies in laying taxes, has been the *method* of collecting them. This has been done by a few officers, with moderate allowances, under the inspection of the respective assemblies. *No more was raised from the subject,* than was used for the intended purposes. But by the late act, a minister may appoint *as many officers as he pleases* for collecting the taxes; may assign them *what salaries he thinks* "adequate;" and they are subject to *no inspection but his own.*

In short, if the late act of parliament takes effect these colonies must dwindle down into "COMMON CORPORATIONS," as their enemies, in the debates concerning the repeal of the *Stamp-Act, strenuously insisted they were;* and it seems not

* *Maryland* and *Pennsylvania* have been engaged in the warmest disputes, in order to obtain an equal and just taxation of their Proprietors' estates: But this late act of parliament does more for those Proprietors, than they themselves would venture to demand. It *totally exempts* them from taxation—tho' their vast estates are to be "secured" by the taxes of other people.

[11] Maryland was originally a proprietary colony, granted by Charles I to George Calvert, the first Lord Baltimore, in 1632. In 1691 it was changed to a royal province, but was re-granted to Charles Calvert, the fourth Lord Baltimore, in 1715. Virginia was originally settled by the Virginia Company, but the original charter was revoked in 1624 when Virginia became a royal colony. Thomas Fairfax, the sixth Lord Fairfax, had inherited an estate of more than five million acres between the Rappahannock and Potomac Rivers from his grandfather, Lord Culpeper. The Penn family's proprietorship over Pennsylvania (originally granted in 1680) and over Delaware (originally granted in 1682) lasted until the Revolution, except for two years, 1692–1694, during which time the colonies were placed under royal rule. The proprietary status of the colony was among the chief sources of pre-Revolutionary tension in Pennsylvania.

improbable that some future historian may thus record our fall.

"The eighth year of this reign was distinguished by *a very memorable event,* the *American* colonies then submitting, for the *FIRST* time, to be *taxed* by the *British* parliament. An attempt of this kind had been made about two years before, but was defeated by the vigorous exertions of the several provinces, in defence of their liberty. Their behavior on that occasion rendered their name very celebrated *for a short time* all over *Europe;* all states being extremely attentive to a dispute between *Great-Britain,* and so considerable a part of her dominions. For as she was thought to be grown too powerful, by the successful conclusion of the late war she had been engaged in, it was hoped by many, that as it had happened before to other kingdoms, civil discords would afford opportunities of revenging all the injuries supposed to be received from her. However, the cause of dissention was removed, by a repeal of the statute that had given offence. This affair rendered the SUBMISSIVE CONDUCT of the colonies so soon after, the more extraordinary; there being *no difference* between the mode of taxation which they opposed, and that to which they submitted, but this, that by the first, they were to be continually *reminded* that they *were taxed,* by certain marks *stamped* on every piece of paper or parchment they used. The authors of *that statute* triumphed greatly on this conduct of the colonies, and insisted, that if the people of *Great-Britain* had persisted in enforcing it, the *Americans* would have been, in a few months, *so fatigued with the efforts of patriotism,* that they would have yielded obedience.

"Certain it is, that tho' they had before their eyes *so many illustrious examples* in their mother country, of *the constant success* attending *firmness* and *perseverance,* in opposition to dangerous encroachments on liberty, yet they quietly gave up a point of the LAST IMPORTANCE. From thence the decline of their freedom began, and its decay was extremely rapid; for as *money* was always raised upon them by the parliament, their *assemblies* grew immediately *useless,* and in a short time *contemptible:* And in less than one hundred years, the people sunk down into that *tameness* and *supineness* of spirit, by which they still continue to be distinguished."

Et majores vestros & posteros cogitate.
Remember your ancestors and your posterity.

A FARMER.

LETTER XI.

My dear COUNTRYMEN,

I have several times, in the course of these letters, mentioned the late act of parliament, as being the *foundation* of future measures injurious to these colonies; and the belief of this truth I wish to prevail, because I think it necessary to our safety.

A perpetual *jealousy*, respecting liberty, is absolutely requisite in all free-states. The very texture of their constitution, in *mixt* governments, demands it. For the *cautions* with which power is *distributed* among the several orders, *imply*, that *each* has that share which is proper for the general welfare, and therefore that any further acquisition must be pernicious. *Machiavel** employs a whole chapter in his discourses, to prove that a state, to be long lived, must be frequently corrected, and reduced to its first principles. But of all states that have existed, there never was any, in which this jealousy could be more proper than in these colonies. For the government here is not only *mixt*, but *dependent*, which circumstance occasions *a peculiarity in its form*, of a very delicate nature.

Two reasons induce me to desire, that this spirit of apprehension may be always kept up among us, in its utmost vigilance. The first is this—that as the happiness of these provinces indubitably consists in their connection with *Great-Britain*, any separation between them is less likely to be occasioned by civil discords, if every disgusting measure is opposed *singly*, and *while it is new:* For in this manner of proceeding, every such measure is most likely to be rectified. On the other hand, oppressions and dissatisfactions being permitted to accumulate—*if ever* the governed throw off the load, *they will do more*. A people does not reform with moderation. The rights of the subject therefore cannot be *too often* considered, explained or asserted: And whoever attempts to do this, shews himself, whatever may be the rash and peevish reflections of pretended wisdom, and pretended duty, a friend to *those* who injudiciously exercise their power, as well as *them* over whom it is so exercised.

Had all the points of prerogative claimed by *Charles* the First, been separately contested and settled in preceding reigns, his fate would in all probability have been very different; and

* *Machiavel's Discources—Book* 3. *Chap.* 1.

the people would have been content with that liberty which is compatible with regal authority. But* he thought, it would be dangerous for him to give up the powers which at any time had been by usurpation exercised by the crown, as those that were legally vested in it. This produced an equal excess on the part of the people. For when their passions were excited by *multiplied* grievances, they thought it would be as dangerous for them to allow the powers that were legally vested in the crown, as those which at any time had been by usurpation exercised by it. Acts, that might *by themselves* have been upon many considerations excused or extenuated, derived a contagious malignancy and odium from other acts, with which they were connected. They were not regarded according to the simple force of each, but as parts of a system of oppression. Every one therefore, however small in itself, became alarming, as an additional evidence of tyrannical designs. It was in vain for prudent and moderate men to insist, that there was no necessity to abolish royalty. Nothing less than the utter destruction of monarchy, could satisfy those who *had* suffered, and thought they had reason to believe, they always *should* suffer under it.

The consequences of these mutual distrusts are well known: But there is no other people mentioned in history, that I recollect, who have been so constantly watchful of their liberty, and so successful in their struggles for it, as the *English*. This consideration leads me to the second reason, why I "desire that the spirit of apprehension may be always kept up among us in its utmost vigilance."

The first principles of government are to be looked for in human nature. Some of the best writers have asserted, and it seems with good reason, that "government is founded on† *opinion.*"

* The author is sensible, that this is putting the gentlest construction on *Charles's* conduct; and that is one reason why he chooses it. Allowances ought to be made for the errors of those men, who are acknowledged to have been possessed of many virtues. The education of this unhappy prince, and his confidence in men not so good or wise as himself, had probably *filled* him with mistaken notions of his own authority, and of the consequences that would attend concessions of any kind to a people, who were represented to him, as aiming at too much power.

† "Opinion is of two kinds, *viz. opinion* of INTEREST, and *opinion* of RIGHT. By *opinion* of *interest,* I chiefly understand, *the sense of the public advantage which is reaped from government;* together with the persuasion, that the particular government which is established, is *equally advantageous* with any other, *that could be easily settled.*"

"*Right* is of two kinds, *right* to *power,* and *right* to *property.* What prevalence *opinion* of the first kind has over mankind, may easily be understood, by observing the attachment which all nations have to their ancient government, and even to those names which have had the sanction of

Custom undoubtedly has a mighty force in producing *opinion,* and reigns in nothing more arbitrarily than in public affairs. It gradually reconciles us to objects even of dread and detestation; and I cannot but think these lines of Mr. *Pope* as applicable to vice in *politics,* as to vice in *ethics*—

> Vice is a monster of so horrid mien,
> As to be hated, needs but to be seen;
> Yet *seen too oft,* familiar with her face,
> We first *endure,* then *pity,* then *embrace.*

When an act injurious to freedom has been *once* done, and the people *bear* it, the *repetition* of it is most likely to meet with *submission.* For as the *mischief* of the one was found to be tolerable, they will hope that of the second will prove so too; and they will not regard the infamy of the last, because they are stained with that of the first.

Indeed nations, in general, are not apt to *think* until they *feel;* and therefore nations in general have lost their liberty: For as violations of the rights of the *governed,* are commonly not only* *specious* but *small* at the beginning, they spread over the multitude in such a manner, as to touch individuals but slightly. †Thus they are disregarded. The power or profit that arises from these violations, *centering in few persons,* is to them considerable. For this reason the *governors* having in view their particular purposes, successively preserve an uniformity of conduct for attaining them. They regularly encrease the first injuries, till at length the inattentive people are compelled to perceive the heaviness of their burthens.—They begin to complain and enquire—but too late. They find their oppressors so strengthened by success, and themselves so entangled in examples of express authority on the part of

---

antiquity. *Antiquity always begets the opinion of right.*" . . . "It is suffciently understood, that the *opinion* of *right* to *property,* is of the greatest moment in all matters of government." *Hume's Essays.*

* Omnia mala exampla ex bonis initiis orta sunt.
SALLUST. *Bell. Cat. S.* 50.

† "The *republic* is always *attacked* with greater vigor, than it is *defended?* For the *audacious* and *profligate,* prompted by their natural enmity to it, are *easily impelled* to act by the *least nod* of their *leaders:* Whereas the honest, I know not why, are generally *slow* and *unwilling* to stir; and *neglecting* always the *BEGINNINGS of things,* are *never roused* to exert themselves, but by the *last necessity:* So that through IRRESOLUTION and DELAY, when they would be glad to compound at last for their QUIET, at the expence even of their HONOR, they *commonly lose them* BOTH."
CICERO's *Orat. for* SEXTIUS.

Such were the sentiments of this great and excellent man, whose vast abilities, and calamities of his country during his time, enabled him, by mournful experience, to form a just judgment on the conduct of the friends and enemies of liberty.

their rulers, and tacit recognition on their own part, that they are quite confounded: For millions entertain no other idea of the *legality* of power, than that it is founded on the *exercise* of power. They voluntarily fasten their chains, by adopting a pusillanimous *opinion,* "that there will be too much *danger* in attempting a remedy,"—or another *opinion* no less fatal,—"that the government has a *right* to treat them as it does." They then seek a wretched relief for their minds, by persuading themselves, that to yield their *obedience,* is to discharge their *duty*. The deplorable *poverty of spirit,* that prostrates all the dignity bestowed by Divine Providence on our nature—*of course succeeds.*

From these reflections I conclude, that every free state should incessantly watch, and instantly take alarm on any addition being made to the power exercised over them. Innumerable instances might be produced to shew, from what slight beginnings the most extensive consequences have flowed: But I shall select two only from the history of *England.*

Henry the Seventh was the *first* monarch of that kingdom, who established A STANDING BODY OF ARMED MEN. This was a band of *fifty* archers, called yeomen of the guard: And this institution, notwithstanding the smallness of the number, was, to prevent discontent,* "disguised under pretence of majesty and grandeur." In 1684 the standing forces were so much augmented, that *Rapin* says—"The king, in order to make his people *fully sensible of their new slavery,* affected to muster his troops, which amounted to 4000 well armed and disciplined men." I think our army, at this time, consists of more than *seventy* regiments.

The method of taxing by EXCISE was first introduced amidst the convulsions of civil wars. Extreme necessity was pretended for it, and its short continuance promised. After the restoration, an excise upon *beer, ale* and *other liquors,* was granted to the† king, one half in fee, the other for life, as an equivalent for the *court of wards*. Upon *James* the Second's accession, the parliament‡ gave him the first *excise,* with an additional duty on *wine, tobacco,* and some *other* things. Since the revolution it has been extended to salt, candles, leather, hides, hops, soap, paper, paste-boards, mill-boards, scale-boards, vellum, parchment, starch, silks, calicoes, linens, stuffs, printed, stained, *&c.* wire, wrought plate, coffee, tea, chocolate, *&c.*

* *Rapin's* History of *England.*
† 12 *Char.* II. Chap. 23 and 24.
‡ 1 *James* II. Chap. 1 and 4.

Thus a *standing army* and *excise* have, from their first slender origins, tho' always *hated,* always *feared,* always *opposed,* at length swelled up to their vast present bulk.

These facts are sufficient to support what I have said. 'Tis true, that all the mischiefs apprehended by our ancestors from a *standing army* and *excise,* have not *yet happened:* But it does not follow from thence, that they *will not happen.* The inside of a house may catch fire, and the most valuable apartments be ruined, before the flames burst out. The question in these cases is not, what evil *has actually attended* particular measures—but, what evil, in the nature of things, *is likely to attend* them. Certain circumstances may for some time delay effects, that *were reasonably expected,* and that *must ensue.* There was a long period, after the *Romans* had prorogued his command to **Q Publilius Philo,* before *that example* destroyed their liberty. All our kings, from the revolution to the present reign, have been *foreigners.* Their *ministers* generally continued but a short time in authority;† and they themselves were *mild* and *virtuous* princes.

A bold, *ambitious* prince, possessed of *great abilities,* firmly *fixed* in his throne *by descent,* served by *ministers like himself,* and rendered either *venerable* or *terrible* by the *glory of his successes,* may execute what his predecessors did not dare to attempt. *Henry* the Fourth tottered in his seat during his whole reign. *Henry* the Fifth drew the strength of that kingdom into *France,* to carry on his wars there, and left the *commons* at home, *protesting,* "that the people were not bound to serve out of the realm."

It is true, that a strong spirit of liberty subsists at present in *Great-Britain,* but what reliance is to be placed in the *temper* of a people, when the prince is possessed of an unconstitutional power, our own history can sufficiently inform us. When *Charles* the Second had strengthened himself by the return of the garrison of *Tangier,* "*England* (says *Rapin*)

* In the year of the city 428, "Duo singularia haec ei viro primum contigere; prorogatio imperii non ante in ullo facta et acto honore triumphus."
Liv. B. 8. *Chap.* 23. 26.

"Had the rest of the *Roman* citizens imitated the example of *L. Quintius,* who refused to have his consulship continued to him, they had never admitted that custom of proroguing of magistrates, and then the prolongation of their commands in the army had never been introduced, *which very thing was at length the ruin of that commonwealth.*" *Machiavel's Discourses, B.* 3. *Chap.* 24.

† I don't know but it may be said, with a good deal of reason, that a quick rotation of ministers is very desirable in *Great Britain.* A minister there has a vast store of materials to work with. *Long Administrations* are rather favorable to the *reputation* of a people abroad, than to their *liberty.*

saw on a sudden an *amazing revolution;* saw herself *stripped of all her rights and privileges,* excepting such as the king should vouchsafe to grant her: And what is *more astonishing,* the *English* themselves *delivered up* these very rights and privileges to *Charles* the Second, which they had so *passionately,* and if I may say it, *furiously* defended against the designs of *Charles* the First." This happened only *thirty-six* years after this last prince had been beheaded.

Some persons are of opinion, that liberty is not violated, but by such *open* acts of force; but they seem to be greatly mistaken. I could mention a period within these forty years, when almost as great a change of disposition was produced by the SECRET measures of a *long* administration, as by *Charles's* violence. Liberty, perhaps, is never exposed to so much danger, as when the people believe there is the least; for it may be subverted, and yet they not think so.

Public disgusting acts are seldom practiced by the ambitious, at the beginning of their designs. Such conduct *silences* and *discourages* the weak, and the wicked, who would otherwise have been their *advocates* or *accomplices.* It is of great consequence, to allow those who, upon any account, are inclined to favor them, something specious to *say* in their defence. Their power may be fully established, tho' it would not be safe for them to do *whatever they please.* For there are things, which, at some times, even *slaves* will not bear. *Julius Cæsar* and *Oliver Cromwell,* did not dare to assume the title of *king.* The *Grand Seignor* dares not lay a *new tax.* The king of *France* dares not be a *protestant.* Certain popular points may be left untouched, and yet freedom be extinguished. The commonalty of *Venice* imagine themselves free, because they are permitted to do what they ought not. But I quit a subject, that would lead me too far from my purpose.

By the late act of parliament, taxes are to be levied upon us, for "defraying the charge of the *administration of justice*—the support of *civil government*—and the expences of *defending* his Majesty's dominions in *America.*"

If any man doubts what ought to be the conduct of these colonies on this occasion, I would ask him these questions.

Has not the parliament *expressly* AVOWED their INTENTION of raising money from us FOR CERTAIN PURPOSES? Is not this scheme *popular* in *Great-Britain?* Will the taxes, imposed by the late act, *answer those purposes?* If it will, must it not take an *immense sum* from us? If it will not, *is it to be expected,* that the parliament will not *fully execute* their INTENTION when it is *pleasing at home,* and *not opposed here?* Must not this be done by imposing NEW *taxes?* Will not every addition thus made to the power of the *British* legislature, by *increasing the number of officers* employed in the collection? Will not every additional tax therefore render it *more difficult* to abrogate any of them? When a branch of revenue is once established, does it not appear to many people *invidious* and *undutiful,* to attempt to abolish it? If taxes, sufficient to *accomplish the* INTENTION of the parliament, are imposed by the parliament, *what taxes will remain* to be imposed by our assemblies? If *no material tax remains* to be imposed by them, what must become of *them,* and the *people* they represent?

*"If any person considers these things, and yet thinks our liberties are in no danger, I wonder at that person's security."

One other argument is to be added, which, by itself, I hope, will be sufficient to convince the most incredulous man on this continent, that the late act of parliament is *only* designed to be a PRECEDENT, whereon the future vassalage of these colonies may be established.

Every duty thereby laid on articles of *British* manufacture, is laid on some commodity, upon the exportation of which from *Great-Britain,* a *drawback* is payable. Those *drawbacks,* in most of the articles, are *exactly double* to the *duties* given by the late act. The parliament therefore might, in *half a dozen lines,* have raised MUCH MORE MONEY, only by *stopping the drawbacks* in the hands of the officers at home, on exportation to these colonies, than by this solemn imposition of taxes upon us, to be collected here. Probably, the artful contrivers of this act formed it in this manner, in order to reserve to themselves, in case of any objections being made to it, this specious pretence—"that the drawbacks are gifts to the colonies, and that the late act only lessens those gifts." But the truth is, that the drawbacks are intended for the encouragement and promotion of *British* manufactures and commerce, and are allowed on exportation to *any foreign parts,* as well as on exportation to these provinces. Besides, care has been taken to slide into the act, some articles on which there are no drawbacks. However, the *whole duties* laid by the late act on *all* the articles therein specified are *so small,* that they will not amount to *as much* as the *drawbacks* which are allowed on *part* of them only. If therefore, *the sum to be ob-*

* Demosthenes's 2d Philippic.

tained by the late act, had been the *sole object* in forming it, there would not have been any occasion for "the COMMONS of *Great-Britain,* to GIVE and GRANT to his Majesty RATES and DUTIES for *raising a revenue* IN *his Majesty's dominions in* America, for making a more certain and adequate provision for defraying the charges of the administration of justice, the support of civil government, and the expence of defending the said dominions;"—nor would there have been any occasion for an* expensive board of commissioners, and all the other new charges to which we are made liable.

Upon the whole, for my part, I regard the late act as an *experiment made of our disposition.* It is a bird sent out over the waters, to discover, whether the waves, that lately agitated this part of the world with such violence, are yet *subsided.* If *this adventurer* gets footing here, we shall quickly find it to be of the† kind described by the poet—

> *"Infelix vates."*
> A direful foreteller of future calamities.

A FARMER.

LETTER XII.

My Dear COUNTRYMEN,

Some states have lost their liberty by *particular accidents:* But this calamity is generally owing to the *decay of virtue.* A *people* is travelling fast to destruction, when *individuals* consider *their* interests as distinct from *those of the public.* Such notions are fatal to their country, and to themselves. Yet how many are there, so *weak* and *sordid* as to *think* they perform *all the offices of life,* if they earnestly endeavor to encrease

* The expence of this board, I am informed, is between Four and Five Thousand Pounds Sterling a year. The establishment of officers, for collectting the revenue in *America,* amounted before to Seven Thousand Six Hundred Pounds *per annum;* and yet, says the author of "The regulation of the colonies," "the whole remittance from *all* the taxes in the colonies, at an average of *thirty years,* has not amounted to One Thousand Nine Hundred Pounds a year, and in that sum Seven or Eight Hundred Pounds *per annum* only, have been remitted from *North America.*"

The smallness of the revenue arising from the duties in *America,* demonstrates that they were intended only as REGULATIONS OF TRADE: And can any person be so blind to truth, so dull of apprehension in a matter of unspeakable importance to his country, as to imagine, that the board of commissioners lately established at such a charge, is instituted to assist in collecting One Thousand Nine Hundred Pounds a year, or the trifling duties imposed by the late act? Surely every man on this continent must perceive, that they are established for the care of a NEW SYSTEM OF REVENUE, which is but now begun.

† "Dira caelaeno," *&c. AEneid* 3.

their own *wealth, power,* and *credit,* without the least regard for the society, under the protection of which they live; who, if they can make an *immediate profit to themselves,* by lending their assistance to those, whose projects plainly tend to the injury of their country, rejoice in their *dexterity,* and believe themselves entitled to the character of *able politicians.* Miserable men! Of whom it is hard to say, whether they ought to be most the objects of *pity* or *contempt:* But whose opinions are certainly as *detestable,* as their practices are *destructive.*

Tho' I always reflect, with a high pleasure, on the integrity and understanding of my countrymen, which, joined with a pure and humble devotion to the great and gracious author of every blessing they enjoy, will, I hope, ensure to them, and their posterity, all temporal and eternal happiness; yet when I consider, that in every age and country there have been bad men, my heart, at this threatening period, is so full of apprehension, as not to permit me to believe, but that there may be some on this continent, *against whom you ought to be upon your guard*—Men, who either* hold, or expect to hold

* It is not intended by these words, to throw any reflection upon gentlemen, because they are possessed of offices: For many of them are certainly men of virtue, and lovers of their country. But supposed obligations of *gratitude,* and *honor,* may induce them to be silent. Whether these obligations *ought to be* regarded or not, is not so much to be considered by others, in the judgment they form of these gentlemen, as whether *they think* they ought to be regarded. Perhaps, therefore, we shall act in the properest manner towards them, if we neither *reproach* nor *imitate* them. The persons meant in this letter, are the *base-spirited wretches,* who may endeavour to *distinguish themselves,* by their sordid zeal in defending and promoting measures, which *they know beyond all question,* to be *destructive* to the *just rights* and *true interests* of their country. It is scarcely possible to speak of *these men* with any degree of *patience*—It is scarcely possible to speak of them with any degree of *propriety*—For no words can truly describe their *guilt* and *meanness* —But every honest bosom, on their being mentioned, will *feel* what cannot be *expressed.*

If their wickedness did not blind them, they might perceive along the coast of these colonies, many men, remarkable instances of wrecked ambition, who after *distinguishing themselves* in the support of the *Stamp-Act,* by a courageous contempt of their country, and of justice, have been left to linger out their miserable existence, without a government, collectorship, secretaryship, or any other commission, to console them *as well as it could,* for loss of virtue and reputation—while numberless offices have been bestowed in these colonies on people from *Great-Britain,* and new ones are continually invented, to be thus bestowed. As a *few great prizes* are put into a lottery to TEMPT *multitudes to lose,* so *here* and *there* an *American* has been raised to a good post.—

"*Apparent* rari nantes *in gurgite vasto.*"

Mr. *Greenville,* indeed, in order to recommend the *Stamp-Act,* had the *unequalled* generosity, to pour down a golden shower of offices upon *Americans;* and yet these *ungrateful* colonies did not thank Mr. *Greenville* for shewing his kindness to their countrymen, nor *them* for accepting it. How must that great statesman have been surprised, to find, that the unpolished colonies could not be reconciled to *infamy* by *treachery?* Such a *bountiful* disposition toward us never appeared in any minister before him, and prob-

certain advantages, by setting examples for servility to their countrymen. Men, who trained to the employment, or self taught by a natural versatility of genius, serve as decoys for drawing the innocent and unaware into snares. It is not to be doubted but that such men will diligently bestir themselves on this and every like occasion, to spread the infection of their meanness as far as they can. On the plans *they* have adopted, this is *their* course. *This* is the method to recommend themselves to their *patrons*.

From *them* we shall learn, how *pleasant* and *profitable* a thing it is, to be for our SUBMISSIVE behavior *well spoken of* at *St. James* or *St. Stephen's;* at *Guildhall,* or the *Royal Exchange*. Specious fallacies will be drest up with all the arts of delusion, to persuade one colony *to distinguish herself from another,* by unbecoming condescensions, *which will serve the ambitious purposes of great men* at home, and therefore will be thought by them *to entitle their assistants in obtaining them* to considerable rewards.

Our fears will be excited. Our hopes will be awakened. It will be insinuated to us, with a plausible affection of *wisdom* and *concern,* how *prudent* it is to please the *powerful*—how *dangerous* to provoke them—and then comes in the perpetual incantation that freezes up every generous purpose of the soul in cold, inactive expectation—"that if there is any request to be made, compliance will obtain a favorable attention."

Our *vigilance* and our *union* are *success* and *safety*. Our *negligence* and our *division* are *distress* and *death*. They are *worse*—they are *shame* and *slavery*. Let us equally shun the benumbing stillness of *overweening sloath,* and the feverish activity of that *ill informed zeal,* which busies itself in maintaining *little, mean,* and *narrow* opinions. Let us, with a truly wise *generosity* and *charity,* banish and discourage all *illiberal distinctions,* which may arise from differences in *situation,* forms of *government,* or modes of *religion*. Let us consider ourselves as MEN—FREEMEN—CHRISTIAN FREEMEN—*separate*

---

ably never will appear again: For it is *evident,* that *such a system* of policy is to be established on this continent, as, in a short time, is to render it utterly unnecessary to use the least *art* in order to *conciliate* our approbation of any measures. Some of our countrymen may be employed to *fix* chains upon us, but *they* will never be permitted to *hold* them afterwards. So that the utmost, that any of them can expect, is only a *temporary provision,* that *may* expire in their own time; but which they may *be assured,* will preclude their children from having any consideration paid to *them*. NATIVES of *America* must sink into total NEGLECT and CONTEMPT, the moment that THEIR COUNTRY loses the constitutional power she now possesses.

from the rest of the world, and *firmly bound together* by the *same rights, interests* and *dangers.* Let *these* keep our attention inflexibly fixed on the GREAT OBJECTS, which we must CONTINUALLY REGARD, in order to *preserve those rights,* to *promote those interests,* and to *avert those dangers.*

Let these *truths* be indelibly impressed on our minds—*that we cannot be* HAPPY, *without being* FREE—that we cannot be free, *without being secure in our property*—that *we* cannot be secure in our property, *if, without our consent, others may, as by right, take it away*—that *taxes imposed on us by parliament,* do thus take it away—that *duties laid for the sole purpose of raising money,* are taxes—that *attempts* to lay such duties *should be instantly and firmly opposed*—that this opposition can never be effectual, *unless it is the united effort of these provinces*—that therefore BENEVOLENCE *of temper towards each other,* and UNANIMITY *of councils,* are essential to the welfare of the whole—and lastly, that for this reason, every man amongst us, who in any manner would encourage either *dissension, diffidence,* or *indifference,* between these colonies, is an enemy to *himself,* and to *his country.*

The belief of these truths, I verily think, my countrymen, is indispensably necessary to your happiness. I beseech you, therefore,* "teach them diligently unto your children, and talk of them when you sit in your houses, and when you walk by the way, and when you lie down, and when you rise up." What have these colonies to *ask,* while they continue free? Or what have they to *dread,* but insidious attempts to subvert their freedom? *Their prosperity* does not depend on *ministerial favors doled* out to *particular* provinces. *They* form *one* political body, of which *each colony* is a *member. Their happiness* is founded on *their constitution;* and is to be promoted, by preserving that constitution in unabated vigor, *throughout every part.* A spot, a speck of decay, however small the limb on which it appears, and however remote it may seem from the vitals, should be alarming. We have *all the rights* requisite for our prosperity. The *legal authority* of *Great-Britain* may indeed lay hard restrictions upon us; but, like the spear of *Telephus,* it will cure as well as wound. Her unkindness will instruct and compel us, after some time, to discover, in our *industry* or *frugality,* surprising remedies—*if our rights continue unviolated:* For as long as the *products* of our *labor,* and the *rewards* of our *care,* can properly be called *our own,*

* Deuteron, vi. 7.

so long it will be worth our while to be *industrious* and *frugal.* But if when we plow—sow—reap—gather—and thresh—we find that we plow—sow—reap—gather—and thresh *for others,* whose PLEASURE is to be the SOLE LIMITATION *how much* they shall *take,* and *how much* they shall *leave,* WHY should we repeat the unprofitable toil? *Horses* and *oxen* are content with *that portion of the fruits of their work,* which their *owners* assign them, in order to keep them strong enough to raise successive crops; but even *these beasts* will not submit to draw for their *masters,* until they are *subdued* by *whips* and *goads.*

Let us take care of our *rights,* and we *therein* take care of *our prosperity.* *"SLAVERY IS EVER PRECEDED BY SLEEP." *Individuals* may be *dependent* on ministers, if they please. STATES SHOULD SCORN IT;—and if *you* are not wanting *to yourselves,* you will have a *proper regard* paid *you* by *those,* to whom if you are not *respectable,* you will be *contemptible.* But—if *we have already forgot* the *reasons* that urged us, with unexampled unanimity, to exert ourselves two years ago—if *our zeal* for the public good is *worn out* before the *homespun cloaths,* which it has caused us to have made—if *our resolutions* are *so faint,* as by our present conduct to *condemn* our own late *successful* example—if *we are not affected* by any reverence for the memory of our ancestors, who transmitted to us that freedom in which they had been blest—if *we are not animated* by any regard for posterity, to whom, by the most sacred obligations, we are bound to deliver down the invaluable inheritance—THEN, indeed, any *minister*—or any *tool* of a minister—or any *creature* of a tool of a minister—or any *lower*† *instrument of*‡ *administration,* if lower there be, is a *personage* whom it may be dangerous to offend.

* *Montesquieu's* Spirits of Laws, Book 14, Chap. 13.

† "Instrumenta regni." *Tacitus's* Ann. *Book* 12, § 66.

‡ If any person shall imagine that he discovers, in these letters, the least dislike of the dependence of these colonies on *Great-Britain,* I beg that such persons will not form any judgment on *particular expressions,* but will consider the *tenor of all the letters taken together.* In that case, I flatter myself, that every unprejudiced reader will be *convinced,* that the true interests of *Great-Britain* are as dear to me, as they ought to be to every good subject.

If I am an *Enthusiast* in any thing, it is in my zeal for the *perpetual dependence* of these colonies on their mother country.—A dependence founded on *mutual benefits,* the continuance of which can be secured only by *mutual affections.* Therefore it is, that with extreme apprehension I view the smallest seeds of discontent, which are unwarily scattered abroad. *Fifty* or *Sixty* years will make astonishing alterations in these colonies; and this consideration should render it the business of *Great-Britain* more and more to cultivate our good dispositions toward her: But the misfortune is, that those *great men,* who are wrestling for power at home, think themselves very slightly interested in the prosperity of their country *Fifty* or *Sixty* years hence,

I shall be extremely sorry, if any man mistakes my meaning in anything I have said. Officers employed by the crown, are, while according to the laws they conduct themselves, entitled to legal obedience, and sincere respect. These it is a duty to render them; and these no good or prudent person will withhold. But when these officers, thro' rashness or design, desire to enlarge their authority beyond its due limits, and expect improper concessions to be made to them, from regard for the employments they bear, their attempts should be considered as equal injuries to the crown and people, and should be courageously and constantly opposed. To suffer our ideas to be confounded by *names* on such occasions, would certainly be an *inexcusable weakness*, and probably an *irremediable error*.

We have reason to believe, that several of his Majesty's present ministers are good men, and friends to our country; and it seems not unlikely, that by a particular concurrence of events, we have been treated a little more severely than they wished we should be. *They* might not think it prudent to stem a torrent. But what is the difference to *us*, whether arbitrary acts take their rise from ministers, or are permitted by them? Ought any point to be allowed to* a good minister, that

---

but are deeply concerned in blowing up a popular clamour for supposed *immediate advantage*.

For my part, I regard *Great-Britain* as a Bulwark, happily fixed between these colonies and the powerful nations of *Europe*. That kingdom remaining safe, we, under its protection, enjoying peace, may diffuse the blessings of religion, science, and liberty, thro' remote wildernesses. It is therefore incontestably our *duty*, and our *interest*, to support the strength of *Great-Britain*. When confiding in that strength, she begins to forget from whence it arose, it will be an easy thing to shew the source. She may readily be reminded of the loud alarm spread among her merchants and tradesmen, by the universal associations of these colonies, at the time of the *Stamp-Act*, not to import any of her MANUFACTURES.

In the year 1718, the *Russians* and *Swedes* entered into an agreement, not to suffer *Great-Britain* to export any NAVAL STORES from their dominions but in *Russian* or *Swedish* ships, and at their own prices. *Great-Britain* was distressed. *Pitch* and *tar* rose to *Three pounds* a barrel. At length she thought of getting these articles from the colonies; and the attempt succeeding, they fell down to *Fifteen shillings*. In the year 1756, *Great-Britain* was threatened with an invasion. An easterly wind blowing for six weeks, she could not MAN her fleet, and the whole nation was thrown into the utmost consternation. The wind changed. The *American* ships arrived. The fleet sailed in ten or fifteen days. There are some other reflections on this subject, worthy of the most deliberate attention of the *British* parliament; but they are of such a nature, that I do not chuse to mention them publicly. I thought it my duty, in the year 1765, while the *Stamp-Act* was in suspence, to write my sentiments to a gentleman of great influence at home, who afterwards distinguished himself, by espousing our cause, in the debates concerning the repeal of that act.

* Ubi imperium ad ignaros aut minus bonos pervenit; *novum illud exemplum*, ad dignis, & idoneis, ad indignos & non idoneos *transfertur*.

Sall. Bell. Cat. § 50.

should be denied to a bad one? The mortality of ministers, is a very frail mortality. A——— may succeed a *Shelburne*—A——— may succeed a *Cornway*.

We find a new kind of minister lately spoken of at home —"THE MINISTER OF THE HOUSE OF COMMONS." The term seems to have peculiar propriety when referred to these colonies, *with a different meaning annexed to it*, from that in which it is taken there. By the word "minister" we may understand not only a *servant of the crown*, but a *man of influence* among the commons, who regard themselves as having a share in the *sovereignty* over us. The "minister OF the house" may, in a point respecting the colonies, be so strong, that the minister of the crown *in* the house, if he is a distinct person, may not choose, even where his sentiments are favorable to us, to come to a pitched battle upon our account. For tho' I have the highest opinion of the deference of the house for the King's minister, yet he may be so good natured, as not to put it to the test, except it be for the mere and immediate profit of his master or himself.

But whatever kind of *minister* he is, that attempts to innovate *a single iota* in the privileges of these colonies, him I hope you will *undauntedly oppose;* and that you will never suffer yourselves to be either *cheated* or *frightened* into any *unworthy obsequiousness*. On such emergencies you may surely, without presumption, believe, that ALMIGHTY GOD himself will look down upon your righteous contest with gracious approbation. You will be a *"band of brothers,"* cemented by the dearest ties,—and strengthened with inconceivable supplies of force and constancy, by that sympathetic ardor, which animates good men, confederated in a good cause. Your *honor* and *welfare* will be, as they now are, most intimately concerned; and besides—*you are assigned by divine providence*, in the appointed order of things, the *protectors of unborn ages*, whose *fate* depends upon your *virtue*. Whether *they* shall arise the *generous* and *indisputable heirs* of the noblest patrimonies, or the *dastardly* and *hereditary drudges* of imperious task-masters, YOU MUST DETERMINE.

To discharge this double duty to *yourselves*, and to your *posterity*, you have nothing to do, but to call forth into use the *good sense* and *spirit* of which you are possessed. You have nothing to do, but to conduct your affairs *peaceably*—*prudently*—*firmly*—*jointly*. By *these means* you will support the character of *freemen*, without losing that of *faithful subjects*—a good character in any government—one of the best under a *British* government—You will *prove,* that *Americans* have that true *magnanimity* of soul, that can resent injuries, without falling into rage; and that tho' your devotion to *Great-Britain* is the most affectionate, yet you can make PROPER DISTINCTIONS, and know what you owe *to yourselves,* as well as to her—You will, at the same time that you advance your *interests,* advance your *reputation*—You will convince the world of the *justice of your demands,* and the *purity of your intentions.*—While all mankind must, with unceasing applauses, confess, that YOU indeed DESERVE liberty, who so *well understand* it, so *passionately love* it, so *temperately enjoy* it, and so *wisely, bravely,* and *virtuously assert, maintain,* and *defend* it.

"Certe ego libertatem, quæ mihi a parente meo tradita est, experiar: Verum id frustra an ob rem faciam, in vestra manu situm est, quirites."

For my part I am resolved to contend for the liberty delivered down to me by my ancestors; but whether I shall do it effectually or not, depends on you, my countrymen.

"How little soever one is able to write, yet when the liberties of one's country are threatened, it is still more difficult to be silent."

A FARMER.

Is there not the strongest probability, that if the universal sense of these colonies is immediately expressed by RESOLVES of the assemblies, in support of their rights, by INSTRUCTIONS to their agents on the subject, and by PETITIONS to the crown and parliament for redress, these measures will have the same success now, that they had in the time of the *Stamp-Act.*

D.

FINIS.

THOMAS JEFFERSON Originally written as instructions for the Virginia delegates to the First Continental Congress in 1774, *A Summary View* was published that same year by a group of Jefferson's friends and admirers, who gave it its present title. With the exception of the Declaration of Independence, it remains Jefferson's most noteworthy and impassioned piece of political writing. Its argument is aggressive, unequivocally stating that the colonies had been settled by free men who owed no allegiance to the British parliament, but who had voluntarily submitted to a "common sovereign." Like Adams in *A Dissertation,* Jefferson is intent on reminding the colonists of their political heritage, of pointing out that the settlement of America was accomplished by "the free inhabitants of the British dominions in Europe . . . [who] possessed a right which nature has given to all men, of departing from the country in which chance, not choice, has placed them, of going in quest of new habitations, and of there establishing new societies, under such laws and regulations as to them shall seem most likely to promote public happiness." The implication of *A Summary View* is that if the British parliament cannot accept the equality and independent status of the colonies, then war is inevitable.

Text: Julian P. Boyd, *et al.,* eds., *The Papers of Thomas Jefferson.* Princeton, 1950—.

A Summary View of the Rights of British America (1774)

[July 1774]

Resolved that it be an instruction to the said deputies when assembled in General Congress with the deputies from the other states of British America to propose to the said Congress that an humble and dutiful address be presented to his majesty begging leave to lay before him as chief magistrate of the British empire the united complaints of his majesty's subjects in America; complaints which are excited by many unwarrantable incroachments and usurpations, attempted to be made by the legislature of one part of the empire, upon those rights which god and the laws have given equally and independently to all. To represent to his majesty that these his states have often individually made humble application to his imperial throne, to obtain thro' it's intervention some redress of their injured rights; to none of which was ever even an answer condescended. Humbly to hope that this their joint address, penned in the language of truth, and divested of those expressions of servility which would persuade his majesty that we are asking favors and not rights, shall obtain from his majesty a more respectful acceptance. And this his majesty will think we have reason to expect when he reflects that he is no more than the chief officer of the people, appointed by the laws, and circumscribed with definite powers, to assist in working the great machine of government erected for their use, and consequently subject to their superintendance. And in order that these our rights, as well as the invasions of them, may be laid more fully before his majesty, to take a view of them from the origin and first settlement of these countries.

To remind him that our ancestors, before their emigration to America, were the free inhabitants of the British dominions in Europe, and possessed a right, which nature has given to all men, of departing from the country in which chance, not choice has placed them, of going in quest of new habitations, and of there establishing new societies, under such laws and regulations as to them shall seem most likely to promote public happiness. That their Saxon ancestors had under this universal law, in like manner, left their native wilds and woods in the North of Europe, had possessed themselves of the island of Britain then less charged with inhabitants, and had established there that system of laws which has so long been the glory and protection of that country. Nor was ever any claim of superiority or dependance asserted over them by that mother country from which they had migrated: and were such a claim made it is believed his majesty's subjects in Great Britain have too firm a feeling of the rights derived to them from their ancestors to bow down the sovereignty of their state before such visionary pretensions. And it is thought that no circumstance has occurred to distinguish materially the British from the Saxon emigration. America was conquered, and her settlements made and firmly established, at the expence of individuals, and not of the British public. Their own blood was spilt in acquiring lands for their settlement, their own fortunes expended in making that settlement effectual. For themselves they fought, for themselves they conquered, and for themselves alone they have right to hold. No shilling was ever issued from the public treasures of his majesty or his ancestors for their assistance, till of very late times, after the colonies had become established on a firm and permanent footing. That then indeed, having become valuable to Great Britain for her commercial purposes, his parliament was pleased to lend them assistance against an enemy who would fain have drawn to herself the benefits of their commerce to the great aggrandisement of herself and danger of Great Britain. Such assistance, and in such circumstances, they had often before given to Portugal and other allied states, with whom they carry on a commercial intercourse. Yet these states never supposed that, by calling in her aid, they thereby submitted themselves to her sovereignty. Had such terms been proposed, they would have rejected them with disdain, and trusted for better to the moderation of their enemies, or to a vigorous exertion of their own force. We do not however mean to underrate those aids, which to us were doubtless valuable, on whatever principles granted: but we would shew that they cannot give a title to that authority which the British parliament would arrogate over us; and that they may amply be repaid, by our giving to the inhabitants of Great Britain such exclusive privileges in trade as may be advantageous to them, and at the same time not too restrictive to ourselves. That settlements having been thus effected in the wilds of America, the emigrants thought proper to adopt that system of laws under which they had hitherto lived in the mother country, and to continue their union with her by submitting themselves to the same common sovereign, who was thereby made the central link connecting the several parts of the empire thus newly multiplied.

But that not long were they permitted, however far they thought themselves removed from the hand of oppression, to hold undisturbed the rights thus acquired at the hazard of their lives and loss of their fortunes. A family of princes was then on the British throne,[1] whose treasonable crimes against their people brought on them afterwards the exertion of those sacred and sovereign rights of punishment, reserved in the hands of the people for cases of extreme necessity, and judged by the constitution unsafe to be delegated to any other judicature. While every day brought forth some new and unjustifiable exertion of power over their subjects on that side the

[1] The Stuart kings.

water, it was not to be expected that those here, much less able at that time to oppose the designs of despotism, should be exempted from injury. Accordingly that country which had been acquired by the lives, the labors and the fortunes of individual adventurers, was by these princes at several times parted out and distributed among the favorites and followers of their fortunes; and by an assumed right of the crown alone were erected into distinct and independent governments; a measure which it is believed his majesty's prudence and understanding would prevent him from imitating at this day; as no exercise of such a power of dividing and dismembering a country has ever occurred in his majesty's realm of England, tho' now of very antient standing; nor could it be justified or acquiesced under there or in any other part of his majesty's empire.

That the exercise of a free trade with all parts of the world, possessed by the American colonists as of natural right, and which no law of their own had taken away or abridged, was next the object of unjust incroachment. Some of the colonies having thought proper to continue the administration of their government in the name and under the authority of his majesty king Charles the first, whom notwithstanding his late deposition by the Common-wealth of England, they continued in the sovereignty of their state, the Parliament for the Common-wealth took the same in high offence, and assumed upon themselves the power of prohibiting their trade with all other parts of the world except the island of Great Britain. This arbitrary act however they soon recalled, and by solemn treaty entered into on the 12th. day of March 1651,[2] between the said Common-wealth by their Commissioners and the colony of Virginia by their house of Burgesses, it was expressly stipulated by the 8th. article of the said treaty that they should have 'free trade as the people of England do enjoy to all places and with all nations according to the laws of that Commonwealth.' But that, upon the restoration of his majesty King Charles the second, their rights of free commerce fell once more a victim to arbitrary power: and by several acts of his reign as well as of some of his successors the trade of the colonies was laid under such restrictions as shew what hopes they might form from the justice of a British parliament

[2] After the execution of Charles I, Virginia proclaimed its continued allegiance to the Stuarts. Parliament then imposed a blockade on Virginia and forced Governor Berkeley and the Council to surrender. The treaty referred to is dated March 12, 1652, not 1651.

were its uncontrouled power admitted over these states. History has informed us that bodies of men as well as individuals are susceptible of the spirit of tyranny. A view of these acts of parliament for regulation, as it has been affectedly called, of the American trade, if all other evidence were removed out of the case, would undeniably evince the truth of this observation.[3] Besides the duties they impose on our articles of export and import, they prohibit our going to any Markets Northward of cape Finesterra in the kingdom of Spain for the sale of commodities which Great Britain will not take from us, and for the purchase of others with which she cannot supply us; and that for no other than the arbitrary purpose of purchasing for themselves by a sacrifice of our rights and interests, certain privileges in their commerce with an allied state, who, in confidence that their exclusive trade with America will be continued while the principles and power of the British parliament be the same, have indulged themselves in every exorbitance which their avarice could dictate, or our necessities extort: have raised their commodities called for in America to the double and treble of what they sold for before such exclusive privileges were given them, and of what better commodities of the same kind would cost us elsewhere; and at the same time give us much less for what we carry thither, than might be had at more convenient ports. That these acts prohibit us from carrying in quest of other purchasers the surplus of our tobaccoes remaining after the consumption of Great Britain is supplied: so that we must leave them with the British merchant for whatever he will please to allow us, to be by him reshipped to foreign markets, where he will reap the benefits of making sale of them for full value. That to heighten still the idea of parliamentary justice, and to shew with what moderation they are like to exercise power, where themselves are to feel no part of it's weight, we take leave to mention to his majesty certain other acts of British parliament, by which they would prohibit us from manufacturing for our own use the articles we raise on our own lands with our own labor. By an act passed in the 5th. year of the reign of his late majesty king George the second an American subject is forbidden to make a hat for himself of the fur which he has taken perhaps on his own soil. An instance of despotism to which no parrallel can be produced in the most arbitrary ages of British history. By one other act passed in the 23d. year

[3] Jefferson is here speaking of all the Acts of Trade and Navigation.

of the same reign, the iron which we make we are forbidden to manufacture; and, heavy as that article is, and necessary in every branch of husbandry, besides commission and insurance, we are to pay freight for it to Great Britain, and freight for it back again, for the purpose of supporting, not men, but machines, in the island of Great Britain.[4] In the same spirit of equal and impartial legislation is to be viewed the act of parliament passed in the 5th. year of the same reign, by which American lands are made subject to the demands of British creditors, while their own lands were still continued unanswerable for their debts; from which one of these conclusions must necessarily follow, either that justice is not the same thing in America as in Britain, or else that the British parliament pay less regard to it here than there. But that we do not point out to his majesty the injustice of these acts with intent to rest on that principle the cause of their nullity, but to shew that experience confirms the propriety of those political principles which exempt us from the jurisdiction of the British parliament. The true ground on which we declare these acts void is that the British parliament has no right to exericse authority over us.

That these exercises of usurped power have not been confined to instances alone in which themselves were interested; but they have also intermeddled with the regulation of the internal affairs of the colonies. The act of the 9th. of Anne for establishing a post office in America seems to have had little connection with British convenience, except that of accomodating his majesty's ministers and favorites with the sale of a lucrative and easy office.[5]

That thus have we hastened thro' the reigns which preceded his majesty's, during which the violation of our rights were less alarming, because repeated at more distant intervals, than that rapid and bold succession of injuries which is likely to distinguish the present from all other periods of American story. Scarcely have our minds been able to emerge from the astonishment into which one stroke of parliamentary thunder has involved us, before another more heavy and more alarming is fallen on us. Single acts of tyranny may be ascribed to the accidental opinion of a day; but a series of oppressions, begun at a distinguished period, and pursued unalterably

[4] The Hat Act of 1732 and the Iron Act of 1750.

[5] In the ninth year of Queen Anne's reign (1710), parliament passed an act which made the Postmaster General of London the Postmaster General of the entire empire.

thro' every change of ministers, too plainly prove a deliberate, systematical plan of reducing us to slavery.

That the act passed in the 4th. year of his majesty's reign intitled 'an act

one other act passed in the 5th. year of his reign intitled 'an act

one other act passed in the 6th. year of his reign intitled 'an act

and one other act passed in the 7th. year of his reign intitled 'an act[6]

form that connected chain of parliamentary usurpation which has already been the subject of frequent applications to his majesty and the houses of Lords and Commons of Great Britain; and, no answers having yet been condescended to any of these, we shall not trouble his majesty with a repetition of the matters they contained.

But that one other act passed in the same 7th. year of his reign, having been a peculiar attempt, must ever require peculiar mention. It is intitled 'an act[7]

One free and independent legislature hereby takes upon itself to suspend the powers of another, free and independent as itself, thus exhibiting a phaenomenon, unknown in nature, the creator and creature of it's own power. Not only the principles of common sense, but the common feelings of human nature must be surrendered up, before his majesty's subjects here can be persuaded to believe that they hold their political existence at the will of a British parliament. Shall these governments be dissolved, their property annihilated, and their people reduced to a state of nature, at the imperious breath of a body of men whom they never saw, in whom they never confided, and over whom they have no powers of punishment or removal, let their crimes against the American public be ever so great? Can any one reason be assigned why 160,000 electors in the island of Great Britain should give law to four millions in the states of America, every individual of whom is equal to every individual of them in virtue, in understanding, and in bodily strength? Were this to be admitted, instead of being a free people, as we have hitherto supposed, and mean to continue, ourselves, we should suddenly be found the slaves, not of one, but of 160,000 tyrants, distinguished too from all others by this singular circumstance that they

[6] The Sugar Act of 1764, the Stamp Act of 1765, the Declaratory Act of 1766, the Townshend Acts of 1767.

[7] The act suspending the New York Legislature's powers.

are removed from the reach of fear, the only restraining motive which may hold the hand of a tyrant.

That by 'an act to discontinue in such manner and for such time as are therein mentioned the landing and discharging lading or shipping of goods wares and merchandize at the town and within the harbor of Boston in the province of Massachusett's bay in North America' which was passed at the last session of British parliament, a large and populous town, whose trade was their sole subsistence, was deprived of that trade, and involved in utter ruin.[8] Let us for a while suppose the question of right suspended, in order to examine this act on principles of justice. An act of parliament had been passed imposing duties on teas to be paid in America, against which act the Americans had protested as inauthoritative. The East India company, who till that time had never sent a pound of tea to America on their own account, step forth on that occasion the asserters of parliamentary right, and send hither many ship loads of that obnoxious commodity. The masters of their several vessels however, on their arrival in America, wisely attended to admonition, and returned with their cargoes. In the province of New England alone the remonstrances of the people were disregarded, and a compliance, after being many days waited for, was flatly refused. Whether in this the master of the vessel was governed by his obstinacy or his instructions, let those who know, say. There are extraordinary situations which require extraordinary interposition. An exasperated people, who feel that they possess power, are not easily restrained within limits strictly regular. A number of them assembled in the town of Boston, threw the tea into the ocean and dispersed without doing any other act of violence. If in this they did wrong, they were known, and were amenable to the laws of the land, against which it could not be objected that they had ever in any instance been obstructed or diverted from their regular course in favor of popular offenders. They should therefore not have been distrusted on this occasion. But that ill-fated colony had formerly been bold in their enmities against the house of Stuart, and were now devoted to ruin by that unseen hand which governs the momentous affairs of this great empire. On the partial representations of a few worthless ministerial dependants, whose constant office it has been to keep

[8] In March, 1774, parliament passed the Boston Port Act, the first of a harsh series of acts, known as the "Coercive Acts," designed to make Massachusetts an example to the other colonies.

that government embroiled, and who by their treacheries hope to obtain the dignity of the British knighthood, without calling for a party accused, without asking a proof, without attempting a distinction between the guilty and the innocent, the whole of that antient and wealthy town is in a moment reduced from opulence to beggary. Men who had spent their lives in extending the British commerce, who had invested in that place the wealth their honest endeavors had merited, found themselves and their families thrown at once on the world for subsistence by it's charities. Not the hundredth part of the inhabitants of that town had been concerned in the act complained of; many of them were in Great Britain and in other parts beyond sea; yet all were involved in one indiscriminate ruin, by a new executive power unheard of till then, that of a British parliament. A property of the value of many millions of money was sacrifised to revenge, not repay, the loss of a few thousands. This is administering justice with a heavy hand indeed! And when is this tempest to be arrested in it's course? Two wharfs are to be opened again when his majesty shall think proper: the residue which lined the extensive shores of the bay of Boston are forever interdicted the exercise of commerce. This little exception seems to have been thrown in for no other purpose than that of setting a precedent for investing his majesty with legislative powers. If the pulse of his people shall beat calmly under this experiment, another and another will be tried till the measure of despotism be filled up. It would be an insult on common sense to pretend that this exception was made in order to restore it's commerce to that great town. The trade which cannot be received at two wharfs alone, must of necessity be transferred to some other place; to which it will soon be followed by that of the two wharfs. Considered in this light it would be an insolent and cruel mockery at the annihilation of the town of Boston.

By the act for the suppression of riots and tumults in the town of Boston, passed also in the last session of parliament, a murder committed there is, if the governor pleases, to be tried in the court of King's bench in the island of Great Britain, by a jury of Middlesex.[9] The witnesses too, on receipt of such a sum as the Governor shall think it reasonable for them to expend, are to enter into recognisance to appear at the trial. This is in other words taxing them to the amount of their

[9] The Administration of Justice Act, another of the "Coercive Acts," was enacted into law on May 20, 1774.

recognisance; and that amount may be whatever a Governor pleases. For who does his majesty think can be prevailed on to cross the Atlantick for the sole purpose of bearing evidence to a fact? His expences are to be borne indeed as they shall be estimated by a Governor; but who are to feed the wife and children whom he leaves behind, and who have had no other subsistence but his daily labor? Those epidemical disorders too, so terrible in a foreign climate, is the cure of them to be estimated among the articles of expence, and their danger to be warded off by the almighty power of a parliament? And the wretched criminal, if he happen to have offended on the American side, stripped of his privilege of trial by peers, of his vicinage, removed from the place where alone full evidence could be obtained, without money, without counsel, without friends, without exculpatory proof, is tried before judges predetermined to condemn. The cowards who would suffer a countryman to be torn from the bowels of their society in order to be thus offered a sacrifice to parliamentary tyranny, would merit that everlasting infamy now fixed on the authors of the act! A clause for a similar purpose had been introduced into an act passed in the 12th. year of his majesty's reign entitled 'an act for the better securing and preserving his majesty's dock-yards, magazines, ships, ammunition and stores,' against which as meriting the same censures the several colonies have already protested.

That these are the acts of power assumed by a body of men foreign to our constitutions, and unacknowledged by our laws; against which we do, on behalf of the inhabitants of British America, enter this our solemn and determined protest. And we do earnestly intreat his majesty, as yet the only mediatory power between the several states of the British empire, to recommend to his parliament of Great Britain the total revocation of these acts, which however nugatory they be, may yet prove the cause of further discontents and jealousies among us.

That we next proceed to consider the conduct of his majesty, as holding the executive powers of the laws of these states, and mark out his deviations from the line of duty. By the constitution of Great Britain as well as of the several American states, his majesty possesses the power of refusing to pass into a law any bill which has already passed the other two branches of legislature. His majesty however and his ancestors, conscious of the impropriety of opposing their single opinion to the united wisdom of two houses of parliament, while their proceedings were unbiassed by interested principles, for several ages past have modestly declined the exercise of this power in that part of his empire called Great Britain. But by change of circumstances, other principles than those of justice simply have obtained an influence on their determinations. The addition of new states to the British empire has produced an addition of new, and sometimes opposite interests. It is now therefore the great office of his majesty to resume the exercise of his negative power, and to prevent the passage of laws by any one legislature of the empire which might bear injuriously on the rights and interests of another. Yet this will not excuse the wanton exercise of this power which we have seen his majesty practice on the laws of the American legislatures. For the most trifling reasons, and sometimes for no conceivable reason at all, his majesty has rejected laws of the most salutary tendency. The abolition of domestic slavery is the great object of desire in those colonies where it was unhappily introduced in their infant state. But previous to the infranchisement of the slaves we have, it is necessary to exclude all further importations from Africa. Yet our repeated attempts to effect this by prohibitions, and by imposing duties which might amount to a prohibition, have been hitherto defeated by his majesty's negative: thus preferring the immediate advantages of a few British corsairs to the lasting interests of the American states, and to the rights of human nature deeply wounded by this infamous practice. Nay the single interposition of an interested individual against a law was scarcely ever known to fail of success, tho' in the opposite scale were placed the interests of a whole country. That this is so shameful an abuse of a power trusted with his majesty for other purposes, as if not reformed would call for some legal restrictions.

With equal inattention to the necessities of his people here, has his majesty permitted our laws to lie neglected in England for years, neither confirming them by his assent, nor annulling them by his negative: so that such of them as have no suspending clause, we hold on the most precarious of all tenures, his majesty's will, and such of them as suspend themselves till his majesty's assent be obtained we have feared might be called into existence at some future and distant period, when time and change of circumstances shall have rendered them destructive to his people here. And to render this grievance still more oppressive, his majesty by his instructions has laid his governors under such restrictions that they can pass no law of any moment unless it have such suspending clause: so that, however immediate may be the call for legislative interposition, the law cannot be executed till it has twice crossed the Atlantic, by which time the evil may have spent it's whole force.

But in what terms reconcileable to majesty and at the same time to truth, shall we speak of a late instruction to his majesty's governor of the colony of Virginia, by which he is forbidden to assent to any law for the division of a county, unless the new county will consent to have no representative in assembly? That colony has as yet affixed no boundary to the Westward. Their Western counties therefore are of indefinite extent. Some of them are actually seated many hundred miles from their Eastern limits. Is it possible then that his majesty can have bestowed a single thought on the situation of those people, who, in order to obtain justice for injuries however great or small, must, by the laws of that colony, attend their county court at such a distance, with all their witnesses, monthly, till their litigation be determined? Or does his majesty seriously wish, and publish it to the world, that his subjects should give up the glorious right of representation, with all the benefits derived from that, and submit themselves the absolute slaves of his sovereign will? Or is it rather meant to confine the legislative body to their present numbers, that they may be the cheaper bargain whenever they shall become worth a purchase?

One of the articles of impeachment against Tresilian and the other judges of Westminster Hall in the reign of Richard the second, for which they suffered death as traitors to their country, was that they had advised the king that he might dissolve his parliament at any time:[10] and succeeding kings have adopted the opinion of these unjust judges. Since the establishment however of the British constitution at the glorious* Revolution on it's free and antient principles, neither his majesty nor his ancestors have exercised such a power of dissolution in the island of Great Britain; and when his majesty was petitioned by the united voice of his people there to dissolve the present parliament, who had become obnoxious to

[10] Sir Robert Tresilian (died 1388) became Chief Justice of the King's Bench in 1381. He was impeached by parliament in 1388 and executed that same year.

* On further enquiry I find two instances of dissolutions before the parl. would of itself have been at an end, viz. the parl. called to meet Aug. 24. 1698. was dissolved by K. Wm. Dec. 19. 1700. & a new one called to meet Feb. 6. 1701. which was also dissolved Nov. 11. 1701. & a new one met Dec. 30. 1701.

them, his ministers were heard to declare in open parliament that his majesty possessed no such power by the constitution. But how different their language and his practice here! To declare as their duty required the known rights of their country, to oppose the usurpation of every foreign judicature, to disregard the imperious mandates of a minister or governor, have been the avowed causes of dissolving houses of representatives in America. But if such powers be really vested in his majesty, can he suppose they are there placed to awe the members from such purposes as these? When the representative body have lost the confidence of their constituents, when they have notoriously made sale of their most valuable rights, when they have assumed to themselves powers which the people never put into their hands, then indeed their continuing in office becomes dangerous to the state, and calls for an exercise of the power of dissolution. Such being the causes for which the representative body should and should not be dissolved, will it not appear strange to an unbiassed observer that that of Great Britain was not dissolved, while those of the colonies have repeatedly incurred that sentence?

But your majesty or your Governors have carried this power beyond every limit known or provided for by the laws. After dissolving one house of representatives, they have refused to call another, so that for a great length of time the legislature provided by the laws has been out of existence. From the nature of things, every society must at all times possess within itself the sovereign powers of legislation. The feelings of human nature revolt against the supposition of a state so situated as that it may not in any emergency provide against dangers which perhaps threaten immediate ruin. While those bodies are in existence to whom the people have delegated the powers of legislation, they alone possess and may exercise those powers. But when they are dissolved by the lopping off one or more of their branches, the power reverts to the people, who may use it to unlimited extent, either assembling together in person, sending deputies, or in any other way they may think proper. We forbear to trace consequences further; the dangers are conspicuous with which this practice is replete.

That we shall at this time also take notice of an error in the nature of our landholdings, which crept in at a very early period of our settlement. The introduction of the Feudal tenures into the kingdom of England, though antient, is well enough understood to set this matter in a proper light. In the earlier ages of the Saxon settlement feudal holdings were certainly altogether unknown, and very few, if any, had been introduced at the time of the Norman conquest. Our Saxon ancestors held their lands, as they did their personal property, in absolute dominion, disencumbered with any superior, answering nearly to the nature of those possessions which the Feudalists term Allodial: William the Norman first introduced that system generally. The lands which had belonged to those who fell in the battle of Hastings, and in the subsequent insurrections of his reign, formed a considerable proportion of the lands of the whole kingdom. These he granted out, subject to feudal duties, as did he also those of a great number of his new subjects, who by persuasions or threats were induced to surrender them for that purpose. But still much was left in the hands of his Saxon subjects, held of no superior, and not subject to feudal conditions. These therefore by express laws, enacted to render uniform the system of military defence, were made liable to the same military duties as if they had been feuds: and the Norman lawyers soon found means to saddle them also with all the other feudal burthens. But still they had not been surrendered to the king, they were not derived from his grant, and therefore they were not holden of him. A general principle indeed was introduced that 'all lands in England were held either mediately or immediately of the crown': but this was borrowed from those holdings which were truly feudal, and only applied to others for the purposes of illustration. Feudal holdings were therefore but exceptions out of the Saxon laws of possession, under which all lands were held in absolute right. These therefore still form the basis or groundwork of the Common law, to prevail wheresoever the exceptions have not taken place. America was not conquered by William the Norman, nor it's lands surrendered to him or any of his successors. Possessions there are undoubtedly of the Allodial nature. Our ancestors however, who migrated hither, were laborers, not lawyers. The fictitious principle that all lands belong originally to the king, they were early persuaded to believe real, and accordingly took grants of their own lands from the crown. And while the crown continued to grant for small sums and on reasonable rents, there was no inducement to arrest the error and lay it open to public view. But his majesty has lately taken on him to advance the terms of purchase and of holding to the double of what they were, by which means the acquisition of lands being rendered difficult, the population of our country is likely to be checked. It is time therefore for us to lay this matter before his majesty, and to declare that he has no right to grant lands of himself. From the nature and purpose of civil institutions, all the lands within the limits which any particular society has circumscribed around itself, are assumed by that society, and subject to their allotment only. This may be done by themselves assembled collectively, or by their legislature to whom they may have delegated sovereign authority: and, if they are allotted in neither of these ways, each individual of the society may appropriate to himself such lands as he finds vacant, and occupancy will give him title.

That, in order to inforce the arbitrary measures before complained of, his majesty has from time to time sent among us large bodies of armed forces, not made up of the people here, nor raised by the authority of our laws. Did his majesty possess such a right as this, it might swallow up all our other rights whenever he should think proper. But his majesty has no right to land a single armed man on our shores; and those whom he sends here are liable to our laws for the suppression and punishment of Riots, Routs, and unlawful assemblies, or are hostile bodies invading us in defiance of law. When in the course of the late war it became expedient that a body of Hanoverian troops should be brought over for the defence of Great Britain, his majesty's grandfather, our late sovereign, did not pretend to introduce them under any authority he possessed. Such a measure would have given just alarm to his subjects in Great Britain, whose liberties would not be safe if armed men of another country, and of another spirit, might be brought into the realm at any time without the consent of their legislature. He therefore applied to parliament who passed an act for that purpose, limiting the number to be brought in and the time they were to continue. In like manner is his majesty restrained in every part of the empire. He possesses indeed the executive power of the laws in every state; but they are the laws of the particular state which he is to administer within that state, and not those of any one within the limits of another. Every state must judge for itself the number of armed men which they may safely trust among them, of whom they are to consist, and under what restrictions they are to be laid. To render these proceedings still more criminal against our laws, instead of subjecting the military to the civil power, his majesty has expressly made the civil subordinate to the military. But can his majesty thus put down all law under his feet? Can he erect a power superior to that which erected himself? He has done it indeed by force; but let him remember that force cannot give right.

That these are our grievances which we have thus laid before his majesty with that freedom of language and sentiment which becomes a free people, claiming their rights as derived from the laws of nature, and not as the gift of their chief magistrate. Let those flatter, who fear: it is not an American art. To give praise where it is not due, might be well from the venal, but would ill beseem those who are asserting the rights of human nature. They know, and will therefore say, that kings are the servants, not the proprietors of the people. Open your breast Sire, to liberal and expanded thought. Let not the name of George the third be a blot in the page of history. You are surrounded by British counsellors, but remember that they are parties. You have no ministers for American affairs, because you have none taken from among us, nor amenable to the laws on which they are to give you advice. It behoves you therefore to think and to act for yourself and your people. The great principles of right and wrong are legible to every reader: to pursue them requires not the aid of many counsellors. The whole art of government consists in the art of being honest. Only aim to do your duty, and mankind will give you credit where you fail. No longer persevere in sacrificing the rights of one part of the empire to the inordinate desires of another: but deal out to all equal and impartial right. Let no act be passed by any one legislature which may infringe on the rights and liberties of another. This is the important post in which fortune has placed you, holding the balance of a great, if a well poised empire. This, Sire, is the advice of your great American council, on the observance of which may perhaps depend your felicity and future fame, and the preservation of that harmony which alone can continue both to Great Britain and America the reciprocal advantages of their connection. It is neither our wish nor our interest to separate from her. We are willing on our part to sacrifice every thing which reason can ask to the restoration of that tranquility for which all must wish. On their part let them be ready to establish union on a generous plan. Let them name their terms, but let them be just. Accept of every commercial preference it is in our power to give for such things as we can raise for their use, or they make for ours. But let them not think to exclude us from going to other markets, to dispose of those commodities which they cannot use, nor to supply those wants which they cannot supply. Still less let it be proposed that our properties within our own territories shall be taxed or regulated by any power on earth but our own. The god who gave us life, gave us liberty at the same time: the hand of force may destroy, but cannot disjoin them. This, Sire, is our last, our determined resolution: and that you will be pleased to interpose with that efficacy which your earnest endeavors may insure to procure redress of these our great grievances, to quiet the minds of your subjects in British America against any apprehensions of future incroachment, to establish fraternal love and harmony thro' the whole empire, and that that may continue to the latest ages of time, is the fervent prayer of all British America.

JAMES WILSON Like John Dickinson, James Wilson was a leader of the conservative forces in Pennsylvania. Although he was one of the signers of the Declaration of Independence, Wilson was, to the last, a believer in the possibility of rapprochement with Great Britain. In part, this *Address* is a final plea to restore moderation and order to a world plunging into violence. Wilson bases his concept of the relationship of man to the state upon the Lockian assumption that "all legitimate authority proceeds" from the people. By imposing an unnatural and unwanted sovereignty upon the colonies, parliament had been guilty of violating that relationship. That he was able to endorse independence is an indication of the clarity of Wilson's thinking. Where Dickinson retreated at so radical a step, Wilson saw that parliament, not the colonies, had defied tradition and brought independence into being.

Text: Worthington C. Ford, *et al.*, eds., *The Journals of the Continental Congress*. Washington, 1904–37.

An Address to the Inhabitants of the Colonies of New Hampshire, Massachusetts Bay, Rhode Island and Providence Plantations, Connecticut, New York, New Jersey, Pennsylvania, The Counties of Newcastle, Kent and Sussex on Delaware, Maryland, Virginia, North Carolina, South Carolina and Georgia from their Delegates in Congress.

[13 February, 1776.]

Friends and Countrymen—

History, we believe, cannot furnish an Example of a Trust, higher and more important than that, which we have received from your Hands. It comprehends in it every Thing that can rouse the Attention and interest the Passions of a People, who will not reflect Disgrace upon their Ancestors nor degrade themselves, nor transmit Infamy to their Descendants. It is committed to us at a Time when every Thing dear and valuable to *such* a People is in imminent Danger. This Danger arises from those, whom we have been accustomed to consider as our Friends; who really were so, while they continued friendly to themselves; and who will again be so, when they shall return to a just Sense of their own Interests. The Calamities, which threaten us, would be attended with a total Loss of those Constitutions, formed upon the venerable Model of British Liberty, which have been long our Pride and Felicity. To avert those *Calamities* we are under the disagreeable Necessity of making temporary Deviations from those *Constitutions.*

Such is the Trust reposed in us. Much does it import you and us, that it be executed with Skill and with Fidelity. That we have discharged it with Fidelity, we enjoy the Testimony of a good Conscience. How far we have discharged it with Skill must be determined by you, who are our Principals and Judges, to whom we esteem it our Duty to render an Account of our Conduct. To enable you to judge of it, as we would wish you to do, it is necessary that you should be made acquainted with the *Situation,* in which your Affairs have been placed; the *Principles,* on which we have acted; and the *Ends,* which we have kept and still keep in View.

That all Power was originally in the People—that all the Powers of Government are derived from them—that all Power, which they have not disposed of, still continues theirs —are Maxims of the *English* Constitution, which, we presume, will not be disputed. The Share of Power, which the King derives from the People, or, in other Words, the Prerogative of the Crown, is well known and precisely ascertained: It is the same in *Great Britain* and in the Colonies. The Share of Power, which the House of Commons derives from the People, is likewise well known: The Manner in which it is conveyed is by Election. But the House of Commons is not elected by the Colonists; and therefore, from *them* that Body can derive no Authority.

Besides; the Powers, which the House of Commons receives from its Constituents, are entrusted by the Colonies to their Assemblies in the several Provinces. Those Assemblies have Authority to propose and assent to Laws for the Government of their Electors, in the same Manner as the House of Commons has Authority to propose and assent to Laws for the Government of the Inhabitants of *Great Britain.* Now the same collective Body cannot delegate the same Powers to distinct representative Bodies. The undeniable Result is, that the *House of Commons* neither has nor can have any Power deriv'd from the *Inhabitants of these Colonies.*

In the Instance of imposing *Taxes,* this Doctrine is clear and familiar: It is true and just in every *other* Instance. If it would be incongruous and absurd, that the same Property should be liable to be taxed by two Bodies independent of each other; would less Incongruity and Absurdity ensue, if the same Offense were to be subjected to different and perhaps inconsistent Punishments? Suppose the Punishment directed by the Laws of one Body to be Death, and that directed by those of the other Body be Banishment for Life; how could both Punishments be inflicted?

Though the Crown possesses the same Prerogative over the Colonies, which it possesses over the Inhabitants of *Great Britain:* Though the Colonists delegate to their Assemblies the same Powers which our Fellow Subjects in *Britain* delegate to the House of Commons: Yet by some inexplicable Mystery in Politics, which is the Foundation of the odious System that we have so much Reason to deplore, *additional* Powers over you are ascribed to the Crown, as a Branch of the British Legislature: And the House of Commons—*a Body which acts solely by derivative Authority*—is supposed entitled to exert over you an Authority, which *you* cannot *give,* and which *it* cannot *receive.*

The Sentence of universal Slavery gone forth against you is; *that the British Parliament have Power to make Laws,* WITHOUT YOUR CONSENT, *building you in* ALL *Cases whatever.* Your Fortunes, your Liberties, your Reputations, your Lives, every Thing that can render you and your Posterity happy, all are the Objects of the Laws: All must be enjoyed, impaired or destroyed as the Laws direct. And are you the Wretches, who have Nothing that you *can* or *ought* to call *your own?* Were all the rich Blessings of Nature, all the Bounties of indulgent Providence poured upon you, not for your own Use; but for the Use of those, upon whom neither Nature nor Providence hath bestowed Qualities or Advantages superior to yours?

From this Root of Bitterness numerous are the Branches of Oppression that have sprung. Your most undoubted and highest-priz'd Rights have been invaded: Heavy and unnecessary Burthens have been imposed on you: Your Interests have been neglected, and sometimes wantonly sacrificed to the Interests, and even to the Caprice of others. When you felt, for your Enemies have not yet made any Laws to divest you of feeling, Uneasiness under your Grievances, and expressed it in the natural Tone of Complaint; your Murmurs were considered and treated as the Language of Faction; and your Uneasiness was ascribed to a restive Disposition, impatient of Controul.

In proportion, however, as your Oppressions were multiplied and increased, your Opposition to them became firm and vigourous. Remonstrances succeeded Petitions: A Resolution carried into Effect, not to import Goods from *Great Britain* succeeded both. The Acts of Parliament then complained of were in Part, repealed. Your Good-Humour and unsuspicious Fondness returned. Short—alas! *too* short—was the Season allowed for indulging them. The former System of Rigour was renewed.

The Colonies, wearied with presenting fruitless Supplications and Petitions *separately;* or prevented, by arbitrary and abrupt Dissolutions of their Assemblies, from using even those fruitless Expedients for Redress, determined to *join* their Counsels and their Efforts. Many of the Injuries flowing from the unconstitutional and ill-advised Acts of the British Legislature, affected all the Provinces equally; and even in those Cases, in which the Injuries were confined, by the Acts, to one or to a few, the *Principles,* on which they were made, extended to all. If common Rights, common Interests, common Dangers and common Sufferings are Principles of Union, what could be more natural than the Union of the Colonies?

Delegates authorised by the several Provinces from Nova Scotia to Georgia to represent them and act in their Behalf, met in GENERAL CONGRESS.[1]

It has been objected, that this Measure was unknown to the Constitution; that the Congress was, of Consequence, an illegal Body; and that its Proceedings could not, in any Manner, be recognised by the Government of Britain. To those, who offer this Objection, and have attempted to vindicate, by its supposed Validity, the Neglect and Contempt, with which the Petition of that Congress to his Majesty was treated by the Ministry, we beg Leave, in our Turn, to propose, that they would explain the Principles of the Constitution, which warranted the *Assembly of the Barons at* RUNNINGMEDE, when

[1] The First Continental Congress met from September 5, 1775 to October 26, 1775. Originally conceived of as an advisory council to the colonies, the Continental Congress became the central government of the colonies, a role it did not relinquish until March 4, 1789, when the first central government under the Constitution was sworn in.

MAGNA CHARTA was signed, the *Convention-Parliament* that recalled Charles 2d, and the *Convention of Lords and Commons* that placed King William on the Throne. When they shall have done this, we shall perhaps, be able to apply their Principles to prove the Necessity and Propriety of a Congress.

But the Objections of those, who have done so much and aimed so much against the Liberties of America, are not confined to the *Meeting* and the *Authority* of the Congress: They are urged with equal Warmth against the *Views* and *Inclinations* of those who composed it. We are told, in the Name of Majesty itself, "that the Authors and Promoters of this *desperate Conspiracy*", as those who have framed his Majesty's Speech are pleased to term our *laudable Resistance;* "have, in the Conduct of it, derived great Advantage from the Difference of his Majesty's Intentions and theirs. That they meant only to amuse by vague Expressions of Attachment to the Parent State, and the strongest Protestations of Loyalty to the King, whilst they were preparing for a general Revolt. That on the Part of his Majesty and the Parliament, the Wish was rather to reclaim than to subdue." It affords us some Pleasure to find that the Protestations of Loyalty to his Majesty, which have been made, are allowed to be strong; and that Attachment to the Parent State is owned to be expressed. Those Protestations of Loyalty and Expressions of Attachment ought, by every Rule of Candour, to be presumed to be sincere, unless Proofs evincing their Insincerity can be drawn from the Conduct of those who used them.

In examining the Conduct of those who directed the Affairs of the Colonies at the Time when, it is said, they were preparing for a general Revolt, we find it an easy Undertaking to shew, that they merited no Reproach from the British Ministry by making any Preparations *for that Purpose.* We wish it were as easy to shew, that they merited no Reproach from their Constituents, by neglecting the necessary Provisions *for their Security.* Has a single Preparation been made, which has not been found requisite for our Defense? Have we not been attacked in places where fatal Experience taught us, we were not sufficiently prepared for a successful Opposition? On which Side of this unnatural Controversy was the *ominous Intimation* first given, that it must be decided by Force? Were Arms and Ammunition imported into *America,* before the Importation of them was prohibited? What Reason can be assigned for this Prohibition, unless it be this, that those who made it had determined upon such a System of

Oppression, as they knew, would *force* the Colonies into Resistance? And yet, they "wished only to reclaim!"

The Sentiments of the Colonies, expressed in the Proceedings of their Delegates assembled in 1774 were far from being disloyal or disrespectful. Was it disloyal to offer a Petition to your Sovereign?[2] Did your still anxious Impatience for [an] answer, which your *Hopes,* founded only on your *Wishes,* as you too soon experienced, flattered you would be a gracious one—did this Impatience indicate a Disposition only to amuse? Did the keen Anguish, with which the Fate of the Petition filled your Breasts, betray an Inclination to avail yourselves of the Indignity with which you were treated, for forwarding favourite Designs of Revolt?

Was the Agreement not to import Merchandise from *Great Britain* or *Ireland;* nor after the tenth Day of September last, to export our Produce to those Kingdoms and the *West Indies*[3] —was this a disrespectful or an hostile Measure? Surely we have a Right to withdraw or to continue our own Commerce. Though the British Parliament have exercised a Power of *directing* and *restraining* our Trade; yet, among all their extraordinary Pretensions, we recollect no Instance of their attempting to *force* it contrary to our Inclinations. It was well known, before this Measure was adopted, that it would be detrimental to our own Interest, as well as to that of our fellow-Subjects. We deplored it on both Accounts. We deplored the Necessity that produced it. But we were willing to sacrifice our Interest to any probable Method of regaining the Enjoyment of those Rights, which, by Violence and Injustice, had been infringed.

Yet even this peaceful Expedient, which Faction surely never suggested, has been represented, and by high Authority too, as a seditious and unwarrantable Combination. We are, we presume, the first Rebels and Conspirators, who commenced their Conspiracy and Rebellion with a System of Conduct, immediately and directly frustrating every Aim, which Ambition or Rapaciousness could propose: Those, whose Fortunes are desperate, may upon slight Evidence be charged with desperate Designs: But how improbable is it, that the Colonists, who have been happy, and have known their

[2] Before adjourning, the Congress drafted a *Petition to the King,* which pledged loyalty to him but affirmed that the colonies were independent of parliament.

[3] Delegates to the Congress pledged to cease both importing from and exporting to England. Extra-legal machinery for carrying out these agreements was set up.

Happiness in the quiet Possession of their Liberties; who see no Situation more to be desired than that, in which, till lately, they have been placed; and whose warmest Wish is to be re-instaled in the Enjoyment of that Freedom, which they claim and are entitled to as Men and as British Subjects—how improbable it is that *such* would, without any Motives that could tempt even the most *profligate* Minds to Crimes, plunge themselves headlong into all the Guilt and Danger and Distress with which those that endeavour to overturn the Constitution of their Country are always surrounded and frequently overwhelmed?

The humble unaspiring Colonists asked only for "Peace, Liberty and Safety". This, we think, was a reasonable Request: Reasonable as it was, it has been refused. Our ministerial Foes, dreading the Effects, which our commercial Opposition might have upon their favourite Plan of reducing the Colonies to Slavery, were determined not to hazard it upon that Issue. They employed military Force to carry it into Execution. Opposition of Force by Force, or unlimited Subjection was now our only Alternative. Which of them did it become Freemen determined never to surrender that Character, to chuse? The Choice was worthily made. We wish for Peace—we wish for Safety: But we will not, to obtain either or both of them, part with our Liberty. The sacred Gift descended to us from our Ancestors: We cannot dispose of it: We are bound by the strongest Ties to transmit it, as we have received it, pure and inviolate to our Posterity.

We have taken up Arms in the best of Causes. We have adhered to the virtuous Principles of our Ancestors, who expressly stipulated, in their Favour, *and in ours,* a Right to resist every Attempt upon their Liberties. We have complied with our Engagements to our Sovereign. He should be the *Ruler* of a *free* People: We will not, as far as his Character depends upon us, permit him to be degraded into a *Tyrant* over *Slaves.*

Our Troops are animated with the Love of Freedom. They have fought and bled and conquered in the Discharge of their Duty as good Citizens as well as brave Soldiers. Regardless of the Inclemency of the Seasons, and of the Length and Fatigue of the March, they go, with Chearfulness, wherever the Cause of Liberty and their Country requires their Service. We confess that they have not the Advantages arising from Experience and Discipline: But Facts have shewn, that native Courage warmed with Patriotism, is sufficient to counterbalance these Advantages. The Experience and Discipline of our Troops will daily increase: Their Patriotism will receive no Diminution: The longer those, who have forced us into this War, oblige us to continue it, the more formidable we shall become.

The Strength and Resources of *America* are not confined to Operations *by Land*. She can exert herself likewise *by Sea*. Her Sailors are hardy and brave: She has all the Materials for Shipbuilding: Her Artificers can Work them into Form. We pretend not to vie with the Royal Navy of England though that Navy had *its Beginnings:* But still we may be able in a great Measure to defend our own Coasts, and may intercept, as we have been hitherto successful in doing, Transports and Vessels laden with Stores and Provisions.

Possessed of so many Advantages; favoured with the Prospect of so many more; Threatened with the Destruction of our constitutional Rights; cruelly and illiberally attacked, because we will not subscribe to our own Slavery; ought we to be animated with Vigour, or to sink into Despondency? When the Forms of our Governments are, by those entrusted with the Direction of them, perverted from their original Design; ought we to submit to this Perversion? Ought we to sacrifice the *Forms,* when the Sacrifice becomes necessary for preserving the *Spirit* of our Constitution? Or ought we to neglect and neglecting, to lose the Spirit by a superstitious Veneration for the Forms? We regard those Forms, and wish to preserve them as long as we can consistently with higher Objects: But much more do we regard essential Liberty, which, at all Events, we are determined not to lose, but with our Lives. In contending for this Liberty, we are willing to go through good Report, and through evil Report.

In our present Situation, in which we are called to oppose an Attack upon your Liberties, made under bold Pretentions of Authority from that Power, to which the executive Part of Government is, in the ordinary Course of affairs, committed—in the Situation, every Mode of Resistance, though directed by Necessity and by Prudence, and authorised by the Spirit of the Constitution, will be exposed to plausible Objections drawn from its Forms. Concerning such Objections, and the Weight that may be allowed to them, we are little solicitous. It will not discourage us to find ourselves represented as "labouring to enflame the Minds of the People of America, and openly avowing Revolt, Hostility and Rebellion." We deem it an Honour to "have raised Troops, and collected a naval Force"; and, *cloathed with the sacred Authority of the People, from* WHOM *all* LEGITIMATE AUTHORITY *proceeds* "to have exercised legislative, executive and judicial Powers." For what Purposes were those Powers instituted? For your Safety and Happiness. You and the World will judge whether those Purposes have been best promoted by us; or by those who claim the Powers, which they charge us with assuming.

But while we feel no Mortification at being misrepresented with Regard to the *Measures* employed by us for accomplishing the great Ends, which you have appointed us to pursue; we cannot sit easy under an Accusation, which charges us with laying aside those *Ends,* and endeavouring to accomplish *such as are very different*. We are accused of carrying on the War "for the Purpose of establishing an independent Empire."

We disavow the Intention. We declare, that what we aim at, and what we are entrusted by you to pursue, *is the Defence and the Re-establishment of the constitutional Rights of the Colonies*. Whoever gives impartial Attention to the Facts, we have already stated, and to the Observations we have already made, must be fully convinced that all the Steps, which have been taken by us in this unfortunate Struggle, can be accounted for as rationally and as satisfactorily by supposing that the Defence and Re-establishment of their Rights were the Objects which the Colonists and their Representatives had in View; as by supposing that an independent Empire was their Aim. Nay, we may safely go farther and affirm, without the most distant Apprehension of being refuted, that many of those steps can be accounted for rationally and satisfactorily only upon the former Supposition, and cannot be accounted for, in that Manner, upon the latter. The numerous Expedients that were tried, though fruitlessly, for avoiding Hostilities: The visible and unfeigned Reluctance and Horrour, with which we entered into them: The Caution and Reserve, with which we have carried them on: The Attempts we have made by petitioning the Throne and by every other Method, which might probably, or could possibly be of any Avail for procuring an accommodation—These are not surely the usual Characteristics of Ambition.

In what Instance have we been the Aggressors? Did our Troops take the Field before the ministerial Forces began their hostile March to *Lexington* and Concord? Did we take Possession, or did we form any Plan for taking Possession of *Canada,* before we knew that it was a Part of the ministerial System to pour the *Canadians* upon our Frontiers? Did we approach the *Canadians,* or have we treated them as Enemies? Did we take the Management of the *Indian* Tribes into our Hands, before we were well assured that the Emissaries of Administration were busy in persuading them to strike us? When we treated with them, did we imitate the barbarous Example? Were not our Views and Persuasions confined to keeping them in a State of Neutrality? Did we seise any Vessel of our Enemies, before our Enemies had seised some of ours? Had we yet seised any, except such as were employed in the Service of Administration, and in supplying those that were in actual Hostilities against us? Cannot our whole Conduct be reconciled to *Principles and Views of Self-Defence?* Whence then the uncandid Imputation of *aiming at an independent Empire?*

Is no regard to be had to the Professions and Protestations made by us, on so many different Occasions, of Attachment to Great Britain, of Allegiance to his Majesty; and of Submission to his Government upon the Terms, on which the Constitution points it out as a Duty, and on which alone a *British Sovereign* has the Right to demand it?

When the Hostilities commenced by the ministerial Forces in Massachusetts Bay, and the imminent Dangers threatening the other Colonies rendered it absolutely necessary that they should be put into a State of Defence—even on that Occasion, we did not forget our Duty to his Majesty, and our Regard for our fellow Subjects in Britain. Our words are these: "But as we most ardently wish for a Restoration of the Harmony formerly subsisting between our Mother-Country and these Colonies, the Interruption of which must at all Events, be exceedingly injurious to both Countries: Resolved, that with a sincere Design of contributing, by all Means in our Power, not incompatible with a just Regard for the undoubted Rights and true Interests of these Colonies, to the Promotion of this most desirable Reconciliation, an humble and dutiful Address be presented to his Majesty."

If the Purposes of establishing an independent Empire has lurked in our Breasts, no fitter Occasion could have been found for giving Intimations of them, than in our Declaration setting forth the Causes and Necessity of our taking up Arms.[4] Yet even there no Pretence can be found for fixing such an

[4] *The Declaration of the Causes and Necessity of Taking up Arms,* drawn up by a committee appointed by Congress which consisted of Franklin, Jay, Livingston, Rutledge, Johnson, Jefferson, and Dickinson, was issued on July 6, 1775. The final draft was the work of Dickinson and Jefferson.

Imputation on us. "Lest this Declaration should disquiet the Minds of our Friends and fellow Subjects in any Part of the Empire, we assure them that we mean not to dissolve that Union, which has so long and so happily subsisted between us, and which we sincerely wish to see restored. Necessity has not yet driven us into that desperate Measure, or induced us to excite any other Nation to war against them. We have not raised Armies with the ambitious Designs of separating from Great Britain, and establishing independent States." Our Petition to the King has the following Asseveration: "By such Arrangements as your Majesty's Wisdom can form for collecting the united Sense of your American People, we are convinced your Majesty would receive such satisfactory Proofs of the Disposition of the Colonists towards their Sovereign and the Parent State, that the wished for Opportunity would be soon restored to them, of evincing the Sincerity of their Professions by every Testimony of Devotion becoming the most dutiful Subjects and the most affectionate Colonists." In our Address to the Inhabitants of Great Britain,[5] we say: "We are accused of aiming at Independence: But how is this Accusation supported? By the Allegations of your Ministers, not by our Actions. Give us leave, most solemnly to assure you, that we have not yet lost Sight of the Object we have ever had in View, a Reconciliation with you on constitutional Principles, and a Restoration of that friendly intercourse, which to the Advantage of both we till lately maintained."

If we wished to detach you from your Allegiance to his Majesty, and to wean your Affections from a Connexion with your fellow-Subjects in Great Britain, is it likely that we would have taken so much Pains, upon every proper Occasion, to place those Objects before you in the most agreeable Points of View?

If any equitable Terms of Accommodation had been offered us, and we had rejected them, there would have been some Foundation for the Charge that we endeavoured to establish an independent Empire. But no Means have been used either by Parliament or by Administration for the Purpose of bringing this Contest to a Conclusion besides Penalties directed by Statutes, or Devastations occasioned by War. Alas! how long will Britons forget that Kindred-Blood flows in your Veins? How long will they strive, with hostile Fury to sluice it out from Bosoms that have already bled in their Cause;

[5] An address drawn up by the First Continental Congress prior to its adjournment.

and, in their Cause, would still be willing to pour out what remains, to the last precious Drop?

We are far from being insensible of the Advantages, which have resulted to the Colonies as well as to Britain from the Connexion which has hitherto subsisted between them: We are far from denying them, or wishing to lessen the Ideas of their Importance. But the Nature of this Connexion, and the Principles, on which it was originally formed and on which alone it can be maintained, seem unhappily to have been misunderstood or disregarded by those, who laid or conducted the late destructive Plan of Colony-Administration. It is a Connexion founded upon mutual Benefits; upon Religion, Laws, Manners, Customs and Habits common to both Countries. Arbitrary Exertions of Power on the Part of Britain, and servile Submission on the [part of the] Colonies, if the Colonies should ever become degenerate enough to [accept] it, would immediately rend every generous Bond asunder. An intimate Connexion between Freemen and Slaves cannot be continued without Danger and, at last, Destruction to the former. Should your Enemies be able to reduce you to Slavery, the baneful Contagion would spread over the whole Empire. We verily believe that the Freedom, Happiness, and Glory of Great Britain, and the Prosperity of his Majesty and his Family depend upon the Success of your Resistance. You are now expending your Blood, and your Treasure in promoting the Welfare and the true Interests of your Sovereign and your fellow-Subjects in Britain, in Opposition to the most dangerous Attacks that have been ever made against them.

The Ideas of deriving Emolument to the Mother Country by taxing you, and depriving you of your Constitutions and Liberties were not introduced till lately. The Experiments, to which those Ideas have given Birth, have proved disastrous: The Voice of Wisdom calls loudly that they should be laid aside. Let them not, however, be removed from View. They may serve as Beacons to prevent future Shipwrecks.

Britain and these Colonies have been Blessings to each other. Sure we are, that they might continue to be so. Some salutary System might certainly be devised, which would remove from both Sides, Jealousies that are ill-founded, and Causes of Jealousies that are well-founded; which would restore to both Countries those important Benefits that Nature seems to have intended them reciprocally to confer and to receive; and which would secure the Continuance and the

Encrease of those Benefits to numerous succeeding Generations. That such a System may be formed is our ardent Wish.

But as such a System must affect the Interest of the Colonies as much as that of the Mother-Country, why should the Colonies be excluded from a Voice in it? Should not, to say the least upon this Subject, their Consent be asked and obtained as to the *general Ends,* which it ought to be calculated to answer? Why should not its Validity depend upon us as well as upon the Inhabitants of Great Britain? No Disadvantage will result to them: An important Advantage will result to [us]. We shall be affected by no Laws, the Authority of which, as far as they regard us, is not *founded on our own Consent.* This Consent may be expressed as well by a solemn Compact, as if the Colonists, by their Representatives, had an immediate Voice in passing the Laws. In a Compact we would *concede* liberally to Parliament: For the *Bounds* of our Concessions would be known.

We are too much attached to the English Laws and Constitution, and know too well their happy Tendency to diffuse Freedom, Prosperity and Peace wherever they prevail, to desire an independent Empire. If one Part of the Constitution be pulled down, it is impossible to foretell whether the other Parts of it may not be shaken, and, perhaps, overthrown. It is a Part of our Constitution to be under Allegiance to the Crown, Limited and ascertained as the Prerogative is, the Position—*that a King can do no wrong*—may be founded in *Fact* as well as in *Law,* if you are not wanting to yourselves.

We trace your Calamities to the House of Commons. *They* have undertaken to *give* and *grant* your Money. From a supposed virtual Representation in *their* House it is argued, that *you* ought to be bound by the Acts of the British Parliament in all Cases whatever. This is no Part of the Constitution. This is the Doctrine, to which we will never subscribe our Assent: This is the Claim, to which we adjure you, as you tender your own Freedom and Happiness, and the Freedom and Happiness of your Prosperity, never to submit. The same Principles, which directed *your Ancestors* to oppose the exorbitant and dangerous Pretensions of the Crown, should direct *you* to oppose the no less exorbitant and dangerous Claims of the House of Commons. Let all Communication of despotic Power through that Channel be cut off, and your Liberties will be safe.

Let neither our Enemies nor our Friends make improper Inferences from the Solicitude, which we have discovered to remove the Imputation of aiming to establish an independent Empire. Though an independent Empire is not our *Wish;* it may—let your Oppressors attend—it may be the Fate of our Countrymen and ourselves. It is in the Power of your Enemies to render Independency or Slavery your and our Alternative. Should we—will you, in such an Event, hesitate a Moment about the Choice? Let those, who drive us to it, answer to their King and to their Country for the Consequences. We are *desirous* to continue Subjects: But we are *determined* to continue Freemen. We shall deem ourselves bound to renounce; and, we hope, you will follow our Example in renouncing the *former* Character whenever it shall become incompatible with the *latter.*

While we shall be continued by you in the very important Trust, which you have committed to us, we shall keep our Eyes constantly and steadily fixed upon the Grand Object of the Union of the Colonies—THE RE-ESTABLISHMENT AND SECURITY OF THEIR CONSTITUTIONAL RIGHTS. Every measure that we employ shall be directed to the Attainment of this great End: No Measure, necessary, in our Opinion, for attaining it, shall be declined. If any such Measure should, against our principal Intention, draw the Colonies into Engagements that may suspend or dissolve their Union with their fellow-Subjects in Great Britain, we shall lament the Effect; but shall hold ourselves justified in adopting the Measure. That the Colonies may continue connected, as they have been, with Britain, is our second Wish: Our first is—THAT AMERICA MAY BE FREE.

[illegible] the Hardships of [illegible] the Fate of [illegible] Constitution and [illegible] it is in the Power of [illegible] independency [illegible] Alternative, [illegible] an Event [illegible] a Moment [illegible] their Rights and [illegible] Country for the [illegible] we are [illegible] that we are determined to [illegible] bound in [illegible] and we hope you will [illegible] become [illegible] with the [illegible]

While we shall be considered by you in the very important Light, which you have [illegible] us, we shall [illegible] constantly and [illegible] upon the Grand Object [illegible] great [illegible] necessary [illegible] our Opinion, for [illegible] shall be [illegible] Mercury [illegible] the Colonies [illegible] their [illegible] with [illegible]

PART II

INDEPENDENCE AND AFTER

The years between the Battle of Lexington and Concord and the Treaty of Paris of 1783, which officially ended the war, were years in which American energy was largely devoted to the task of winning the war. But these years were also a period in which the American political character was being formed and in which added impetus was given to the concept of an American nationality that grew out of the Declaration of Independence. This is not to say that an American character, or even an American political character, did not exist prior to the war; a glance at colonial newspapers of the 1750's suggests that the outlines of what Hector St. John de Crèvecœur was to call "this new man" were already being sketched. But prior to the achievement of independence, the American had so identified himself and his political rights with England that it was virtually impossible for him not to view himself as an appendage of England. The rights for which he went to war were the rights of Englishmen; the philosophers and statesmen whose words and actions he drew upon to defend his own words and actions were, for the most part, Englishmen; and the constitutional heritage which he claimed as his due was recognized as an English heritage dating back to the *Magna Charta*.

Where the struggle with England prior to independence had been based on a special awareness of the relationship of colonies to mother country, independence not only removed the necessity of re-shaping that relationship but forced the colonists to observe themselves, to turn inward, to create a national government that, in turn, could inspire national confidence. From independence to the close of the war, the Founding Fathers focused not merely on the constitutional aspects of nationhood but also on formulating a preliminary answer to the question of the nation's destiny. And that destiny, as Paine noted in *Common Sense*, rested wholly upon the ability of the people to accept the responsibilities of self-government. That they did so, and that they did so successfully, was due both to their heritage as a largely self-governing people and to their obvious desire, instilled in them by training and temperament, to be their own masters.

The two most basic political problems which faced the emergent nation were the relationship of the individual to the state and of the state to the nation. Once the colonists' attitude toward Great Britain had been solved with a decisive move in the direction of independence, they were forced to decide whether the country was to be a united nation, or whether it was to be thirteen independent states loosely bound together in a confederation. The Declaration of Independence, while it speaks of "Free and Independent States," conveys a singular as well as plural meaning, since it was composed under instructions issued by the Second Continental Congress, a legislative body acting for all of the states and endowed, however inadequately, with all the requirements of a central government. A month before independence was declared, this same congress had appointed a committee to draft a document which would codify and define the government the new-born nation was to have. The committee which drafted the Articles of Confederation did little more than to sanction a government that already existed, the Continental Congress.

Whether the government under the Articles of Confederation was or was not successful cannot be our main concern here; what is important is that it was a fairly adequate reflection of what most Americans wanted in a government at that time. No one has ever successfully refuted Charles Beard's thesis that the government brought into being with the adoption of the Constitution in 1787 was not the government that the majority of Americans desired. While unification was undoubtedly important to the former colonists, most of them did not want unification at the expense of individual liberty. They had seen themselves and their country victimized by a highly centralized and authoritarian government, and they were most conscious of the injuries they had suffered and fully determined not to repeat their causes when it came time to create their own government. "The fact that the Articles of Confederation were supplanted by another constitution is no proof either of their success or of their failure. Any valid opinion as to the merits of the Articles must be based on a detailed and unbiased study of the confederation period."[1]

[1] Merrill Jensen, *The Articles of Confederation: An Interpretation of the Social-Constitutional History of the American Revolution, 1774–1781,* 3rd Printing, p. 239.

There can be little doubt that the Articles were a better reflection of the philosophy expressed in the Declaration of Independence than was the Constitution that replaced it in 1787. Liberal thought of the time saw in any strong central government a built-in despotism, and the state governments were sufficiently jealous of their sovereignty and sufficiently experienced with the government of England to demand safeguards against the overwhelming power of a strong central government. The Articles gave them this power by granting them the power of the purse. Congress was permitted to requisition the states for money, but there was nothing in the Articles which granted Congress the power to force the states to meet its requisitions. By maintaining the power of the purse in their own hands, the states, in effect, seized the power of government. Because in our own age state governments have generally been more conservative than the national government, it is somewhat difficult to understand that, for the generation of Americans which fought the War of Independence, the reverse was usually true.

By 1776, most of the former colonies had begun to change their colonial charters into written constitutions, and, almost invariably, the constitutions were more liberal than the charters had been. Most of them granted specific civil liberties and rights to the people, which government could not negate except under the most extraordinary circumstances. Standing armies were forbidden, as were general warrants; trial by jury, freedom of the press, and the right to petition were guaranteed; and the powers of the executive and the judiciary were considerably weakened by making these elective offices and by creating constitutional safeguards against any possible abuse of their powers. Some states, for instance, specifically denied the governor the right to veto acts of the legislature; other states forbade the governor to dissolve or prorogue legislative assemblies; in still other states, the governor was elected by the legislature, which retained the power to impeach him. Pennsylvania went so far as to abolish the office of governor altogether.

But the liberalism of the period is best reflected in the numerous changes that colonial society was undergoing. The relationship of the individual to the state was being significantly changed, and the change was one which usually granted more rights to the individual. As Americans became more conscious of their identity as Americans, they began to discard certain features of English society, just as they were discarding English political rule. The movement toward political democracy was spurred by the movement toward economic democracy; the great Tory estates which had been seized after the war's outbreak were divided into numerous individual farms, few of them more than five hundred acres; primogeniture and entail, both of which had worked toward the creation and sustenance of a landed gentry, were abandoned; the right to vote was generally extended; religious qualifications for voting were seriously questioned, and, in most states, repealed, while established churches came in for censure or were disestablished; Negro slavery came under serious attack, to the point where some northern states outlawed it altogether and even some southern states, most notable among them Virginia, discouraged it (Virginia passed a law permitting the manumission of slaves).

By the war's end, the colonists had not merely freed themselves from English political domination, but they had pulled even further away from the social and class divisions which were seemingly endemic to English life. It would be stretching a point to claim that the American Revolution brought into existence a radical new government and nation, dedicated solely to the promulgation of democracy and the democratic ethos. But the nation created by the Declaration of Independence and the nation governed under the Articles of Confederation was certainly a far more radical political and social innovation than anything the rest of the world had to offer. If the former colonists agreed on nothing else, they agreed that the establishment of the United States of America had signaled the birth of a nation whose form and purpose were to be different from those of the nations of the Old World.

THOMAS PAINE Paine's later writings, especially *Agrarian Justice* and *The Rights of Man,* are marked by what was, for his own age, an extreme radicalism which made him a favorite of the political left and anathema to the political right. Although he was to occupy this very position during his own lifetime, his first important pamphlet, *Common Sense,* was greeted in the colonies by conservatives and radicals alike when it was issued in Philadelphia on January 10, 1776. The pamphlet had an immediate and far-reaching effect, for in it Paine said, better than anyone else before him had said, that the purpose of the colonies was so different from the purpose of Great Britain that independence was to be desired, not feared. Where other colonial thinkers had argued that the colonists were bound to Great Britain only through a mutual sovereign, the king, Paine attacked not only George III but the very concept of monarchy itself, condemning it as artificial and corrupt. Using the Old Testament and English history as his two chief sources, he effectively destroyed the idea of hereditary monarchy as possessing any validity whatsoever for Americans. He followed this with an analysis of the possibilities of an independent America's economic growth.

Paine has frequently been dismissed as no more than a propagandist. In the sense that all of the Founding Fathers were propagandists, the label may justly be applied to him. But it should also be pointed out that, as well as any other colonial thinker, he evolved a distinctly American synthesis of what he had learned. *Common Sense* is no more original than the Declaration of Independence, but it remains, with that document, the most important voice of an aspiring America to be heard at the beginning of the Revolution.

Text: *Common Sense.* Philadelphia, 1776.*

* Paine expanded *Common Sense* after its first two printings. The text is taken from the edition published by W. & T. Bradford, which is the first printing of the expanded text.

Common Sense (1776)

INTRODUCTION

Perhaps the sentiments contained in the following pages, are not *yet* sufficiently fashionable to procure them general favor; a long habit of not thinking a thing *wrong*, gives it a superficial appearance of being *right*, and raises at first a formidable outcry in defence of custom. But the tumult soon subsides. Time makes more converts than reason.

As a long and violent abuse of power, is generally the Means of calling the right of it in question (and in Matters too which might never have been thought of, had not the Sufferers been aggravated into the inquiry) and as the King of England hath undertaken in his *own Right*, to support the Parliament in what he calls *Theirs*, and as the good people of this country are grievously oppressed by the combination, they have an undoubted privilege to inquire into the pretensions of both, and equally to reject the usurpation of either.

In the following sheets, the author hath studiously avoided every thing which is personal among ourselves. Compliments as well as censure to individuals make no part thereof. The wise, and the worthy, need not the triumph of a pamphlet; and those whose sentiments are injudicious, or unfriendly, will cease of themselves unless too much pains are bestowed upon their conversion.

The cause of America is in a great measure the cause of all mankind. Many circumstances hath, and will arise, which are not local, but universal, and through which the principles of all Lovers of Mankind are affected, and in the Event of which, their Affections are interested. The laying a Country desolate with Fire and Sword, declaring War against the natural rights of all Mankind, and extirpating the Defenders thereof from the Face of the Earth, is the Concern of every Man to whom Nature hath given the Power of feeling; of which Class, regardless of Party Censure, is the

AUTHOR.

P. S. The Publication of this new Edition hath been delayed, with a View of taking notice (had it been necessary) of any Attempt to refute the Doctrine of Independence: As no Answer hath yet appeared, it is now presumed that none will, the Time needful for getting such a Performance ready for the Public being considerably past.

Who the Author of this Production is, is wholly unnecessary to the Public, as the Object for Attention is the *Doctrine itself*, not the *Man*. Yet it may not be unnecessary to say, That he is unconnected with any Party, and under no sort of Influence public or private, but the influence of reason and principle.

Philadelphia, February 14, 1776

Of the origin and design of government in general. With concise remarks on the English constitution

Some writers have so confounded society with government, as to leave little or no distinction between them; whereas they are not only different, but have different origins. Society is produced by our wants, and government by our wickedness; the former promotes our happiness *positively* by uniting our affections, the latter *negatively* by restraining our vices. The one encourages intercourse, the other creates distinctions. The first is a patron, the last a punisher.

Society in every state is a blessing, but government even in its best state is but a necessary evil; in its worst state an intolerable one; for when we suffer, or are exposed to the same miseries *by a government*, which we might expect in a country *without government*, our calamity is heightened by reflecting that we furnish the means by which we suffer. Government, like dress, is the badge of lost innocence; the palaces of kings are built on the ruins of the bowers of paradise. For were the impulses of conscience clear, uniform, and irresistibly obeyed, man would need no other lawgiver; but that not being the case, he finds it necessary to surrender up a part of his property to furnish means for the protection of the rest; and this he is induced to do by the same prudence which in every other case advises him out of two evils to choose the least. *Wherefore,* security being the true design and end of government, it unanswerably follows, that whatever *form* thereof appears most likely to ensure it to us, with the least expence and greatest benefit, is preferable to all others.

In order to gain a clear and just idea of the design and end of government, let us suppose a small number of persons settled in some sequestered part of the earth, unconnected with the rest, they will then represent the first peopling of any country, or of the world. In this state of natural liberty, society will be their first thought. A thousand motives will excite them thereto, the strength of one man is so unequal to his wants, and his mind so unfitted for perpetual solitude, that he is soon obliged to seek assistance and relief of another, who in his turn requires the same. Four or five united would be able to raise a tolerable dwelling in the midst of a wilderness, but *one* man might labour out of the common period of life without accomplishing any thing; when he had felled his timber he could not remove it, nor erect it after it was removed; hunger in the mean time would urge him from his work, and every different want call him a different way. Disease, nay even misfortune would be death, for though neither might be mortal, yet either would disable him from living, and reduce him to a state in which he might rather be said to perish than to die.

Thus necessity, like a gravitating power, would soon form our newly arrived emigrants into society, the reciprocal blessings of which, would supersede, and render the obligations of law and government unnecessary while they remained perfectly just to each other; but as nothing but heaven is impregnable to vice, it will unavoidably happen, that in proportion as they surmount the first difficulties of emigration, which bound them together in a common cause, they will begin to relax in their duty and attachment to each other; and this remissness will point out the necessity of establishing some form of government to supply the defect of moral virtue.

Some convenient tree will afford them a State-House, under the branches of which, the whole colony may assemble to deliberate on public matters. It is more than probable that their first laws will have the title only of REGULATIONS, and be enforced by no other penalty than public disesteem. In this first parliament every man, by natural right, will have a seat.

But as the colony increases, the public concerns will increase likewise, and the distance at which the members may be separated, will render it too inconvenient for all of them to meet on every occasion as at first, when their number was small, their habitations near, and the public concerns few and trifling. This will point out the convenience of their consenting to leave the legislative part to be managed by a select number chosen from the whole body, who are supposed to have the same concerns at stake which those have who appointed them, and who will act in the same manner as the whole body would act, were they present. If the colony continue increasing, it will become necessary to augment the number of the representatives, and that the interest of every part of the colony may be attended to, it will be found best to divide the whole into convenient parts, each part sending its proper number; and that the *elected* might never form to themselves an interest separate from the *electors*, prudence will point out the propriety of having elections often; because as the *elected* might by that means return and mix again with the general body of the *electors* in a few months, their fidelity to the public will be secured by the prudent reflexion of not making a rod for themselves. And as this frequent interchange will establish a common interest with every part of the community, they will mutually and naturally support each other, and on this (not on the unmeaning name of king) depends the *strength of government, and the happiness of the governed.*

Here then is the origin and rise of government; namely, a mode rendered necessary by the inability of moral virtue to govern the world; here too is the design and end of government, viz. freedom and security. And however our eyes may be dazzled with show, or our ears deceived by sound; however, prejudice may warp our wills, or interest darken our understanding, the simple voice of nature and of reason will say, it is right.

I draw my idea of the form of government from a principle in nature, which no art can overturn, viz. that the more simple any thing is, the less liable it is to be disordered, and the easier repaired when disordered; and with this maxim in view, I offer a few remarks on the so much boasted constitution of England. That it was noble for the dark and slavish times in which it was erected, is granted. When the world was overrun with tyranny the least remove therefrom was a glorious rescue. But that it is imperfect, subject to convulsions, and incapable of producing what it seems to promise, is easily demonstrated.

Absolute governments (tho' the disgrace of human nature) have this advantage with them, that they are simple; if the people suffer, they know the head from which their suffering springs, know likewise the remedy, and are not bewildered by a variety of causes and cures. But the constitution of England is so exceedingly complex, that the nation may suffer for years together without being able to discover in which part the fault lies; some will say in one and some in another, and every political physician will advise a different medicine.

I know it is difficult to get over local or long standing prejudices, yet if we will suffer ourselves to examine the component parts of the English constitution, we shall find them to be the base remains of two ancient tyrannies, compounded with some new republican materials.

First.—The remains of monarchical tyranny in the person of the king.

Secondly.—The remains of aristocratical tyranny in the persons of the peers.

Thirdly.—The new republican materials in the persons of the commons, on whose virtue depends the freedom of England.

The two first, by being hereditary, are independent of the people; wherefore in a *constitutional sense* they contribute nothing towards the freedom of the state.

To say that the constitution of England is a *union* of three powers reciprocally *checking* each other, is farcical, either the words have no meaning, or they are flat contradictions.

To say that the commons is a check upon the king, presupposes two things:

First.—That the king is not to be trusted without being looked after, or in other words, that a thirst for absolute power is the natural disease of monarchy.

Secondly.—That the commons, by being appointed for that purpose, are either wiser or more worthy of confidence than the crown.

But as the same constitution which gives the commons a power to check the king by withholding the supplies, gives afterwards the king a power to check the commons, by empowering him to reject their other bills; it again supposes that the king is wiser than those whom it has already supposed to be wiser than him. A mere absurdity!

There is something exceedingly ridiculous in the composition of monarchy; it first excludes a man from the means of information, yet empowers him to act in cases where the highest judgment is required. The state of a king shuts him from the world, yet the business of a king requires him to know it thoroughly; wherefore the different parts, by unnaturally opposing and destroying each other, prove the whole character to be absurd and useless.

Some writers have explained the English constitution thus: The king, say they, is one, the people another; the peers are an house in behalf of the king, the commons in behalf of the people; but this hath all the distinctions of an house divided against itself; though the expressions be pleasantly arranged, yet when examined, they appear idle and ambiguous; and it will always happen, that the nicest construction that words are capable of, when applied to the description of some thing which either cannot exist, or is too incomprehensible to be within the compass of description, will be words of sound only, and though they may amuse the ear, they cannot inform the mind, for this explanation includes a previous question, viz. *How came the king by a power which the people are afraid to trust, and always obliged to check?* Such a power could not be the gift of a wise people, neither can any power, *which needs checking,* be from God; yet the provision, which the constitution makes, supposes such a power to exist.

But the provision is unequal to the task; the means either cannot or will not accomplish the end, and the whole affair is a felo de se; for as the greater weight will always carry up the less, and as all the wheels of a machine are put in motion by one, it only remains to know which power in the constitution has the most weight, for that will govern; and though the others, or a part of them, may clog, or, as the phrase is, check the rapidity of its motion, yet so long as they cannot stop it, their endeavours will be ineffectual; the first moving power will at last have its way, and what it wants in speed, is supplied by time.

That the crown is this overbearing part in the English constitution, needs not be mentioned, and that it derives its whole consequence merely from being the giver of places and pensions, is self-evident, wherefore, though we have been wise enough to shut and lock a door against absolute monarchy, we at the same time have been foolish enough to put the crown in possession of the key.

The prejudice of Englishmen in favour of their own government by king, lords and commons, arises as much or more from national pride than reason. Individuals are undoubtedly safer in England than in some other countries, but the *will* of the king is as much the *law* of the land in Britain as in France, with this difference, that instead of proceeding directly from his mouth, it is handed to the people under the more formidable shape of an act of parliament. For the fate of Charles the First hath only made kings more subtle—not more just.

Wherefore, laying aside all national pride and prejudice in favour of modes and forms, the plain truth is, that *it is wholly owing to the constitution of the people, and not to the con-*

stitution of the government, that the crown is not as oppressive in England as in Turkey.

An inquiry into the *constitutional errors* in the English form of government is at this time highly necessary; for as we are never in a proper condition of doing justice to others, while we continue under the influence of some leading partiality, so neither are we capable of doing it to ourselves while we remain fettered by any obstinate prejudice. And as a man, who is attached to a prostitute, is unfitted to choose or judge a wife, so any prepossession in favour of a rotten constitution of government will disable us from discerning a good one.

Of monarchy and hereditary succession

Mankind being originally equals in the order of creation, the equality could only be destroyed by some subsequent circumstance; the distinctions of rich, and poor, may in a great measure be accounted for, and that without having recourse to the harsh, ill-sounding names of oppression and avarice. Oppression is often the *consequence,* but seldom or never the *means* of riches; and though avarice will preserve a man from being necessitously poor, it generally makes him too timorous to be wealthy.

But there is another and greater distinction, for which no truly natural or religious reason can be assigned, and that is, the distinction of men into KINGS and SUBJECTS. Male and female are the distinctions of nature, good and bad the distinctions of heaven; but how a race of men came into the world so exalted above the rest, and distinguished like some new species, is worth inquiring into, and whether they are the means of happiness or of misery to mankind.

In the early ages of the world, according to the scripture chronology, there were no kings; the consequence of which was, there were no wars; it is the pride of kings which throw mankind into confusion. Holland without a king hath enjoyed more peace for this last century than any of the monarchical governments in Europe. Antiquity favours the same remark; for the quiet and rural lives of the first patriarchs hath a happy something in them, which vanishes away when we come to the history of Jewish royalty.

Government by kings was first introduced into the world by the Heathens, from whom the children of Israel copied the custom. It was the most prosperous invention the Devil ever set on foot for the promotion of idolatry. The Heathens paid divine honors to their deceased kings, and the Christian world hath improved on the plan, by doing the same to their living ones. How impious is the title of sacred majesty applied to a worm, who in the midst of his splendor is crumbling into dust!

As the exalting one man so greatly above the rest cannot be justified on the equal rights of nature, so neither can it be defended on the authority of scripture; for the will of the Almighty, as declared by Gideon and the prophet Samuel, expressly disapproves of government by kings. All anti-monarchical parts of scripture have been very smoothly glossed over in monarchical governments, but they undoubtedly merit the attention of countries which have their governments yet to form. *"Render unto Cæsar the things which are Cæsar's"* is the scripture doctrine of courts, yet it is no support of monarchical government, for the Jews at that time were without a king, and in a state of vassalage to the Romans.

Near three thousand years passed away from the Mosaic account of the creation, till the Jews under a national delusion requested a king. Till then their form of government (except in extraordinary cases, where the Almighty interposed) was a kind of republic administered by a judge and the elders of the tribes. Kings they had none, and it was held sinful to acknowledge any being under that title but the Lord of Hosts. And when a man seriously reflects on the idolatrous homage which is paid to the persons of kings, he need not wonder that the Almighty, ever jealous of his honor, should disapprove of a form of government which so impiously invades the prerogative of heaven.

Monarchy is ranked in scripture as one of the sins of the Jews, for which a curse in reserve is denounced against them. The history of that transaction is worth attending to.

The children of Israel being oppressed by the Midianites, Gideon marched against them with a small army, and victory, thro' the divine interposition, decided in his favour. The Jews, elate with success, and attributing it to the generalship of Gideon, proposed making him a king, saying, *Rule thou over us, thou and thy son and thy son's son.* Here was temptation in its fullest extent; not a kingdom only, but an hereditary one, but Gideon in the piety of his soul replied, *I will not rule over you, neither shall my son rule over you,* THE LORD SHALL RULE OVER YOU. Words need not be more explicit; Gideon doth not decline the honor, but denieth their right to give it; neither doth he compliment them with invented declarations of his thanks, but in the positive stile of a prophet charges them with disaffection to their proper Sovereign, the King of heaven.

About one hundred and thirty years after this, they fell again into the same error. The hankering which the Jews had for the idolatrous customs of the Heathens, is something exceedingly unaccountable; but so it was, that laying hold of the misconduct of Samuel's two sons, who were entrusted with some secular concerns, they came in an abrupt and clamorous manner to Samuel, saying, *Behold thou art old, and thy sons walk not in thy ways, now make us a king to judge us, like all the other nations.* And here we cannot but observe that their motives were bad, viz. that they might be *like* unto other nations, i.e. the Heathens, whereas their true glory laid in being as much *unlike* them as possible. *But the thing displeased Samuel when they said, Give us a king to judge us; and Samuel prayed unto the Lord, and the Lord said unto Samuel, Hearken unto the voice of the people in all that they say unto thee, for they have not rejected thee, but they have rejected me,* THAT I SHOULD NOT REIGN OVER THEM. *According to all the works which they have done since the day that I brought them up out of Egypt, even unto this day; wherewith they have forsaken me and served other Gods; so do they also unto thee. Now therefore hearken unto their voice, howbeit, protest solemnly unto them and shew them the manner of the king that shall reign over them, i. e.* not of any particular king, but the general manner of the kings of the earth, whom Israel was so eagerly copying after. And notwithstanding the great distance of time and difference of manners, the character is still in fashion. *And Samuel told all the words of the Lord unto the people, that asked of him a king. And he said, This shall be the manner of the king that shall reign over you; he will take your sons and appoint them for himself, for his chariots, and to be his horsemen, and some shall run before his chariots* (this description agrees with the present mode of impressing men) *and he will appoint him captains over thousands and captains over fifties, and will set them to ear his ground and to reap his harvest, and to make his instruments of war, and instruments of his chariots; and he will take your daughters to be confectionaries, and to be cooks and to be bakers* (this describes the expence and luxury as well as the oppression of kings) *and he will take your fields and your olive yards, even the best of them, and give them to his servants; and he will take the tenth of your seed, and of your vineyards, and give them to his officers and to his servants* (by which we see that bribery, corruption and favouritism are the standing vices of kings) *and he will take the tenth of your men servants, and your maid servants, and your goodliest young men and your asses, and put them to his work; and he will take the tenth of your sheep, and ye shall be his servants, and ye shall cry out in that day because of your king which ye shall have chosen,* AND THE LORD WILL NOT HEAR YOU IN THAT DAY. This accounts for the continuation of monarchy; neither do the characters of the few good kings which have lived since, either sanctify the title, or blot out the sinfulness of the origin; the high encomium given of David takes no notice of him *officially as a king,* but only as a *man* after God's own heart. *Nevertheless the people refused to obey the voice of Samuel, and they said, Nay, but we will have a king over us that we may be like all the nations, and that our king may judge us, and go out before us, and fight our battles.* Samuel continued to reason with them, but to no purpose; he set before them their ingratitude, but all would not avail; and seeing them fully bent on their folly, he cried out, *I will call unto the Lord, and he shall send thunder and rain* (which then was a punishment, being in the time of wheat harvest) *that ye may perceive and see that your wickedness is great which ye have done in the sight of the Lord,* IN ASKING YOU A KING. *So Samuel called unto the Lord, and the Lord sent thunder and rain that day, and all the people greatly feared the Lord and Samuel. And all the people said unto Samuel, pray for thy servants unto the Lord thy God that we die not, for* WE HAVE ADDED UNTO OUR SINS THIS EVIL, TO ASK A KING. These portions of scripture are direct and positive. They admit of no equivocal construction. That the Almighty hath here entered his protest against monarchical government, is true, or the scripture is false. And a man hath good reason to believe that there is as much of king-craft, as priest-craft, in withholding the scripture from the public in Popish countries. For monarchy in every instance is the Popery of government.

To the evil of monarchy we have added that of hereditary succession; and as the first is a degradation and lessening of ourselves, so the second, claimed as a matter of right, is an insult and an imposition on posterity. For all men being originally equals, no *one* by *birth* could have a right to set up his own family in perpetual preference to all others for ever, and though himself might deserve *some* decent degree of honors of his cotemporaries, yet his descendants might be far too unworthy to inherit them. One of the strongest *natural* proofs of the folly of hereditary right in kings, is, that nature disapproves it, otherwise she would not so frequently turn it into ridicule by giving mankind an *Ass for a Lion.*

Secondly, as no man at first could possess any other public honors than were bestowed upon him, so the givers of those honors could have no power to give away the right of posterity. And though they might say, "We choose you for *our* head," they could not, without manifest injustice to their children, say "that your children and your childrens children shall reign over *ours* for ever." Because such an unwise, unjust, unnatural compact might (perhaps) in the next succession put them under the government of a rogue or a fool. Most wise men, in their private sentiments, have ever treated hereditary right with contempt; yet it is one of those evils, which when once established is not easily removed; many submit from fear, others from superstition, and the more powerful part shares with the king the plunder of the rest.

This is supposing the present race of kings in the world to have had an honorable origin; whereas it is more than probable, that could we take off the dark covering of antiquity, and trace them to their first rise, that we should find the first of them nothing better than the principal ruffian of some restless gang, whose savage manners or pre-eminence in subtilty obtained him the title of chief among plunderers; and who by increasing in power, and extending his depredations, overawed the quiet and defenceless to purchase their safety by frequent contributions. Yet his electors could have no idea of giving hereditary right to his descendants, because such a perpetual exclusion of themselves was incompatible with the free and unrestrained principles they professed to live by. Wherefore, hereditary succession in the early ages of monarchy could not take place as a matter of claim, but as something casual or complimental; but as few or no records were extant in those days, and traditionary history stuffed with fables, it was very easy, after the lapse of a few generations, to trump up some superstitious tale, conveniently timed, Mahomet like, to cram hereditary right down the throats of the vulgar. Perhaps the disorders which threatened, or seemed to threaten, on the decease of a leader and the choice of a new one (for elections among ruffians could not be very orderly) induced many at first to favor hereditary pretensions; by which means it happened, as it hath happened since, that what at first was submitted to as a convenience, was afterwards claimed as a right.

England, since the conquest, hath known some few good monarchs, but groaned beneath a much larger number of bad ones; yet no man in his senses can say that their claim under William the Conqueror is a very honorable one. A French bastard landing with an armed banditti, and establishing himself king of England against the consent of the natives, is in plain terms a very paltry rascally original.—It certainly hath no divinity in it. However, it is needless to spend much time in exposing the folly of hereditary right; if there are any so weak as to believe it, let them promiscuously worship the ass and lion, and welcome. I shall neither copy their humility, nor disturb their devotion.

Yet I should be glad to ask how they suppose kings came at first? The question admits but of three answers, viz. either by lot, by election, or by usurpation. If the first king was taken by lot, it establishes a precedent for the next, which excludes hereditary succession. Saul was by lot, yet the succession was not hereditary, neither does it appear from that transaction there was any intention it ever should. If the first king of any country was by election, that likewise establishes a precedent for the next; for to say, that the *right* of all future generations is taken away, by the act of the first electors, in their choice not only of a king, but of a family of kings for ever, hath no parallel in or out of scripture but the doctrine of original sin, which supposes the free will of all men lost in Adam; and from such comparison, and it will admit of no other, hereditary succession can derive no glory. For as in Adam all sinned, and as in the first electors all men obeyed; as in the one all mankind were subjected to Satan, and in the other to Sovereignty; as our innocence was lost in the first, and our authority in the last; and as both disable us from reassuming some former state and privilege, it unanswerably follows that original sin and hereditary succession are parallels. Dishonorable rank! Inglorious connexion! Yet the most subtile sophist cannot produce a juster simile.

As to usurpation, no man will be so hardy as to defend it; and that William the Conqueror was an usurper is a fact not to be contradicted. The plain truth is, that the antiquity of English monarchy will not bear looking into.

But it is not so much the absurdity as the evil of hereditary succession which concerns mankind. Did it ensure a race of good and wise men it would have the seal of divine authority, but as it opens a door to the *foolish,* the *wicked,* and the *improper,* it hath in it the nature of oppression. Men who look upon themselves born to reign, and others to obey, soon grow insolent; selected from the rest of mankind their minds are early poisoned by importance; and the world they act in differs so materially from the world at large, that they have but little opportunity of knowing its true interests, and when they succeed to the government are frequently the most ignorant and unfit of any throughout the dominions.

Another evil which attends hereditary succession is, that the throne is subject to be possessed by a minor at any age; all which time the regency, acting under the cover of a king, have every opportunity and inducement to betray their trust. The same national misfortune happens, when a king, worn out with age and infirmity, enters the last stage of human weakness. In both these cases the public becomes a prey to every miscreant, who can tamper successfully with the follies either of age or infancy.

The most plausible plea, which hath ever been offered in favour of hereditary succession, is, that it preserves a nation from civil wars; and were this true, it would be weighty; whereas, it is the most barefaced falsity ever imposed upon mankind. The whole history of England disowns the fact. Thirty kings and two minors have reigned in that distracted kingdom since the conquest, in which time there have been (including the Revolution) no less than eight civil wars and nineteen rebellions. Wherefore instead of making for peace, it makes against it, and destroys the very foundation it seems to stand on.

The contest for monarchy and succession, between the houses of York and Lancaster, laid England in a scene of blood for many years. Twelve pitched battles, besides skirmishes and sieges, were fought between Henry and Edward. Twice was Henry prisoner to Edward, who in his turn was prisoner to Henry. And so uncertain is the fate of war and the temper of a nation, when nothing but personal matters are the ground of a quarrel, that Henry was taken in triumph from a prison to a palace, and Edward obliged to fly from a palace to a foreign land; yet, as sudden transitions of temper are seldom lasting, Henry in his turn was driven from the throne, and Edward recalled to succeed him. The parliament always following the strongest side.

This contest began in the reign of Henry the Sixth, and was not entirely extinguished till Henry the Seventh, in whom the families were united. Including a period of 67 years, viz. from 1422 to 1489.

In short, monarchy and succession have laid (not this or that kingdom only) but the world in blood and ashes. 'Tis a form of government which the word of God bears testimony against, and blood will attend it.

If we inquire the business of a king, we shall find that in some countries they have none; and after sauntering away their lives without pleasure to themselves or advantage to the nation, withdraw from the scene, and leave their successors to tread the same idle ground. In absolute monarchies the whole weight of business, civil and military, lies on the king; the children of Israel in their request for a king, urged this plea "that he may judge us, and go out before us and fight our battles." But in countries where he is neither a judge nor a general, as in England, a man would be puzzled to know what *is* his business.

The nearer any government approaches to a republic the less business there is for a king. It is somewhat difficult to find a proper name for the government of England. Sir William Meredith calls it a republic,[1] but in its present state it is unworthy of the name, because the corrupt influence of the crown, by having all the places in its disposal, hath so effectually swallowed up the power, and eaten out the virtue of the house of commons (the republican part in the constitution) that the government of England is nearly as monarchical as that of France or Spain. Men fall out with names without understanding them. For it is the republican and not the monarchical part of the constitution of England which Englishmen glory in, viz. the liberty of choosing an house of commons from out of their own body—and it is easy to see that when republican virtue fails, slavery ensues. Why is the constitution of England sickly, but because monarchy hath poisoned the republic, the crown hath engrossed the commons?

In England a king hath little more to do than to make war and give away places; which in plain terms, is to impoverish the nation and set it together by the ears. A pretty business indeed for a man to be allowed eight hundred thousand sterling a year for, and worshipped into the bargain! Of more worth is one honest man to society and in the sight of God, than all the crowned ruffians that ever lived.

[1] Sir William Meredith (1726?–1790) was a Whig politician and writer who became an Admiralty Lord in 1765.

Thoughts on the present state of American affairs

In the following pages I offer nothing more than simple facts, plain arguments, and common sense; and have no other preliminaries to settle with the reader, than that he will divest himself of prejudice and prepossession, and suffer his reason and his feelings to determine for themselves; that he will put *on,* or rather that he will not put *off* the true character of a man, and generously enlarge his views beyond the present day.

Volumes have been written on the subject of the struggle between England and America. Men of all ranks have embarked in the controversy, from different motives, and with various designs; but all have been ineffectual, and the period of debate is closed. Arms, as the last resource, decide the contest; the appeal was the choice of the king, and the continent hath accepted the challenge.

It hath been reported of the late Mr. Pelham (who tho' an able minister was not without his faults) that on his being attacked in the house of commons, on the score, that his measures were only of a temporary kind, replied *"they will last my time."*[2] Should a thought so fatal and unmanly possess the colonies in the present contest, the name of ancestors will be remembered by future generations with detestation.

The sun never shined on a cause of greater worth. 'Tis not the affair of a city, a county, a province, or a kingdom, but of a continent—of at least one eighth part of the habitable globe. 'Tis not the concern of a day, a year, or an age; posterity are virtually involved in the contest, and will be more or less affected, even to the end of time, by the proceedings now. Now is the seed-time of continental union, faith and honor. The least fracture now will be like a name engraved with the point of a pin on the tender rind of a young oak; the wound will enlarge with the tree, and posterity read it in full grown characters.

By referring the matter from argument to arms, a new æra for politics is struck; a new method of thinking hath arisen. All plans, proposals, &c. prior to the nineteenth of April, *i. e.* to the commencement of hostilities, are like the almanacks of the last year;[3] which, though proper then are superseded

[2] Henry Pelham (1695?–1754) was a rather timid, peace-loving politician whose parliamentary influence was maintained through an elaborate system of corruption.

[3] The Battle of Lexington and Concord was fought on April 19, 1775.

and useless now. Whatever was advanced by the advocates on either side of the question then, terminated in one and the same point, viz. a union with Great-Britain; the only difference between the parties was the method of effecting it; the one proposing force, the other friendship; but it hath so far happened that the first hath failed, and the second hath withdrawn her influence.

As much hath been said of the advantages of reconciliation, which, like an agreeable dream, hath passed away and left us as we were, it is but right, that we should examine the contrary side of the argument, and inquire into some of the many material injuries which these colonies sustain, and always will sustain, by being connected with, and dependant on Great-Britain: To examine that connexion and dependance, on the principles of nature and common sense, to see what we have to trust to, if separated, and what we are to expect, if dependant.

I have heard it asserted by some, that as America hath flourished under her former connexion with Great-Britain, that the same connexion is necessary towards her future happiness, and will always have the same effect. Nothing can be more fallacious than this kind of argument. We may as well assert that because a child has thrived upon milk, that it is never to have meat, or that the first twenty years of our lives is to become a precedent for the next twenty. But even this is admitting more than is true, for I answer roundly, that America would have flourished as much, and probably much more, had no European power had any thing to do with her. The commerce, by which she hath enriched herself, are the necessaries of life, and will always have a market while eating is the custom of Europe.

But she has protected us, say some. That she has engrossed us is true, and defended the continent at our expence as well as her own is admitted, and she would have defended Turkey from the same motive, viz. the sake of trade and dominion.

Alas, we have been long led away by ancient prejudices, and made large sacrifices to superstition. We have boasted the protection of Great-Britain, without considering, that her motive was *interest* not *attachment;* that she did not protect us from *our enemies* on *our account,* but from *her enemies* on *her own account,* from those who had no quarrel with us on any *other account,* and who will always be our enemies on the *same account.* Let Britain wave her pretensions to the continent, or the continent throw off the dependance, and we should be at peace with France and Spain were they at war with Britain. The miseries of Hanover last war ought to warn us against connexions.

It has lately been asserted in parliament, that the colonies have no relation to each other but through the parent country, *i. e.* that Pennsylvania and the Jerseys, and so on for the rest, are sister colonies by the way of England; this is certainly a very round-about way of proving relationship, but it is the nearest and only true way of proving enemyship, if I may so call it. France and Spain never were, nor perhaps ever will be our enemies as *Americans,* but as our being the *subjects of Great-Britain.*

But Britain is the parent country, say some. Then the more shame upon her conduct. Even brutes do not devour their young, nor savages make war upon their families; wherefore the assertion, if true, turns to her reproach; but it happens not to be true, or only partly so, and the phrase *parent* or *mother country* hath been jesuitically adopted by the king and his parasites, with a low papistical design of gaining an unfair bias on the credulous weakness of our minds. Europe, and not England, is the parent country of America. This new world hath been the asylum for the persecuted lovers of civil and religious liberty from *every part* of Europe. Hither have they fled, not from the tender embraces of the mother, but from the cruelty of the monster; and it is so far true of England, that the same tyranny which drove the first emigrants from home, pursues their descendants still.

In this extensive quarter of the globe, we forget the narrow limits of three hundred and sixty miles (the extent of England) and carry our friendship on a larger scale; we claim brotherhood with every European Christian, and triumph in the generosity of the sentiment.

It is pleasant to observe by what regular gradations we surmount the force of local prejudice, as we enlarge our acquaintance with the world. A man born in any town in England divided into parishes, will naturally associate most with his fellow-parishioners (because their interests in many cases will be common) and distinguish him by the name of *neighbour;* if he meet him but a few miles from home, he drops the narrow idea of a street, and salutes him by the name of *townsman;* if he travel out of the county, and meet him in any other, he forgets the minor divisions of street and town, and calls him *countryman,* i. e. *countyman;* but if in their foreign excursions they should associate in France or any other part of *Europe,* their local remembrance would be enlarged into that of *Englishmen.* And by a just parity of reasoning, all Europeans meeting in America, or any other quarter of the globe, are *countrymen;* for England, Holland, Germany, or Sweden, when compared with the whole, stand in the same places on the larger scale, which the divisions of street, town, and county do on the smaller ones; distinctions too limited for continental minds. Not one third of the inhabitants, even of this province,[4] are of English descent. Wherefore I reprobate the phrase of parent or mother country applied to England only, as being false, selfish, narrow and ungenerous.

But admitting, that we were all of English descent, what does it amount to? Nothing. Britain, being now an open enemy, extinguishes every other name and title: And to say that reconciliation is our duty, is truly farcical. The first king of England, of the present line (William the Conqueror) was a Frenchman, and half the Peers of England are descendants from the same country; wherefore, by the same method of reasoning, England ought to be governed by France.

Much hath been said of the united strength of Britain and the colonies, that in conjunction they might bid defiance to the world. But this is mere presumption; the fate of war is uncertain, neither do the expressions mean any thing; for this continent would never suffer itself to be drained of inhabitants, to support the British arms in either Asia, Africa, or Europe.

Besides what have we to do with setting the world at defiance? Our plan is commerce, and that, well attended to, will secure us the peace and friendship of all Europe; because, it is the interest of all Europe to have America a *free port.* Her trade will always be a protection, and her barrenness of gold and silver secure her from invaders.

I challenge the warmest advocate for reconciliation, to shew, a single advantage that this continent can reap, by being connected with Great-Britain. I repeat the challenge, not a single advantage is derived. Our corn will fetch its price in any market in Europe, and our imported goods must be paid for buy them where we will.

But the injuries and disadvantages we sustain by that connection, are without number; and our duty to mankind at large, as well as to ourselves, instruct us to renounce the

[4] Pennsylvania.

alliance: Because, any submission to, or dependance on Great-Britain, tends directly to involve this continent in European wars and quarrels; and sets us at variance with nations, who would otherwise seek our friendship, and against whom, we have neither anger nor complaint. As Europe is our market for trade, we ought to form no partial connection with any part of it. It is the true interest of America to steer clear of European contentions, which she never can do, while by her dependance on Britain, she is made the make-weight in the scale of British politics.

Europe is too thickly planted with kingdoms to be long at peace, and whenever a war breaks out between England and any foreign power, the trade of America goes to ruin, *because of her connection with Britain*. The next war may not turn out like the last, and should it not, the advocates for reconciliation now, will be wishing for separation then, because, neutrality in that case, would be a safer convoy than a man of war. Every thing that is right or natural pleads for separation. The blood of the slain, the weeping voice of nature cries, 'TIS TIME TO PART. Even the distance at which the Almighty hath placed England and America, is a strong and natural proof, that the authority of the one, over the other, was never the design of Heaven. The time likewise at which the continent was discovered, adds weight to the argument, and the manner in which it was peopled encreases the force of it. The reformation was preceded by the discovery of America, as if the Almighty graciously meant to open a sanctuary to the persecuted in future years, when home should afford neither friendship nor safety.

The authority of Great-Britain over this continent, is a form of government, which sooner or later must have an end: And a serious mind can draw no true pleasure by looking forward, under the painful and positive conviction, that what he calls "the present constitution" is merely temporary. As parents, we can have no joy, knowing that *this government* is not sufficiently lasting to ensure any thing which we may bequeath to posterity: And by a plain method of argument, as we are running the next generation into debt, we ought to do the work of it, otherwise we use them meanly and pitifully. In order to discover the line of our duty rightly, we should take our children in our hand, and fix our station a few years farther into life; that eminence will present a prospect, which a few present fears and prejudices conceal from our sight.

Though I would carefully avoid giving unnecessary offence,

yet I am inclined to believe, that all those who espouse the doctrine of reconciliation, may be included within the following descriptions. Interested men, who are not to be trusted; weak men, who *cannot* see; prejudiced men, who *will not* see; and a certain set of moderate men, who think better of the European world than it deserves; and this last class, by an ill-judged deliberation, will be the cause of more calamities to this continent, than all the other three.

It is the good fortune of many to live distant from the scene of sorrow; the evil is not sufficient brought to *their* doors to make *them* feel the precariousness with which all American property is possessed. But let our imaginations transport us for a few moments to Boston, that seat of wretchedness will teach us wisdom, and instruct us for ever to renounce a power in whom we can have no trust.[5] The inhabitants of that unfortunate city, who but a few months ago were in ease and affluence, have now, no other alternative than to stay and starve, or turn out to beg. Endangered by the fire of their friends if they continue within the city, and plundered by the soldiery if they leave it. In their present condition they are prisoners without the hope of redemption, and in a general attack for their relief, they would be exposed to the fury of both armies.

Men of passive tempers look somewhat lightly over the offences of Britain, and, still hoping for the best, are apt to call out, *"Come, come, we shall be friends again, for all this."* But examine the passions and feelings of mankind, Bring the doctrine of reconciliation to the touchstone of nature, and then tell me, whether you can hereafter love, honor, and faithfully serve the power that hath carried fire and sword into your land? If you cannot do all these, then are you only deceiving yourselves, and by your delay bringing ruin upon posterity. Your future connexion with Britain, whom you can neither love nor honor, will be forced and unnatural, and being formed only on the plan of present convenience, will in a little time fall into a relapse more wretched than the first. But if you say, you can still pass the violations over, then I ask, Hath your house been burnt? Hath your property been destroyed before your face? Are your wife and children destitute of a bed to lie on, or bread to live on? Have you lost a parent or a child by their hands, and yourself the ruined

[5] The citizens of Boston had suffered greatly as a result of the "Coercive Acts." See notes 8 and 9, Jefferson's *A Summary View of the Rights of British America.*

and wretched survivor? If you have not, then are you not a judge of those who have. But if you have, and still can shake hands with the murderers, then are you unworthy the name of husband, father, friend, or lover, and whatever may be your rank or title in life, you have the heart of a coward, and the spirit of a sycophant.

This is not inflaming or exaggerating matters, but trying them by those feelings and affections which nature justifies, and without which, we should be incapable of discharging the social duties of life, or enjoying the felicities of it. I mean not to exhibit horror for the purpose of provoking revenge, but to awaken us from fatal and unmanly slumbers, that we may pursue determinedly some fixed object. It is not in the power of Britain or of Europe to conquer America, if she do not conquer herself by *delay* and *timidity*. The present winter is worth an age if rightly employed, but if lost or neglected, the whole continent will partake of the misfortune; and there is no punishment which that man will not deserve, be he who, or what, or where he will, that may be the means of sacrificing a season so precious and useful.

It is repugnant to reason, to the universal order of things, to all examples from former ages, to suppose, that this continent can longer remain subject to any external power. The most sanguine in Britain does not think so. The utmost stretch of human wisdom cannot, at this time, compass a plan short of separation, which can promise the continent even a year's security. Reconciliation is *now* a fallacious dream. Nature hath deserted the connexion, and Art cannot supply her place. For, as Milton wisely expresses, "never can true reconcilement grow, where wounds of deadly hate have pierc'd so deep."

Every quiet method for peace hath been ineffectual. Our prayers have been rejected with disdain; and only tended to convince us, that nothing flatters vanity, or confirms obstinacy in Kings more than repeated petitioning—and nothing hath contributed more than that very measure to make the Kings of Europe absolute: Witness Denmark and Sweden. Wherefore, since nothing but blows will do, for God's sake, let us come to a final separation, and not leave the next generation to be cutting throats, under the violated unmeaning names of parent and child.

To say, they will never attempt it again is idle and visionary, we thought so at the repeal of the stamp-act, yet a year or two undeceived us; as well may we suppose that nations, which have been once defeated, will never renew the quarrel.

As to government matters, it is not in the power of Britain to do this continent justice: The business of it will soon be too weighty, and intricate, to be managed with any tolerable degree of convenience, by a power so distant from us, and so very ignorant of us; for if they cannot conquer us, they cannot govern us. To be always running three or four thousand miles with a tale or a petition, waiting four or five months for an answer, which when obtained requires five or six more to explain it in, will in a few years be looked upon as folly and childishness—There was a time when it was proper, and there is a proper time for it to cease.

Small islands not capable of protecting themselves, are the proper objects for kingdoms to take under their care, but there is something very absurd, in supposing a continent to be perpetually governed by an island. In no instance hath nature made the satellite larger than its primary planet, and as England and America, with respect to each other, reverses the common order of nature, it is evident they belong to different systems; England to Europe, America to itself.

I am not induced by motives of pride, party, or resentment to espouse the doctrine of separation and independance; I am clearly, positively, and conscientiously persuaded that it is the true interest of this continent to be so; that every thing short of *that* is mere patchwork, that it can afford no lasting felicity, —that it is leaving the sword to our children, and shrinking back at a time, when, a little more, a little farther, would have rendered this continent the glory of the earth.

As Britain hath not manifested the least inclination towards a compromise, we may be assured that no terms can be obtained worthy the acceptance of the continent, or any ways equal to the expence of blood and treasure we have been already put to.

The object, contended for, ought always to bear some just proportion to the expence. The removal of North, or the whole detestable junto, is a matter unworthy the millions we have expended. A temporary stoppage of trade, was an inconvenience, which would have sufficiently balanced the repeal of all the acts complained of, had such repeals been obtained; but if the whole continent must take up arms, if every man must be a soldier, it is scarcely worth our while to fight against a contemptible ministry only. Dearly, dearly, do we pay for the repeal of the acts, if that is all we fight for; for in a just estimation, it is as great a folly to pay a Bunker-hill price for law, as for land. As I have always considered the independancy of this continent, as an event, which sooner or later must arrive, so from the late rapid progress of the continent to maturity, the event could not be far off. Wherefore, on the breaking out of hostilities, it was not worth while to have disputed a matter, which time would have finally redressed, unless we meant to be in earnest; otherwise, it is like wasting an estate on a suit at law, to regulate the trespasses of a tenant, whose lease is just expiring. No man was a warmer wisher for reconciliation than myself, before the fatal nineteenth of April 1775,* but the moment the event of that day was made known, I rejected the hardened, sullen tempered Pharaoh of England for ever; and disdain the wretch, that with the pretended title of FATHER OF HIS PEOPLE can unfeelingly hear of their slaughter, and composedly sleep with their blood upon his soul.

But admitting that matters were now made up, what would be the event? I answer, the ruin of the continent. And that for several reasons.

First. The powers of governing still remaining in the hands of the king, he will have a negative over the whole legislation of this continent. And as he hath shewn himself such an inveterate enemy to liberty, and discovered such a thirst for arbitrary power; is he, or is he not, a proper man to say to these colonies, *"You shall make no laws but what I please."* And is there any inhabitant in America so ignorant, as not to know, that according to what is called the *present constitution,* that this continent can make no laws but what the king gives leave to; and is there any man so unwise, as not to see, that (considering what has happened) he will suffer no law to be made here, but such as suit *his* purpose. We may be as effectually enslaved by the want of laws in America, as by submitting to laws made for us in England. After matters are made up (as it is called) can there be any doubt, but the whole power of the crown will be exerted, to keep this continent as low and humble as possible? Instead of going forward we shall go backward, or be perpetually quarrelling or ridiculously petitioning.—We are already greater than the king wishes us to be, and will he not hereafter endeavour to make us less? To bring the matter to one point. Is the power who is jealous of our prosperity, a proper power to govern us? Whoever says *No* to this question, is an *independent,* for inde-

* Massacre at Lexington.

pendancy means no more, than, whether we shall make our own laws, or whether the king, the greatest enemy this continent hath, or can have, shall tell us *"there shall be no laws but such as I like."*

But the king you will say has a negative in England; the people there can make no laws without his consent. In point of right and good order, there is something very ridiculous, that a youth of twenty-one (which hath often happened) shall say to several millions of people, older and wiser than himself, I forbid this or that act of yours to be law. But in this place I decline this sort of reply, though I will never cease to expose the absurdity of it, and only answer, that England being the King's residence, and America not so, makes quite another case. The king's negative *here* is ten times more dangerous and fatal than it can be in England, for *there* he will scarcely refuse his consent to a bill for putting England into as strong a state of defence as possible, and in America he would never suffer such a bill to be passed.

America is only a secondary object in the system of British politics, England consults the good of *this* country, no farther than it answers her *own* purpose. Wherefore, her own interest leads her to suppress the growth of *ours* in every case which doth not promote her advantage, or in the least interferes with it. A pretty state we should soon be in under such a secondhand government, considering what has happened! Men do not change from enemies to friends by the alteration of a name: And in order to shew that reconciliation *now* is a dangerous doctrine, I affirm, *that it would be policy in the king at this time, to repeal the acts for the sake of reinstating himself in the government of the provinces;* in order, that HE MAY ACCOMPLISH BY CRAFT AND SUBTILTY, IN THE LONG RUN, WHAT HE CANNOT DO BY FORCE AND VIOLENCE IN THE SHORT ONE. Reconciliation and ruin are nearly related.

Secondly. That as even the best terms, which we can expect to obtain, can amount to no more than a temporary expedient, or a kind of government by guardianship, which can last no longer than till the colonies come of age, so the general face and state of things, in the interim, will be unsettled and unpromising. Emigrants of property will not choose to come to a country whose form of government hangs but by a thread, and who is every day tottering on the brink of commotion and disturbance; and numbers of the present inhabitants would lay hold of the interval, to dispose of their effects, and quit the continent.

But the most powerful of all arguments, is, that nothing but independance, i. e. a continental form of government, can keep the peace of the continent and preserve it inviolate from civil wars. I dread the event of a reconciliation with Britain now, as it is more than probable, that it will be followed by a revolt somewhere or other, the consequences of which may be far more fatal than all the malice of Britain.

Thousands are already ruined by British barbarity; (thousands more will probably suffer the same fate) Those men have other feelings than us who have nothing suffered. All they *now* possess is liberty, what they before enjoyed is sacrificed to its service, and having nothing more to lose, they disdain submission. Besides, the general temper of the colonies, towards a British government, will be like that of a youth, who is nearly out of his time; they will care very little about her. And a government which cannot preserve the peace, is no government at all, and in that case we pay our money for nothing; and pray what is it that Britain can do, whose power will be wholly on paper, should a civil tumult break out the very day after reconciliation? I have heard some men say, many of whom I believe spoke without thinking, that they dreaded an independance, fearing that it would produce civil wars. It is but seldom that our first thoughts are truly correct, and that is the case here; for there are ten times more to dread from a patched up connexion than from independance. I make the sufferers case my own, and I protest, that were I driven from house and home, my property destroyed, and my circumstances ruined, that as man, sensible of injuries, I could never relish the doctrine of reconciliation, or consider myself bound thereby.

The colonies have manifested such a spirit of good order and obedience to continental government, as is sufficient to make every reasonable person easy and happy on that head. No man can assign the least pretence for his fears, on any other grounds, than such as are truly childish and ridiculous, viz. that one colony will be striving for superiority over another.

Where there are no distinctions there can be no superiority, perfect equality affords no temptation. The republics of Europe are all (and we may say always) in peace. Holland and Swisserland are without wars, foreign or domestic: Monarchical governments, it is true, are never long at rest; the crown itself is a temptation to enterprizing ruffians at *home;* and that degree of pride and insolence ever attendant on regal authority, swells into a rupture with foreign powers, in instances, where a republican government, by being formed on more natural principles, would negotiate the mistake.

If there is any true cause of fear respecting independance, it is because no plan is yet laid down. Men do not see their way out—Wherefore, as an opening into that business, I offer the following hints; at the same time modestly affirming, that I have no other opinion of them myself, than that they may be the means of giving rise to something better. Could the straggling thoughts of individuals be collected, they would frequently form materials for wise and able men to improve into useful matter.

LET the assemblies be annual, with a President only. The representation more equal. Their business wholly domestic, and subject to the authority of a Continental Congress.

Let each colony be divided into six, eight, or ten, convenient districts, each district to send a proper number of delegates to Congress, so that each colony send at least thirty. The whole number in Congress will be at least 390. Each Congress to sit and to choose a president by the following method. When the delegates are met, let a colony be taken from the whole thirteen colonies by lot, after which, let the whole Congress choose (by ballot) a president from out of the delegates of *that* province. In the next Congress, let a colony be taken by lot from twelve only, omitting that colony from which the president was taken in the former Congress, and so proceeding on till the whole thirteen shall have had their proper rotation. And in order that nothing may pass into a law but what is satisfactorily just, not less than three fifths of the Congress to be called a majority—He that will promote discord, under a government so equally formed as this, would have joined Lucifer in his revolt.

But as there is a peculiar delicacy, from whom, or in what manner, this business must first arise, and as it seems most agreeable and consistent, that it should come from some intermediate body between the governed and the governors, that is, between the Congress and the people, let a CONTINENTAL CONFERENCE be held, in the following manner, and for the following purpose.

A committee of twenty-six members of Congress, viz. two for each colony. Two Members from each House of Assembly, or Provincial Convention; and five representatives of the people at large, to be chosen in the capital city or town of each province, for and in behalf of the whole province, by as many qualified voters as shall think proper to attend from all parts of the province for that purpose; or, if more convenient, the representatives may be chosen in two or three of the most populous parts thereof. In this conference, thus assembled, will be united, the two grand principles of business *knowledge* and *power*. The members of Congress, Assemblies, or Conventions, by having had experience in national concerns, will be able and useful counsellors, and the whole, being impowered by the people, will have a truly legal authority.

The conferring members being met, let their business be to frame a CONTINENTAL CHARTER, or Charter of the United Colonies; (answering to what is called the Magna Charta of England) fixing the number and manner of choosing members of Congress, members of Assembly, with their date of sitting, and drawing the line of business and jurisdiction between them: (Always remembering, that our strength is continental, not provincial:) Securing freedom and property to all men, and above all things, the free exercise of religion, according to the dictates of conscience; with such other matter as is necessary for a charter to contain. Immediately after which, the said Conference to dissolve, and the bodies which shall be chosen comformable to the said charter, to be the legislators and governors of this continent for the time being: Whose peace and happiness may God preserve, Amen.

Should any body of men be hereafter delegated for this or some similar purpose, I offer them the following extracts from that wise observer on governments *Dragonetti.* "The science" says he "of the politician consists in fixing the true point of happiness and freedom. Those men would deserve the gratitude of ages, who should discover a mode of government that contained the greatest sum of individual happiness, with the least national expence.

Dragonetti on virtue and rewards."

But where, says some, is the King of America? I'll tell you. Friend, he reigns above, and doth not make havoc of mankind like the Royal Brute of Britain. Yet that we may not appear to be defective even in earthly honors, let a day be solemnly set apart for proclaiming the charter; let it be brought forth placed on the divine law, the word of God; let a crown be placed thereon, by which the world may know, that so far we approve of monarchy, that in America THE LAW IS KING. For as in absolute governments the King is law, so in free countries the law *ought* to be King; and there ought to be no other. But lest any ill use should afterwards arise, let the crown at the conclusion of the ceremony, be demolished, and scattered among the people whose right it is.

A government of our own is our natural right: And when a man seriously reflects on the precariousness of human affairs, he will become convinced, that it is infinitely wiser and safer, to form a constitution of our own in a cool deliberate manner, while we have it in our power, than to trust such an interesting event to time and chance. If we omit it now, some* Massanello may hereafter arise, who laying hold of popular disquietudes, may collect together the desperate and the discontented, and by assuming to themselves the powers of government, may sweep away the liberties of the continent like a deluge. Should the government of America return again into the hands of Britain, the tottering situation of things will be a temptation for some desperate adventurer to try his fortune; and in such a case, what relief can Britain give? Ere she could hear the news, the fatal business might be done; and ourselves suffering like the wretched Britons under the oppression of the Conqueror. Ye that oppose independance now, ye know not what ye do; ye are opening a door to eternal tyranny, by keeping vacant the seat of government. There are thousands, and tens of thousands, who would think it glorious to expel from the continent that barbarous and hellish power, which hath stirred up the Indians and Negroes to destroy us; the cruelty hath a double guilt, it is dealing brutally by us, and treacherously by them.

To talk of friendship with those in whom our reason forbids us to have faith, and our affections wounded through a thousand pores instruct us to detest, is madness and folly. Every day wears out the little remains of kindred between us and them, and can there be any reason to hope, that as the relationship expires, the affection will increase, or that we shall agree better, when we have ten times more and greater concerns to quarrel over than ever?

Ye that tell us of harmony and reconciliation, can ye restore to us the time that is past? Can ye give to prostitution its former innocence? Neither can ye reconcile Britain and America. The last cord now is broken, the people of England

* Thomas Anello otherwise Massanello a fisherman of Naples, who after spiriting up his countrymen in the public market-place, against the oppressions of the Spaniards, to whom the place was then subject prompted them to revolt, and in the space of a day became king.

are presenting addresses against us. There are injuries which nature cannot forgive; she would cease to be nature if she did. As well can the lover forgive the ravisher of his mistress, as the continent forgive the murders of Britain. The Almighty hath implanted in us these unextinguishable feelings for good and wise purposes. They are the guardians of his image in our hearts. They distinguish us from the herd of common animals. The social compact would dissolve, and justice be extirpated the earth, or have only a casual existence were we callous to the touches of affection. The robber, and the murderer, would often escape unpunished, did not the injuries which our tempers sustain, provoke us into justice.

O ye that love mankind! Ye that dare oppose, not only the tyranny, but the tyrant, stand forth! Every spot of the old world is overrun with oppression. Freedom hath been hunted round the globe. Asia, and Africa, have long expelled her—Europe regards her like a stranger, and England hath given her warning to depart. O! receive the fugitive, and prepare in time an asylum for mankind.

Of the present ABILITY *of* AMERICA, *with some miscellaneous* REFLEXIONS

I have never met with a man, either in England or America, who hath not confessed his opinion, that a separation between the countries, would take place one time or other: And there is no instance, in which we have shewn less judgment, than in endeavouring to describe, what we call the ripeness or fitness of the Continent for independance.

As all men allow the measure, and vary only in their opinion of the time, let us, in order to remove mistakes, take a general survey of things, and endeavour, if possible, to find out the *very* time. But we need not go far, the inquiry ceases at once, for, the *time hath found us.* The general concurrence, the glorious union of all things prove the fact.

It is not in numbers, but in unity, that our great strength lies; yet our present numbers are sufficient to repel the force of all the world. The Continent hath, at this time, the largest body of armed and disciplined men of any power under Heaven; and is just arrived at that pitch of strength, in which no single colony is able to support itself, and the whole, when united, can accomplish the matter, and either more, or, less than this, might be fatal in its effects. Our land force is already sufficient, and as to naval affairs, we cannot be insensible, that Britain would never suffer an American man of war to be built, while the continent remained in her hands. Wherefore, we should be no forwarder an hundred years hence in that branch, than we are now; but the truth is, we should be less so, because the timber of the country is every day diminishing, and that, which will remain at last, will be far off and difficult to procure.

Were the continent crowded with inhabitants, her sufferings under the present circumstances would be intolerable. The more seaport towns we had, the more should we have both to defend and to lose. Our present numbers are so happily proportioned to our wants, that no man need be idle. The diminution of trade affords an army, and the necessities of an army create a new trade.

Debts we have none; and whatever we may contract on this account will serve as a glorious memento of our virtue. Can we but leave posterity with a settled form of government, an independant constitution of its own, the purchase at any price will be cheap. But to expend millions for the sake of getting a few vile acts repealed, and routing the present ministry only, is unworthy the charge, and is using posterity with the utmost cruelty; because it is leaving them the great work to do, and a debt upon their backs, from which they derive no advantage. Such a thought is unworthy a man of honor, and is the true characteristic of a narrow heart and a peddling politician.

The debt we may contract doth not deserve our regard, if the work be but accomplished. No nation ought to be without a debt. A national debt is a national bond; and when it bears no interest, is in no case a grievance. Britain is oppressed with a debt of upwards of one hundred and forty millions sterling, for which she pays upwards of four millions interest. And as a compensation for her debt, she has a large navy; America is without a debt, and without a navy; yet for the twentieth part of the English national debt, could have a navy as large again. The navy of England is not worth, at this time, more than three millions and an half sterling.

The first and second editions of this pamphlet were published without the following calculations, which are now given as a proof that the above estimation of the navy is a just one. *See Entic's naval history, intro.* page 56.

The charge of building a ship of each rate, and furnishing her with masts, yards, sails and rigging, together with a proportion of eight months boatswain's and carpenter's sea-stores, as calculated by Mr. Burchett, Secretary to the navy.[6]

		£.
For a ship of a 100 guns	....	35,553
90	....	29,886
80	....	23,638
70	....	17,785
60	....	14,197
50	....	10,606
40	....	7,558
30	....	5,846
20	....	3,710

And from hence it is easy to sum up the value, or cost rather, of the whole British navy, which in the year 1757, when it was at its greatest glory consisted of the following ships and guns:

Ships.		Guns.		Cost of one.		Cost of all.
6	—	100	—	35,553*l.*	———	213,318*l.*
12	—	90	—	29,886	———	358,632
12	—	80	—	23,638	———	283,656
43	—	70	—	17,785	———	764,755
35	—	60	—	14,197	———	496,895
40	—	50	—	10,606	———	424,240
45	—	40	—	7,558	———	340,110
58	—	20	—	3,710	———	215,180
85	Sloops, bombs, and fireships, one with another,		}	2,000		170,000
					Cost	3,266,786
	Remains for guns,			———		233,214
						3,500,000

No country on the globe is so happily situated, or so internally capable of raising a fleet as America. Tar, timber, iron, and cordage are her natural produce. We need go abroad for nothing. Whereas the Dutch, who make large profits by hiring out their ships of war to the Spaniards and Portuguese, are obliged to import most of their materials they use. We

[6] Josiah Burchett (1666?–1746) was Secretary of the Admiralty, a member of parliament, and a writer on naval history.

ought to view the building a fleet as an article of commerce, it being the natural manufactory of this country. It is the best money we can lay out. A navy when finished is worth more than it cost. And is that nice point in national policy, in which commerce and protection are united. Let us build; if we want them not, we can sell; and by that means replace our paper currency with ready gold and silver.

In point of manning a fleet, people in general run into great errors; it is not necessary that one fourth part should be sailors. The Terrible privateer, Captain Death, stood the hottest engagement of any ship last war, yet had not twenty sailors on board, though her complement of men was upwards of two hundred. A few able and social sailors will soon instruct a sufficient number of active landmen in the common work of a ship. Wherefore, we never can be more capable to begin on maritime matters than now, while our timber is standing, our fisheries blocked up, and our sailors and shipwrights out of employ. Men of war of seventy and eighty guns were built forty years ago in New-England, and why not the same now? Ship-building is America's greatest pride, and in which she will in time excel the whole world. The great empires of the east are mostly inland, and consequently excluded from the possibility of rivalling her. Africa is in a state of barbarism; and no power in Europe hath either such an extent of coast, or such an internal supply of materials. Where nature hath given the one, she has withheld the other; to America only hath she been liberal of both. The vast empire of Russia is almost shut out from the sea: wherefore, her boundless forests, her tar, iron, and cordage are only articles of commerce.

In point of safety, ought we to be without a fleet? We are not the little people now, which we were sixty years ago; at that time we might have trusted our property in the streets, or fields rather; and slept securely without locks or bolts to our doors or windows. The case now is altered, and our methods of defence ought to improve with our increase of property. A common pirate, twelve months ago, might have come up the Delaware, and laid the city of Philadelphia under instant contribution, for what sum he pleased; and the same might have happened to other places. Nay, any daring fellow, in a brig of fourteen or sixteen guns might have robbed the whole continent, and carried off half a million of money. These are circumstances which demand our attention, and point out the necessity of naval protection.

Some, perhaps, will say, that after we have made it up with Britain, she will protect us. Can we be so unwise as to mean, that she shall keep a navy in our harbours for that purpose? Common sense will tell us, that the power which hath endeavoured to subdue us, is of all others the most improper to defend us. Conquest may be effected under the pretence of friendship; and ourselves after a long and brave resistance, be at last cheated into slavery. And if her ships are not to be admitted into our harbours, I would ask, how is she to protect us? A navy three or four thousand miles off can be of little use, and on sudden emergencies, none at all. Wherefore, if we must hereafter protect ourselves, why not do it for ourselves? Why do it for an other?

The English list of ships of war, is long and formidable, but not a tenth part of them are at any one time fit for service, numbers of them not in being; yet their names are pompously continued in the list, if only a plank be left of the ship: and not a fifth part of such as are fit for service, can be spared on any one station at one time. The East and West Indies, Mediterranean, Africa, and other parts over which Britain extends her claim, make large demands upon her navy. From a mixture of prejudice and inattention, we have contracted a false notion respecting the navy of England, and have talked as if we should have the whole of it to encounter at once, and for that reason, supposed, that we must have one as large; which not being instantly practicable, have been made use of by a set of disguised Tories to discourage our beginning thereon. Nothing can be farther from truth than this; for if America had only a twentieth part of the naval force of Britain, she would be by far an overmatch for her; because, as we neither have, nor claim any foreign dominion, our whole force would be employed on our own coast, where we should, in the long run, have two to one the advantage of those who had three or four thousand miles to sail over, before they could attack us, and the same distance to return in order to refit and recruit. And although Britain, by her fleet, hath a check over our trade to Europe, we have as large a one over her trade to the West-Indies, which, by laying in the neighbourhood of the continent, is entirely at its mercy.

Some method might be fallen on to keep up a naval force in time of peace, if we should not judge it necessary to support a constant navy. If premiums were to be given to merchants, to build and employ in their service ships mounted with twenty, thirty, forty or fifty guns, (the premiums to be in proportion to the loss of bulk to the merchants) fifty or sixty of those ships, with a few guardships on constant duty, would keep up a sufficient navy, and that without burdening ourselves with the evil so loudly complained of in England, of suffering their fleet, in time of peace to lie rotting in the docks. To unite the sinews of commerce and defence is sound policy; for when our strength and our riches play into each other's hand, we need fear no external enemy.

In almost every article of defence we abound. Hemp flourishes even to rankness, so that we need not want cordage. Our iron is superior to that of other countries. Our small arms equal to any in the world. Cannon we can cast at pleasure. Saltpetre and gunpowder we are every day producing. Our knowledge is hourly improving. Resolution is our inherent character, and courage hath never yet forsaken us. Wherefore, what is it that we want? Why is it that we hesitate? From Britain we can expect nothing but ruin. If she is once admitted to the government of America again, this Continent will not be worth living in. Jealousies will be always arising; insurrections will be constantly happening; and who will go forth to quell them? Who will venture his life to reduce his own countrymen to a foreign obedience? The difference between Pennsylvania and Connecticut, respecting some unlocated lands, shews the insignificance of a British government, and fully proves, that nothing but Continental authority can regulate Continental matters.

Another reason why the present time is preferable to all others, is, that the fewer our numbers are, the more land there is yet unoccupied, which instead of being lavished by the king on his worthless dependants, may be hereafter applied, not only to the discharge of the present debt, but to the constant support of government. No nation under heaven hath such an advantage at this.

The infant state of the Colonies, as it is called, so far from being against, is an argument in favor of independance. We are sufficiently numerous, and were we more so, we might be less united. It is a matter worthy of observation, that the more a country is peopled, the smaller their armies are. In military numbers, the ancients far exceeded the moderns: and the reason is evident, for trade being the consequence of population, men become too much absorbed thereby to attend to any thing else. Commerce diminishes the spirit, both of patriotism and military defence. And history sufficiently informs us, that the bravest achievements were always accomplished in the non-age of a nation. With the increase of commerce, England hath lost its spirit. The city of London, notwithstanding its numbers, submits to continued insults with the patience of a coward. The more men have to lose, the less willing are they to venture. The rich are in general slaves to fear, and submit to courtly power with the trembling duplicity of a Spaniel.

Youth is the seed time of good habits, as well in nations as in individuals. It might be difficult, if not impossible, to form the Continent into one government half a century hence. The vast variety of interests, occasioned by an increase of trade and population, would create confusion. Colony would be against colony. Each being able might scorn each other's assistance: and while the proud and foolish gloried in their little distinctions, the wise would lament, that the union had not been formed before. Wherefore, the *present time* is the *true time* for establishing it. The intimacy which is contracted in infancy, and the friendship which is formed in misfortune, are, of all others, the most lasting and unalterable. Our present union is marked with both these characters: we are young, and we have been distressed; but our concord hath withstood our troubles, and fixes a memorable æra for posterity to glory in.

The present time, likewise, is that peculiar time, which never happens to a nation but once, *viz.* the time of forming itself into a government. Most nations have let slip the opportunity, and by that means have been compelled to receive laws from their conquerors, instead of making laws for themselves. First, they had a king, and then a form of government; whereas, the articles or charter of government, should be formed first, and men delegated to execute them afterward: but from the errors of other nations, let us learn wisdom, and lay hold of the present opportunity—*To begin government at the right end.*

When William the Conqueror subdued England, he gave them law at the point of the sword; and until we consent, that the seat of government, in America, be legally and authoritatively occupied, we shall be in danger of having it filled by some fortunate ruffian, who may treat us in the same manner, and then, where will be our freedom? where our property?

As to religion, I hold it to be the indispensable duty of all government, to protect all conscientious professors thereof, and I know of no other business which government hath to do therewith, Let a man throw aside that narrowness of soul, that selfishness of principle, which the niggards of all professions are so unwilling to part with, and he will be at once delivered of his fears on that head. Suspicion is the companion of mean souls, and the bane of all good society. For myself, I fully and conscientiously believe, that it is the will of the Almighty, that there should be diversity of religious opinions among us: It affords a larger field for our Christian kindness. Were we all of one way of thinking, our religious dispositions would want matter for probation; and on this liberal principle, I look on the various denominations among us, to be like children of the same family, differing only, in what is called, their Christian names.

In page forty, I threw out a few thoughts on the propriety of a Continental Charter, (for I only presume to offer hints, not plans) and in this place, I take the liberty of re-mentioning the subject, by observing, that a charter is to be understood as a bond of solemn obligation, which the whole enters into, to support the right of every separate part, whether of religion, personal freedom, or property. A firm bargain and a right reckoning make long friends.

In a former page I likewise mentioned the necessity of a large and equal representation; and there is no political matter which more deserves our attention. A small number of electors, or a small number of representatives, are equally dangerous. But if the number of the representatives be not only small, but unequal, the danger is increased. As an instance of this, I mention the following; when the Associators petition was before the House of Assembly of Pennsylvania; twenty-eight members only were present, all the Bucks county members, being eight, voted against it, and had seven of the Chester members done the same, this whole province had been governed by two counties only, and this danger it is always exposed to. The unwarrantable stretch likewise, which that house made in their last sitting, to gain an undue authority over the Delegates of that province, ought to warn the people at large, how they trust power out of their own hands. A set of instructions for the Delegates were put together, which in point of sense and business would have dishonored a schoolboy, and after being approved by a *few*, a *very few* without doors, were carried into the House, and there passed *in behalf of the whole colony;* whereas, did the whole colony know, with what ill-will that House hath entered on some necessary public measures, they would not hesitate a moment to think them unworthy of such a trust.

Immediate necessity makes many things convenient, which if continued would grow into oppressions. Expedience and right are different things. When the calamities of America required a consultation, there was no method so ready, or at that time so proper, as to appoint persons from the several Houses of Assembly for that purpose; and the wisdom with which they have proceeded hath preserved this continent from ruin. But as it is more than probable that we shall never be without a CONGRESS, every well wisher to good order, must own, that the mode for choosing members of that body, deserves consideration. And I put it as a question to those, who make a study of mankind, whether *representation and election* is not too great a power for one and the same body of men to possess? When we are planning for posterity, we ought to remember, that virtue is not hereditary.

It is from our enemies that we often gain excellent maxims, and are frequently surprised into reason by their mistakes, Mr. Cornwall (one of the Lords of the Treasury) treated the petition of the New-York Assembly with contempt,[7] because *that* House, he said, consisted but of twenty-six members, which trifling number, he argued, could not with decency be put for the whole. We thank him for his involuntary honesty.*

TO CONCLUDE, however strange it may appear to some, or however unwilling they may be to think so, matters not, but many strong and striking reasons may be given, to shew, that nothing can settle our affairs so expeditiously as an open and determined declaration for independence. Some of which are,

First.—It is the custom of nations, when any two are at war, for some other powers, not engaged in the quarrel, to step in as mediators, and bring about the preliminaries of a peace: but while America calls herself the Subject of Great-Britain, no power, however well disposed she may be, can offer her mediation. Wherefore, in our present state we may quarrel on for ever.

Secondly.—It is unreasonable to suppose, that France or Spain will give us any kind of assistance, if we mean only, to make use of that assistance for the purpose of repairing the breach, and strengthening the connection between Britain and America; because, those powers would be sufferers by the consequences.

[7] Charles Wolfran Cornwall (1735–1789) was an English politician who became Speaker of the House of Commons in 1780.

* Those who would fully understand of what great consequence a large and equal representation is to a state, should read Burgh's political Disquisitions.

Thirdly.—While we profess ourselves the subjects of Britain, we must, in the eye of foreign nations, be considered as rebels. The precedent is somewhat dangerous to *their peace,* for men to be in arms under the name of subjects; we, on the spot, can solve the paradox: but to unite resistance and subjection, requires an idea much too refined for common understanding.

Fourthly.—Were a manifesto to be published, and despatched to foreign courts, setting forth the miseries we have endured, and the peaceable methods we have ineffectually used for redress; declaring, at the same time, that not being able, any longer, to live happily or safely under the cruel disposition of the British court, we had been driven to the necessity of breaking off all connections with her; at the same time, assuring all such courts of our peaceable disposition towards them, and of our desire of entering into trade with them: Such a memorial would produce more good effects to this Continent, than if a ship were freighted with petitions to Britain.

Under our present denomination of British subjects, we can neither be received nor heard abroad: The custom of all courts is against us, and will be so, until, by an independance, we take rank with other nations.

These proceedings may at first appear strange and difficult; but, like all other steps which we have already passed over, will in a little time become familiar and agreeable; and, until an independance is declared, the Continent will feel itself like a man who continues putting off some unpleasant business from day to day, yet knows it must be done, hates to set about it, wishes it over, and is continually haunted with the thoughts of its necessity.

APPENDIX

Since the publication of the first edition of this pamphlet, or rather, on the same day on which it came out, the King's Speech made its appearance in this city. Had the spirit of prophecy directed the birth of this production, it could not have brought it forth, at a more seasonable juncture, or a more necessary time. The bloody mindedness of the one, shew the necessity of pursuing the doctrine of the other. Men read by way of revenge. And the Speech, instead of terrifying, prepared a way for the manly principles of Independance.

Ceremony, and even, silence, from whatever motive they may arise, have a hurtful tendency, when they give the least degree of countenance to base and wicked performances; wherefore, if this maxim be admitted, it naturally follows, that the King's Speech, as being a piece of finished villany, deserved, and still deserves, a general execration both by the Congress and the people. Yet, as the domestic tranquillity of a nation, depends greatly, on the *chastity* of what may properly be called NATIONAL MANNERS, it is often better, to pass some things over in silent disdain, than to make use of such new methods of dislike, as might introduce the least innovation, on that guardian of our peace and safety. And, perhaps, it is chiefly owing to this prudent delicacy, that the King's Speech, hath not, before now, suffered a public execution. The Speech if it may be called one, is nothing better than a wilful audacious libel against the truth, the common good, and the existence of mankind; and is a formal and pompous method of offering up human sacrifices to the pride of tyrants. But this general massacre of mankind, is one of the privileges, and the certain consequence of Kings; for as nature knows them *not,* they know *not her,* and although they are beings of our *own* creating, they know not *us,* and are become the gods of their creators. The Speech hath one good quality, which is, that it is not calculated to deceive, neither can we, even if we would, be deceived by it. Brutality and tyranny appear on the face of it. It leaves us at no loss: And every line convinces, even in the moment of reading, that He, who hunts the woods for prey, the naked and untutored Indian, is less a Savage than the King of Britain.

Sir John Dalrymple, the putative father of a whining jesuitical piece, fallaciously called, *"The Address of the people of* ENGLAND *to the inhabitants of* AMERICA,"[8] hath, perhaps, from a vain supposition, that the people *here* were to be frightened at the pomp and description of a king, given, (though very unwisely on his part) the real character of the present one: "But," says this writer, "if you are inclined to pay compliments to an administration, which we do not complain of," (meaning the Marquis of Rockingham's at the repeal of the Stamp Act) "it is very unfair in you to withhold them from that prince, *by whose* NOD ALONE *they were permitted to do any thing."* This is toryism with a witness! Here is idolatry even without a mask: And he who can calmly hear, and digest

[8] Sir John Dalrymple (1726–1810) was a Scottish judge and writer.

such doctrine, hath forfeited his claim to rationality—an apostate from the order of manhood; and ought to be considered—as one, who hath not only given up the proper dignity of man, but sunk himself beneath the rank of animals, and contemptibly crawl through the world like a worm.

However, it matters very little now, what the king of England either says or does; he hath wickedly broken through every moral and human obligation, trampled nature and conscience beneath his feet; and by a steady and constitutional spirit of insolence and cruelty, procured for himself an universal hatred. It is *now* the interest of America to provide for herself. She hath already a large and young family, whom it is more her duty to take care of, than to be granting away her property, to support a power who is become a reproach to the names of men and christians—YE, whose office it is to watch over the morals of a nation, of whatsoever sect or denomination ye are of, as well as ye, who, are more immediately the guardians of the public liberty, if ye wish to preserve your native country uncontaminated by European corruption, ye must in secret wish a separation—But leaving the moral part to private reflection, I shall chiefly confine my farther remarks to the following heads.

First. That it is the interest of America to be separated from Britain.

Secondly. Which is the easiest and most practicable plan, RECONCILIATION or INDEPENDANCE? with some occasional remarks.

In support of the first, I could, if I judged it proper, produce the opinion of some of the ablest and most experienced men on this continent; and whose sentiments, on that head, are not yet publicly known. It is in reality a self-evident position: For no nation in a state of foreign dependance, limited in its commerce, and cramped and fettered in its legislative powers, can ever arrive at any material eminence. America doth not yet know what opulence is; and although the progress which she hath made stands unparalleled in the history of other nations, it is but childhood, compared with what she would be capable of arriving at, had she, as she ought to have, the legislative powers in her own hands. England is, at this time, proudly coveting what would do her no good, were she to accomplish it; and the Continent hesitating on a matter, which will be her final ruin if neglected. It is the commerce and not the conquest of America, by which England is to be benefited, and that would in a great measure continue, were the countries as independant of each other as France and Spain; because in many articles, neither can go to a better market. But it is the independance of this country on Britain or any other, which is now the main and only object worthy of contention, and which, like all other truths discovered by necessity, will appear clearer and stronger every day.

First. Because it will come to that one time or other.

Secondly. Because, the longer it is delayed the harder it will be to accomplish.

I have frequently amused myself both in public and private companies, with silently remarking, the specious errors of those who speak without reflecting. And among the many which I have heard, the following seems the most general, viz. that had this rupture happened forty or fifty years hence, instead of *now*, the Continent would have been more able to have shaken off the dependance. To which I reply, that our military ability, *at this time*, arises from the experience gained in the last war,[9] and which in forty or fifty years time, would have been totally extinct. The Continent, would not, by that time, have had a General, or even a military officer left; and we, or those who may succeed us, would have been as ignorant of martial matters as the ancient Indians: And this single position, closely attended to, will unanswerably prove, that the present time is preferable to all others. The argument turns thus—at the conclusion of the last war, we had experience, but wanted numbers; and forty or fifty years hence, we should have numbers, without experience; wherefore, the proper point of time, must be some particular point between the two extremes, in which a sufficiency of the former remains, and a proper increase of the latter is obtained: And that point of time is the present time.

The reader will pardon this digression, as it does not properly come under the head I first set out with, and to which I again return by the following position, viz.

Should affairs be patched up with Britain, and she to remain the governing and sovereign power of America, (which, as matters are now circumstanced, is giving up the point entirely) we shall deprive ourselves of the very means of sinking

[9] The reference is to the French and Indian Wars, 1756–1763.

the debt we have, or may contract. The value of the back lands which some of the provinces are clandestinely deprived of, by the unjust extension of the limits of Canada, valued only at five pounds sterling per hundred acres, amount to upwards of twenty-five millions, Pennsylvania currency; and the quit-rents at one penny sterling per acre, to two millions yearly.[10]

It is by the sale of those lands that the debt may be sunk, without burthen to any, and the quit-rent reserved thereon, will always lessen, and in time, will wholly support the yearly expence of government. It matters not how long the debt is in paying, so that the lands when sold be applied to the discharge of it, and for the execution of which, the Congress for the time being, will be the continental trustees.

I proceed now to the second head, viz. Which is the easiest and most practicable plan, RECONCILIATION or INDEPENDANCE; with some occasional remarks.

He who takes nature for his guide is not easily beaten out of his argument, and on that ground, I answer *generally—That* INDEPENDANCE *being a* SINGLE SIMPLE LINE, *contained within ourselves; and reconciliation, a matter exceedingly perplexed and complicated, and in which, a treacherous capricious court is to interfere, gives the answer without a doubt.*

The present state of America is truly alarming to every man who is capable of reflexion. Without law, without government, without any other mode of power than what is founded on, and granted by courtesy. Held together by an unexampled concurrence of sentiment, which, is nevertheless subject to change, and which, every secret enemy is endeavouring to dissolve. Our present condition, is, Legislation without law; wisdom without a plan; a constitution without a name; and, what is strangely astonishing, perfect Independance contending for dependance. The instance is without a precedent; the case never existed before; and who can tell what may be the event? The property of no man is secure in the present unbraced system of things. The mind of the multitude is left at random, and seeing no fixed object before them, they pursue such as fancy or opinion starts. Nothing is criminal; there is no such thing as treason; wherefore, every one thinks himself at liberty to act as he pleases. The Tories dared not have as-

[10] Under the Quebec Act of 1774, Canada's boundaries were extended to the Ohio River, an area in which Virginia, Connecticut, and Massachusetts had claims.

sembled offensively, had they known that their lives, by that act, were forfeited to the laws of the state. A line of distinction should be drawn, between, English soldiers taken in battle, and inhabitants of America taken in arms. The first are prisoners, but the latter traitors. The one forfeits his liberty, the other his head.

Notwithstanding our wisdom, there is a visible feebleness in some of our proceedings which gives encouragement to dissensions. The Continental Belt is too loosely buckled. And if something is not done in time, it will be too late to do any thing, and we shall fall into a state, in which, neither *Reconciliation* nor *Independance* will be practicable. The king and his worthless adherents are got at their old game of dividing the Continent, and there are not wanting among us, Printers, who will be busy in spreading specious falsehoods. The artful and hypocritical letter which appeared a few months ago in two of the New-York papers, and likewise in two others, is an evidence that there are men who want either judgment or honesty.

It is easy getting into holes and corners and talking of reconciliation: But do such men seriously consider, how difficult the task is, and how dangerous it may prove, should the Continent divide thereon. Do they take within their view, all the various orders of men whose situation and circumstances, as well as their own, are to be considered therein. Do they put themselves in the place of the sufferer whose *all* is *already* gone, and of the soldier, who hath quitted *all* for the defence of his country. If their ill judged moderation be suited to their own private situations *only*, regardless of others, the event will convince them, that "they are reckoning without their Host."

Put us, says some, on the footing we were on in sixty-three: To which I answer, the request is not *now* in the power of Britain to comply with, neither will she propose it; but if it were, and even should be granted, I ask, as a reasonable question, By what means is such a corrupt and faithless court to be kept to its engagements? Another parliament, nay, even the present, may hereafter repeal the obligation, on the pretence, of its being violently obtained, or unwisely granted; and in that case, Where is our redress?—No going to law with nations; cannon are the barristers of Crowns; and the sword, not of justice, but of war, decides the suit. To be on the footing of sixty-three, it is not sufficient, that the laws only be put on the same state, but, that our circumstances, likewise, be put on the same state; Our burnt and destroyed towns repaired or built up, our private losses made good, our public debts (contracted for defence) discharged; otherwise, we shall be millions worse than we were at that enviable period. Such a request, had it been complied with a year ago, would have won the heart and soul of the Continent—but now it is too late, "The Rubicon is passed."

Besides, the taking up arms, merely to enforce the repeal of a pecuniary law, seems as unwarrantable by the divine law, and as repugnant to human feelings, as the taking up arms to enforce obedience thereto. The object, on either side, doth not justify the means; for the lives of men are too valuable to be cast away on such trifles. It is the violence which is done and threatened to our persons; the destruction of our property by an armed force; the invasion of our country by fire and sword, which conscientiously qualifies the use of arms: And the instant, in which such a mode of defence became necessary, all subjection to Britain ought to have ceased; and the independancy of America, should have been considered, as dating its æra from, and published by, *the first musket that was fired against her*. This line is a line of consistency; neither drawn by caprice, nor extended by ambition; but produced by a chain of events, of which the colonies were not the authors.

I shall conclude these remarks, with the following timely and well intended hints. We ought to reflect, that there are three different ways, by which an independancy may hereafter be effected; and that *one* of those *three*, will one day or other, be the fate of America, viz. By the legal voice of the people in Congress; by a military power; or by a mob: It may not always happen that our soldiers are citizens, and the multitude a body of reasonable men; virtue, as I have already remarked, is not hereditary, neither is it perpetual. Should an independancy be brought about by the first of those means, we have every opportunity and every encouragement before us, to form the noblest purest constitution on the face of the earth. We have it in our power to begin the world over again. A situation, similar to the present, hath not happened since the days of Noah until now. The birthday of a new world is at hand, and a race of men, perhaps as numerous as all Europe contains, are to receive their portion of freedom from the event of a few months. The Reflexion is awful—and in this point of view, How trifling, how ridiculous, do the little, paltry cavillings, of a few weak or interested men appear, when weighed against the business of a world.

Should we neglect the present favorable and inviting period, and an Independance be hereafter effected by any other means, we must charge the consequence to ourselves, or to those rather, whose narrow and prejudiced souls, are habitually opposing the measure, without either inquiring or reflecting. There are reasons to be given in support of Independance, which men should rather privately think of, than be publicly told of. We ought not now to be debating whether we shall be independant or not, but, anxious to accomplish it on a firm, secure, and honorable basis, and uneasy rather that it is not yet began upon. Every day convinces us of its necessity. Even the Tories (if such beings yet remain among us) should, of all men, be the most solicitous to promote it; for, as the appointment of committees at first, protected them from popular rage, so, a wise and well established form of government, will be the only certain means of continuing it securely to them. *Wherefore*, if they have not virtue enough to be WHIGS, they ought to have prudence enough to wish for Independance.

In short, Independance is the only BOND that can tye and keep us together. We shall then see our object, and our ears will be legally shut against the schemes of an intriguing, as well, as a cruel enemy. We shall then too, be on a proper footing, to treat with Britain; for there is reason to conclude, that the pride of that court, will be less hurt by treating with the American states for terms of peace, than with those, whom she denominates, "rebellious subjects," for terms of accommodation. It is our delaying it that encourages her to hope for conquest, and our backwardness tends only to prolong the war. As we have, without any good effect therefrom, withheld our trade to obtain a redress of our grievances, let us *now* try the alternative, by *independantly* redressing them ourselves, and then offering to open the trade. The mercantile and reasonable part in England, will be still with us; because, peace *with* trade, is preferable to war *without* it. And if this offer be not accepted, other courts may be applied to.

On these grounds I rest the matter. And as no offer hath yet been made to refute the doctrine contained in the former editions of this pamphlet, it is a negative proof, that either the doctrine cannot be refuted, or, that the party in favour of it are too numerous to be opposed. WHEREFORE, instead of gazing at each other with suspicious or doubtful curiosity, let each of us, hold out to his neighbour the hearty hand of friendship, and unite in drawing a line, which, like an act of oblivion shall bury in forgetfulness every former dissension.

Let the names of Whig and Tory be extinct; and let none other be heard among us, than those of *a good citizen, an open and resolute friend, and a virtuous supporter of the* RIGHTS *of* MANKIND *and of the* FREE AND INDEPENDANT STATES OF AMERICA.

To the Representatives of the Religious Society of the People called Quakers, or to so many of them as were concerned in publishing a late piece, entitled "The ANCIENT TESTIMONY and PRINCIPLES of the People called QUAKERS renewed, with Respect to the KING and GOVERNMENT, and touching the COMMOTIONS now prevailing in these and other parts of AMERICA addressed to the PEOPLE IN GENERAL."

The Writer of this, is one of those few, who never dishonors religion either by ridiculing, or cavilling at any denomination whatsoever. To God, and not to man, are all men accountable on the score of religion. Wherefore, this epistle is not so properly addressed to you as a religious, but as a political body, dabbling in matters, which the professed Quietude of your Principles instruct you not to meddle with.

As you have, without a proper authority for so doing, put yourselves in the place of the whole body of the Quakers, so, the writer of this, in order to be on an equal rank with yourselves, is under the necessity, of putting himself in the place of all those, who, approve the very writings and principles, against which, your testimony is directed: And he hath chosen this singular situation, in order, that you might discover in him that presumption of character which you cannot see in yourselves. For neither he nor you can have any claim or title to *Political Representation.*

When men have departed from the right way, it is no wonder that they stumble and fall. And it is evident from the manner in which ye have managed your testimony, that politics, (as a religious body of men) is not your proper Walk; for however well adapted it might appear to you, it is, nevertheless, a jumble of good and bad put unwisely together, and the conclusion drawn therefrom, both unnatural and unjust.

The two first pages, (and the whole doth not make four) we give you credit for, and expect the same civility from you, because the love and desire of peace is not confined to Quakerism, it is the *natural,* as well the religious wish of all denominations of men. And on this ground, as men laboring to establish an Independant Constitution of our own, do we exceed all others in our hope, end, and aim. *Our plan is peace for ever.* We are tired of contention with Britain, and can see no real end to it but in a final separation. We act consistently, because for the sake of introducing an endless and uninterrupted peace, do we bear the evils and burthens of the present day. We are endeavoring, and will steadily continue to endeavor, to separate and dissolve a connexion which hath already filled our land with blood; and which, while the name of it remains, will be the fatal cause of future mischiefs to both countries.

We fight neither for revenge nor conquest; neither from pride nor passion; we are not insulting the world with our fleets and armies, nor ravaging the globe for plunder. Beneath the shade of our own vines are we attacked; in our own houses, and on our own lands, is the violence committed against us. We view our enemies in the character of Highwaymen and Housebreakers, and having no defence for ourselves in the civil law, are obliged to punish them by the military one, and apply the sword, in the very case, where you have before now, applied the halter— Perhaps we feel for the ruined and insulted sufferers in all and every part of the continent, with a degree of tenderness which hath not yet made its way into some of your bosoms. But be ye sure that ye mistake not the cause and ground of your Testimony. Call not coldness of soul, religion; nor put the *Bigot* in the place of the *Christian.*

O ye partial ministers of your own acknowledged principles. If the bearing arms be sinful, the first going to war must be more so, by all the difference between wilful attack and unavoidable defence. Wherefore, if ye really preach from conscience, and mean not to make a political hobbyhorse of your religion, convince the world thereof, by proclaiming your doctrine to our enemies, *for they likewise bear* ARMS. Give us proof of your sincerity by publishing it at St. James's, to the commanders in chief at Boston, to the Admirals and Captains who are piratically ravaging our coasts, and to all the murdering miscreants who are acting in authority under HIM whom ye profess to serve. Had ye the honest soul of* *Barclay*

* "Thou hast tasted of prosperity and adversity; thou knowest what it is to be banished thy native country, to be over-ruled as well as to rule, and set upon the throne; and being *oppressed* thou has reason to know how *hateful* the *oppressor* is both to God and man: If after all these warnings and advertisements, thou dost not turn unto the Lord with all thy heart, but forget him who remembered thee in thy distress, and give up thyself to follow lust and vanity, surely great will be thy condemnation.—Against which snare, as well as the temptation of those who may or do feed thee, and prompt thee to evil, the most excellent and prevalent remedy will be, to apply thyself

ye would preach repentance to *your* king;[11] Ye would tell the Royal Wretch his sins, and warn him of eternal ruin. Ye would not spend your partial invectives against the injured and the insulted only, but, like faithful ministers, would cry aloud and *spare none*. Say not that ye are persecuted, neither endeavour to make us the authors of that reproach, which, ye are bringing upon yourselves; for we testify unto all men, that we do not complain against you because ye are *Quakers,* but because ye pretend to *be* and are NOT Quakers.

Alas! it seems by the particular tendency of some part of your testimony, and other parts of your conduct, as if, all sin was reduced to, and comprehended in, *the act of bearing arms,* and that by the *people only*. Ye appear to us, to have mistaken party for conscience; because, the general tenor of your actions wants uniformity: And it is exceedingly difficult to us to give credit to many of your pretended scruples; because, we see them made by the same men, who, in the very instant that they are exclaiming against the mammon of this world, are nevertheless, hunting after it with a step as steady as Time, and an appetite as keen as Death.

The quotation which ye have made from Proverbs, in the third page of your testimony, that, "when a man's ways please the Lord, he maketh even his enemies to be at peace with him"; is very unwisely chosen on your part; because, it amounts to a proof, that the king's ways (whom ye are so desirous of supporting) do *not* please the Lord, otherwise, his reign would be in peace.

I now proceed to the latter part of your testimony, and that, for which all the foregoing seems only an introduction, viz.

"It hath ever been our judgment and principle, since we were called to profess the light of Christ Jesus, manifested in our consciences unto this day, that the setting up and putting down kings and governments, is God's peculiar prerogative; for causes best known to himself: And that it is not our business to have any hand or contrivance therein; nor to be busy bodies above our station, much less to plot and contrive the ruin, or overturn of any of them, but to pray for the king, and safety of our nation, and good of all men: That we may live

---

to that light of Christ which shineth in thy conscience, and which neither can, nor will flatter thee, nor suffer thee to be at ease in thy sins."

Barclay's Address to Charles II.

[11] David Barclay (1610–1686) was a Scottish soldier and political supporter of Oliver Cromwell. He became a Quaker in 1666.

a peaceable and quiet life, in all godliness and honesty; *under the government which God is pleased to set over us*."—If these are *really* your principles why do ye not abide by them? Why do ye not leave that, which ye call God's Work, to be managed by himself? These very principles instruct you to wait with patience and humility, for the event of all public measures, and to receive *that event* as the divine will towards you. *Wherefore*, what occasion is there for your *political testimony* if you fully believe what it contains? And the very publishing it proves, that either, ye do not believe what ye profess, or have not virtue enough to practise what ye believe.

The principles of Quakerism have a direct tendency to make a man the quiet and inoffensive subject of any, and every government *which is set over him*. And if the setting up and putting down of kings and governments is God's peculiar prerogative, he most certainly will not be robbed thereof by us; wherefore, the principle itself leads you to approve of every thing, which ever happened, or may happen to kings as being his work. OLIVER CROMWELL thanks you. CHARLES, then, died not by the hands of man; and should the present Proud Imitators of him, come to the same untimely end, the writers and publishers of the Testimony, are bound, by the doctrine it contains, to applaud the fact. Kings are not taken away by miracles, neither are changes in governments brought about by any other means than such as are common and human; and such as we are now using. Even the dispersion of the Jews, though foretold by our Saviour, was effected by arms. Wherefore, as ye refuse to be the means on one side, ye ought not to be meddlers on the other; but to wait the issue in silence; and unless ye can produce divine authority, to prove, that the Almighty who hath created and placed this *new* world, at the greatest distance it could possibly stand, east and west, from every part of the old, doth, nevertheless, disapprove of its being independent of the corrupt and abandoned court of Britain, unless I say, ye can shew this, how can ye on the ground of your principles, justify the exciting and stirring up the people "firmly to unite in the *abhorrence* of all such *writings*, and *measures*, as evidence a desire and design to break off the *happy* connexion we have hitherto enjoyed, with the kingdom of Great-Britain, and our just and necessary subordination to the king, and those who are lawfully placed in authority under him." What a slap of the face is here! the men, who in the very paragraph before, have quietly and passively resigned up the ordering, altering, and disposal of kings and governments, into the hands of God, are now, recalling their principles, and putting in for a share of the business. Is it possible, that the conclusion, which is here justly quoted, can any ways follow from the doctrine laid down? The inconsistency is too glaring not to be seen; the absurdity too great not to be laughed at; and such as could only have been made by those, whose understandings were darkened by the narrow and crabby spirit of a despairing political party; for ye are not to be considered as the whole body of the Quakers but only as a factional and fractional part thereof.

Here ends the examination of your testimony; (which I call upon no man to abhor, as ye have done, but only to read and judge of fairly;) to which I subjoin the following remark; "That the setting up and putting down of kings," most certainly mean, the making him a king, who is yet not so, and the making him no king who is already one. And pray what hath this to do in the present case? We neither mean to *set up* nor to *put down,* neither to *make* nor to *unmake,* but to have nothing to *do* with them. Wherefore, your testimony in whatever light it is viewed serves only to dishonor your judgement, and for many other reasons had better have been let alone than published.

First, Because it tends to the decrease and reproach of all religion whatever, and is of the utmost danger to society, to make it a party in political disputes.

Secondly, Because it exhibits a body of men, numbers of whom disavow the publishing political testimonies, as being concerned therein and approvers thereof.

Thirdly, Because it hath a tendency to undo that continental harmony and friendship which yourselves by your late liberal and charitable donations hath lent a hand to establish; and the preservation of which, is of the utmost consequence to us all.

And here without anger or resentment I bid you farewel. Sincerely wishing, that as men and christians, ye may always fully and uninterruptedly enjoy every civil and religious right; and be, in your turn, the means of securing it to others; but that the example which ye have unwisely set, of mingling religion with politics, *may be disavowed and reprobated by every inhabitant of* AMERICA.

FINIS.

THOMAS JEFFERSON In a letter written to Henry Lee a year before he died, Jefferson claimed that the Declaration of Independence "was intended to be an expression of the American mind, and to give to that expression the proper tone and spirit called for by the occasion." The Declaration is simply a natural affirmation of Enlightenment political philosophy combined with a recapitulation of the controversy with Great Britain. Its importance has nothing to do with its originality, for it was never intended to be an original contribution to political philosophy. But as a statement of the observations and needs of the colonists after more than a decade of struggle with England, it leaves nothing to be desired. And as an impassioned plea for human liberty and equality, it has remained one of the most significant documents ever penned. The essence of what Jefferson said so well was to question a conception of man which saw him as fit for no more than servitude. Few things written before or since, certainly nothing written by an American, have so effectively denied the relationship of sovereign to populace based upon power alone. The "history of repeated injuries and usurpations" with which Jefferson indicts George III is an accusation of England itself, based upon its refusal to accept its responsibilities toward the colonies. The absorption of the Enlightenment mind into the American experience is apparent in the Declaration.

Jefferson was only one member of a committee consisting of himself, Franklin, John Adams, Roger Sherman and Robert Livingston which had been appointed by the Second Continental Congress to draft a resolution of independence. The changes that the other committee members made in Jefferson's draft are, for the most part, stylistic, although one can also detect a desire to make the document somewhat less emphatic.

Text: Julian Boyd, *et al.*, eds., *The Papers of Thomas Jefferson*. Princeton, 1950—.

"Original Rough Draft" of the Declaration of Independence (1776)

A Declaration of the Representatives of the UNITED STATES OF AMERICA, in General Congress assembled.

When in the course of human events it becomes necessary for a people to advance from that subordination in which they have hitherto remained, & to assume among the powers of the earth the equal & independant station to which the laws of nature & of nature's god entitle them, a decent respect to the opinions of mankind requires that they should declare the causes which impel them to the change.

We hold these truths to be sacred & undeniable, that all men are created equal & independant, that from that equal creation they derive rights inherent & inalienable, among which are the preservation of life, & liberty, & the pursuit of happiness; that to secure these ends, governments are instituted among men, deriving their just powers from the consent of the governed; that whenever any form of government shall become destructive of these ends, it is the right of the people to alter or to abolish it, & to institute new government, laying it's foundation on such principles & organising it's powers in such form, as to them shall seem most likely to effect their safety & happiness. prudence indeed will dictate that governments long established should not be changed for light & transient causes: and accordingly all experience hath shewn that mankind are more disposed to suffer while evils are sufferable, than to right themselves by abolishing the forms to which they are accustomed. but when a long train of abuses & usurpations, begun at a distinguished period, & pursuing invariably the same object, evinces a design to subject them to arbitrary power, it is their right, it is their duty, to throw off such government & to provide new guards for their future security. such has been the patient sufferance of these colonies; & such is now the necessity which constrains them to expunge their former systems of government. the history of his present majesty, is a history of unremitting injuries and usurpations, among which no one fact stands single or solitary to contradict the uniform tenor of the rest, all of which have in direct object the establishment of an absolute tyranny over these states. to prove this, let facts be submitted to a candid world, for the truth of which we pledge a faith yet unsullied by falsehood.

he has refused his assent to laws the most wholesome and necessary for the public good:

he has forbidden his governors to pass laws of immediate & pressing importance, unless suspended in their operation till his assent should be obtained; and when so suspended, he has neglected utterly to attend to them.

he has refused to pass other laws for the accomodation of large districts of people unless those people would relinquish the right of representation, a right inestimable to them, & formidable to tyrants alone:

he has dissolved Representative houses repeatedly & continually, for opposing with manly firmness his invasions on the rights of the people:

he has refused for a long space of time to cause others to be elected, whereby the legislative powers, incapable of annihilation, have returned to the people at large for their exercise, the state remaining in the mean time exposed to all the dangers of invasion from without, & convulsions within:

he has endeavored to prevent the population of these states; for that purpose obstructing the laws for naturalization of foreigners; refusing to pass others to encourage their migrations hither; & raising the conditions of new appropriations of lands:

he has suffered the administration of justice totally to cease in some of these colonies, refusing his assent to laws for establishing judiciary powers:

he has made our judges dependant on his will alone, for the tenure of their offices, and amount of their salaries:

he has erected a multitude of new offices by a self-assumed power, & sent hither swarms of officers to harrass our people & eat out their substance:

he has kept among us in times of peace standing armies & ships of war:

he has affected to render the military, independant of & superior to the civil power:

he has combined with others to subject us to a jurisdiction foreign to our constitutions and unacknoleged by our laws; giving his assent to their pretended acts of legislation, for quartering large bodies of armed troops among us;

for protecting them by a mock-trial from punishment for any murders they should commit on the inhabitants of these states;

for cutting off our trade with all parts of the world;

for imposing taxes on us without our consent;
for depriving us of the benefits of trial by jury;
for transporting us beyond seas to be tried for pretended offences:
for taking away our charters, & altering fundamentally the forms of our governments;
for suspending our own legislatures & declaring themselves invested with power to legislate for us in all cases whatsoever:

he has abdicated government here, withdrawing his governors, & declaring us out of his allegiance & protection:

he has plundered our seas, ravaged our coasts, burnt our towns & destroyed the lives of our people:

he is at this time transporting large armies of foreign mercenaries to compleat the works of death, desolation & tyranny, already begun with circumstances of cruelty & perfidy unworthy the head of a civilized nation:

he has endeavored to bring on the inhabitants of our frontiers the merciless Indian savages, whose known rule of warfare is an undistinguished destruction of all ages, sexes, & conditions of existence:

he has incited treasonable insurrections in our fellow-subjects, with the allurements of forfeiture & confiscation of our property:

he has waged cruel war against human nature itself, violating it's most sacred rights of life & liberty in the persons of a distant people who never offended him, captivating & carrying them into slavery in another hemisphere, or to incur miserable death in their transportation thither. this piratical warfare, the opprobrium of *infidel* powers, is the warfare of the CHRISTIAN king of Great Britain. determined to keep open a market where MEN should be bought & sold, he has prostituted his negative for suppressing every legislative attempt to prohibit or to restrain this execrable commerce: and that this assemblage of horrors might want no fact of distinguished die, he is now exciting those very people to rise in arms among us, and to purchase that liberty of which *he* has deprived them, by murdering the people upon whom *he* also obtruded them; thus paying off former crimes committed against the *liberties* of one people, with crimes which he urges them to commit against the *lives* of another.

in every stage of these oppressions we have petitioned for redress in the most humble terms; our repeated petitions have been answered by repeated injury. a prince whose character is thus marked by every act which may define a tyrant, is unfit to be the ruler of a people who mean to be free. future ages will scarce believe that the hardiness of one man, adventured within the short compass of 12 years only, on so many acts of tyranny without a mask, over a people fostered & fixed in principles of liberty.

Nor have we been wanting in attentions to our British brethren. we have warned them from time to time of attempts by their legislature to extend a jurisdiction over these our states. we have reminded them of the circumstances of our emigration & settlement here, no one of which could warrant so strange a pretension: that these were effected at the expence of our own blood & treasure, unassisted by the wealth or the strength of Great Britain: that in constituting indeed our several forms of government, we had adopted one common king, thereby laying a foundation for perpetual league & amity with them: but that submission to their parliament was no part of our constitution, nor ever in idea, if history may be credited: and we appealed to their native justice & magnanimity, as well as to the ties of our common kindred to disavow these usurpations which were likely to interrupt our correspondence & connection. they too have been deaf to the voice of justice & of consanguinity, & when occasions have been given them, by the regular course of their laws, of removing from their councils the disturbers of our harmony, they have by their free election re-established them in power. at this very time too they are permitting their chief magistrate to send over not only soldiers of our common blood, but Scotch & foreign mercenaries to invade & deluge us in blood. these facts have given the last stab to agonizing affection, and manly spirit bids us to renounce for ever these unfeeling brethren. we must endeavor to forget our former love for them, and to hold them as we hold the rest of mankind, enemies in war, in peace friends. we might have been a free & a great people together; but a communication of grandeur & of freedom it seems is below their dignity. be it so, since they will have it: the road to glory & happiness is open to us too; we will climb it in a separate state, and acquiesce in the necessity which pronounces our everlasting Adieu!

We therefore the representatives of the United States of America in General Congress assembled do, in the name & by authority of the good people of these states, reject and renounce all allegiance & subjection to the kings of Great Britain

& all others who may hereafter claim by, through, or under them; we utterly dissolve & break off all political connection which may have heretofore subsisted between us & the people or parliament of Great Britain; and finally we do assert and declare these colonies to be free and independant states, and that as free & independant states they shall hereafter have power to levy war, conclude peace, contract alliances, establish commerce, & to do all other acts and things which independant states may of right do. And for the support of this declaration we mutually pledge to each other our lives, our fortunes, & our sacred honour.

The Declaration of Independence as Adopted by Congress

IN CONGRESS, JULY 4, 1776.

THE UNANIMOUS DECLARATION OF THE THIRTEEN UNITED STATES OF AMERICA,

When in the Course of human events, it becomes necessary for one people to dissolve the political bands which have connected them with another, and to assume among the powers of the earth, the separate and equal station to which the Laws of Nature and of Nature's God entitle them, a decent respect to the opinions of mankind requires that they should declare the causes which impel them to the separation. We hold these truths to be self-evident, that all men are created equal, that they are endowed by their Creator with certain unalienable Rights, that among these are Life, Liberty and the pursuit of Happiness. That to secure these rights, Governments are instituted among Men, deriving their just powers from the consent of the governed, That whenever any Form of Government becomes destructive of these ends, it is the Right of the People to alter or to abolish it, and to institute new Government, laying its foundation on such principles and organizing its powers in such form, as to them shall seem most likely to effect their Safety and Happiness. Prudence, indeed, will dictate that Governments long established should not be changed for light and transient causes; and accordingly all experience hath shewn, that mankind are more disposed to suffer, while evils are sufferable, than to right themselves by abolishing the forms to which they are accustomed. But when a long train of abuses and usurpations, pursuing invariably the same Object evinces a design to reduce them under absolute Despotism, it is their right, it is their duty, to throw off such Government, and to provide new Guards for their future security. Such has been the patient sufferance of these Colonies; and such is now the necessity which constrains them to alter their former Systems of Government. The history of the present King of Great Britain is a history of repeated injuries and usurpations, all having in direct object the establishment of an absolute Tyranny over these States. To prove this, let Facts be submitted to a candid world. He has refused his Assent to Laws, the most wholesome and necessary for the public good. He has forbidden his Governors to pass Laws of immediate and pressing importance, unless suspended in their operation till his Assent should be obtained; and when so suspended, he has utterly neglected to attend to them. He has refused to pass other Laws for the accommodation of large districts of people, unless those people would relinquish the right of Representation in the Legislature, a right inestimable to them and formidable to tyrants only. He has called together legislative bodies at places unusual, uncomfortable, and distant from the depository of their public Records, for the sole purpose of fatiguing them into compliance with his measures. He has dissolved Representative Houses repeatedly, for opposing with manly firmness his invasions on the rights of the people. He has refused for a long time, after such dissolutions, to cause others to be elected; whereby the Legislative powers, incapable of Annihilation, have returned to the People at large for their exercise; the State remaining in the mean time exposed to all the dangers of invasion from without, and convulsions within. He has endeavoured to prevent the population of these States; for that purpose obstructing the Laws for Naturalization of Foreigners; refusing to pass others to encourage their migrations hither, and raising the conditions of new Appropriations of Lands. He has obstructed the Administration of Justice, by refusing his Assent to Laws for establishing Judiciary powers. He has made Judges dependent on his Will alone, for the tenure of their offices, and the amount and payment of their salaries. He has erected a multitude of New Offices, and sent hither swarms of Officers to harrass our people, and eat out their substance. He has kept among us, in times of peace, standing Armies without the Consent of our legislatures. He has affected to render the Military independent of and superior to the Civil power. He has combined with others to subject us to a jurisdiction foreign to our constitution, and unacknowledged by our laws; giving his Assent to their Acts of pretended Legislation: For Quartering large bodies of armed troops among us: For protecting them, by a mock Trial, from punishment for any Murders which they should commit on the Inhabitants of these States: For cutting off our Trade with all parts of the world: For imposing Taxes on us without our Consent: For depriving us in many cases of the benefits of Trial by Jury: For transporting us beyond Seas to be tried for pretended offences: For abolishing the free System of English Laws in a neighbouring Province, establishing therein an Arbitrary government, and enlarging its Boundaries so as to render it at once an example and fit instrument for introducing the same absolute rule into these Colonies: For taking away our Charters, abolishing our most valuable Laws, and altering fundamentally the Forms of our Governments: For suspending our own Legislatures, and declaring themselves invested with power to legislate for us in all cases whatsoever. He has abdicated Government here, by declaring us out of his Protection and waging War against us. He has plundered our seas, ravaged our Coasts, burnt our towns, and destroyed the Lives of our people. He is at this time transporting large Armies of foreign Mercenaries to compleat the works of death, desolation and tyranny, already begun with circumstances of Cruelty & perfidy scarcely paralleled in the most barbarous ages, and totally unworthy the Head of a civilized nation. He has constrained our fellow Citizens taken Captive on the high Seas to bear Arms against their Country, to become the executioners of their friends and Brethren, or to fall themselves by their Hands. He has excited domestic insurrections amongst us, and has endeavoured to bring on the inhabitants of our frontiers, the merciless Indian Savages, whose known rule of warfare, is an undistinguished destruction of all ages, sexes and conditions. In every stage of these Oppressions We have Petitioned for Redress in the most humble terms: Our repeated Petitions have been answered only by repeated injury. A Prince, whose character is thus marked by every act which may define a Tyrant, is unfit to be the ruler of a free people. Nor have We been wanting in attentions to our British brethren. We have warned them from time to time of attempts by their legislature to extend an unwarrantable jurisdiction over us. We have reminded them of the circumstances of our emigration and settlement here. We have appealed to their native justice and magnanimity, and we have conjured them by the ties of our common kindred to disavow these usurpations, which, would inevitably interrupt our connections and correspondence. They too have been deaf to the voice of justice and of consanguinity. We must, therefore, acquiesce in the necessity, which denounces our Separation, and hold them, as we hold the rest of mankind, Enemies in War, in Peace Friends.

We, therefore, the Representatives of the united States of America, in General Congress, Assembled, appealing to the Supreme Judge of the world for the rectitude of our intentions, do, in the Name, and by Authority of the good People of these Colonies, solemnly publish and declare, That these United Colonies are, and of Right ought to be Free and Independent States; that they are Absolved from all Allegiance to the British Crown, and that all political connection between them and the State of Great Britain, is and ought to be totally dissolved; and that as Free and Independent States, they have full Power to levy War, conclude Peace, contract Alliances, establish Commerce, and to do all other Acts and Things which Independent States may of right do. And for the support of this Delaration, with a firm reliance on the protection of divine Providence, we mutually pledge to each other our Lives, our Fortunes and our sacred Honor.

John Hancock

Button Gwinnett
Lyman Hall
Geo Walton.
Wm. Hooper
Joseph Hewes,
John Penn
Edward Rutledge.
Thos. Heyward Junr.
Thomas Lynch Junr.
Arthur Middleton
Samuel Chase
Wm. Paca
Thos. Stone
Charles Carroll of Carrollton
George Wythe
Richard Henry Lee
Th: Jefferson
Benja. Harrison

Thos. Nelson jr.
Francis Lightfoot Lee
Carter Braxton
Robt. Morris
Benjamin Rush
Benja. Franklin
John Morton
Geo Clymer
Jas. Smith.
Geo. Taylor
James Wilson
Geo. Ross
Cæsar Rodney
Geo Read
Tho M:Kean
Wm. Floyd
Phil. Livingston
Frans. Lewis
Lewis Morris

Richd. Stockton
Jno Witherspoon
Fras. Hopkinson
John Hart
Abra Clark
Josiah Bartlett
Wm: Whipple
Saml. Adams
John Adams
Robt. Treat Paine
Elbridge Gerry
Step. Hopkins
William Ellery
Roger Sherman
Saml. Huntington
Wm. Williams
Oliver Wolcott
Matthew Thornton

THOMAS PAINE All of Paine's *Crisis Papers* were written in response to a critical aspect of the war, in language that had the broadest popular appeal. The *Papers* reflect the conditions under which they were written; their tone is invariably inspirational and propagandistic. *Crisis Number I,* with its famous opening line, was written on a drumhead during the retreat of Washington's army across New Jersey, the nadir of the American war effort. Washington ordered the pamphlet read to his embattled troops just before he launched the successful surprise attack on the Hessian garrison in Trenton on Christmas Eve, 1776. *Crisis Number XIII* appeared four days after Congress had ratified the provisional Treaty of Peace drawn up in Paris. In this most important of *The Crisis Papers,* Paine warned Americans to maintain their sovereignty and to establish a firm union of states. His argument is an attack upon the theory of states' rights and sectional divisions and a plea for a strong centralized government.

Text: *The Crisis.* Albany, 1792.

The Crisis Papers

NUMBER I

December 23, 1776

These are the times that try men's souls: The summer soldier and the sunshine patriot will, in this crisis, shrink from the service of his country; but he that stands it NOW, deserves the love and thanks of man and woman. Tyranny, like hell, is not easily conquered; yet we have this consolation with us, that the harder the conflict, the more glorious the triumph. What we obtain too cheap, we esteem too lightly: 'Tis dearness only that gives every thing its value. Heaven knows how to put a proper price upon its goods; and it would be strange indeed, if so celestial an article as FREEDOM should not be highly rated. Britain, with an army to enforce her tyranny, has declared that she has a right (*not only to* TAX) but "*to* BIND *us in* ALL CASES WHATSOEVER," and if being *bound in that manner,* is not slavery, then is there not such a thing as slavery upon earth.[1] Even the expression is impious, for so unlimited a power can belong only to GOD.

Whether the independence of the continent was declared too soon, or delayed too long, I will not now enter into as an argument; my own simple opinion is, that had it been eight months earlier, it would have been much better. We did not make a proper use of last winter, neither could we, while we were in a dependant state. However, the fault, if it were one, was all our own; we have none to blame but ourselves. But no great deal is lost yet; all that Howe has been doing for this month past is rather a ravage than a conquest, which the spirit of the Jerseys a year ago would have quickly repulsed, and which time and a little resolution will soon recover.

I have as little superstition in me as any man living, but my secret opinion has ever been, and still is, that God Almighty will not give up a people to military destruction, or leave them unsupportedly to perish, who had so earnestly and so repeatedly sought to avoid the calamities of war, by every decent method which wisdom could invent. Neither have I so much of the infidel in me, as to suppose that HE has relinquished the government of the world, and given us up to the care of devils; and as I do not, I cannot see on what grounds the king of Britain can look up to Heaven for help against us: A common murderer, a highwayman, or a house-breaker has as good a pretence as he.

'Tis surprising to see how rapidly a panic will sometimes run through a country. All nations and ages have been subject to them: Britain has trembled like an ague at the report of a French fleet of flat bottomed boats; and in the fourteenth century the whole English army, after ravaging the kingdom of France, was driven back like men petrified with fear,[2] and this brave exploit was performed by a few broken forces collected and headed by a woman, Joan of Arc. Would, that Heaven might inspire some Jersey maid to spirit up her countrymen, and save her fair fellow sufferers from ravage and ravishment! Yet panics, in some cases, have their uses, they produce as much good as hurt. Their duration is always short; the mind soon grows through them, and acquires a firmer habit than before. But their peculiar advantage is, that they are the touchstones of sincerity and hypocrisy, and bring things and men to light, which might otherwise have lain for ever

[1] "To bind us in all cases whatsoever" is a quotation from the Declaratory Act.
[2] Paine means the fifteenth century.

undiscovered. In fact, they have the same effect on secret traitors, which an imaginary apparition would have upon a private murderer. They sift out the hidden thoughts of man, and hold them up in public to the world. Many a disguised tory has lately shewn his head, that shall penitentially solemnize with curses the day on which Howe arrived upon the Delaware.

As I was with the troops at Fort-Lee, and marched with them to the edge of Pennsylvania, I am well acquainted with many circumstances, which those, who lived at a distance, know but little or nothing of.[3] Our situation there was exceedingly cramped, the place being on a narrow neck of land between the North-River and the Hackensack. Our force was inconsiderable, being not one fourth so great as Howe could bring against us. We had no army at hand to have relieved the garrison, had we shut ourselves up and stood on the defence. Our ammunition, light artillery, and the best part of our stores, had been removed upon the apprehension that Howe would endeavor to penetrate the Jerseys, in which case Fort-Lee could be of no use to us; for it must occur to every thinking man, whether in the army or not, that these kind of field forts are only for temporary purposes, and last in use no longer than the enemy directs his force against the particular object, which such forts are raised to defend. Such was our situation and condition at Fort-Lee on the morning of the 20th of November, when an officer arrived with information that the enemy with 200 boats had landed about seven or eight miles above: Major General Greene, who commanded the garrison, immediately ordered them under arms, and sent express to his Excellency General Washington at the town of Hackensack, distant by the way of the ferry six miles. Our first object was to secure the bridge over the Hackensack, which laid up the river between the enemy and us, about six miles from us, and three from them. General Washington arrived in about three quarters of an hour, and marched at the head of the troops towards the bridge, which place I expected we should have a brush for; however they did not choose to dispute it with us, and the greatest part of our troops went over the bridge, the rest over the ferry, except some which passed at a mill on a small creek, between the bridge and the ferry, and made their way through some marshy grounds up to the

[3] In September, 1776, Paine, who had enlisted a month earlier in a Pennsylvania regiment, was stationed at Fort Lee, New Jersey, where he was appointed aide-de-camp to General Nathanael Greene.

town of Hackensack, and there passed the river. We brought off as much baggage as the waggons could contain, the rest was lost. The simple object was to bring off the garrison, and to march them on till they could be strengthened by the Jersey or Pennsylvania militia, so as to be enabled to make a stand. We staid four days at Newark, collected in our outposts with some of the Jersey militia, and marched out twice to meet the enemy on information of their being advancing, though our numbers were greatly inferior to theirs. Howe, in my little opinion, committed a great error in generalship in not throwing a body of forces off from Staten-Island through Amboy, by which means he might have seized all our stores at Brunswick, and intercepted our march into Pennsylvania: But if we believe the power of hell to be limited, we must likewise believe that their agents are under some providential controul.

I shall not now attempt to give all the particulars of our retreat to the Delaware; suffice it for the present to say, that both officers and men, though greatly harassed and fatigued, frequently without rest, covering, or provision, the inevitable consequences of a long retreat, bore it with a manly and a martial spirit. All their wishes were one, which was, that the country would turn out and help them to drive the enemy back. Voltaire has remarked that King William never appeared to full advantage but in difficulties and in action; the same remark may be made on General Washington, for the character fits him. There is a natural firmness in some minds which cannot be unlocked by trifles, but which, when unlocked, discovers a cabinet of fortitude; and I reckon it among those kind of public blessings, which we do not immediately see, that GOD hath blest him with uninterrupted health, and given him a mind that can even flourish upon care.

I shall conclude this paper with some miscellaneous remarks on the state of our affairs; and shall begin with asking the following question, Why is it that the enemy have left the New-England provinces, and made these middle ones the seat of war?[4] The answer is easy: New-England is not infested with tories, and we are. I have been tender in raising the cry against these men, and used numberless arguments to shew them their danger, but it will not do to sacrifice a world to

[4] In March, 1776, Howe evacuated Boston. He landed on Staten Island in July and fought a number of successful battles against Washington, finally forcing Washington to evacuate New York City and to retreat across New Jersey into Pennsylvania.

either their folly or their baseness. The period is now arrived, in which either they or we must change our sentiments, or one or both must fall. And what is a tory? Good GOD! what is he? I should not be afraid to go with an hundred whigs against a thousand tories, were they to attempt to get into arms. Every tory is a coward, for a servile, slavish, self-interested fear is the foundation of toryism; and a man under such influence, though he may be cruel, never can be brave.

But, before the line of irrecoverable separation be drawn between us, let us reason the matter together: Your conduct is an invitation to the enemy, yet not one in a thousand of you has heart enough to join him. Howe is as much deceived by you as the American cause is injured by you. He expects you will all take up arms, and flock to his standard with muskets on your shoulders. Your opinions are of no use to him, unless you support him personally, for 'tis soldiers, and not tories, that he wants.

I once felt all that kind of anger, which a man ought to feel, against the mean principles that are held by the tories: A noted one, who kept a tavern at Amboy, was standing at his door, with as pretty a child in his hand, about eight or nine years old, as most I ever saw, and after speaking his mind as freely as he thought was prudent, finished with this unfatherly expression, *"Well! give me peace in my day."* Not a man lives on the continent but fully believes that a separation must some time or other finally take place, and a generous parent should have said, *"If there must be trouble, let it be in my day that my child may have peace;"* and this single reflection, well applied, is sufficient to awaken every man to duty. Not a place upon earth might be so happy as America. Her situation is remote from all the wrangling world, and she has nothing to do but to trade with them. A man may easily distinguish in himself between temper and principle, and I am as confident, as I am that GOD governs the world, that America will never be happy till she gets clear of foreign dominion. Wars, without ceasing, will break out till that period arrives, and the continent must in the end be conqueror; for though the flame of liberty may sometimes cease to shine, the coal never can expire.

America did not, nor does not want force; but she wanted a proper application of that force. Wisdom is not the purchase of a day, and it is no wonder that we should err at first setting off. From an excess of tenderness, we were unwilling to raise an army, and trusted our cause to the temporary defence of a well-meaning militia. A summer's experience has now taught us better; yet with those troops, while they were collected, we were able to set bounds to the progress of the enemy, and, thank GOD! they are again assembling. I always considered a militia as the best troops in the world for a sudden exertion, but they will not do for a long campaign. Howe, it is probable, will make an attempt on this city,[5] should he fail on this side the Delaware, he is ruined; If he succeeds, our cause is not ruined. He stakes all on his side against a part on ours; admitting he succeeds, the consequence will be, that armies from both ends of the continent will march to assist their suffering friends in the middle states; for he cannot go every where, it is impossible. I consider Howe as the greatest enemy the tories have; he is bringing a war into their country, which, had it not been for him and partly for themselves, they had been clear of. Should he now be expelled, I wish with all the devotion of a Christian, that the names of whig and tory may never more be mentioned; but should the tories give him encouragement to come, or assistance if he come, I as sincerely wish that our next year's arms may expel them from the continent, and the congress appropriate their possessions to the relief of those who have suffered in well-doing. A single successful battle next year will settle the whole. America could carry on a two years war by the confiscation of the property of disaffected persons, and be made happy by their expulsion. Say not that this is revenge, call it rather the soft resentment of a suffering people, who, having no object in view but the GOOD of ALL, have staked thier OWN ALL upon a seemingly doubtful event. Yet it is folly to argue against determined hardness; eloquence may strike the ear, and the language of sorrow draw forth the tear of compassion, but nothing can reach the heart that is steeled with prejudice.

Quitting this class of men, I turn with the warm ardor of a friend to those who have nobly stood, and are yet determined to stand the matter out: I call not upon a few, but upon all; not on THIS state or THAT state, but on EVERY state; up and help us; lay your shoulders to the wheel; better have too much force than too little, when so great an object is at stake. Let it be told to the future world, that in the depth of winter, when nothing but hope and virtue could survive, that the city and the country, alarmed at one common danger, came forth to meet and to repulse it. Say not, that thousands are gone,

[5] Philadelphia, where Paine had gone to arrange publication of *The Crisis Number I.*

turn out your tens of thousands; throw not the burden of the day upon Providence, but *"shew your faith by your works,"* that God may bless you. It matters not where you live, or what rank of life you hold, the evil or the blessing will reach you all. The far and the near, the home counties and the back, the rich and the poor, will suffer or rejoice alike. The heart that feels not now, is dead: The blood of his children will curse his cowardice, who shrinks back at a time when a little might have saved the whole, and made *them* happy. I love the man that can smile in trouble, that can gather strength from distress, and grow brave by reflection. 'Tis the business of little minds to shrink; but he whose heart is firm, and whose conscience approves his conduct, will pursue his principles unto death. My own line of reasoning is to myself as strait and clear as a ray of light. Not all the treasures of the world, so far as I believe, could have induced me to support an offensive war, for I think it murder; but if a thief break into my house, burn and destroy my property, and kill or threaten to kill me, or those that are in it, and to *"bind me in all cases whatsoever,"* to his absolute will, am I to suffer it? What signifies it to me, whether he who does it, is a king or a common man; my countryman or not my countryman? whether it is done by an individual villain, or an army of them? If we reason to the root of things we shall find no difference; neither can any just cause be assigned why we should punish in the one case and pardon in the other. Let them call me rebel, and welcome, I feel no concern from it; but I should suffer the misery of devils, were I to make a whore of my soul by swearing allegiance to one whose character is that of a sottish, stupid, stubborn, worthless, brutish man. I conceive likewise a horrid idea in receiving mercy from a being, who at the last day shall be shrieking to the rocks and mountains to cover him, and fleeing with terror from the orphan, the widow, and the slain of America.

There are cases which cannot be overdone by language, and this is one. There are persons too who see not the full extent of the evil which threatens them, they solace themselves with hopes that the enemy, if they succeed, will be merciful. It is the madness of folly to expect mercy from those who have refused to do justice; and even mercy, where conquest is the object, is only a trick of war: The cunning of the fox is as murderous as the violence of the wolf; and we ought to guard equally against both. Howe's first object is partly by threats and partly by promise, to terrify or seduce the people to deliver up their arms, and receive mercy. The ministry recommended the same plan to Gage, and this is what the tories call making their peace; *"a peace which passeth all understanding" indeed!* A peace which would be the immediate forerunner of a worse ruin than any we have yet thought of. Ye men of Pennsylvania, do reason upon these things! Were the back counties to give up their arms, they would fall an easy prey to the Indians, who are all alarmed: This perhaps is what some tories would not be sorry for. Were the home counties to deliver up their arms, they would be exposed to the resentment of the back counties, who would then have it in their power to chastise their defection at pleasure. And were any one state to give up its arms, THAT state must be garrisoned by all Howe's army of Britons and Hessians to preserve it from the anger of the rest. Mutual fear is a principal link in the chain of mutual love, and woe be to that state that breaks the compact. Howe is mercifully inviting you to barbarous destruction, and men must be either rogues or fools that will not see it. I dwell not upon the powers of imagination; I bring reason to your ears; and in language as plain as A, B, C, hold up truth to your eyes.

I thank GOD that I fear not. I see no real cause for fear. I know our situation well, and can see the way out of it. While our army was collected, Howe dared not risk a battle, and it is no credit to him that he decamped from the White Plains, and waited a mean opportunity to ravage the defenceless Jerseys; but it is great credit to us, that, with a handful of men, we sustained an orderly retreat for near an hundred miles, brought off our ammunition, all our field-pieces, the greatest part of our stores, and had four rivers to pass. None can say that our retreat was precipitate, for we were near three weeks in performing it, that the country might have time to come in. Twice we marched back to meet the enemy and remained out till dark. The sign of fear was not seen in our camp, and had not some of the cowardly and disaffected inhabitants spread false alarms through the country, the Jerseys had never been ravaged. Once more we are again collected and collecting; our new army at both ends of the continent is recruiting fast, and we shall be able to open the next campaign with sixty thousand men, well armed and cloathed. This is our situation, and who will may know it. By perseverance and fortitude we have the prospect of a glorious issue; by cowardice and submission, the sad choice of a variety of evils—a ravaged country—a depopulated city—habitations without safety, and slavery without hope—our homes turned into barracks and bawdy-houses for Hessians, and a future race to provide for whose fathers we shall doubt of. Look on this picture and weep over it! and if there yet remains one thoughtless wretch who believes it not, let him suffer it unlamented.

NUMBER XIII

Philadelphia, April 19, 1783[1]

"The times that tried men's souls,"* are over—and the greatest and completest revolution the world ever knew, gloriously and happily accomplished.

But to pass from the extremes of danger to safety—from the tumult of war, to the tranquility of peace, though sweet in contemplation, requires a gradual composure of the senses to receive it. Even calmness has the power of stunning, when it opens too instantly upon us. The long and raging hurricane that should cease in a moment, would leave us in a state rather of wonder than enjoyment; and some moments of recollection must pass, before we could be capable of tasting the full felicity of repose. There are but few instances, in which the mind is fitted for sudden transitions: It takes in its pleasures by reflection and comparison, and those must have time to act, before the relish for new scenes is complete.

In the present case—the mighty magnitude of the object—the various uncertainties of fate it has undergone—the numerous and complicated dangers we have suffered or escaped—the eminence we now stand on, and the vast prospect before us, must all conspire to impress us with contemplation.

To see it in our power to make a world happy—to teach mankind the art of being so—to exhibit on the theatre of the universe, a character hitherto unknown—and to have, as it were, a creation entrusted to our hands, are honors that command reflection, and can neither be too highly estimated, nor too gratefully received.

In this pause then of recollection—while the storm is ceasing, and the long agitated mind vibrating to a rest, let us look back on the scenes we have passed, and learn from experience what is yet to be done.

[1] The date of publication of *The Crisis, Number XIII,* marked the eighth anniversary of the Battle of Lexington and Concord. On February 4, 1783, Britain officially proclaimed a cessation of hostilities.

* "These are the times that try men's souls." Crisis No. I, published December 19, 1776.

Never, I say, had a country so many openings to happiness as this. Her setting out into life, like the rising of a fair morning, was unclouded and promising. Her cause was good. Her principles just and liberal. Her temper serene and firm. Her conduct regulated by the nicest steps, and every thing about her wore the mark of honor.

It is not every country (perhaps there is not another in the world) that can boast so fair an origin. Even the first settlement of America corresponds with the character of the revolution. Rome, once the proud mistress of the universe, was originally a band of ruffians. Plunder and rapine made her rich, and her oppression of millions made her great. But America needs never be ashamed to tell her birth, nor relate the stages by which she rose to empire.

The remembrance then of what is past, if it operates rightly, must inspire her with the most laudable of all ambition, that of adding to the fair fame she began with. The world has seen her great in adversity. Struggling without a thought of yielding beneath accumulated difficulties. Bravely, nay proudly, encountering distress, and rising in resolution as the storm encreased. All this is justly due to her, for her fortitude has merited the character. Let then the world see that she can bear prosperity: and that her honest virtue in time of peace, is equal to the bravest virtue in time of war.

She is now descending to the scenes of quiet and domestic life. Not beneath the cypress shade of disappointment, but to enjoy in her own land, and under her own vine, the sweet of her labors, and the reward of her toil—In this situation, may she never forget that a fair national reputation, is of as much importance as independence. That it possesses a charm which wins upon the world, and makes even enemies civil. That it gives a dignity which is often superior to power, and commands a reverence where pomp and splendor fail.

It would be a circumstance ever to be lamented and never to be forgotten, were a single blot, from any cause whatever, suffered to fall on a revolution, which to the end of time must be an honor to the age that accomplished it: and which has contributed more to enlighten the world, and diffuse a spirit of freedom and liberality among mankind, than any human event (if this may be called one) that ever preceded it.

It is not among the least of the calamities of a long continued war, that it unhinges the mind from those nice sensations which at other times appear so amiable. The continual spectacle of woe, blunts the finer feelings, and the necessity of bearing with the sight, renders it familiar. In like manner, are many of the moral obligations of society weakened, till the custom of acting by necessity, becomes an apology where it is truly a crime. Yet let but a nation conceive rightly of its character, and it will be chastly just in protecting it. None ever began with a fairer than America, and none can be under a greater obligation to preserve it.

The debt which America has contracted, compared with the cause she has gained, and the advantages to flow from it, ought scarcely to be mentioned. She has it in her choice to do, and to live, as happily, as she pleases. The world is in her hands. She has no foreign power to monopolize her commerce, perplex her legislation, or controul her prosperity. The struggle is over, which must one day have happened, and, perhaps, never could have happened at a better time.* And instead of a domineering master, she has gained an *ally*, whose exemplary greatness, and universal liberality, have extorted a confession even from her enemies.

With the blessings of peace, independence, and an uni-

* That the revolution began at the exact period of time best fitted to the purpose, is sufficiently proved by the event—But the great hinge on which the whole machine turned is the UNION OF THE STATES: and this union was naturally produced by the inability of any one state to support itself against any foreign enemy without the assistance of the rest.

Had the states severally been less able than they were when the war began, their united strength would not have been equal to the undertaking, and they must, in all human probability, have failed—And on the other hand, had they severally been more able, they might not have seen, or, what is more, might not have felt the necessity of uniting; and either by attempting to stand alone, or in small confederacies, would have been separately conquered.

Now, as we cannot see a time (and many years must pass away before it can arrive) when the strength of any one state, or several united, can be equal to the whole of the present United States, and as we have seen the extreme difficulty of collectively prosecuting the war to a successful issue, and preserving our national importance in the world, therefore, from the experience we have had, and the knowledge we have gained, we must, unless we make a waste of wisdom, be strongly impressed with the advantage, as well as the necessity of strengthening that happy union which has been our salvation, and without which we should have been a ruined people.

While I was writing this note, I cast my eye on the pamphlet COMMON SENSE, from which I shall make an extract, as it applies exactly to the case. It is as follows:

"I have never met with a man, either in England or America, who hath not confessed his opinion that a separation between the countries would take place one time or other: And there is no instance in which we have shewn less judgment, than in endeavoring to describe, what we call, the ripeness or fitness of the continent for independence.

"As all men allow the measure, and differ only in their opinion of the time, let us, in order to remove mistakes, take a general survey of things, and endeavor, if possible, to find out the VERY TIME. But we need not go far, the enquiry ceases at once, for, THE TIME HATH FOUND US. The general concurrence, the glorious union of all things prove the fact.

"It is not in numbers, but in a union, that our great strength lies. The continent is just arrived at that pitch of strength, in which no single colony is able to support itself, and the whole, when united, can accomplish the matter; and either more or less than this, might be fatal in its effects."

versal commerce, the states individually and collectively, will have leisure and opportunity to regulate and establish their domestic concerns, and to put it beyond the power of calumny to throw the least reflection on their honor. Character is much easier kept than recovered, and that man, if any such there be, who, from any sinister views, or littleness of soul, lends unseen his hand to injure it, contrives a wound it will never be in his power to heal.

As we have established an inheritance for posterity, let that inheritance descend, with every mark of an honorable conveyance. The little it will cost, compared with the worth of the states, the greatness of the object, and the value of national character, will be a profitable exchange.

But that which must more forcibly strike a thoughtful penetrating mind, and which includes and renders easy all inferior concerns, is the UNION OF THE STATES. On this, our great national character depends. It is this which must give us importance abroad and security at home. It is through this only that we are, or can be nationally known in the world. It is the flag of the United States which renders our ships and commerce safe on the seas, or in a foreign port. Our Mediterranean passes must be obtained under the same stile. All our treaties whether of alliance, peace or commerce, are formed under the sovereignty of the United States, and Europe knows us by no other name or title.

The division of the empire into states is for our own convenience, but abroad this distinction ceases. The affairs of each state are local. They can go no farther than to itself. And were the whole worth of even the richest of them expended in revenue, it would not be sufficient to support sovereignty against a foreign attack. In short, we have no other national sovereignty than as United States. It would even be fatal for us if we had—too expensive to be maintained, and impossible to be supported. Individuals or individual states may call themselves what they please; but the world, and especially the world of enemies, is not to be held in awe by the whistling of a name. Sovereignty must have power to protect all the parts that compose and constitute it: and as UNITED STATES we are equal to the importance of the title, but otherwise we are not. Our union well and wisely regulated and cemented, is the cheapest way of being great—the easiest way of being powerful, and the happiest invention in government which the circumstances of America can admit of—Because it collects from each state, that which, by being inadequate, can be of no use to it, and forms an aggregate that serves for all.

The states of Holland are an unfortunate instance of the effects of individual sovereignty. Their disjointed condition exposes them to numerous intrigues, losses, calamities and enemies; and the almost impossibility of bringing their measures to a decision, and that decision into execution, is to them, and would be to us, a source of endless misfortune.

It is with confederated states as with individuals in society; something must be yielded up to make the whole secure. In this view of things we gain by what we give, and draw an annual interest greater than the capital.—I ever feel myself hurt when I hear the union, that great palladium of our liberty and safety, the least irreverently spoken of. It is the most sacred thing in the constitution of America, and that which every man should be most proud and tender of. Our citizenship in the United States is our national character. Our citizenship in any particular state is only our local distinction. By the latter we are known at home, by the former to the world. Our great title is, AMERICANS—our inferior one varies with the place.

So far as my endeavors could go, they have all been directed to conciliate the affections, unite the interests and draw and keep the mind of the country together; and the better to assist in this foundation-work of the revolution, I have avoided all places of profit or office, either in the state I live in, or in the United States; kept myself at a distance from all parties and party connections, and even disregarded all private and inferior concerns: and when we take into view the great work we have gone through, and feel, as we ought to feel, the just importance of it, we shall then see, that the little wranglings and indecent contentions of personal parly, are as dishonorable to our characters, as they are injurious to our repose.

It was the cause of America that made me an author. The force with which it struck my mind, and the dangerous condition the country appeared to me in, by courting an impossible and an unnatural reconciliation with those who were determined to reduce her, instead of striking out into the only line that could cement and save her, A DECLARATION OF INDEPENDENCE, made it impossible for me, feeling as I did, to be silent: and if, in the course of more than seven years, I have rendered her any service, I have likewise added something to the reputation of literature, by freely and disinterestedly employing it in the great cause of mankind, and shewing there may be genius without prostitution.

Independence always appeared to me practicable and probable; provided the sentiment of the country could be formed and held to the object: and there is no instance in the world, where a people so extended, and wedded to former habits of thinking, and under such a variety of circumstances, were so instantly and effectually pervaded, by a turn in politics, as in the case of independence, and who supported their opinion, undiminished, through such a succession of good and ill fortune, till they crowned it with success.

But as the scenes of war are closed, and every man preparing for home and happier times, I therefore take my leave of the subject. I have most sincerely followed it from beginning to end, and through all its turns and windings: and whatever country I may hereafter be in, I shall always feel an honest pride at the part I have taken and acted, and a gratitude to Nature and Providence for putting it in my power to be of some use to mankind.

COMMON SENSE

THE ARTICLES OF CONFEDERATION In July, 1776, John Dickinson's draft of "Articles of Confederation and Perpetual Union" was reported to Congress. For the next year, the articles were debated; on November 15, 1777, they were adopted and sent to the states for ratification. The Articles were not formally ratified until March 1, 1781, when Maryland finally agreed to them.

The form of government established by the Articles of Confederation was an extension of the informal arrangement that had developed during the Revolution. While one cannot speak of the Articles as a radical document, they reflect the deep suspicion with which the colonists viewed any strong, centralized government at the beginning of the Revolution. Such suspicion was natural enough, for the colonists had seen a strong, centralized government transformed into what they considered to be a tyrannous government in the decade preceding the Revolution. The government which the Articles brought into being was responsible to the states which had created it, and there was no question but that those states were superior to the central government. Power resided in the states, and what little power was granted to the central government was difficult, if not impossible, to enforce without the will of the states behind it.

Text: Worthington C. Ford, *et al.*, eds., *Journals of the Continental Congress, 1774–1789*. Washington, 1904–37.

The Articles of Confederation (1776)

ARTICLE 1. The stile of this confederacy shall be "The United States of America."

ART. 2. Each State retains its sovereignty, freedom and independence, and every power, jurisdiction, and right, which is not by this confederation expressly delegated to the United States, in Congress assembled.

ART. 3. The said states hereby severally enter into a firm league of friendship with each other for their common defence, the security of their liberties and their mutual and general welfare; binding themselves to assist each other against all force offered to, or attacks made upon them, or any of them, on account of religion, sovereignty, trade, or any other pretence whatever.

ART. 4. The better to secure and perpetuate mutual friendship and intercourse among the people of the different states in this union, the free inhabitants of each of these states, paupers, vagabonds, and fugitives from justice excepted, shall be entitled to all privileges and immunities of free citizens in the several states; and the people of each State shall have free ingress and regress to and from any other State, and shall enjoy therein all the privileges of trade and commerce, subject to the same duties, impositions, and restrictions, as the inhabitants thereof respectively; provided, that such restrictions shall not extend so far as to prevent the removal of property, imported into any State, to any other State of which the owner is an inhabitant; provided also, that no imposition, duties, or restriction, shall be laid by any State on the property of the United States, or either of them.

If any person guilty of, or charged with treason, felony, or other high misdemeanor in any State, shall flee from justice and be found in any of the United States, he shall, upon demand of the governor or executive power of the State from which he fled, be delivered up and removed to the State having jurisdiction of his offence.

Full faith and credit shall be given in each of these states to the records, acts, and judicial proceedings of the courts and magistrates of every other State.

ART. 5. For the more convenient management of the general interests of the United States, delegates shall be annually appointed, in such manner as the legislature of each State shall direct, to meet in Congress, on the 1st Monday in November in every year, with a power reserved to each State to recal its delegates, or any of them, at any time within the year, and to send others in their stead for the remainder of the year.

No State shall be represented in Congress by less than two, nor by more than seven members; and no person shall be capable of being a delegate for more than three years in any term of six years; nor shall any person, being a delegate, be capable of holding any office under the United States, for which he, or any other for his benefit, receives any salary, fees, or emolument of any kind.

Each State shall maintain its own delegates in a meeting of

the states, and while they act as members of the committee of the states.

In determining questions in the United States, in Congress assembled, each State shall have one vote.

Freedom of speech and debate in Congress shall not be impeached or questioned in any court or place out of Congress: and the members of Congress shall be protected in their persons from arrests and imprisonments, during the time of their going to and from, and attendance on Congress, *except for treason,* felony, or breach of the peace.

ART. 6. No State, without the consent of the United States, in Congress assembled, shall send any embassy to, or receive any embassy from, or enter into any conference, agreement, alliance, or treaty with any king, prince, or state; nor shall any person, holding any office of profit or trust under the United States, or any of them, accept of any present, emolument, office or title, of any kind whatever, from any king, prince, or foreign state; nor shall the United States, in Congress assembled, or any of them, grant any title of nobility.

No two or more states shall enter into any treaty, confederation, or alliance, whatever, between them, without the consent of the United States, in Congress assembled, specifying accurately the purposes for which the same is to be entered into, and how long it shall continue.

No state shall lay any imposts or duties which may interfere with any stipulations in treaties entered into by the United States, in Congress assembled, with any king, prince, or state, in pursuance of any treaties already proposed by Congress to the courts of France and Spain.

No vessels of war shall be kept up in time of peace by any State, except such number only as shall be deemed necessary by the United States, in Congress assembled, for the defence of such State or its trade; nor shall any body of forces be kept up by any State, in time of peace, except such number only as, in the judgment of the United States, in Congress assembled, shall be deemed requisite to garrison the forts necessary for the defence of such State; but every State shall always keep up a well regulated and disciplined militia, sufficiently armed and accoutred, and shall provide, and constantly have ready for use, in public stores, a due number of field pieces and tents, and a proper quantity of arms, ammunition and camp equipage.

No State shall engage in any war without the consent of the

United States, in Congress assembled, unless such State be actually invaded by enemies, or shall have received certain advice of a resolution being formed by some nation of Indians to invade such State, and the danger is so imminent as not to admit of a delay till the United States, in Congress assembled, can be consulted; nor shall any State grant commissions to any ships or vessels of war, nor letters of marque or reprisal, except it be after a declaration of war by the United States, in Congress assembled, and then only against the kingdom or state, and the subjects thereof, against which war has been so declared, and under such regulations as shall be established by the United States, in Congress assembled, unless such State be infested by pirates, in which case vessels of war may be fitted out for that occasion, and kept so long as the danger shall continue, or until the United States, in Congress assembled, shall determine otherwise.

ART. 7. When land forces are raised by any State for the common defence, all officers of or under the rank of colonel, shall be appointed by the legislature of each State respectively, by whom such forces shall be raised, or in such manner as such State shall direct; and all vacancies shall be filled up by the State which first made the appointment.

ART. 8. All charges of war and all other expences, that shall be incurred for the common defence or general welfare, and allowed by the United States, in Congress assembled, shall be defrayed out of a common treasury, which shall be supplied by the several states, in proportion to the value of all land within each State, granted to or surveyed for any person, as such land and the buildings and improvements thereon shall be estimated according to such mode as the United States, in Congress assembled, shall, from time to time, direct and appoint.

The taxes for paying that proportion shall be laid and levied by the authority and direction of the legislatures of the several states, within the time agreed upon by the United States, in Congress assembled.

ART. 9. The United States, in Congress assembled, shall have the sole and exclusive right and power of determining on peace and war, except in the cases mentioned in the 6th article; of sending and receiving ambassadors; entering into treaties and alliances, provided that no treaty of commerce shall be made, whereby the legislative power of the respective states shall be restrained from imposing such imposts and duties on foreigners as their own people are subjected to, or from prohibiting the exportation or importation of any species of goods or commodities whatsoever; of establishing rules for deciding, in all cases, what captures on land or water shall be legal, and in what manner prizes, taken by land or naval forces in the service of the United States, shall be divided or appropriated; of granting letters of marque and reprisal in times of peace; appointing courts for the trial of piracies and felonies committed on the high seas, and establishing courts for receiving and determining, finally, appeals in all cases of captures; provided, that no member of Congress shall be appointed a judge of any of the said courts.

The United States, in Congress assembled, shall also be the last resort on appeal in all disputes and differences now subsisting, or that hereafter may arise between two or more states concerning boundary, jurisdiction or any other cause whatever; which authority shall always be exercised in the manner following: whenever the legislative or executive authority, or lawful agent of any State, in controversy with another, shall present a petition to Congress, stating the matter in question, and praying for a hearing, notice thereof shall be given, by order of Congress, to the legislative or executive authority of the other State in controversy, and a day assigned for the appearance of the parties by their lawful agents, who shall then be directed to appoint, by joint consent, commissioners or judges to constitute a court for hearing and determining the matter in question; but, if they cannot agree, Congress shall name three persons out of each of the United States, and from the list of such persons each party shall alternately strike out one, the petitioners beginning, until the number shall be reduced to thirteen; and from that number not less than seven, nor more than nine names, as Congress shall direct, shall, in the presence of Congress, be drawn out by lot, and the persons whose names shall be so drawn, or any five of them, shall be commissioners or judges to hear and finally determine the controversy, so always as a major part of the judges who shall hear the cause shall agree in the determination; and if either party shall neglect to attend at the day appointed, without shewing reasons which Congress shall judge sufficient, or, being present, shall refuse to strike, the Congress shall proceed to nominate three persons out of each State, and the secretary of Congress shall strike in behalf of such party absent or refusing; and the judgment and sentence of the court to be appointed, in the manner before prescribed, shall be final and conclusive; and if any of the parties shall refuse to submit to the authority of such court, or to appear or defend their claim or cause, the court shall nevertheless proceed to pronounce sentence or judgment, which shall, in like manner, be final and decisive, the judgment or sentence and other proceedings being, in either case, transmitted to Congress, and lodged among the acts of Congress for the security of the parties concerned: provided, that every commissioner, before he sits in judgment, shall take an oath, to be administered by one of the judges of the supreme or superior court of the State where the cause shall be tried, "well and truly to hear and determine the matter in question, according to the best of his judgment, without favour, affection, or hope of reward:" provided, also, that no State shall be deprived of territory for the benefit of the United States.

All controversies concerning the private right of soil, claimed under different grants of two or more states, whose jurisdictions, as they may respect such lands and the states which passed such grants, are adjusted, the said grants, or either of them, being at the same time claimed to have originated antecedent to such settlement of jurisdiction, shall, on the petition of either party to the Congress of the United States, be finally determined, as near as may be, in the same manner as is before prescribed for deciding disputes respecting territorial jurisdiction between different states.

The United States, in Congress assembled, shall also have the sole and exclusive right and power of regulating the alloy and value of coin struck by their own authority, or by that of the respective states; fixing the standard of weights and measures throughout the United States; regulating the trade and managing all affairs with the Indians not members of any of the states; provided that the legislative right of any State within its own limits be not infringed or violated; establishing and regulating post offices from one State to another throughout all the United States, and exacting such postage on the papers passing through the same as may be requisite to defray the expences of the said office; appointing all officers of the land forces in the service of the United States, excepting regimental officers; appointing all the officers of the naval forces, and commissioning all officers whatever in the service of the United States; making rules for the government and regulation of the said land and naval forces, and directing their operations.

The United States, in Congress assembled, shall have authority to appoint a committee to sit in the recess of Congress, to be denominated "a Committee of the States," and to consist of one delegate from each State, and to appoint such other committees and civil officers as may be necessary for managing the general affairs of the United States, under their direction; to appoint one of their number to preside; provided that no person be allowed to serve in the office of president more than one year in any term of three years; to ascertain the necessary sums of money to be raised for the service of the United States, and to appropriate and apply the same for defraying the public expences; to borrow money or emit bills on the credit of the United States, transmitting, every half year, to the respective states, an account of the sums of money so borrowed or emitted; to build and equip a navy; to agree upon the number of land forces, and to make requisitions from each State for its quota, in proportion to the number of white inhabitants in such State; which requisitions shall be binding; and, thereupon, the legislature of each State shall appoint the regimental officers, raise the men, and cloathe, arm, and equip, them in a soldier-like manner, at the expence of the United States; and the officers and men so cloathed, armed, and equipped, shall march to the place appointed and within the time agreed on by the United States, in Congress assembled; but if the United States, in Congress assembled, shall, on consideration of circumstances, judge proper that any State should not raise men, or should raise a smaller number than its quota, and that any other State should raise a greater number of men than the quota thereof, such extra number shall be raised, officered, cloathed, armed, and equipped in the same manner as the quota of such State, unless the legislature of such State shall judge that such extra number cannot be safely spared out of the same, in which case they shall raise, officer, cloathe, arm, and equip as many of such extra number as they judge can be safely spared. And the officers and men so cloathed, armed, and equipped, shall march to the place appointed and within the time agreed on by the United States, in Congress assembled.

The United States, in Congress assembled, shall never engage in a war, nor grant letters of marque and reprisal in time of peace, nor enter into any treaties or alliances, nor coin money, nor regulate the value thereof, nor ascertain the sums and expences necessary for the defence and welfare of the United States, or any of them: nor emit bills, nor borrow money on the credit of the United States, nor appropriate money, nor agree upon the number of vessels of war to be built or purchased, or the number of land or sea forces to be raised, nor appoint a commander in chief of the army or navy, unless nine states assent to the same; nor shall a question on any other point, except for adjourning from day to day, be determined, unless by the votes of a majority of the United States, in Congress assembled.

The Congress of the United States shall have power to adjourn to any time within the year, and to any place within the United States, so that no period of adjournment be for a longer duration than the space of six months, and shall publish the journal of their proceedings monthly, except such parts thereof, relating to treaties, alliances or military operations, as, in their judgment, require secrecy; and the yeas and nays of the delegates of each State on any question shall be entered on the journal, when it is desired by any delegate; and the delegates of a State, or any of them, at his, or their request, shall be furnished with a transcript of the said journal, except such parts as are above excepted, to lay before the legislatures of the several states.

ART. 10. The committee of the states, or any nine of them, shall be authorized to execute, in the recess of Congress, such of the powers of Congress as the United States, in Congress assembled, by the consent of nine states, shall, from time to time, think expedient to vest them with; provided, that no power be delegated to the said committee, for the exercise of which, by the articles of confederation, the voice of nine states, in the Congress of the United States assembled, is requisite.

ART. 11. Canada acceding to this confederation, and joining in the measures of the United States, shall be admitted into and entitled to all the advantages of this union; but no other colony shall be admitted into the same, unless such admission be agreed to by nine states.

ART. 12. All bills of credit emitted, monies borrowed and debts contracted by, or under the authority of Congress before the assembling of the United States, in pursuance of the present confederation, shall be deemed and considered as a charge against the United States, for payment and satisfaction whereof the said United States and the public faith are hereby solemnly pledged.

ART. 13. Every State shall abide by the determinations of the United States, in Congress assembled, on all questions which, by this confederation, are submitted to them. And the articles of this confederation shall be inviolably observed by every State, and the union shall be perpetual; nor shall any alteration at any time hereafter be made in any of them, unless such alteration be agreed to in a Congress of the United States, and be afterwards confirmed by the legislatures of every State.

These articles shall be proposed to the legislatures of all the United States, to be considered, and if approved of by them, they are advised to authorize their delegates to ratify the same in the Congress of the United States; which being done, the same shall become conclusive.

THOMAS JEFFERSON Jefferson's *Notes on Virginia* was first published in Paris in 1784 (the edition is dated 1782, the time of composition), after Jefferson had succeeded Benjamin Franklin as American Minister to France. The book was written as an answer to a series of inquiries put to Jefferson by the Marquis de Marbois, Secretary of the French Legation at Philadelphia. Jefferson's acute scientific observations, along with his rigorous political thinking, produced what remains the most impressive book-length manuscript any of the Founding Fathers wrote. In "Query XIII," Jefferson traces the history of Virginia, from early attempts at settlement through his own administration as governor of the state, which ended with his resignation in 1781. "Query XIV" begins with a description of the political and legal institutions of the state, passes into a reflection on the nature and extent of slavery and the relations between the races in Virginia, and concludes with a plea for the extension of public education. Jefferson's remarks about slavery and the relationship between Negro and white are of particular interest; the remarks of a liberal, democratic thinker, they depict the moral burden of slavery on the enlightened eighteenth-century mind, even while we see Jefferson's own "deep-rooted prejudices" forcing him to subscribe to a "suspicion . . . that the blacks . . . are inferior to the whites in the endowments both of body and mind."

Text: Paul Leicester Ford, ed., *The Works of Thomas Jefferson*. New York, 1904.

Notes on Virginia (1782)

QUERY XIII

The constitution of the State and its several charters?

Queen Elizabeth by her letters patent, bearing date March 25, 1584, licensed Sir Walter Raleigh to search for remote heathen lands, not inhabited by Christian people, and granted to him in fee simple, all the soil within 200 leagues of the places where his people should, within six years, make their dwellings or abidings,[1] reserving only to herself and her successors, their allegiance and one fifth part of all the gold and silver ore they should obtain. Sir Walter immediately sent out two ships, which visited Wococon island in North Carolina, and the next year despatched seven with 107 men, who settled in Roanoke Island about latitude 35°. 50′. Here Okisko, king of the Weopomeiocs, in a full council of his people is said to have acknowledged himself the homager of the Queen of England, and, after her, of Sir Walter Raleigh. A supply of 50 men were sent in 1586, and 150 in 1587. With these last Sir Walter sent a Governor, appointed him twelve assistants, gave them a charter of incorporation, and instructed them to settle on Chesapeak bay. They landed, however, at Hatorask. In 1588, when a fleet was ready to sail with a new supply of colonists and necessaries, they were detained by the Queen to assist against the Spanish armada. Sir Walter having now expended 40,000£ in these enterprises, obstructed occasionally by the crown without a shilling of aid from it, was under a necessity of engaging others to adventure their money. He, therefore, by deed bearing date the 7th of March 1589, by the name of Sir Walter Raleigh, Chief Governor of Assamàcomòc, (probably Acomàc,) alias Wingadacoia, alias Virginia, granted to Thomas Smith and others, in consideration of their adventuring certain sums of money, liberty to trade to this new country free from all customs and taxes for seven years, excepting the fifth part of the gold and silver ore to be obtained; and stipulated with them and the other assistants, then in Virginia, that he would confirm the deed of incorporation which he had given in 1587, with all the prerogatives, jurisdictions, royalties and privileges granted to him by the Queen. Sir Walter, at different times sent five other adventurers hither, the last of which was in 1602; for in 1603 he was attainted and put into close imprisonment, which put an end to his cares over his infant colony. What was the particular fate of the colonists he had before sent and seated, has never been known; whether they were murdered, or incorporated with the savages.[2]

[1] This was actually an extension of the patent granted to Sir Humphrey Gilbert, Raleigh's half-brother, in 1578.

[2] Sir Richard Grenville left fifteen men at Roanoke Island in June, 1586. In July, 1587, an expedition under John White arrived at Roanoke, found no survivors of the previous expedition, and left a new group of colonists (including Virginia Dare, White's granddaughter and the first English child born in what is now the United States). Because of a war with Spain, White was unable to return to Roanoke until August, 1590. He found no traces of the colonists except the letters CRO cut in a tree and the word CROATAN carved on a doorpost.

Some gentlemen and merchants, supposing that by the attainder of Sir Walter Raleigh the grant to him was forfeited, not enquiring over carefully whether the sentence of an English court could affect lands not within the jurisdiction of that court, petitioned king James for a new grant of Virginia to them. He accordingly executed a grant to Sir Thomas Gates and others, bearing date the 9th of March, 1607, under which, in the same year, a settlement was affected at Jamestown, and ever after maintained. Of this grant, however, no particular notice need be taken, as it was superceded by letters patent of the same king, of May 23, 1609, to the Earl of Salisbury and others, incorporating them by the name of 'The Treasurer and company of Adventurers and Planters of the City of London for the first colony in Virginia,' granting to them and their successors all the lands in Virginia from Point Comfort along the sea-coast, to the northward 200 miles, and from the same point along the sea coast to the southward two hundred miles, and all the space from this precinct on the sea coast up into the land, West and North west, from sea to sea, and the islands within one hundred miles of it, with all the commodities, jurisdictions, royalties, privileges, franchises, and pre-eminences, within the same, and thereto and thereabouts, by sea and land, appertaining in as ample manner as had before been granted to any adventurer; to be held of the king and his successors, in common soccage, yielding one-fifth part of the gold and silver ore to be therein found, for all manner of services; establishing a council in England for the direction of the enterprise, the members of which were to be chosen and displaced by the voice of the majority of the company and adventurers, and were to have the nomination and revocation of the governors, officers, and ministers, which by them should be thought needful for the colony, the power of establishing laws and forms of government and magistracy, obligatory not only within the colony, but also on the seas in going and coming to and from it; authorizing them to carry thither any persons who should consent to go, freeing them forever from all taxes and impositions on any goods or merchandise on importation into the colony, or exportation out of it, except the five per cent. due for customs on all goods imported into the British dominions, according to the ancient trade of merchants; which five per cent. only being paid they might, within 13 months, re-export the same goods into foreign parts, without any custom, tax, or other duty, to the king or any his officers, or deputies; with powers of waging war against those who should annoy them; giving to the inhabitants of the colony all the rights of natural subjects, as if born and abiding in England; and declaring that these letters should be construed, in all doubtful parts, in such manner as should be most for the benefit of the grantees.

Afterwards on the 12th of March 1612, by other letters patent, the king added to his former grants, all islands in any part of the ocean between the 30th and 41st degrees of latitude, and within 300 leagues of any of the parts before granted to the treasurer and company not being possessed or inhabited by any other Christian prince or state, nor within the limits of the northern colony.

In pursuance of the authorities given to the company by these charters, and more especially of that part in the charter of 1609, which authorized them to establish a form of government, they on the 24th of July 1621, by charter under their common seal, declared that from thence forward there should be two supreme councils in Virginia, the one to be called the council of state, to be placed and displaced by the treasurer, council in England, and company from time to time, whose office was to be that of assisting and advising the governor; the other to be called the general assembly, to be convened by the governor once yearly or oftener, which was to consist of the council of state, and two burgesses out of every town, hundred, or plantation, to be respectively chosen by the inhabitants. In this all matters were to be decided by the greater part of the votes present; reserving to the governor a negative voice; and they were to have power to treat, consult, and conclude all emergent occasions concerning the public weal, and to make laws for the behoof and government of the colony, imitating and following the laws and policy of England as nearly as might be; providing that these laws should have no force till ratified in a general quarter court of the company in England, and returned under their common seal; and declaring that, after the government of the colony should be well framed and settled, no orders of the council in England should bind the colony unless ratified in the said general assembly. The king and company quarrelled, and by a mixture of law and force, the latter were ousted of all their rights without retribution, after having expended 100,000£ in establishing the colony, without the smallest aid from government. King James suspended their powers by proclamation of July 15, 1624, and Charles I. took the government into his own hands. Both sides had their partisans in the colony; but, in truth, the people of the colony in general thought themselves little concerned in the dispute. There being three parties interested in these several charters, what passed between the first and second, it was thought could not affect the third. If the king seized on the powers of the company, they only passed into other hands, without increase or diminution, while the rights of the people remained as they were. But they did not remain so long. The northern parts of their country were granted away to the lords Baltimore and Fairfax; the first of these obtaining also the rights of separate jurisdiction and government. And in 1650 the parliament, considering itself as standing in the place of their deposed king, and as having succeeded to all his powers, without as well as within the realm, began to assume a right over the colonies, passing an act for inhibiting their trade with foreign nations. This succession to the exercise of kingly authority gave the first color for parliamentary interference with the colonies, and produced that fatal precedent which they continued to follow, after they had retired, in other respects, within their proper functions. When this colony, therefore, which still maintained its opposition to Cromwell and the parliament, was induced in 1651 to lay down their arms, they previously secured their most essential rights by a solemn convention, which, having never seen in print, I will here insert literally from the records.[3]

"ARTICLES agreed on & concluded at James Cittie in Virginia for the surrendering and settling of that plantation under ye obedience and government of the commonwealth of England by the commissioners of the Councill of State by authoritie of the parliamt of England, and by the Grand assembly of the Governour, Councill, & Burgesses of that countrey.

"First it is agreed & consted that the plantation of Virginia, & all the inhabitants thereof, shall be and remaine in due obedience and subjection to the Comonwealth of England, according to ye lawes there established, and that this submission and subscription bee acknowledged a voluntary act not forced nor constrained by a conquest upon the countrey, and that they shall have and enjoy such freedoms and priviledges as belong to the free borne people of England, and that the

[3] Virginia became a refuge for prominent Cavaliers fleeing England after the execution of Charles I. See Note 2, Jefferson's *A Summary View of the Rights of British America.*

former government by the Commissions and Instructions be void and null.

"2ly, Secondly, that the Grand assembly as formerly shall convene & transact the affairs of Virginia, wherein nothing is to be acted or done contrairie to the government of the Comonwealth of England & the lawes there established.

"3ly, That there shall be a full and totall remission and indempnitie of all acts, words, or writeings done or spoken against the parliament of England in relation to the same.

"4ly, That Virginia shall have & enjoy ye antient bounds and lymitts granted by the charters of the former kings, and that we shall seek a new charter from the parliament to that purpose against any that have intrencht upon ye rights thereof.

"5ly, That all the pattents of land granted under the collony seale by any of the precedent governours shall be & remaine in their full force & strength.

"6ly, That the priviledge of haveing ffiftie acres of land for every person transported in that collonie shall continue as formerly granted.

"7ly, That ye people of Virginia have free trade as ye people of England do enjoy to all places and with all nations according to ye lawes of that commonwealth, and that Virginia shall enjoy all priviledges equall with any English plantations in America.

"8ly, That Virginia shall be free from all taxes, customs & impositions whatsoever, & none to be imposed on them without consent of the Grand assembly. And soe that neither fforts nor castles bee erected or garrisons maintained without their consent.

"9ly, That noe charge shall be required from this country in respect of this present ffleet.

"10ly, That for the future settlement of the countrey in their due obedience, the Engagement shall be tendered to all ye inhabitants according to act of parliament made to that purpose, that all persons who shall refuse to subscribe the said engagement, shall have a yeare's time if they please to remove themselves and their estates out of Virginia, & in the meantime during the said yeare to have equall justice as formerly.

"11ly, That ye use of the booke of common prayer shall be permitted for one yeare ensueinge with referrence to the consent of ye major part of the parishes, provided that those which relate to kingshipp or that government be not used publiquely, and the continuance of ministers in their places, they not misdemeaning themselves, and the payment of their accustomed dues and agreements made with them respectively shall be left as they now stand dureing this ensueing yeare.

"12ly, That no man's cattell shall be questioned as ye companies, unles such as have been entrusted with them or have disposed of them without order.

"13ly, That all ammunition, powder and armes, other than for private use, shall be delivered up, securitie being given to make satisfaction for it.

"14ly, That all goods all readie brought hither by ye Dutch or others which are now on shoar shall be free from surprizall.

"15ly, That the quittrents granted unto us by the late kinge for seaven yeares bee confirmed.

"16ly, That ye commissioners for the parliament subscribeing these articles engage themselves & the honour of parliament for the full performance thereof: and that the present governour, & ye councill, and the burgesses do likewise subscribe and engage the whole collony on their parts.

RICH. BENNETT.—Seale.
WM. CLAIBORNE.—Seale.
EDMOND CURTIS.—Seale.

"Theise articles were signed and sealed by the Commissioners of the Councill of state for the Commonwealth of England the twelveth day of March 1651."

Then follow the articles stipulated by the governor and council, which relate merely to their own persons and property, and then the ensuing instrument:

"An act of indempnitie made att the surrender of the countrey.

"Whereas, by the authoritie of the parliament of England wee the commissioners appointed by the councill of state authorized thereto, having brought a ffleet and force before James cittie in Virginia to reduce that collonie under the obedience of the commonwealth of England, and finding force raised by the Governour and countrey to make opposition against the said ffleet, whereby assured danger appearinge of the ruine and destruction of the plantation, for prevention whereof the burgesses of all the severall plantations being called to advise and assist therein, uppon long and serious debate, and in sad contemplation of the greate miseries and certaine destruction which were soe neerely hovering over the whole countrey; Wee the said Commissioners have thought fitt and condescending and granted to signe and confirme under our hands, seales and by our oath, Articles bearing date with theise presents, and do further declare that by the authoritie of the parliament and commonwealth of England derived unto us their commissioners, that according to the articles in generall wee have granted an act of indempnitie and oblivion to all the inhabitants of this colloney from all words, actions, or writings that have been spoken acted or writt against the parliament or comonwealth of England or any other person from the beginning of the world to this daye. And this we have done that all the inhabitants of the collonie may live quietly and securely under the comonwealth of England. And we do promise that the parliament and commonwealth of England shall confirm and make good all those transactions of ours. Witenes our hands and seales this 12th of March 1651.

RICHARD BENNETT.—Seale.
WILLIAM CLAIBORNE.—Seale.
EDMOND CURTIS.—Seale.

The colony supposed, that, by this solemn convention, entered into with arms in their hands, they had secured the antient limits of their country, its free trade its exemption from taxation but by their own assembly, and exclusion of military force from among them. Yet in every of these points was this convention violated by subsequent kings and parliaments, and other infractions of their constitution, equally dangerous, committed. Their General Assembly, which was composed of the council of state and burgesses, sitting together and deciding by plurality of voices, was split into two houses, by which the council obtained a separate negative on their laws. Appeals from their supreme court, which had been fixed by law in their general assembly, were arbitrarily revoked to England, to be there heard before the king and council. Instead of four hundred miles on the seacoast, they were reduced, in the space of thirty years, to about one hundred miles. Their trade with foreigners was totally suppressed, and when carried to Great Britain, was there loaded with imposts. It is unnecessary, however, to glean up the several instances of injury, as scattered through American and British history, and the more especially as, by passing on to the accession of the present king, we shall find specimens of them all, aggravated, multiplied and crouded within a small compass of time, so as to evince a fixed design of considering our rights natural, conventional and chartered as mere nullities. The following is an epitome of the first sixteen years of his reign. The colonies were taxed internally and externally; their essential interests sacrificed to individuals in Great Britain; their legislatures suspended; charters annulled; trials by juries taken away; their persons subjected to transportation across the Atlantic, and to trial before foreign judicatories; their supplications for redress thought beneath answer; themselves published as cowards in the councils of their mother country and courts of Europe; armed troops sent among them to enforce submission to these violences; and actual hostilities commenced against them. No alternative was presented but resistance, or unconditional submission. Between these could be no hesitation. They closed in the appeal to arms. They declared themselves independent states. They confederated together into one great republic; thus securing to every state the benefit of an union of their whole force. In each state separately a new form of government was established. Of ours particularly the following are the outlines. The executive powers are lodged in the hands of a governor, chosen annually, and incapable of acting more than three years in seven. He is assisted by a council of eight members. The judiciary powers are divided among several courts, as will be hereafter explained. Legislation is exercised by two houses of assembly, the one called the house of delegates, composed of two members from each county, chosen annually by the citizens, possessing an estate for life in 100 acres of uninhabited land, or 25 acres with a house on it, or in a house or lot in some town: the other called the Senate, consisting of 24 members, chosen quadrennially by the same electors, who for this purpose are distributed into 24 districts. The concurrence of both houses is necessary to the passage of a law. They have the appointment of the governor and council, the judges of the superior courts, auditors, attorney general, treasurer, register of the land office, and delegates to congress. As the dismemberment of the state had never had its confirmation, but, on the contrary, had always been the subject of protestation and complaint, that it might never be in our own power to raise scruples on that subject, or to disturb the harmony of our new confederacy, the grants to Maryland, Pennsylvania and the two Carolinas were ratified.

This constitution was formed when we were new and unexperienced in the science of government. It was the first, too, which was formed in the whole United States. No wonder then that time and trial have discovered very capital defects in it.

1. The majority of the men in the state, who pay and fight for its support, are unrepresented in the legislature, the roll of freeholders entitled to vote not including generally the half of those on the roll of the militia, or the tax-gatherers.

2. Among those who share the representation, the shares are very unequal. Thus the county of Warwick, with only one hundred fighting men, has an equal representation with the county of Loudon, which has 1746. So that every man in Warwick has as much influence in the government as 17 men in Loudon. But lest it should be thought that an equal interpersion of small among large counties, through the whole state, may prevent any danger of injury to particular parts of it, we will divide it into districts, and shew the proportions of land, or fighting men, and of representation in each:

	Square miles.	*Fighting Men.*	*Delegates.*	*Senators.*
Between the sea-coast and falls of the rivers	*11,205	19,012	71	12
Between the falls of the rivers and Blue Ridge of mountains	18,759	18,828	46	8
Between the Blue Ridge and the Alleghany	11,911	7,673	16	2
Between the Alleghany and Ohio	†79,650	4,458	16	2
Total	121,525	49,971	149	24

* Of these, 542 are on the eastern shore.

† Of these, 22,616 are Eastward of the meridian of the mouth of the Great Kanhaway.

An inspection of this table will supply the place of commentaries on it. It will appear at once that nineteen thousand men, living below the falls of the rivers, possess half of the senate, and want four members only of possessing a majority of the house of delegates; a want more than supplied by the vicinity of their situation to the seat of government, and of course the greater degree of convenience and punctuality with which their members may and will attend in the legislature. These nineteen thousand, therefore, living in one part of the country, give law to upwards of thirty thousand living in another, and appoint all their chief officers executive and judiciary. From the difference of their situation and circumstances, their interests will often be very different.

3. The senate is, by its constitution, too homogenous with the house of delegates. Being chosen by the same electors, at the same time, and out of the same subjects, the choice falls of course on men of the same description. The purpose of establishing different houses of legislation is to introduce the influence of different interests or different principles. Thus in Great Britain it is said their constitution relies on the house of commons for honesty, and the lords for wisdom; which would be a rational reliance, if honesty were to be bought with money, and if wisdom were hereditary. In some of the American States, the delegates and senators are so chosen, as that the first represent the persons, and the second the property of the State. But with us, wealth and wisdom have equal chance for admission into both houses. We do not, therefore, derive from the separation of our legislature into two houses, those benefits which a proper complication of principles is capable of producing, and those which alone can compensate the evils which may be produced by their dissensions.

4. All the powers of government, legislative, executive, and judiciary, result to the legislative body. The concentrating these in the same hands is precisely the definition of despotic government. It will be no alleviation that these powers will be exercised by a plurality of hands, and not by a single one. 173 despots would surely be as oppressive as one. Let those who doubt it turn their eyes on the republic of Venice. As little will it avail us that they are chosen by ourselves. An *elective despotism* was not the government we fought for, but one which should not only be founded on free principles, but in which the powers of government should be so divided and balanced among several bodies of magistracy, as that no one could transcend their legal limits, without being effectually checked and restrained by the others. For this reason that convention, which passed the ordinance of government laid its foundation on this basis, that the legislative, executive and judiciary departments should be separate and distinct, so that no person should exercise the powers of more than one of them at the same time. But no barrier was provided between these several powers. The judiciary and executive members were left dependent on the legislative, for their subsistence in office, and some of them for their continuance in it. If therefore the legislature assumes executive and judiciary powers, no opposition is likely to be made; nor, if made, can it be

effectual; because in that case they may put their proceedings into the form of an act of assembly, which will render them obligatory on the other branches. They have accordingly in many instances, decided rights which should have been left to judiciary controversy: and the direction of the executive, during the whole time of their session, is becoming habitual and familiar. And this is done with no ill intention. The views of the present members are perfectly upright. When they are led out of their regular province, it is by art in others, and inadvertence in themselves. And this will probably be the case for some time to come. But it will not be a very long time. Mankind soon learn to make interested uses of every right and power which they possess, or may assume. The public money and public liberty, intended to have been deposited with three branches of magistracy, but found inadvertently to be in the hands of one only, will soon be discovered to be sources of wealth and dominion to those who hold them; distinguished, too, by this tempting circumstance, that they are the instrument, as well as the object, of acquisition. With money we will get men, said Cæsar, and with men we will get money. Nor should our assembly be deluded by the integrity of their own purposes, and conclude that these unlimited powers will never be abused, because themselves are not disposed to abuse them. They should look forward to a time, and that not a distant one, when a corruption in this, as in the country from which we derive our origin, will have seized the heads of government, and be spread by them through the body of the people; when they will purchase the voices of the people, and make them pay the price. Human nature is the same on every side of the Atlantic, and will be alike influenced by the same causes. The time to guard against corruption and tyranny, is before they shall have gotten hold of us. It is better to keep the wolf out of the fold, than to trust to drawing his teeth and talons after he shall have entered. To render these considerations the more cogent, we must observe in addition:

5. That the ordinary legislature may alter the constitution itself. On the discontinuance of assemblies, it became necessary to substitute in their place some other body, competent to the ordinary business of government, and to the calling forth the powers of the State for the maintenance of our opposition to Great Britain. Conventions were therefore introduced, consisting of two delegates from each county, meeting together and forming one house, on the plan of the former

house of Burgesses, to whose places they succeeded. These were at first chosen anew for every particular session. But in March 1775, they recommended to the people to choose a convention, which should continue in office a year. This was done, accordingly, in April 1775, and in the July following that convention passed an ordinance for the election of delegates in the month of April annually. It is well known, that in July 1775, a separation from Great Britain and establishment of republican government, had never yet entered into any person's mind. A convention, therefore, chosen under that ordinance, cannot be said to have been chosen for the purposes which certainly did not exist in the minds of those who passed it. Under this ordinance, at the annual election in April 1776, a convention for the year was chosen. Independance, and the establishment of a new form of government, were not even yet the objects of the people at large.[4] One extract from the pamphlet called Common sense had appeared in the Virginia papers in February, and copies of the pamphlet itself had got in a few hands. But the idea had not been opened to the mass of the people in April, much less can it be said that they had made up their minds in its favor. So that the electors of April 1776, no more than the legislators of July 1775, not thinking of independance and a permanent republic, could not mean to vest in these delegates powers of establishing them, or any authorities other than those of the ordinary legislature. So far as a temporary organization of government was necessary to render our opposition energetic, so far their organization was valid. But they received in their creation no powers but what were given to every legislature before and since. They could not, therefore, pass an act transcendent to the powers of other legislatures. If the present assembly pass an act, and declare it shall be irrevocable by subsequent assemblies, the declaration is merely void, and the act repealable, as other acts are. So far, and no farther authorized, they organized the government by the ordinance entituled a Constitution or Form of government. It pretends to no higher authority than the other ordinance of the same session; it does not say that it shall be perpetual; that it shall

[4] By April, 1776, independence was certainly being talked of. Hostilities had commenced a year earlier at Lexington and Concord. Paine's *Common Sense* had been read by many people in Virginia, despite what Jefferson says in the next sentence; and in a letter to Thomas Nelson, dated May 16, 1776, he admitted having "enquire[d] into the sentiments of the people on that head [independence] in the upper counties I think I may safely say nine out of ten are for it."

be unalterable by other legislatures; that it shall be transcendent above the powers of those who they knew would have equal power with themselves. Not only the silence of the instrument is a proof they thought it would be alterable, but their own practice also; for this very convention, meeting as a House of Delegates in General assembly with the Senate in the autumn of that year, passed acts of assembly in contradiction of their ordinance of government; and every assembly from that time to this has done the same. I am safe therefore in the position that the constitution itself is alterable by the ordinary legislature. Though this opinion seems founded on the first elements of common sense, yet is the contrary maintained by some persons. 1. Because, say they, the conventions were vested with every power necessary to make effectual opposition to Great Britain. But to complete this argument, they must go on, and say further, that effectual opposition could not be made to Great Britain without establishing a form of government perpetual and unalterable by the legislature; which is not true. An opposition which at some time or other was to come to an end, could not need a perpetual institution to carry it on: and a government amendable as its defects should be discovered, was likely to make effectual resistance, as one that should be unalterably wrong. Besides, the assemblies were as much vested with all powers requisite for resistance as the Conventions were. If therefore these powers included that of modelling the form of government in the one case, they did so in the other. The assemblies then as well as the conventions may model the government; that is, they may alter the ordinance of government. 2. They urge that if the convention had meant that this instrument should be alterable, as their other ordinances were, they would have called it an ordinance; but they have called it a *constitution,* which *ex vi termini,* means "an act above the power of the ordinary legislature." I answer that *constitutio, constitutum, statutum, lex,* are convertible terms. "*Constitutio* dicitur jus quod a principe conditur." "*Constitutum,* quod ab imperatoribus rescriptum statutumve est." "*Statutum,* idem quod lex." Calvini Lexicon juridicum. *Constitution* and *statute* were originally terms of the* civil law, and from thence introduced by Ecclesiastics into the English law. Thus in the statute 25 Hen. VIII. c. 19, §. 1, "*Constitutions* and *ordinances*" are used as synonimous. The term *constitution* has many other

* To bid, to set, was the ancient legislative word of the English. Ll. Hlotharri and Eadrici. Ll. Inae. Ll. Eadwerdi. Ll. Aeathelstani.

significations in physics and politics; but in Jurisprudence, whenever it is applied to any act of the legislature, it invariably means a statute, law, or ordinance, which is the present case. No inference then of a different meaning can be drawn from the adoption of this title: on the contrary, we might conclude that, by their affixing to it a term synonimous with ordinance or statute, they meant it to be an ordinance or statute. But of what consequence is their meaning, where their power is denied? If they meant to do more than they had power to do, did this give them power? It is not the name, but the authority which renders an act obligatory. Lord Coke says, 'an article of the statute, 11. R. II. c. 5. that no person should attempt to revoke any ordinance then made, is repealed, for that such restraint is against the jurisdiction and power of the parliament.' 4. inst. 42. and again, 'though divers parliaments, have attempted to restrain subsequent parliaments, yet could they never effect it; for the latter parliament hath ever power to abrogate, suspend, qualify, explain, or make void the former in the whole or in any part thereof, notwithstanding any words of restraint, prohibition, or penalty, in the former; for it is a maxim in the laws of the parliament, 'quod leges posteriores priores contrarias abrogant.' 4. inst. 43.—To get rid of the magic supposed to be in the word *constitution,* let us translate it into its definition as given by those who think it above the power of the law; and let us suppose the convention, instead of saying, 'We the ordinary legislature, establish a *constitution,*' had said, 'We the ordinary legislature, establish an act *above the power of the ordinary legislature.*' Does not this expose the absurdity of the attempt? 3. But, say they, the people have acquiesced, and this has given it an authority superior to the laws. It is true that the people did not rebel against it: and was that a time for the people to rise in rebellion? Should a prudent acquiescence, at a critical time, be construed into a confirmation of every illegal thing done during that period? Besides, why should they rebel? At an annual election they had chosen delegates for the year, to exercise the ordinary powers of legislation, and to manage the great contest in which they were engaged. These delegates thought the contest would be best managed by an organized government. They therefore, among others, passed an ordinance of government. They did not presume to call it perpetual and unalterable. They well knew they had no power to make it so; that our choice of them had been for no such purpose, and at a time when we could have no such purpose in contemplation. Had an unalterable form of government been meditated, perhaps we should have chosen a different set of people. There was no cause then for the people to rise in rebellion. But to what dangerous lengths will this argument lead? Did the acquiescence of the colonies under the various acts of power exercised by Great Britain in our infant state, confirm these acts, and so far invest them with the authority of the people as to render them unalterable, and our present resistance wrong? On every unauthoritative exercise of power by the legislature must the people rise in rebellion, or their silence be construed into a surrender of that power to them? If so, how many rebellions should we have had already? One certainly for every session of assembly. The other states in the union have been of opinion that to render a form of government unalterable by ordinary acts of assembly, the people must delegate persons with special powers. They have accordingly chosen special conventions to form and fix their governments. The individuals then who maintain the contrary opinion in this country, should have the modesty to suppose it possible that they may be wrong, and the rest of America right. But if there be only a possibility of their being wrong, if only a plausible doubt remains of the validity of the ordinance of government, is it not better to remove that doubt by placing it on a bottom which none will dispute? If they be right we shall only have the unnecessary trouble of meeting once in convention. If they be wrong, they expose us to the hazard of having no fundamental rights at all. True it is, this is no time for deliberating on forms of government. While an enemy is within our bowels, the first object is to expel him. But when this shall be done, when peace shall be established, and leisure given us for intrenching within good forms, the rights for which we have bled, let no man be found indolent enough to decline a little more trouble for placing them beyond the reach of question. If anything more be requisite to produce a conviction of the expediency of calling a convention at a proper season to fix our form of government, let it be the reflection:

6. That the assembly exercises a power of determining the quorum of their own body which may legislate for us. After the establishment of the new form they adhered to the *Lex majoris partis*, founded in common law as well as common right. It is the natural law of every assembly of men, whose numbers are not fixed by any other law. They continued for some time to require the presence of a majority of their whole

number, to pass an act. But the British parliament fixes its own quorum; our former assemblies fixed their own quorum; and one precedent in favor of power is stronger than an hundred against it. The house of delegates, therefore, have* lately voted that, during the present dangerous invasion, forty members shall be a house to proceed to business. They have been moved to this by the fear of not being able to collect a house. But this danger could not authorize them to call that a house which was none; and if they may fix it at one number, they may at another, till it loses its fundamental character of being a representative body. As this vote expires with the present invasion, it is probable the former rule will be permitted to revive; because at present no ill is meant. The power, however, of fixing their own quorum has been avowed, and a precedent set. From forty it may be reduced to four, and from four to one; from a house to a committee, from a committee to a chairman or speaker, and thus an oligarchy or monarchy be substituted under forms supposed to be regular. 'Omnia mala exempla ex bonis orta sunt; sed ubi imperium ad ignaros aut minus bonos pervenit, novum illud exemplum ab dignis et idoneis ad indignos et non idoneos fertur.' When, therefore, it is considered, that there is no legal obstacle to the assumption by the assembly of all the powers legislative, executive, and judiciary, and that these may come to the hands of the smallest rag of delegation, surely the people will say, and their representatives, while yet they have honest representatives, will advise them to say, that they will not acknowledge as laws any acts not considered and assented to by the major part of their delegates.

In enumerating the defects of the constitution, it would be wrong to count among them what is only the error of particular persons. In December 1776, our circumstances being much distressed, it was proposed in the house of delegates to create a *dictator*, invested with every power legislative, executive, and judiciary, civil and military, of life and of death, over our persons and over our properties: and in June 1781, again under calamity, the same proposition was repeated, and wanted a few votes only of being passed.[5]—One who entered into this contest from a pure love of liberty, and a sense of injured rights, who determined to make every sacri-

* June 4, 1781.

[5] The proposed dictator was originally believed to have been Patrick Henry. However, in a letter to Jefferson dated September 8, 1818, Archibald Stuart, who was present at the Assembly of 1781, claimed that Washington was the choice of those delegates who wanted a dictator.

fice, and to meet every danger, for the re-establishment of those rights on a firm basis, who did not mean to expend his blood and substance for the wretched purpose of changing this master for that, but to place the powers of governing him in a plurality of hands of his own choice, so that the corrupt will of no one man might in future oppress him, must stand confounded and dismayed when he is told, that a considerable portion of that plurality had meditated the surrender of them into a single hand, and, in lieu of a limited monarch, to deliver him over to a despotic one! How must he find his efforts and sacrifices abused and baffled, if he may still, by a single vote, be laid prostrate at the feet of one man! In God's name, from whence have they derived this power? Is it from our ancient laws? None such can be produced. Is it from any principle in our new constitution expressed or implied? Every lineament of that expressed or implied, is in full opposition to it. Its fundamental principle is, that the state shall be governed as a commonwealth. It provides a republican organization, proscribes under the name of *prerogative* the exercise of all powers undefined by the laws; places on this basis the whole system of our laws; and by consolidating them together, chooses that they shall be left to stand or fall together, never providing for any circumstances, nor admitting that such could arise, wherein either should be suspended; no, not for a moment. Our antient laws expressly declare, that those who are but delegates themselves shall not delegate to others powers which require judgment and integrity in their exercise. Or was this proposition moved on a supposed right in the movers, of abandoning their posts in a moment of distress? The same laws forbid the abandonment of that post, even on ordinary occasions; and much more a transfer of their powers into other hands and other forms, without consulting the people. They never admit the idea that these, like sheep or cattle, may be given from hand to hand without an appeal to their own will.—Was it from the necessity of the case? Necessities which dissolve a government, do not convey its authority to an oligarchy or a monarchy. They throw back, into the hands of the people, the powers they had delegated, and leave them as individuals to shift for themselves. A leader may offer, but not impose himself, nor be imposed on them. Much less can their necks be submitted to his sword, their breath be held at his will or caprice. The necessity which should operate these tremendous effects should at least be palpable and irresistible. Yet in both instances, where it was feared, or pretended with us, it was belied by the event. It was belied, too, by the preceding experience of our sister states, several of whom had grappled through greater difficulties without abandoning their forms of government. When the proposition was first made, Massachusets had found even the government of committees sufficient to carry them through an invasion. But we at the time of that proposition, were under no invasion. When the second was made, there had been added to this example those of Rhode-Island, New-York, New-Jersey, and Pennsylvania, in all of which the republican form had been found equal to the task of carrying them through the severest trials. In this state alone did there exist so little virtue, that fear was to be fixed in the hearts of the people, and to become the motive of their exertions, and the principle of their government? The very thought alone was treason against the people; was treason against mankind in general; as rivetting forever the chains which bow down their necks by giving to their oppressors a proof, which they would have trumpeted through the universe, of the imbecility of republican government, in times of pressing danger, to shield them from harm. Those who assume the right of giving away the reins of government in any case, must be sure that the herd, whom they hand on to the rods and hatchet of the dictator, will lay their necks on the block when he shall nod to them. But if our assemblies supposed such a resignation in the people, I hope they mistook their character. I am of opinion, that the government, instead of being braced and invigorated for greater exertions under their difficulties, would have been thrown back upon the bungling machinery of county committees for administration, till a convention could have been called, and its wheels again set into regular motion. What a cruel moment was this for creating such an embarrassment, for putting to the proof the attachment of our countrymen to republican government! Those who meant well, of the advocates for this measure, (and most of them meant well, for I know them personally, had been their fellow-labourers in the common cause, and had often proved the purity of their principles,) had been seduced in their judgment by the example of an antient republic, whose constitution and circumstances were fundamentally different. They had sought this precedent in the history of Rome, where alone it was to be found, and where at length, too, it had proved fatal. They had taken it from a republic rent by the most bitter factions and tumults, where the government was of a heavy-handed unfeeling aristocracy, over a people ferocious, and rendered desperate by poverty and wretchedness; tumults which could not be allayed under the most trying circumstances, but by the omnipotent hand of a single despot. Their constitution, therefore, allowed a temporary tyrant to be erected, under the name of a Dictator; and that temporary tyrant, after a few examples, became perpetual. They misapplied this precedent to a people mild in their dispositions, patient under their trial, united for the public liberty, and affectionate to their leaders. But if from the constitution of the Roman government there resulted to their Senate a power of submitting all their rights to the will of one man, does it follow that the assembly of Virginia have the same authority? What clause in our constitution has submitted that of Rome, by way of residuary provision, for all cases not otherwise provided for? Or if they may step ad libitum into any other form of government for precedents to rule us by, for what oppression may not a precedent be found in this world of the bellum omnium in omnia? Searching for the foundations of this proposition, I can find none which may pretend a colour of right or reason, but the defect before developed, that there being no barrier between the legislative, executive, and judiciary departments, the legislature may seize the whole: that having seized it, and possessing a right to fix their own quorum, they may reduce that quorum to one, whom they may call a chairman, speaker, dictator, or by any other name they please.—Our situation is indeed perilous, and I hope my countrymen will be sensible of it, and will apply, at a proper season, the proper remedy; which is a convention to fix the constitution, to amend its defects, to bind up the several branches of government by certain laws, which, when they transgress, their acts shall become nullities; to render unnecessary an appeal to the people, or in other words a rebellion, on every infraction of their rights, on the peril that their acquiescence shall be construed into an intention to surrender those rights.

QUERY XIV

The administration of justice and description of the laws?

The state is divided into counties. In every county are appointed magistrates, called justices of the peace, usually from eight to thirty or forty in number, in proportion to the size of the county, of the most discreet and honest inhabitants. They are nominated by their fellows, but commissioned by the governor, and act without reward. These magistrates have jurisdiction both criminal and civil. If the question before them be a question of law only, they decide on it themselves; but if it be a fact, or of fact and law combined, it must be referred to a jury. In the latter case, of a combination of law and fact, it is usual for the jurors to decide the fact, and to refer the law arising on it to the decision of the judges. But this division of the subject lies with their discretion only. And if the question relate to any point of public liberty, or if it be one of those in which the judges may be suspected of bias, the jury undertake to decide both law and fact. If they be mistaken, a decision against right, which is casual only, is less dangerous to the state, and less afflicting to the loser, than one which makes part of a regular and uniform system. In truth, it is better to toss up cross and pile in a cause, than to refer it to a judge whose mind is warped by any motive whatever, in that particular case. But the common sense of twelve honest men gives still a better chance of just decision, than the hazard of cross and pile. These judges execute their process by the sheriff or coroner of the county, or by constables of their own appointment. If any free person commit an offence against the commonwealth, if it be below the degree of felony, he is bound by a justice to appear before their court, to answer it on indictment or information. If it amount to felony, he is committed to jail; a court of these justices is called; if they on examination think him guilty, they send him to the jail of the general court, before which court he is to be tried first by a grand jury of 24, of whom 13 must concur in opinion; if they find him guilty, he is then tried by a jury of 12 men of the county where the offence was committed, and by their verdict, which must be unanimous, he is acquitted or condemned without appeal. If the criminal be a slave, the trial by the county court is final. In every case, however, except that of high treason, there resides in the governor a power of pardon. In high treason the pardon can only flow from the general assembly. In civil matters these justices have jurisdiction in all cases of whatever value, not appertaining to the department of the admiralty. This jurisdiction is twofold. If the matter in dispute be of less value than 4⅙ dollars, a single member may try it at any time and place within his county, and may award execution on the goods of the party cast. If it be of that or greater value, it is determinable before the county court, which consists of four at the least of those justices and assemblies at the court-house of the county on a certain day in every month. From their determination, if the matter be of the value of ten pounds sterling, or concern the title or bounds of lands, an appeal lies to one of the superior courts.

There are three superior courts, to wit, the high court of chancery, the general court, and court of admiralty. The first and second of these receive appeals from the county courts, and also have original jurisdiction, where the subject of controversy is of the value of ten pounds sterling, or where it concerns the title or bounds of lands. The jurisdiction of the admiralty is original altogether. The high court of chancery is composed of three judges, the general court of five, and the court of admiralty of three. The two first hold their sessions at Richmond at stated times, the chancery twice in the year, and the general court twice for business civil and criminal, and twice more for criminal only. The court of admiralty sits at Williamsburg whenever a controversy arises.

There is one supreme court, called the court of appeals, composed of the judges of the three superior courts, assembling twice a year at stated times at Richmond. This court receives appeals in all civil cases from each of the superior courts, and determines them finally. But it has no original jurisdiction.

If a controversy arise between two foreigners of a nation in alliance with the United States, it is decided by the Consul for their State, or, if both parties chuse it, by the ordinary courts of justice. If one of the parties only be such a foreigner, it is triable before the courts of justice of the country. But if it shall have been instituted in a county court, the foreigner may remove it into the general court, or court of chancery, who are to determine it at their first sessions, as they must also do if it be originally commenced before them. In cases of life and death, such foreigners have a right to be tried by a jury, the one-half foreigners, the other natives.

All public accounts are settled with a board of auditors, consisting of three members appointed by the general assembly, any two of whom may act. But an individual, dissatisfied with the determination of that board, may carry his case into the proper superior court.

A description of the laws.

The general assembly was constituted, as has been already shown, by letters-patent of March the 9th, 1607, in the 4th year of the reign of James the first. The laws of England seem to have been adopted by consent of the settlers, which might easily enough be done whilst they were few and living all together. Of such adoption, however, we have no other proof than their practice till the year 1661, when they were expressly adopted by an act of the assembly, except so far as 'a difference of condition' rendered them inapplicable. Under this adoption, the rule, in our courts of judicature was, that the common law of England, and the general statutes previous to the 4th of James, were in force here; but that no subsequent statutes were, *unless we were named in them,* said the judges and other partisans of the crown, but *named or not named,* said those who reflected freely. It will be unnecessary to attempt a description of the laws of England, as that may be found in English publications. To those which were established here, by the adoption of the legislature, have been since added a number of acts of assembly passed during the monarchy, and ordinances of convention and acts of assembly enacted since the establishment of the republic. The following variations from the British model are perhaps worthy of being specified:

Debtors unable to pay their debts, and making faithful delivery of their whole effects, are released from confinement, and their persons forever discharged from restraint for such previous debts: but any property they may afterwards acquire will be subject to their creditors.

The poor, unable to support themselves, are maintained by an assessment on the titheable persons in their parish. This assessment is levied and administered by twelve persons in each parish, called vestrymen, originally chosen by the housekeepers of the parish, but afterwards filling vacancies in their own body by their own choice. These are usually the most discreet farmers, so distributed through their parish, that every part of it may be under the immediate eye of some one of them. They are well acquainted with the details and œconomy of private life, and they find sufficient inducements to execute their charge well, in their philanthropy, in the approbation of their neighbors, and the distinction which that gives them. The poor who have neither property, friends, nor strength to labour, are boarded in the houses of good farmers, to whom a stipulated sum is annually paid. To those who are able to help themselves a little, or have friends from whom they derive some succours, inadequate however to their full maintenance, supplementary aids are given which enable them to live comfortably in their own houses, or in the houses of their friends. Vagabonds without visible property or vocation, are placed in work houses, where they are well clothed, fed, lodged, and made to labour. Nearly the same methods of providing for the poor prevails through all our states; and from Savannah to Portsmouth you will seldom meet a beggar. In the larger towns, indeed, they sometimes present themselves. These are usually foreigners, who have never obtained a settlement in any parish. I never yet saw a native American begging in the streets or highways. A subsistence is easily gained here: and if, by misfortunes, they are thrown on the charities of the world, those provided by their own country are so comfortable and so certain, that they never think of relinquishing them to become strolling beggars. Their situation too, when sick, in the family of a good farmer, where every member is emulous to do them kind offices, where they are visited by all the neighbors, who bring them the little rarities which their sickly appetites may crave, and who take by rotation the nightly watch over them, when their condition requires it, is without comparison better than in a general hospital, where the sick, the dying and the dead are crammed together in the same rooms, and often in the same beds. The disadvantages, inseparable from general hospitals, are such as can never be counterpoised by all the regularities of medicine and regimen. Nature and kind nursing save a much greater proportion in our plain way, at a smaller expense, and with less abuse. One branch only of hospital institution is wanting with us; that is a general establishment for those laboring under difficult cases of chirurgery. The aids of this art are not equivocal. But an able chirurgeon cannot be had in every parish. Such a receptacle should therefore be provided for those patients: but no others should be admitted.

Marriages must be solemnized either on special licence, granted by the first magistrate of the county, on proof of the consent of the parent or guardian of either party under age, or after solemn publication, on three several sundays, at some place of religious worship, in the parishes where the parties reside. The act of solemnization may be by the minister of any society of christians, who shall have been previously licensed for this purpose by the court of the county. Quakers and Menonists however are exempted from all these conditions, and marriage among them is to be solemnized by the society itself.

A foreigner of any nation, not in open war with us, becomes naturalized by removing to the state to reside, and taking an oath of fidelity: and thereupon acquires every right of a native citizen: and citizens may divest themselves of that character, by declaring, by solemn deed, or in open court, that they mean to expatriate themselves, and no longer to be citizens of this state.

Conveyances of land must be registered in the court of the county wherein they lie, or in the general court, or they are void, as to creditors, and subsequent purchasers.

Slaves pass by descent and dower as lands do. Where the descent is from a parent, the heir is bound to pay an equal share of their value in money to each of his brothers and sisters.

Slaves, as well as lands, were entailable during the monarchy; but, by an act of the first republican assembly, all donees in tail, present and future, were vested with the absolute dominion of the entailed subject.

Bills of exchange, being protested, carry 10 per cent. interest from their date.

No person is allowed, in any other case, to take more than five per centum per annum simple interest for the loan of moneys.

Gaming debts are made void, and monies actually paid to discharge such debts (if they exceed 40 shillings) may be recovered by the payer within three months, or by any other person afterwards.

Tobacco, flour, beef, pork, tar, pitch, and turpentine must be inspected by persons publicely appointed before they can be exported.

The erecting iron-works and mills is encouraged by many privileges; with necessary cautions however to prevent their dams from obstructing the navigation of the water courses. The general assembly have on several occasions shewn a great desire to encourage the opening the great falls of James and Patowmac rivers. As yet, however, neither of these have been effected.

The laws have also descended to the preservation and improvement of the races of useful animals, such as horses, cattle, deer; to the extirpation of those which are noxious, as wolves, squirrels, crows, blackbirds; and to the guarding our citizens against infectious disorders, by obliging suspected vessels coming into the state, to perform quarantine, and by regulating the conduct of persons having such disorders within the state.

The mode of acquiring lands, in the earliest times of our settlement, was by petition to the general assembly. If the lands prayed for were already cleared of the Indian title, and the assembly thought the prayer reasonable, they passed the property by their vote to the petitioner. But if they had not yet been ceded by the Indians, it was necessary that the petitioner should previously purchase their right. This purchase the assembly verified, by enquiries of the Indian proprietors; and being satisfied of its reality and fairness, proceeded further to examine the reasonableness of the petition, and its consistence with policy; and according to the result either granted or rejected the petition. The company also sometimes, though very rarely, granted lands, independently of the general assembly. As the colony increased, and individual applications for land multiplied, it was found to give too much occupation to the general assembly to inquire into and execute the grant in every special case. They therefore thought it better to establish general rules, according to which all grants should be made, and to leave to the governor the execution of them, under these rules. This they did by what have been usually called the land laws, amending them from time to time, as their defects were developed. According to these laws, when an individual wished a portion of unappropriated land, he was to locate and survey it by a public officer, appointed for that purpose: its breadth was to bear a certain proportion to its length: the grant was to be executed by the governor: and the lands were to be improved in a certain manner, within a given time. From these regulations there resulted to the state a sole and exclusive power of taking conveyances of the Indian right of soil; since, according to them an Indian conveyance alone could give no right to an individual, which the laws would acknowledge. The state, or the crown, thereafter, made general purchases of the Indians from time to time, and the governor parcelled them out by special grants, conformed to the rules before described, which it was not in his power, or in that of the crown, to dispense with. Grants, unaccompanied by their proper legal circumstances, were set aside regularly by *scire facias,* or by bill in Chancery. Since the establishment of our new government, this order of things is but little changed. An individual, wishing to appropriate to himself lands still unappropriated by any other, pays to the public treasurer a sum of money proportioned to the quantity he wants. He carries the treasurer's receipt to the auditors of public accompts, who thereupon debit the treasurer with the sum, and order the register of the land-office to give the party a warrant for his land. With this warrant from the register, he goes to the surveyor of the county where the land lies on which he has cast his eye. The Surveyor lays it off for him, gives him its exact description, in the form of a certificate, which certificate he returns to the land-office, where a grant is made out, and is signed by the governor. This vests in him a perfect dominion in his lands, transmissible to whom he pleases by deed or will, or by descent to his heirs, if he die intestate.

Many of the laws which were in force during the monarchy being relative merely to that form of government, or inculcating principles inconsistent with republicanism, the first assembly which met after the establishment of the commonwealth, appointed a committee to revise the whole code, to reduce it into proper form and volume, and report it to the assembly. This work has been executed by three gentlemen, and reported; but probably will not be taken up till a restoration of peace shall leave to the legislature leisure to go through such a work.[1]

The plan of the revisal was this. The common law of England, by which is meant that part of the English law which was anterior to the date of the oldest statutes extant, is made the basis of the work. It was thought dangerous to attempt to reduce it to a text: it was therefore left to be collected from the usual monuments of it. Necessary alterations in that, and so much of the whole body of the British statutes, and of acts of assembly, as were thought proper to be retained, were digested into 126 new acts, in which simplicity of style was aimed at, as far as was safe. The following are the most remarkable alterations proposed:

To change the rules of descent, so as that the lands of any person dying intestate shall be divisible equally among all his children, or other representatives, in equal degree.

To make slaves distributable among the next of kin, as other movables.

[1] On October 12, 1776, Jefferson, then a member of the Virginia House of Delegates, moved for the revision of state laws in order to adapt them to republican principles. Along with George Wythe and Edmund Pendleton, he drew up the *Report of the Revisors*, which was presented to the House on June 18, 1778. Almost all of the "alterations" which Jefferson describes were eventually adopted, leaving Virginia among the most liberal states in the new union.

To have all public expences, whether of the general treasury, or of a parish or county, (as for the maintenance of the poor, building bridges, courthouses, &c.,) supplied by assessments on the citizens, in proportion to their property.

To hire undertakers for keeping the public roads in repair, and indemnify individuals through whose lands new roads shall be opened.

To define with precision the rules whereby aliens should become citizens, and citizens make themselves aliens.

To establish religious freedom on the broadest bottom.

To emancipate all slaves born after passing the act. The bill reported by the revisers does not itself contain this proposition; but an amendment containing it was prepared, to be offered to the legislature whenever the bill should be taken up, and further directing, that they should continue with their parents to a certain age, then be brought up, at the public expence, to tillage, arts, or sciences, according to their geniusses, till the females should be eighteen, and the males twenty-one years of age, when they should be colonized to such place as the circumstances of the time should render most proper, sending them out with arms, implements of household and of the handicraft arts, seeds, pairs of the useful domestic animals, &c. to declare them a free and independent people, and extend to them our alliance and protection, till they shall have acquired strength; and to send vessels at the same time to other parts of the world for an equal number of white inhabitants; to induce whom to migrate hither, proper encouragements were to be proposed. It will probably be asked, Why not retain and incorporate the blacks into the state, and thus save the expence of supplying by importation of white settlers, the vacancies they will leave? Deep rooted prejudices entertained by the whites; ten thousand recollections, by the blacks; of the injuries they have sustained; new provocations; the real distinctions which nature has made; and many other circumstances will divide us into parties, and produce convulsions, which will probably never end but in the extermination of the one or the other race.—To these objections, which are political, may be added others, which are physical and moral. The first difference which strikes us in that of colour. Whether the black of the negro resides in the reticular membrane between the skin and scarfskin, or in the scarfskin itself; whether it proceeds from the colour of the blood, the colour of the bile, or from that of some other secretion, the difference is fixed in nature, and is as real as if its seat and cause were better known to us. And is this difference of no importance? Is it not the foundation of a greater or less share of beauty in the two races? Are not the fine mixtures of red and white, the expressions of every passion by greater or less suffusions of colour in the one, preferable to that eternal monotony, which reigns in the countenances, that immovable veil of black which covers all the emotions of the other race? Add to these, flowing hair, a more elegant symmetry of form, their own judgment in favour of the whites, declared by their preference of them as uniformly as is the preference of the Oran ootan for the black woman over those of his own species. The circumstance of superior beauty, is thought worthy attention in the propagation of our horses, dogs, and other domestic animals; why not in that of man? Besides those of colour, figure, and hair, there are other physical distinctions proving a difference of race. They have less hair on the face and body. They secrete less by the kidnies, and more by the glands of the skin, which gives them a very strong and disagreeable odour. This greater degree of transpiration, renders them more tolerant of heat, and less so of cold than the whites. Perhaps too a difference of structure in the pulmonary apparatus, which a late ingenious experimentalist has discovered to be the principal regulator of animal heat, may have disabled them from extricating, in the act of inspiration, so much of that fluid from the outer air, or obliged them in expiration, to part with more of it. They seem to require less sleep. A black after hard labour through the day, will be induced by the slightest amusements to sit up till midnight or later, though knowing he must be out with the first dawn of the morning. They are at least as brave, and more adventuresome. But this may perhaps proceed from a want of forethought, which prevents their seeing a danger till it be present. When present, they do not go through it with more coolness or steadiness than the whites. They are more ardent after their female; but love seems with them to be more an eager desire, than a tender delicate mixture of sentiment and sensation. Their griefs are transient. Those numberless afflictions, which render it doubtful whether heaven has given life to us in mercy or in wrath, are less felt, and sooner forgotten with them. In general, their existence appears to participate more of sensation than reflection. To this must be ascribed their disposition to sleep when abstracted from their diversions, and unemployed in labour. An animal whose body is at rest, and who does not reflect, must be disposed to sleep of course.

Comparing them by their faculties of memory, reason, and imagination, it appears to me that in memory they are equal to the whites; in reason much inferior, as I think one could scarcely be found capable of tracing and comprehending the investigations of Euclid: and that in imagination they are dull, tasteless, and anomalous. It would be unfair to follow them to Africa for this investigation. We will consider them here, on the same stage with the whites, and where the facts are not apochryphal on which a judgment is to be formed. It will be right to make great allowances for the difference of condition, of education, of conversation, of the sphere in which they move. Many millions of them have been brought to, and born in America. Most of them, indeed, have been confined to tillage, to their own homes, and their own society: yet many have been so situated, that they might have availed themselves of the conversation of their masters; many have been brought up to the handicraft arts, and from that circumstance have always been associated with the whites. Some have been liberally educated, and all have lived in countries where the arts and sciences are cultivated to a considerable degree, and have had before their eyes samples of the best works from abroad. The Indians, with no advantages of this kind, will often carve figures on their pipes not destitute of design and merit. They will crayon out an animal, a plant, or a country, so as to prove the existence of a germ in their minds which only wants cultivation. They astonish you with strokes of the most sublime oratory; such as prove their reason and sentiment strong, their imagination glowing and elevated. But never yet could I find that a black had uttered a thought above the leval of plain narration; never seen even an elementary trait of painting or sculpture. In music they are more generally gifted than the whites, with accurate ears for tune and time, and they have been found capable of imagining a small catch.* Whether they will be equal to the composition of a more extensive run of melody, or of complicated harmony, is yet to be proved. Misery is often the parent of the most affecting touches in poetry.—Among the blacks is misery enough, God knows, but no poetry. Love is the peculiar œstrum of the poet. Their love is ardent, but it kindles the senses only, not the imagination. Religion, indeed, has pro-

* The instrument proper to them is the Banjar, which they brought hither from Africa, and which is the original of the guitar, its chords being precisely the four lower chords of the guitar.

duced a Phyllis Whately; but it could not produce a poet.[2] The compositions published under her name are below the dignity of criticism. The heroes of the Dunciad are to her, as Hercules to the author of that poem. Ignatius Sancoh has approached nearer to merit in composition; yet his letters do more honour to the heart than the head.[3] They breathe the purest effusions of friendship and general philanthropy, and show how great a degree of the latter may be compounded with strong religious zeal. He is often happy in the turn of his compliments, and his style is easy and familiar, except when he affects a Shandean fabrication of words. But his imagination is wild and extravagant, escapes incessantly from every restraint of reason and taste, and, in the course of its vagaries, leaves a tract of thought as incoherent and eccentric, as is the course of a meteor through the sky. His subjects should often have led him to a process of sober reasoning; yet we find him always substituting sentiment for demonstration. Upon the whole, though we admit him to the first place among those of his own color who have presented themselves to the public judgment, yet when we compare him with the writers of the race among whom he lived and particularly with the epistolary class in which he has taken his own stand, we are compelled to enrol him at the bottom of the column. This criticism supposes the letters published under his name to be genuine, and to have received amendment from no other hand; points which would not be of easy investigation. The improvement of the blacks in body and mind, in the first instance of their mixture with the whites, has been observed by every one, and proves that their inferiority is not the effect merely of their condition of life. We know that among the Romans, about the Augustan age especially, the condition of their slaves was much more deplorable than that of the blacks on the continent of America. The two sexes were confined in separate apartments, because to raise a child cost the master more than to buy one. Cato, for a very restricted indulgence to his slaves in this particular,* took from them a certain price. But in this country the slaves multiply as fast as the free inhabitants.

[2] Phyllis Wheatley was an eighteenth-century Negro poetess whose verse was highly religious and rather unoriginal.

[3] Ignatius Sancho (1729–1780) was a Negro writer born on a slave ship. His *Letters,* the style of which derives from Laurence Sterne, were published in 1782. The "Shandean fabrication of words" refers to Sterne's *Tristam Shandy.*

*Τους δουλους εταξεν ὡρισμενου νομισματος ὁμιλειν ταις θεραπαινισν.—Plutarch. Cato.

Their situation and manners place the commerce between the two sexes almost without restraint.—The same Cato, on a principle of economy, always sold his sick and superannuated slaves. He gives it as a standing precept to a master visiting his farm, to sell his old oxen, old waggons, old tools, old and diseased servants, and everything else become useless. 'Vendat boves vetulos, plaustrum vetus, feramenta vetera, servum senem, servum morbosum, si quid aliud supersit vendat.' Cato de re rusticâ, c. 2. The American slaves cannot enumerate this among the injuries and insults they receive. It was the common practice to expose in the island AEsculapius, in the Tyber, diseased slaves whose cure was like to become tedious.* The Emperor Claudius, by an edict, gave freedom to such of them as should recover, and first declared that if any person chose to kill rather than to expose them, it should be deemed homicide. The exposing them is a crime of which no instance has existed with us; and were it to be followed by death, it would be punished capitally. We are told of a certain Vedius Pollio, who, in the presence of Augustus, would have given a slave as food to his fish, for having broken a glass. With the Romans, the regular method of taking the evidence of their slaves was under torture. Here it has been thought better never to resort to their evidence. When a master was murdered, all his slaves, in the same house, or within hearing, were condemned to death. Here punishment falls on the guilty only, and as precise proof is required against him as against a freeman. Yet notwithstanding these and other discouraging circumstances among the Romans, their slaves were often their rarest artists. They excelled too in science, insomuch as to be usually employed as tutors to their master's children. Epictetus, Terence, and Phædrus, were slaves. But they were of the race of whites. It is not their condition then, but nature, which has produced the distinction.—Whether further observation will or will not verify the conjecture, that nature has been less bountiful to them in the endowments of the head, I believe that in those of the heart she will be found to have done them justice. That disposition to theft with which they have been branded, must be ascribed to their situation, and not to any depravity of the moral sense. The man in whose favour no laws of property exist, probably feels himself less bound to respect those made in favour of others. When arguing for ourselves, we lay it down as a fundamental, that laws,

* Suet. Claud. 25.

to be just, must give a reciprocation of right: that, without this, they are mere arbitrary rules of conduct, founded in force, and not in conscience; and it is a problem which I give to the master to solve, whether the religious precepts against the violation of property were not framed for him as well as his slave? And whether the slave may not as justifiably take a little from one who has taken all from him, as he may slay one who would slay him? That a change in the relations in which a man is placed should change his ideas of moral right and wrong, is neither new, nor peculiar to the colour of the blacks. Homer tells us it was so 2600 years ago.

> 'Ημισυ, γὰρ τ' ἀρετῆς ἀποαίνυται εὐρύοπα Ζεὺ
> 'Αφνερος, ευτ' ἂν μιν κατὰ δουλιον ἦμαρ ἕλησιν.
> —Od. 17, 323.

> Jove fix'd it certain, that whatever day
> Makes man a slave, takes half his worth away.

But the slaves of which Homer speaks were whites. Notwithstanding these considerations which must weaken their respect for the laws of property, we find among them numerous instances of the most rigid integrity, and as many as among their better instructed masters, of benevolence, gratitude, and unshaken fidelity. The opinion that they are inferior in the faculties of reason and imagination, must be hazarded with great diffidence. To justify a general conclusion, requires many observations, even where the subject may be submitted to the Anatomical knife, to Optical glasses, to analysis by fire or by solvents. How much more then where it is a faculty, not a substance, we are examining; where it eludes the research of all the senses; where the conditions of its existence are various and variously combined; where the effects of those which are present or absent bid defiance to calculation; let me add too, as a circumstance of great tenderness, where our conclusion would degrade a whole race of men from the rank in the scale of beings which their Creator may perhaps have given them. To our reproach it must be said, that though for a century and a half we have had under our eyes the races of black and of red men, they have never yet been viewed by us as subjects of natural history. I advance it, therefore, as a suspicion only, that the blacks, whether originally a distinct race, or made distinct by time and circumstances, are inferior to the whites in the endowments both of body and mind. It is not against experience to suppose that different species of the same genus, or varieties of the same species, may possess different qualifications. Will not a lover of natural history then, one who views the gradations in all the races of animals with the eye of philosophy, excuse an effort to keep those in the department of man as distinct as nature has formed them? This unfortunate difference of colour, and perhaps of faculty, is a powerful obstacle to the emancipation of these people. Many of their advocates, while they wish to vindicate the liberty of human nature, are anxious also to preserve its dignity and beauty. Some of these, embarrassed by the question, 'What further is to be done with them?' join themselves in opposition with those who are actuated by sordid avarice only. Among the Romans emancipation required but one effort. The slave, when made free, might mix with, without staining the blood of his master. But with us a second is necessary, unknown to history. When freed, he is to be removed beyond the reach of mixture.

The revised code further proposes to proportion crimes and punishments. This is attempted in the following scale.

I. Crimes whose punishment extends to *Life*.

1. High Treason.		Death by hanging. Forfeiture of lands and goods to the commonwealth.
2. Petty treason.		Death by hanging. Dissection. Forfeiture of half the lands and goods to the representatives of the party slain.
3. Murder.	1. By poison.	Death by poison. Forfeiture of one-half, as before.
	2. In duel.	Death by hanging. Gibbeting, if the challenger. Forfeiture of one-half as before, unless it be the party challenged, then the forfeiture is to the commonwealth.
	3. In any other way.	Death by hanging. Forfeiture of one-half as before.
4. Manslaughter.		The second offence is murder.

II. Crimes whose punishment goes to *Limb*.

1. Rape .... 2. Sodomy	Dismemberment.
3. Maiming ...... 4. Disfiguring	Retaliation, and the forfeiture of half of the land and goods to the sufferer.

III. Crimes punishable by *Labour*.

1. Manslaughter, 1st offence.	Labor VII. years for the public.	Forfeiture of half, as in murder.
2. Counterfeiting money.	Labor VI. years.	Forfeiture of lands and goods to the commonwealth.
3. Arson 4. Asportation of vessels.	Labor V. years.	Reparation threefold.
5. Robbery 6. Burglary.	Labor IV. years.	Reparation double.
7. House-breaking. 8. Horse-stealing.	Labor III. years.	Reparation.
9. Grand larceny.	Labor II. years.	Reparation. Pillory.
10. Petty larceny.	Labor I. year.	Reparation. Pillory.
11. Pretensions to witchcraft, &c.	Ducking.	Stripes.
12. Excusable homicide. 13. Suicide. 14. Apostacy. Heresy.	To be pitied, not punished.	

Pardon and privilege of clergy are proposed to be abolished; but if the verdict be against the defendant, the court in their discretion may allow a new trial. No attainder to cause a corruption of blood, or forfeiture of dower. Slaves guilty of offences punishable in others by labour, to be transported to Africa, or elsewhere, as the circumstances of the time admit, there to be continued in slavery. A rigorous regimen proposed for those condemned to labour.

Another object of the revisal is, to diffuse knowledge more generally through the mass of the people.[4] This bill proposes to lay off every country into small districts of five or six miles square, called hundreds and in each of them to establish a

[4] Jefferson's proposals for revising the educational system were never enacted. They were as far in advance of his own time as anything he ever conceived. His attempts to revise the constitution of William and Mary College, which he had attended from 1760 to 1762, along with his attempts to establish a public library, also failed.

school for teaching, reading, writing, and arithmetic. The tutor to be supported by the hundred, and every person in it entitled to send their children three years gratis, and as much longer as they please, paying for it. These schools to be under a visitor who is annually to chuse the boy of best genius in the school, of those whose parents are too poor to give them further education, and to send him forward to one of the grammar schools, of which twenty are proposed to be erected in different parts of the country, for teaching Greek, Latin, geography, and the higher branches of numerical arithmetic. Of the boys thus sent in any one year, trial is to be made at the grammar schools one or two years, and the best genius of the whole selected, and continued six years, and the residue dismissed. By this means twenty of the best geniuses will be raked from the rubbish annually, and be instructed, at the public expence, so far as the grammar schools go. At the end of six years instruction, one half are to be discontinued (from among whom the grammar schools will probably be supplied with future masters); and the other half, who are to be chosen for the superiority of their parts and disposition, are to be sent and continued three years in the study of such sciences as they shall chuse, at William and Mary college, the plan of which is proposed to be enlarged, as will be hereafter explained, and extended to all the useful sciences. The ultimate result of the whole scheme of education would be the teaching all the children of the State reading, writing, and common arithmetic; turning out ten annually, of superior genius, well taught in Greek, Latin, geography, and the higher branches of arithmetic; turning out ten others annually, of still superior parts, who, to those branches of learning, shall have added such of the sciences as their genius shall have them led to; the furnishing to the wealthier part of the people convenient schools at which their children may be educated at their own expence.—The general objects of this law are to provide an education adapted to the years, to the capacity, and the condition of every one, and directed to their freedom and happiness. Specific details were not proper for the law. These must be the business of the visitors entrusted with its execution. The first stage of this education being the schools of the hundreds, wherein the great mass of the people will receive their instruction, the principal foundations of future order will be laid here. Instead, therefore, of putting the Bible and Testament into the hands of the children at an age when their judgments are not sufficiently matured for religious inquiries, their memories may here be stored with the most useful facts from Grecian, Roman, European, and American history. The first elements of morality too may be instilled into their minds; such as, when further developed as their judgments advance in strength, may teach them how to work out their own greatest happiness, by shewing them that it does not depend on the condition of life in which chance has placed them, but is always the result of a good conscience, good health, occupation, and freedom in all just pursuits.—Those whom either the wealth of their parents or the adoption of the state shall destine to higher degrees of learning, will go on to the grammar schools, which constitute the next stage, there to be instructed in the languages. The learning Greek and Latin, I am told, is going into disuse in Europe. I know not what their manners and occupations may call for: but it would be very ill-judged in us to follow their example in this instance. There is a certain period of life, say from eight to fifteen or sixteen years of age, when the mind like the body is not yet firm enough for laborious and close operations. If applied to such, it falls an early victim to premature exertion; exhibiting, indeed, at first, in these young and tender subjects, the flattering appearance of their being men while they are yet children, but ending in reducing them to be children when they should be men. The memory is then most susceptible and tenacious of impressions; and the learning of languages being chiefly a work of memory, it seems precisely fitted to the powers of this period, which is long enough too for acquiring the most useful languages, antient and modern. I do not pretend that language is science. It is only an instrument for the attainment of science. But that time is not lost which is employed in providing tools for future operation: more especially as in this case the books put into the hands of the youth for this purpose may be such as will at the same time impress their minds with useful facts and good principles. If this period be suffered to pass in idleness, the mind becomes lethargic and impotent, as would the body it inhabits if unexercised during the same time. The sympathy between body and mind during their rise, progress and decline, is too strict and obvious to endanger our being misled while we reason from the one to the other.—As soon as they are of sufficient age, it is supposed they will be sent on from the grammar schools to the university, which constitutes our third and last stage, there to study those sciences which may be adapted to their views.—By that part of our plan which prescribes the selection of the youths of genius from among the classes of the poor, we hope to avail the state of those talents which nature has shown as liberally among the poor as the rich, but which perish without use, if not sought for and cultivated.—But of all the views of this law none is more important, none more legitimate, than that of rendering the people the safe, as they are the ultimate, guardians of their own liberty. For this purpose the reading in the first stage, where *they* will receive their whole education, is proposed, as has been said, to be chiefly historical. History, by apprising them of the past, will enable them to judge of the future; it will avail them of the experience of other times and other nations; it will qualify them as judges of the actions and designs of men; it will enable them to know ambition under every disguise it may assume; and knowing it, to defeat its views. In every government on earth is some trace of human weakness, some germ of corruption and degeneracy, which cunning will discover, and wickedness insensibly open, cultivate and improve. Every government degenerates when trusted to the rulers of the people alone. The people themselves therefore are its only safe depositories. And to render even them safe, their minds must be improved to a certain degree. This indeed is not all that is necessary, though it be essentially necessary. An amendment of our constitution must here come in aid of the public education. The influence over government must be shared among all the people. If every individual which composes their mass participates of the ultimate authority, the government will be safe; because the corrupting the whole mass will exceed any private resources of wealth; and public ones cannot be provided but by levies on the people. In this case every man would have to pay his own price. The government of Great Britain has been corrupted, because but one man in ten has a right to vote for members of parliament. The sellers of the government, therefore, get nine-tenths of their price clear. It has been thought that corruption is restrained by confining the right of suffrage to a few of the wealthier of the people: but it would be more effectually restrained by an extension of that right to such members as would bid defiance to the means of corruption.

Lastly, it is proposed, by a bill in this revisal, to begin a public library and gallery, by laying out a certain sum annually in books, paintings, and statues.

PART III

THE EMERGENCE OF THE NATION

The Philadelphia Convention, which, in Hamilton's words, was "to render the constitution of the Federal Government adequate to the exigencies of the Union," officially opened on May 25, 1787. Its purpose appeared vague enough to permit its functioning with the secrecy most of the delegates deemed necessary. The Convention had grown out of the Annapolis Convention of 1786, in which the representatives of five states, ostensibly summoned to discuss interstate commercial problems, called upon all states to convene a new convention at Philadelphia in May of the following year for the purpose of discussing both commercial matters and possible revision of the Articles of Confederation. Congress endorsed the plan, although with no great degree of enthusiasm and with the rather firm stipulation that the Convention was to assemble "for the sole and express purpose of revising the Articles of Confederation and reporting to Congress and the several legislatures such alterations and provisions therein."

The Philadelphia Convention, then, was called not to create a new constitution but to make certain suggestions as to how the already existing one could be changed for the better. The Articles of Confederation were sufficiently to the liking of most Americans, and, despite the veneration with which every American schoolboy is taught to look upon the Constitution, the Articles might have been better adapted to the problems that arose in certain periods of American history than the document composed in Philadelphia in 1787. It is conceivable that the government created by the Articles might have evolved into an efficient copy of the English parliamentary system; it is even more conceivable that such a government might be better able to handle the problems of our own time with far greater efficiency and skill than the government created by our present Constitution, with its highly praised but possibly outdated system of "checks and balances." But speculation on this point, however interesting, is basically fruitless, since it is only into what history has given us that we can rightfully inquire.

Ever since 1913, when Charles Beard's highly influential *An Economic Interpretation of the Constitution* was published, historians have disagreed as to how much the Constitution that was drafted in Philadelphia represented the triumph of American political principles and how much it represented the mercenary desires of the delegates, most of whom were holders of public securities. Beard's argument implied that the delegates who created the Constitution were primarily interested in the establishment of a government in which property would be "safer" than it had been under the Articles, and that most of the delegates were interested in the protection of private property because they were representatives of the wealthier classes who stood to gain most by a strong national government.[1] Regardless of whether Beard's thesis is or is not valid, the fact remains that the Constitution created a more conservative political atmosphere than had existed under the Articles of Confederation.

This is not to say that power was taken away from the people; no attempt was made to disfranchise the large numbers of the American electorate, nor was any attempt made to dictate to the states who was to have the right to vote. But the Framers of the Constitution were intent on creating a greater distance between the electorate and the government. While the Constitution provided for members of the House of Representatives to be directly elected by the people, Senators were to be chosen by state legislatures and the President was to be elected by "a Number of Electors, equal to the whole Number of Senators and Representatives to which the State may be entitled in Congress"; the judiciary was to be wholly independent of popular influence and control, the responsi-

[1] Beard's influence is apparent in the work of a number of American historians. Perhaps it is most apparent in two books by Merrill Jensen, *The Articles of Confederation: An Interpretation of the Social-Constitutional History of the American Revolution, 1774–1781*, and *The New Nation: A History of the United States During the Confederation, 1781–1789*. More recently, the Beard thesis has been decisively challenged, especially by Robert E. Brown in *Middle-Class Democracy and the Revolution in Massachusetts, 1691–1780* and *Charles Beard and the Constitution: A Critical Analysis of "An Economic Interpretation of the Constitution."* In *The Birth of the Republic, 1763–89*, Edmund S. Morgan asserts that the same patriotism which "led responsible Americans to invest in public securities in wartime . . . guided their efforts to revise the languishing nation which their money and blood had purchased." The money and blood, however, were not exclusively the money and blood of the Framers of the Constitution. The farmers and laborers who benefited from stay laws and the issuance of cheap paper money had, after all, fought in and supported the Revolution. Had they been eloquent enough, they might have argued that the money and blood were theirs.

bility of Congress alone. That the electoral college system did not work out as the delegates to the Convention had intended simply points to the course of American democratic development; to the men who created the Constitution, however, the electoral college was meant to prevent excessive popular control of government. Their commitment was essentially a republican commitment, and their chief problem, as they conceived of it, was to create a strong central government that would not be subject to the whims of mob rule. There were those delegates, Alexander Hamilton and John Dickinson were foremost among them, who so desired to remove government from the whims of the people that they conceived of a constitutional monarchy along with a Senate modeled on the English House of Lords as a proper form of government for the new nation. But most of the delegates, while they strongly distrusted "the leveling spirit" of democracy, approached the problems of creating a government from a decidedly republican vantage point which insisted that all power ultimately be derived from the people. "The people do not want virtue, but are the dupes of pretended patriots," said Elbridge Gerry to his fellow delegates, as he noted that the infant republic was suffering from an "excess of democracy." It was the responsibility of the delegates to create a government strong enough to maintain its independence from popular pressure.

That the Framers of the Constitution were adept at the art of political compromise is well known. But their ability to compromise was due to the fact that they shared certain fundamental assumptions about the nature of government. On the third day of the Convention, when Edmund Randolph presented a series of resolutions drafted by James Madison, the heart of what was to emerge three and a half months later as the Constitution of the United States of America was already apparent. While there was a great deal of opposition to the Virginia Plan, as the resolutions came to be known, the opposition was almost invariably on specific details rather than on the kind of government the plan conceived of. The New Jersey Plan, presented by William Paterson as a counter to the Virginia Plan, was overwhelmingly rejected by the delegates because, by erecting a national government which was exclusively under the control of Congress, it incorporated many of the weaknesses of the government under the Articles of Confederation. The New Jersey Plan would have given greater voice in the new government to the small states than what they were granted in the Virginia Plan. The small states desired representation by state, but the large states desired representation by population. The conflict over representation led to the most significant of the Convention's compromises, representation by states in the Senate and by population in the House of Representatives. The compromise was a victory for the small states, for it gave them equality in one branch of the legislature. After this "great compromise," the work of the Convention was relatively simple and clear-cut. The only other issue which created a serious political division was the question of slavery, and this was solved by the adoption of the "three fifths clause," which specified that Negro slaves were to be counted as "three fifths of all other Persons" as far as representation and taxation were concerned. Congress was also prevented from interfering with the importation of slaves into the country before 1808, although it was granted the power to impose a tax of not more than ten dollars per imported slave until that time.

But the greatest victory of the delegates to the Constitutional Convention was that they forced a nation which was largely opposed to the Constitution to accept it. No other feat of the Framers of the Constitution seems so impressive today as their ability to unite behind it and persuade the nation that its ratification was the greatest single guarantee of American longevity. To achieve this in the face of a generally hostile, suspicious population was no minor accomplishment. Their political skill and intellectual persuasiveness is most in evidence here. In state after state, sometimes employing such questionable tactics as physically forcing members of a state legislature to be present at a quorum, the advocates of the Constitution managed to override the objections of its opponents and to clear the way for its rapid adoption. On September 28, 1787, Congress called upon the state legislatures to submit the proposed Constitution to special ratifying conventions. The speed with which ratification was accomplished was amazing. Before the year's end, Delaware, Pennsylvania, and New Jersey had ratified it; early in January of 1788, Georgia and Connecticut ratified it; Massachusetts, in which anti-Federalist strength was estimated to be greater than that of the Federalists, assented to the new constitution along with nine proposed amendments early in February; Maryland, South Carolina, and New Hampshire followed in that order; Virginia and New York, where anti-Federalist sentiment had been high, both ratified the new constitution by the summer of 1788. In their ratifying conventions, five states had suggested that the Constitution be immediately amended, and the first Congress to serve under the new government soon submitted twelve proposed amendments to the states, ten of which were eventually adopted as the Bill of Rights. The Constitution was then accepted by North Carolina and Rhode Island (the one state which had not sent delegates to the Constitutional Convention and which had tested the proposed constitution's popularity with a public referendum in which ratification was overwhelmingly defeated by 2,945 votes to 237 votes), and the thirteen original colonies had entered into their "more perfect Union."

On April 30, 1789, George Washington was sworn in as the first President of the United States of America, twenty-five years after the passage of the Sugar Act had set into motion a series of events from which was to emerge a nation as powerful and as independent as any ever known in the Old or New Worlds.

RICHARD HENRY LEE It was Richard Henry Lee who introduced the resolution calling for a declaration of independence in the Second Continental Congress. It was also Lee who helped persuade Virginia to cede its western lands to the national government, a move which forced Maryland to ratify the Articles of Confederation in 1781. As a man who had served as President of Congress (1784–85), Lee was a natural choice to be named a delegate to the Constitutional Convention. That he declined is an indication of the strength of his opposition to the proposed Constitution. Lee's argument against the Constitution was not so much for what was contained in it as for what had been left out of it. One of the more radical of the Fathers, he opposed the Constitution on the grounds that it denied certain essential republican rights to the people and was far too restrictive as far as its legislative construction was concerned. Many of his objections were met by the addition of the First Ten Amendments to the Constitution, the Bill of Rights, which made the Constitution a more liberal document than some of its Framers had intended.

Text: Paul Leicester Ford, ed., *Pamphlets on the Constitution of the United States, 1787–88*. Brooklyn, 1888.

Letters from the Federal Farmer to the Republican (1787)

LETTER I.

OCTOBER 8th, 1787.

DEAR SIR,

My letters to you last winter, on the subject of a well balanced national government for the United States, were the result of a free enquiry; when I passed from the subject to enquiries relative to our commerce, revenues, past administration, &c. I anticipated the anxieties I feel, on carefully examining the plan of government proposed by the convention. It appears to be a plan retaining some federal features; but to be the first important step, and to aim strongly at one consolidated government of the United States. It leaves the powers of government, and the representation of the people, so unnaturally divided between the general and state governments, that the operations of our system must be very uncertain. My uniform federal attachments, and the interest I have in the protection of property, and a steady execution of the laws, will convince you, that, if I am under any bias at all, it is in favor of any general system which shall promise those advantages. The instability of our laws increases my wishes for firm and steady government; but then, I can consent to no government, which, in my opinion, is not calculated equally to preserve the rights of all orders of men in the community. My object has been to join with those who have endeavoured to supply the defects in the forms of our governments by a steady and proper administration of them. Though I have long apprehended that fraudulent debtors, and embarrassed men, on the one hand, and men, on the other, unfriendly to republican equality, would produce an uneasiness among the people and prepare the way, not for cool and deliberate reforms in the governments, but for changes calculated to promote the interests of particular orders of men. Acquit me, sir, of any agency in the formation of the new system; I shall be satisfied with seeing, if it shall be adopted with a prudent administration. Indeed I am so much convinced of the truth of Pope's maxim, that "That which is best administered is best," that I am much inclined to subscribe to it from experience. I am not disposed to unreasonably contend about forms. I know our situation is critical, and it behoves us to make the best of it. A federal government of some sort is necessary. We have suffered the present to languish; and whether the confederation was capable or not originally of answering any valuable purposes, it is now but of little importance. I will pass by the men, and states, who have been particularly instrumental in preparing the way for a change, and perhaps, for governments not very favourable to the people at large. A constitution is now presented which we may reject, or which we may accept with or without amendments, and to which point we ought to direct our exertions is the question. To determine this question with propriety; we must attentively examine the system itself, and the probable consequences of either step. This I shall endeavour to do, so far as I am able, with candor and fairness; and leave you to decide upon the propriety of my opinions, the weight of my reasons, and how far my conclusions are well drawn. Whatever may be the conduct of others, on the present occasion, I do not mean hastily and positively to decide on the merits of the constitution proposed. I shall be open to conviction and always disposed to adopt that which, all things considered, shall appear to me to be most for the happiness of the community. It must be granted, that if men hastily and blindly adopt a system of government, they will as hastily and as blindly be led to alter or abolish it; and changes must ensue, one after another, till the peaceable and better part of the community will grow weary with changes, tumults and disorders, and be disposed to accept any government however despotic, that shall promise stability and firmness.

The first principal question that occurs, is, Whether, considering our situation, we ought to precipitate the adoption of the proposed constitution? If we remain cool and temperate, we are in no immediate danger of any commotions; we are in a state of perfect peace, and in no danger of invasions; the state governments are in the full exercise of their powers; and our governments answer all present exigencies, except the regulation of trade, securing credit, in some cases, and providing for the interest, in some instances, of the public debts; and whether we adopt a change three or nine months hence, can make but little odds with the private circumstances of individuals; their happiness and prosperity, after all, depend principally upon their own exertions. We are hardly recovered from a long and distressing war: The farmers, fishmen. &c. have not fully repaired the waste made by it. Industry and frugality are again assuming their proper station. Private debts are lessened, and public debts incurred by the war have been, by various ways, diminished; and the public lands have now become a productive source for diminishing them much more. I know uneasy men, who with very much to precipitate, do not admit all these facts; but they are facts well known to all men who are thoroughly informed in the affairs of this country. It must, however, be admitted, that our federal system is defective, and that some of the state governments are not well administered; but, then, we impute to the defects in our governments many evils and embarrassments which are most clearly the result of the late war. We must allow men to conduct on the present occasion, as on all similar one's. They will urge a thousand pretences to answer their purposes on both sides. When we want a man to change his condition, we describe it as wretched, miserable, and despised; and draw a pleasing picture of that which we would have him assume. And when we wish the contrary, we reverse our descriptions. Whenever a clamor is raised, and idle men get to work, it is highly necessary to examine facts carefully, and without unreasonably suspecting men of falsehood, to examine, and enquire attentively, under what impressions they act. It is too often the case in political concerns that men state facts not as they are, but as they wish them to be; and almost every man, by calling to mind past scenes, will find this to be true.

Nothing but the passions of ambitious, impatient, or disorderly men, I conceive, will plunge us into commotions, if time should be taken fully to examine and consider the system proposed. Men who feel easy in their circumstances, and such as are not sanguine in their expectations relative to the consequences of the proposed change, will remain quiet under the existing governments. Many commercial and monied men, who are uneasy, not without just cause, ought to be respected; and by no means, unreasonably disappointed in their expectations and hopes; but as to those who expect employments under the new constitution; as to those weak and ardent men who always expect to be gainers by revolutions, and whose lot it generally is to get out of one difficulty into another, they are very little to be regarded; and as to those who designedly avail themselves of this weakness and ardor, they are to be despised. It is natural for men, who wish to hasten the adoption of a measure, to tell us, now is the crisis —now is the critical moment which must be seized or all will be lost; and to shut the door against free enquiry, whenever conscious the thing presented has defects in it, which time and investigation will probably discover. This has been the custom of tyrants, and their dependants in all ages. If it is true, what has been so often said, that the people of this country cannot change their condition for the worse, I presume it still behoves them to endeavour deliberately to change it for the better. The fickle and ardent, in any community are the proper tools for establishing despotic government. But it is deliberate and thinking men, who must establish and secure governments on free principles. Before they decide on the plan proposed, they will enquire whether it will probably be a blessing or a curse to this people.

The present moment discovers a new face in our affairs. Our object has been all along, to reform our federal system, and to strengthen our governments—to establish peace, order and justice in the community—but a new object now presents. The plan of government now proposed is evidently calculated totally to change, in time, our condition as a people. Instead of being thirteen republics, under a federal head, it is clearly designed to make us one consolidated government. Of this, I think, I shall fully convince you, in my following letters on this subject. This consolidation of the states has been the object of several men in this country for some time past. Whether such a change can ever be effected, in any manner; whether it can be effected without convulsions and civil wars; whether such a change will not totally destroy the liberties of this country—time only can determine.

To have a just idea of the government before us, and to shew that a consolidated one is the object in view, it is necessary not only to examine the plan, but also its history, and the politics of its particular friends.

The confederation was formed when great confidence was placed in the voluntary exertions of individuals, and of the respective states; and the framers of it, to guard against usurpation, so limited, and checked the powers, that, in many respects, they are inadequate to the exigencies of the union. We find, therefore, members of congress urging alterations in the federal system almost as soon as it was adopted. It was early proposed to vest congress with powers to levy an impost, to regulate trade, &c. but such was known to be the caution of the states in parting with power, that the vestment even of these, was proposed to be under several checks and limitations. During the war, the general confusion, and the introduction of paper money, infused in the minds of people vague ideas respecting government and credit. We expected too much from the return of peace, and of course we have been disappointed. Our governments have been new and unsettled; and several legislatures, by making tender, suspension, and paper money laws, have given just cause of uneasiness to creditors. By these and other causes, several orders of men in the community have been prepared, by degrees, for a change of government; and this very abuse of power in the legislatures, which in some cases has been charged upon the democratic part of the community, has furnished aristocratical men with those very weapons, and those very means, with which, in great measure, they are rapidly effecting their favourite object. And should an oppressive government be the consequence of the proposed change, prosperity may reproach not only a few overbearing, unprincipled men, but those parties in the states which have misused their powers.

The conduct of several legislatures, touching paper money, and tender laws, has prepared many honest men for changes in government, which otherwise they would not have thought of

—when by the evils, on the one hand, and by the secret instigations of artful men, on the other, the minds of men were become sufficiently uneasy, a bold step was taken, which is usually followed by a revolution, or a civil war. A general convention for mere commercial purposes was moved for—the authors of this measure saw that the people's attention was turned solely to the amendment of the federal system; and that, had the idea of a total change been started, probably no state would have appointed members to the convention. The idea of destroying ultimately, the state government, and forming one consolidated system, could not have been admitted —a convention, therefore, merely for vesting in congress power to regulate trade was proposed. This was pleasing to the commercial towns; and the landed people had little or no concern about it. September, 1786, a few men from the middle states met at Annapolis, and hastily proposed a convention to be held in May, 1787, for the purpose, generally, of amending the confederation——this was done before the delegates of Massachusetts, and of the other states arrived[1]——still not a word was said about destroying the old constitution, and making a new one—The states still unsuspecting, and not aware that they were passing the Rubicon, appointed members to the new convention, for the sole and express purpose of revising and amending the confederation——and, probably, not one man in ten thousand in the United States, till within these ten or twelve days, had an idea that the old ship was to be destroyed, and he put to the alternative of embarking in the new ship presented, or of being left in danger of sinking—The States, I believe, universally supposed the convention would report alterations in the confederation, which would pass an examination in congress, and after being agreed to there, would be confirmed by all the legislatures, or be rejected. Virginia made a very respectable appointment, and placed at the head of it the first man in America.[2] In this appointment there was a mixture of political characters; but Pennsylvania appointed principally those men who were esteemed aristocratical. Here the favourite moment for changing the government was evidently discerned by a few men, who seized it with ad-

[1] The Annapolis Convention was sponsored by Virginia. Georgia, South Carolina, Connecticut; strangely enough, Maryland did not name delegates to represent it at the Convention, while the delegates from Massachusetts, New Hampshire, Rhode Island, and North Carolina failed to reach Annapolis in time to attend. Thus, the Constitutional Convention that met at Philadelphia the following year was called by the delegates of five states—New York, New Jersey, Pennsylvania, Delaware, and Virginia.

[2] George Washington was President of the Convention.

dress. Ten other states appointed, and tho' they chose men principally connected with commerce and the judicial department yet they appointed many good republican characters—had they all attended we should now see, I am persuaded, a better system presented. The non-attendance of eight or nine men, who were appointed members of the convention, I shall ever consider as a very unfortunate event to the United States.——Had they attended, I am pretty clear that the result of the convention would not have had that strong tendency to aristocracy now discernable in every part of the plan. There would not have been so great an accumulation of powers, especially as to the internal police of this country in a few hands as the constitution reported proposes to vest in them—the young visionary men, and the consolidating aristocracy, would have been more restrained than they have been. Eleven states met in the convention, and after four months close attention presented the new constitution, to be adopted or rejected by the people.[3] The uneasy and fickle part of the community may be prepared to receive any form of government; but I presume the enlightened and substantial part will give any constitution presented for their adoption a candid and thorough examination; and silence those designing or empty men, who weakly and rashly attempt to precipitate the adoption of a system of so much importance—We shall view the convention with proper respect——and, at the same time, that we reflect there were men of abilities and integrity in it, we must recollect how disproportionately the democratic and aristocratic parts of the community were represented——Perhaps the judicious friends and opposers of the new constitution will agree, that it is best to let it rely solely on its own merits, or be condemned for its own defects.

In the first place, I shall premise, that the plan proposed is a plan of accommodation—and that it is in this way only, and by giving up a part of our opinions, that we can ever expect to obtain a government founded in freedom and compact. This circumstance candid men will always keep in view, in the discussion of this subject.

The plan proposed appears to be partly federal, but principally however, calculated ultimately to make the states one consolidated government.

The first interesting question, therefore suggested, is, how

[3] Twelve states met in the Constitutional Convention. The delegates from New Hampshire did not arrive until the Convention was two months old. Only Rhode Island ignored it.

far the states can be consolidated into one entire government on free principles. In considering this question extensive objects are to be taken into view, and important changes in the forms of government to be carefully attended to in all their consequences. The happiness of the people at large must be the great object with every honest statesman, and he will direct every movement to this point. If we are so situated as a people, as not to be able to enjoy equal happiness and advantages under one government, the consolidation of the states cannot be admitted.

There are three different forms of free government under which the United States may exist as one nation; and now is, perhaps, the time to determine to which we will direct our views. 1. Distinct republics connected under a federal head. In this case the respective state governments must be the principal guardians of the peoples rights, and exclusively regulate their internal police; in them must rest the balance of government. The congress of the states, or federal head, must consist of delegates amenable to, and removable by the respective states: The congress must have general directing powers; powers to require men and monies of the states; to make treaties; peace and war; to direct the operations of armies, &c. Under this federal modification of government, the powers of congress would be rather advisary or recommendatory than coercive. 2. We may do away the federal state governments, and form or consolidate all the states into one entire government, with one executive, one judiciary, and one legislature, consisting of senators and representatives collected from all parts of the union: In this case there would be a compleat consolidation of the states. 3. We may consolidate the states as to certain national objects, and leave them severally distinct independent republics, as to internal police generally. Let the general government consist of an executive, a judiciary, and balanced legislature, and its powers extend exclusively to all foreign concerns, causes arising on the seas to commerce, imports, armies, navies, Indian affairs, peace and war, and to a few internal concerns of the community; to the coin, post-offices, weights and measures, a general plan for the militia, to naturalization, *and, perhaps to bankruptcies,* leaving the internal police of the community, in other respects, exclusively to the state governments; as the administration of justice in all causes arising internally, the laying and collecting of internal taxes, and the forming of the militia according to a general plan prescribed. In this case there would be a compleat consolidation, *quoad* certain objects only.

Touching the first, or federal plan, I do not think much can be said in its favor: The sovereignity of the nation, without coercive and efficient powers to collect the strength of it, cannot always be depended on to answer the purposes of government; and in a congress of representatives of foreign states, there must necessarily be an unreasonable mixture of powers in the same hands.

As to the second, or compleat consolidating plan, it deserves to be carefully considered at this time by every American: If it be impracticable, it is a fatal error to model our governments, directing our views ultimately to it.

The third plan, or partial consolidation, is, in my opinion, the only one that can secure the freedom and happiness of this people. I once had some general ideas that the second plan was practicable, but from long attention, and the proceedings of the convention, I am fully satisfied, that this third plan is the only one we can with safety and propriety proceed upon. Making this the standard to point out, with candor and fairness, the parts of the new constitution which appear to be improper, is my object. The convention appears to have proposed the partial consolidation evidently with a view to collect all powers ultimately, in the United States into one entire government; and from its views in this respect, and from the tenacity of the small states to have an equal vote in the senate, probably originated the greatest defects in the proposed plan.

Independent of the opinions of many great authors, that a free elective government cannot be extended over large territories, a few reflections must evince, that one government and general legislation alone never can extend equal benefits to all parts of the United States: Different laws, customs, and opinions exist in the different states, which by a uniform system of laws would be unreasonably invaded. The United States contain about a million of square miles, and in half a century will, probably, contain ten millions of people; and from the center to the extremes is about 800 miles.

Before we do away the state governments or adopt measures that will tend to abolish them, and to consolidate the states into one entire government several principles should be considered and facts ascertained:——These, and my examination into the essential parts of the proposed plan, I shall pursue in my next.

Your's, &c.

THE FEDERAL FARMER.

LETTER II.

OCTOBER 9, 1787.

DEAR SIR,

The essential parts of a free and good government are a full and equal representation of the people in the legislature, and the jury trial of the vicinage in the administration of justice—a full and equal representation, is that which possesses the same interests, feelings, opinions, and views the people themselves would were they all assembled—a fair representation, therefore, should be so regulated, that every order of men in the community, according to the common course of elections, can have a share in it—in order to allow professional men, merchants, traders, farmers, mechanics, &c. to bring a just proportion of their best informed men respectively into the legislature, the representation must be considerably numerous—We have about 200 state senators in the United States. and a less number than that of federal representatives cannot, clearly, be a full representation of this people, in the affairs of internal taxation and police, were there but one legislature for the whole union. The representation cannot be equal, or the situation of the people proper for one government only—if the extreme parts of the society cannot be represented as fully as the central—It is apparently impracticable that this should be the case in this extensive country——it would be impossible to collect a representation of the parts of the country five, six, and seven hundred miles from the seat of government.

Under one general government alone, there could be but one judiciary, one supreme and a proper number of inferior courts. I think it would be totally impracticable in this case to preserve a due administration of justice, and the real benefits of the jury trial of the vicinage——there are now supreme courts in each state in the union, and a great number of county and other courts subordinate to each supreme court——most of these supreme and inferior courts are itinerant, and hold their sessions in different parts every year of their respective states, counties and districts—with all these moving courts, our citizens, from the vast extent of the country, must travel very considerable distances from home to find the place where justice is administered. I am not for bringing justice so near to individuals as to afford them any temptation to engage in law suits; though I think it one of the greatest benefits in a good government, that each citizen should find a court of justice within a reasonable distance, perhaps, within a day's travel of his home; so that, without great inconveniences and enormous expense, he may have the advantages of his witnesses and jury—it would be impracticable to derive these advantages from one judiciary——the one supreme court at most could only set in the centre of the union, and move once a year into the centre of the eastern and southern extremes of it—and, in this case, each citizen, on an average, would travel 150 to 200 miles to find this court——that, however, inferior courts might be properly placed in the different counties, and districts of the union, the appellate jurisdiction would be intolerable and expensive.

If it were possible to consolidate the states, and preserve the features of a free government, still it is evident that the middle states, the parts of the union, about the seat of government, would enjoy great advantages, while the remote states would experience the many inconveniences of remote provinces. Wealth, offices, and the benefits of government would collect in the centre: and the extreme states; and their principal towns, become much less important.

There are other considerations which tend to prove that the idea of one consolidated whole, on free principles, is ill-founded—the laws of a free government rest on the confidence of the people, and operate gently—and never can extend the influence very far——if they are executed on free principles, about the centre, where the benefits of the government induce the people to support it voluntarily; yet they must be executed on the principles of fear and force in the extremes——This has been the case with every extensive republic of which we have any accurate account.

There are certain unalienable and fundamental rights, which in forming the social compact, ought to be explicitly ascertained and fixed—a free and enlightened people, in forming this compact, will not resign all their rights to those who govern, and they will fix limits to their legislators and rulers, which will soon be plainly seen by those who are governed, as well as by those who govern: and the latter will know they cannot be passed unperceived by the former, and without giving a general alarm——These rights should be made the basis of every constitution; and if a people be so situated, or have such different opinions that they cannot agree in ascertaining and fixing them, it is a very strong argument against their attempting to form one entire society, to live under one system of laws only.——I confess, I never thought the people of these states differed essentially in these respects; they having derived all these rights from one common source, the British systems; and having in the formation of their state constitutions, discovered that their ideas relative to these rights are very similar. However, it is now said that the states differ so essentially in these respects, and even in the important article of the trial by jury, that when assembled in convention, they can agree to no words by which to establish that trial, or by which to ascertain and establish many other of these rights, as fundamental articles in the social compact. If so, we proceed to consolidate the states on no solid basis whatever.

But I do not pay much regard to the reasons given for not bottoming the new constitution on a better bill of rights. I still believe a complete federal bill of rights to be very practicable. Nevertheless I acknowledge the proceedings of the convention furnish my mind with many new and strong reasons, against a complete consolidation of the states. They tend to convince me, that it cannot be carried with propriety very far—that the convention have gone much farther in one respect than they found it practicable to go in another; that is, they propose to lodge in the general government very extensive powers—*powers* nearly, if not altogether, complete and unlimited, over the purse and the sword. But, in its organization, they furnish the strongest proof that the proper limbs, or parts of a government, to support and execute those powers on proper principles (or in which they can be safely lodged) cannot be formed. These powers must be lodged somewhere in every society; but then they should be lodged where the strength and guardians of the people are collected. They can be wielded, or safely used, in a free country only by an able executive and judiciary, a respectable senate, and a secure, full, and equal representation of the people. I think the principles I have premised or brought into view, are well founded—I think they will not be denied by any fair reasoner. It is in connection with these, and other solid principles, we are to examine the constitution. It is not a few democratic phrases, or a few well formed features, that will prove its merits; or a few small omissions that will produce its rejection among men of sense; they will enquire what are the essential powers in a community, and what are nominal ones; where and how the essential powers shall be lodged to secure government, and to secure true liberty.

In examining the proposed constitution carefully, we must clearly perceive an unnatural separation of these powers from the substantial representation of the people. The state government will exist, with all their governors, senators, representatives, officers and expences; in these will be nineteen twentieths of the representatives of the people; they will have a near connection, and their members an immediate intercourse with the people; and the probability is, that the state governments will possess the confidence of the people, and be considered generally as their immediate guardians.

The general government will consist of a new species of executive, a small senate, and a very small house of representatives. As many citizens will be more than three hundred miles from the seat of this government as will be nearer to it, its judges and officers cannot be very numerous, without making our governments very expensive. Thus will stand the state and the general governments, should the constitution be adopted without any alterations in their organization; but as to powers, the general government will possess all essential ones, at least on paper, and those of the states a mere shadow of power. And therefore, unless the people shall make some great exertions to restore to the state governments their powers in matters of internal police; as the powers to lay and collect, exclusively, internal taxes, to govern the militia, and to hold the decisions of their own judicial courts upon their own laws final, the balance cannot possibly continue long; but the state governments must be annihilated, or continue to exist for no purpose.

It is however to be observed, that many of the essential powers given the national government are not exclusively given; and the general government may have prudence enough to forbear the exercise of those which may still be exercised by the respective states. But this cannot justify the impropriety of giving powers, the exercise of which prudent men will not attempt, and imprudent men will, or probably can, exercise only in a manner destructive of free government. The general government, organized as it is, may be adequate to many valuable objects, and be able to carry its laws into execution on proper principles in several cases; but I think its warmest friends will not contend, that it can carry all the powers proposed to be lodged in it into effect, without calling to its aid a military force, which must very soon destroy all elective governments in the country, produce anarchy, or establish despotism. Though we cannot have now a complete idea of what will be the operations of the proposed system, we may, allowing things to have their common course, have a very tolerable one. The powers lodged in the general government, if exercised by it, must intimately effect the internal police of the states, as well as external concerns; and there is no reason to expect the numerous state governments, and their connections, will be very friendly to the execution of federal laws in those internal affairs, which hitherto have been under their own immediate management. There is more reason to believe, that the general government, far removed from the people, and none of its members elected oftener than once in two years, will be forgot or neglected, and its laws in many cases disregarded, unless a multitude of officers and military force be continually kept in view, and employed to enforce the execution of the laws, and to make the government feared and respected. No position can be truer than this. That in this country either neglected laws, or a military execution of them, must lead to a revolution, and to the destruction of freedom. Neglected laws must first lead to anarchy and confusion; and a military execution of laws is only a shorter way to the same point—despotic government.

Your's, &c.

THE FEDERAL FARMER.

LETTER III.

OCTOBER 10th, 1787.

DEAR SIR,

The great object of a free people must be so to form their government and laws, and so to administer them, as to create a confidence in, and respect for the laws; and thereby induce the sensible and virtuous part of the community to declare in favor of the laws, and to support them without an expensive military force. I wish, though I confess I have not much hope, that this may be the case with the laws of congress under the new constitution. I am fully convinced that we must organize the national government on different principals, and make the parts of it more efficient, and secure in it more effectually the different interests in the community; or else leave in the state governments some powers proposed to be lodged in it—at least till such an organization shall be found to be practicable. Not sanguine in my expectations of a good federal administration, and satisfied, as I am, of the impracticability of consolidating the states, and at the same time of preserving the rights of the people at large, I believe we ought still to leave some of those powers in the state governments, in which the people, in fact, will still be represented—to define some other powers proposed to be vested in the general government, more carefully, and to establish a few principles to secure a proper exercise of the powers given it. It is not my object to multiply objections, or to contend about inconsiderable powers or amendments. I wish the system adopted with a few alterations; but those, in my mind, are essential ones; if adopted without, every good citizen will acquiesce, though I shall consider the duration of our governments, and the liberties of this people, very much dependant on the administration of the general government. A wise and honest administration, may make the people happy under any government; but necessity only can justify even our leaving open avenues to the abuse of power, by wicked, unthinking, or ambitious men, I will examine, first, the organization of the proposed government, in order to judge; 2d, with propriety, what powers are improperly, at least prematurely lodged in it. I shall examine, 3d, the undefined powers; and 4th, those powers, the exercise of which is not secured on safe and proper ground.

First. As to the organization——the house of representatives, the democrative branch, as it is called, is to consist of 65 members: that is, about one representative for fifty thousand inhabitants, to be chosen biennially——the federal legislature may increase this number to one for each thirty thousand inhabitants, abating fractional numbers in each state.——Thirty-three representatives will make a quorum for doing business, and a majority of those present determine the sense of the house.——I have no idea that the interests, feelings, and opinions of three or four millions of people, especially touching internal taxation, can be collected in such a house.——In the nature of things, nine times in ten, men of the elevated classes in the community only can be chosen——Connecticut, for instance, will have five representatives——not one man in a hundred of those who form the democrative branch in the state legislature, will, on a fair computation, be one of the five.—The people of this country, in one sense, may all be democratic; but if we make the proper distinction between the few men of wealth and abilities, and consider them, as we ought, as the natural aristocracy of the country, and the great body of the people, the middle and lower classes, as the democracy, this federal representative branch will have but very little democracy in it, even this small representation is not secured on proper principles.——The branches of the legislature are essential parts of the fundamental compact, and ought to be so fixed by the people, that the legislature cannot alter itself by modifying the elections of its own members. This, by a part of Art. I, Sect. 4, the general legislature may do, it may evidently so regulate elections as to secure the choice of any particular description of men.——It may make the whole state one district—make the capital, or any places in the state, the place or places of election—it may declare that the five men (or whatever the number may be the state may chuse) who shall have the most votes shall be considered as chosen. ——In this case it is easy to perceive how the people who live scattered in the inland towns will bestow their votes on different men—and how a few men in a city, in any order or profession, may unite and place any five men they please highest among those that may be voted for——and all this may be done constitutionally, and by those silent operations, which are not immediately perceived by the people in general. ——I know it is urged, that the general legislature will be disposed to regulate elections on fair and just principles:——This may be true—good men will generally govern well with almost any constitution: but why in laying the foundation of the social system, need we unnecessarily leave a door open to improper regulations?—This is a very general and unguarded clause, and many evils may flow from that part which authorises the congress to regulate elections.——Were it omitted, the regulations of elections would be solely in the respective states, where the people are substantially represented; and where the elections ought to be regulated, otherwise to secure a representation from all parts of the community, in making the constitutions, we ought to provide for dividing each state into a proper number of districts, and for confining the electors in each district to the choice of some men, who shall have a permanent interest and residence in it; and also for this essential object, that the representative elected shall have a majority of the votes of those electors who shall attend and give their votes.

In considering the practicability of having a full and equal representation of the people from all parts of the union, not only distances and different opinions, customs and views, common in extensive tracts of country, are to be taken into view, but many differences peculiar to Eastern, Middle, and Southern States. These differences are not so perceivable among the members of congress, and men of general information in the states, as among the men who would properly form the democratic branch. The Eastern states are very democratic, and composed chiefly of moderate freeholders; they have but few rich men and no slaves; the Southern states are composed chiefly of rich planters and slaves; they have but few moderate freeholders, and the prevailing influence, in them is generally a dissipated aristocracy: The Middle states partake partly of the Eastern and partly of the Southern character.

Perhaps, nothing could be more disjointed, unwieldy and incompetent to doing business with harmony and dispatch, than a federal house of representatives properly numerous for the great objects of taxation, &c. collected from the federal states; whether such men would ever act in concert; whether they would not worry along a few years, and then be the means of separating the parts of the union, is very problematical?——View this system in whatever form we can, propriety brings us still to this point, a federal government possessed of general and complete powers, as to those national objects which cannot well come under the cognizance of the internal laws of the respective states, and this federal government, accordingly, consisting of branches not very numerous.

The house of representatives is on the plan of consolidation, but the senate is entirely on the federal plan; and Delaware will have as much constitutional influence in the senate, as the largest state in the union: and in this senate are lodged legislative, executive and judicial powers: Ten states in this union urge that they are small states, nine of which were present in the convention.—They were interested in collecting large powers into the hands of the senate, in which each state still will have its equal share of power. I suppose it was impracticable for the three large states, as they were called, to get the senate formed on any other principles: But this only proves, that we cannot form one general government on equal and just principles—and proves, that we ought not to lodge in it such extensive powers before we are convinced of the practicability of organizing it on just and equal principles. The senate will consist of two members from each state, chosen by the state legislatures, every sixth year. The clause referred to, respecting the elections of representatives, empowers the general legislature to regulate the elections of senators also, "except as to the places of chusing senators."—There is, therefore, but little more security in the elections than in those of representatives: Fourteen senators make a quorum for business, and a majority of the senators present give the vote of the senate, except in giving judgment upon an impeachment, or in making treaties, or in expelling a member, when two-thirds of the senators present must agree—The members of the legislature are not excluded from being elected to any military offices, or any civil offices, except those created, or the emoluments of which shall be increased by themselves: two-thirds of the members present, of either house, may expel a member at pleasure. The senate is an independant branch of the legislature, a court for trying impeachments, and also a part of the executive, having a negative in the making of all treaties, and in appointing almost all officers.

The vice president is not a very important, if not an unnecessary part of the system—he may be a part of the senate at one period, and act as the supreme executive magistrate at another——The election of this officer, as well as of the president of the United States seems to be properly secured; but when we examine the powers of the president, and the forms of the executive, we shall perceive that the general government, in this part, will have a strong tendency to aristocracy, or the government of the few. The executive is, in fact, the president and senate in all transactions of any importance; the president is connected with, or tied to the senate; he may always act with the senate, but never can effectually counteract its views: The president can appoint no officer, civil or military, who shall not be agreeable to the senate; and the presumption is, that the will of so important a body will not be very easily controuled, and that it will exercise its powers with great address.

In the judicial department, powers ever kept distinct in well balanced governments, are no less improperly blended in the hands of the same men—in the judges of the supreme court is lodged the law, the equity and the fact. It is not necessary to pursue the minute organical parts of the general government proposed.–-There were various interests in the convention, to be reconciled, especially of large and small states; of carrying and non-carrying states; and of states more and states less democratic—vast labour and attention were by the convention bestowed on the organization of the parts of the constitution offered; still it is acknowledged there are many things radically wrong in the essential parts of this constitution—but it is said that these are the result of our situation: On a full examination of the subject, I believe it; but what do the laborious inquiries and determination of the convention prove? If they prove any thing, they prove that we cannot consolidate the states on proper principles: The organization of the government presented proves, that we cannot form a general government in which all power can be safely lodged; and a little attention to the parts of the one proposed will make it appear very evident, that all the powers proposed to be lodged in it, will not be then well deposited, either for the purposes of government, or the preservation of liberty. I will suppose no abuse of power in those cases, in which the abuse of it is not well guarded against—I will suppose the words authorizing the general government to regulate the elections of its own members struck out of the plan, or free district elections, in each state, amply secured.—That the small representation provided for shall be as fair and equal as it is capable of being made—I will suppose the judicial department regulated on pure principles, by future laws, as far as it can be by the constitution, and consist with the situation of the country—still there will be an unreasonable accumulation of powers in the general government if all be granted, enumerated in the plan proposed. The plan does not present a well balanced government: The senatorial branch of the legislative and the executive are substantially united, and the president, or the state executive magistrate, may aid the senatorial interest when weakest, but never can effectually support the democratic, however it may be opposed;—the excellency, in my mind, of a well-balanced government is that it consists of distinct branches, each sufficiently strong and independant to keep its own station, and to aid either of the other branches which may occasionally want aid.

The convention found that any but a small house of representatives would be expensive, and that it would be impracticable to assemble a large number of representatives. Not only the determination of the convention in this case, but the situation of the states, proves the impracticability of collecting, in any one point, a proper representation.

The formation of the senate, and the smallness of the house, being, therefore, the result of our situation, and the actual state of things, the evils which may attend the exercise of many powers in this national government may be considered as without a remedy.

All officers are impeachable before the senate only—before the men by whom they are appointed, or who are consenting to the appointment of these officers. No judgment of conviction, on an impeachment, can be given unless two thirds of the senators agree. Under these circumstances the right of impeachment, in the house, can be of but little importance; the house cannot expect often to convict the offender; and, therefore, probably, will but seldom or never exercise the right. In addition to the insecurity and inconveniences attending this organization beforementioned, it may be observed, that it is extremely difficult to secure the people against the fatal effects of corruption and influence. The power of making any law will be in the president, eight senators, and seventeen representatives, relative to the important objects enumerated in the constitution. Where there is a small representation a sufficient number to carry and measure, may, with ease, be influenced by bribes, offices and civilities; they easily form private juntoes, and out-door meetings, agree on measures, and carry them by silent votes.

Impressed, as I am, with a sense of the difficulties there are in the way of forming the parts of a federal government on proper principles, and seeing a government so unsubstantially organized, after so arduous an attempt has been made, I am led to believe, that powers ought to be given to it with great care and caution.

In the second place it is necessary, therefore, to examine the extent, and the probable operations of some of those extensive powers proposed to be vested in this government. These powers, legislative, executive, and judicial, respect internal as well as external objects. Those respecting external objects, as all foreign concerns, commerce, imposts, all causes arising on the seas, peace and war, and Indian affairs, can be lodged no where else, with any propriety, but in this government. Many powers that respect internal objects ought clearly to be lodged in it; as those to regulate trade between the states, weights and measures, the coin or current monies, post-offices, naturalization, &c. These powers may be exercised without essentially effecting the internal police of the respective states: But powers to lay and collect internal taxes, to form the militia, to make bankrupt laws, and to decide on appeals, questions arising on the internal laws of the respective states, are of a very serious nature, and carry with them almost all other powers. These taken in connection with the others, and powers to raise armies and build navies, proposed to be lodged in this government, appear to me to comprehend all the essential powers in this community, and those which will be left to the states will be of no great importance.

A power to lay and collect taxes at discretion, is, in itself, of very great importance. By means of taxes, the government may command the whole or any part of the subject's property. Taxes may be of various kinds; but there is a strong distinction between external and internal taxes. External taxes are import duties, which are laid on imported goods; they may usually be collected in a few seaport towns, and of a few individuals, though ultimately paid by the consumer; a few officers can collect them, and they can be carried no higher than trade will bear, or smuggling permit—that in the very nature of commerce, bounds are set to them. But internal taxes, as poll and land taxes, excises, duties on all written instruments, &c. may fix themselves on every person and species of property in the community; they may be carried to any lengths, and in proportion as they are extended, numerous officers must be employed to assess them, and to enforce the collection of them. In the United Netherlands the general government has compleat powers, as to external taxation; but as to internal taxes, it makes requisitions on the provinces. Internal taxation in this country is more important, as the country is so very extensive. As many assessors and collectors of federal taxes will be above three hundred miles from the seat of the federal government as will be less. Besides, to lay and collect taxes, in this extensive country, must require a great number of congressional ordinances, immediately operating upon the body of the people; these must continually interfere with the state laws, and thereby produce disorder and general dissatisfaction, till the one system of laws or the other, operating on the same subjects, shall be abolished. These ordinances alone, to say nothing of those respecting the militia, coin, commerce, federal judiciary, &c. &c. will probably soon defeat the operations of the state laws and governments.

Should the general government think it politic, as some administration (if not all) probably will, to look for a support in a system of influence, the government will take every occasion to multiply laws, and officers to execute them, considering these as so many necessary props for its own support. Should this system of policy be adopted, taxes more productive than the impost duties will, probably, be wanted to support the government, and to discharge foreign demands, without leaving any thing for the domestic creditors. The internal sources of taxation then must be called into operation, and internal tax laws and federal assessors and collectors spread over this immense country. All these circumstances considered, is it wise, prudent, or safe, to vest the powers of laying and collecting internal taxes in the general government, while imperfectly organized and inadequate; and to trust to amending it hereafter, and making it adequate to this purpose? It is not only unsafe but absurd to lodge power in a government before it is fitted to receive it? It is confessed that this power and representation ought to go together. Why give the power first? Why give the power to the few, who, when possessed of it, may have address enough to prevent the increase of representation? Why not keep the power, and, when necessary, amend the constitution, and add to its other parts this power, and a proper increase of representation at the same time? Then men who may want the power will be under strong inducements to let in the people, by their representatives, into the government, to hold their due proportion of this power. If a proper representation be impracticable, then we shall see this power resting in the states, where it at present ought to be, and not inconsiderately given up.

When I recollect how lately congress, conventions, legislatures, and people contended in the cause of liberty, and carefully weighed the importance of taxation, I can scarcely believe we are serious in proposing to vest the powers of laying and collecting internal taxes in a government so imperfectly organized for such purposes. Should the United States be taxed by a house of representatives of two hundred members, which would be about fifteen members for Connecticut, twenty-five for Massachusetts, &c. still the middle and lower classes of people could have no great share, in fact, in taxation. I am aware it is said, that the representation proposed by the new constitution is sufficiently numerous; it may be for many purposes; but to suppose that this branch is sufficiently numerous to guard the rights of the people in the administration of the government, in which the purse and sword is placed, seems to argue that we have forgot what the true meaning of representation is. I am sensible also, that it is said that congress will not attempt to lay and collect internal taxes; that it is necessary for them to have the power, though it cannot probably be exercised.———I admit that it is not probable that any prudent congress will attempt to lay and collect internal taxes, especially direct taxes: but this only proves, that the power would be improperly lodged in congress, and that it might be abused by imprudent and designing men.

I have heard several gentlemen, to get rid of objections to this part of the constitution, attempt to construe the powers relative to direct taxes, as those who object to it would have them; as to these, it is said, that congress will only have power to make requisitions, leaving it to the states to lay and collect them. I see but very little colour for this construction, and the attempt only proves that this part of the plan cannot be defended. By this plan there can be no doubt, but that the powers of congress will be complete as to all kinds of taxes whatever—Further, as to internal taxes, the state governments will have concurrent powers with the general government, and both may tax the same objects in the same year: and the objection that the general government may suspend a state tax, as a necessary measure for the promoting the collection of a federal tax, is not without foundation.——As the states owe large debts, and have large demands upon them individually, there clearly will be a propriety in leaving in their possession exclusively, some of the internal sources of taxation, at least until the federal representation shall be properly encreased: The power in the general government to lay and collect internal taxes, will render its powers respecting armies, navies and the militia, the more exceptionable. By the constitution it is proposed that congress shall have power "to raise and support armies, but no appropriation of money to that use shall be for a longer term than two years; to provide and maintain a navy; to provide for calling forth the militia to execute the laws of the union; suppress insurrections, and repel invasions: to provide for organizing, arming, and disciplining the militia;" reserving to the states the right to appoint the officers, and to train the militia according to the discipline prescribed by congress; congress will have unlimited power to raise armies, and to engage officers and men for any number of years; but a legislative act applying money for their support can have operation for no longer term than two years, and if a subsequent congress do not within the two years renew the appropriation, or further appropriate monies for the use of the army, the army will be left to take care of itself. When an army shall once be raised for a number of years, it is not probable that it will find much difficulty in getting congress to pass laws for applying monies to its support. I see so many men in America fond of a standing army, and especially among those who probably will have a large share in administering the federal system; it is very evident to me, that we shall have a large standing army as soon as the monies to support them can be possibly found. An army is not a very agreeable place of employment for the young gentlemen of many families. A power to raise armies must be lodged some where; still this will not justify the lodging this power in a bare majority of so few men without any checks; or in the government in which the great body of the people, in the nature of things, will be only nominally represented. In the state governments the great body of the people, the yeomanry, &c. of the country, are represented: It is true they will chuse the members of congress, and may now and then chuse a man of their own way of thinking; but it is not impossible for forty, or thirty thousand people in this country, one time in ten to find a man who can possess similar feelings, views, and interests with themselves: Powers to lay and collect taxes and to raise armies are of the greatest moment; for carrying them into effect, laws need not be frequently made, and the yeomanry, &c. of the country ought substantially to have a check upon the passing of these laws; this check ought to be placed in the legislatures, or at least, in the few men the common people of the country, will, probably, have in congress, in the true sense of the word, "from among themselves." It is true, the yeomanry of the country possess the lands, the weight of property, possess arms, and are too strong a body of men to be openly offended—and, therefore, it is urged, they will take care of themselves, that men who shall govern will not dare pay any disrespect to their opinions. It is easily perceived, that if they have not their proper negative upon passing laws in congress, or on the passage of laws relative to taxes and armies, they may in twenty or thirty years be by means imperceptible to them, totally deprived of that boasted weight and strength: This may be done in a great measure by congress, if disposed to do it, by modelling the militia. Should one fifth or one eighth part of the men capable of bearing arms, be made a select militia, as has been proposed, and those the young and ardent part of the community, possessed of but little or no property, and all the others put upon a plan that will render them of no importance, the former will answer all the purposes of an army, while the latter will be defenceless. The state must train the militia in such form and according to such systems and rules as congress shall prescribe: and the only actual influence the respective states will have respecting the militia will be in appointing the officers. I see no provision made for calling out the *posse comitatus* for executing the laws of the union, but provision is made for congress to call forth the militia for the execution of them—and the militia in general, or any select part of it, may be called out under military officers, instead of the sheriff to enforce an execution of federal laws, in the first instance, and thereby introduce an entire military execution of the laws. I know that powers to raise taxes, to regulate the military strength of the community on some uniform plan, to provide for its defence and internal order, and for duly executing the laws, must be lodged somewhere; but still we ought not so to lodge them, as evidently to give one order of men in the community, undue advantages over others; or commit the many to the mercy, prudence, and moderation of the few. And so far as it may be necessary to lodge any of the peculiar powers in the general government, a more safe exercise of them ought to be secured, by requiring the consent of two-thirds or three-fourths of congress thereto—until the federal representation can be increased, so that the democratic members in congress may stand some tolerable chance of a reasonable negative, in behalf of the numerous, important, and democratic part of the community.

I am not sufficiently acquainted with the laws and internal police of all the states to discern fully, how general bankrupt laws, made by the union, would effect them, or promote the public good. I believe the property of debtors, in the several states, is held responsible for their debts in modes and forms very different. If uniform bankrupt laws can be made without producing real and substantial inconveniences, I wish them to be made by congress.

There are some powers proposed to be lodged in the general government in the judicial department, I think very unnecessarily, I mean powers respecting questions arising upon the internal laws of the respective states. It is proper the federal judiciary should have powers co-extensive with the federal legislature—that is, the power of deciding finally on the laws of the union. By Art. 3, Sec. 2. the powers of the federal judiciary are extended (among other things) to all cases between a state and citizens of another state—between citizens of different states—between a state or the citizens thereof, and foreign states, citizens or subjects. Actions in all these cases, except against a state government, are now brought and finally determined in the law courts of the states respectively and as there are no words to exclude these courts of their jurisdiction in these cases, they will have concurrent jurisdiction with the inferior federal courts in them; and, therefore, if the new constitution be adopted without any amendment in this respect, all those numerous actions, now brought in the state courts between our citizens and foreigners, between citizens of different states, by state governments against foreigners, and by state governments against citizens of other states, may also be brought in the federal courts; and an appeal will lay in them from the state courts or federal inferior courts to the supreme judicial court of the union. In almost all these cases, either party may have the trial by jury in the state courts; except paper money and tender laws, which are wisely guarded against in the proposed constitution; justice may be obtained in these courts on reasonable terms; they must be more competent to proper decisions on the laws of their respective states, than the federal states can possibly be. I do not, in any point of view, see the need of opening a new jurisdiction in these causes—of opening a new scene of expensive law suits, of suffering foreigners, and citizens of different states, to drag each other many hundred miles into the federal courts. It is true, those courts may be so organized by a wise and prudent legislature, as to make the obtaining of justice in them tolerably easy; they may in general be organized on the common law principles of the country: But this benefit is by no means secured by the constitution. The trial by jury is secured only in those few criminal cases, to which the federal laws will extend—as crimes committed on the seas, against the laws of nations, treason and counterfeiting the federal securities and coin: But even in these cases, the jury trial of the vicinage is not secured—particularly in the large states, a citizen may be tried for a crime committed in the state, and yet tried in some states 500 miles from the place where it was committed; but the jury trial is not secured at all in civil causes. Though the convention have not established this trial, it is to be hoped that congress, in putting the new system into execution, will do it by a legislative act, in all cases in which it can be done with propriety. Whether the jury trial is not excluded the supreme judicial court is an important question. By Art. 3. Sec. 2, all cases affecting ambassadors, other public ministers, and consuls, and in those cases in which a state shall be party, the supreme court shall have jurisdiction. In all the other cases beforementioned, the supreme court shall have appellate jurisdiction, both as to *law and fact,* with such exception, and under such regulations as the congress shall make. By court is understood a court consisting of judges; and the idea of a jury is excluded. This court, or the judges, are to have jurisdiction on appeals, in all the cases enumerated, as to law and fact; the judges are to decide the law and try the fact, and the trial of the fact being assigned to the judges by the constitution, a jury for trying the fact is excluded; however, under the exceptions and powers to make regulations, congress may, perhaps, introduce the jury, to try the fact in most necessary cases.

There can be but one supreme court in which the final jurisdiction will centre in all federal causes—except in cases where appeals by law shall not be allowed: The judicial powers of the federal courts extend in law and equity to certain cases: and, therefore, the powers to determine on the law, in equity, and as to the fact, all will concentrate in the supreme court:—These powers, which by this constitution are blended in the same hands, the same judges, are in Great-Britain deposited in different hands—to wit, the decision of the law in the law judges, the decision in equity in the chancellor, and the trial of the fact in the jury. It is a very dangerous thing to vest in the same judge power to decide on the law, and also general powers in equity; for if the law restrain him, he is only to step into his shoes of equity, and give what judgment his reason or opinion may dictate; we have no precedents in this country, as yet, to regulate the divisions in equity as in Great Britain; equity, therefore, in the supreme court for many years will be mere discretion. I confess in the constitution of this supreme court, as left by the constitution, I do not see a spark of freedom or a shadow of our own or the British common law.

This court is to have appellate jurisdiction in all the other cases before mentioned: Many sensible men suppose that cases before mentioned respect, as well the criminal cases as the civil ones mentioned antecedently in the constitution, if so an appeal is allowed in criminal cases—contrary to the usual sense of law. How far it may be proper to admit a foreigner or the citizen of another state to bring actions against state governments, which have failed in performing so many promises made during the war is doubtful: How far it may be proper so to humble a state, as to oblige it to answer to an individual in a court of law, is worthy of consideration; the states are now subject to no such actions; and this new jurisdiction will subject the states, and many defendants to actions, and processes, which were not in the contemplation of the parties, when the contract was made; all engagements existing between citizens of different states, citizens and foreigners, states and foreigners; and states and citizens of other states were made the parties contemplating the remedies then existing on the laws of the states——and the new remedy proposed to be given in the federal courts, can be founded on no principle whatever.

Your's, &c,

THE FEDERAL FARMER.

LETTER IV.

OCTOBER 12th, 1787.

DEAR SIR,

It will not be possible to establish in the federal courts the jury trial of the vicinage so well as in the state courts.

Third, there appears to me to be not only a premature deposit of some important powers in the general government—but many of those deposited there are undefined, and may be used to good or bad purposes as honest or designing men shall prevail. By Art. 1. Sec. 2, representatives and direct taxes shall be apportioned among the several states, &c.——same art. sec. 8, the congress shall have powers to lay and collect taxes, duties, &c. for the common defence and general welfare, but all duties, imposts, and excises, shall be uniform throughout the United States: By the first recited clause, direct taxes shall be apportioned on the states. This seems to favour the idea suggested by some sensible men and writers that congress, as to direct taxes, will only have power to make requisitions; but the latter clause, power to lay and collect taxes, &c. seems clearly to favour the contrary opinion, and, in my mind, the true one, the congress shall have power to tax immediately individuals, without the intervention of the state legislatures, in fact the first clause appears to me only to provide that each state shall pay a certain portion of the tax, and the latter to provide that congress shall have power to lay and collect taxes, that is to assess upon, and to collect of the individuals in the state, the states quota; but these still I consider as undefined powers, because judicious men understand them differently.

It is doubtful whether the vice-president is to have any qualifications; none are mentioned; but he may serve as president, and it may be inferred, he ought to be qualified therefore as the president; but the qualifications of the president are required only of the person to be elected president. By art. 2, sect. 2, "But the congress may by law vest the appointment of such inferior officers as they think proper in the president alone, in the courts of law, or in the heads of the departments:" Who are inferior officers? May not a congress disposed to vest the appointment of all officers in the president, under this clause, vest the appointment of almost every officer in the president alone, and destroy the check mentioned in the first part of the clause, and lodged in the senate. It is true, this check is badly lodged, but then some check upon the first magistrate in appointing officers, ought it appears by the opinion of the convention, and by the general opinion, to be established in the constitution. By art. 3, sect. 2, the supreme court shall have appellate jurisdiction as to law and facts with such exceptions, &c. to what extent is it intended the exceptions shall be carried——Congress may carry them so far as to annihilate substantially the appellate jurisdiction, and the clause be rendered of very little importance.

4th. There are certain rights which we have always held sacred in the United States, and recognized in all our constitutions, and which, by the adoption of the new constitution in its present form, will be left unsecured. By article 6, the proposed constitution, and the laws of the United States, which shall be made in pursuance thereof; and all treaties made, or which shall be made under the authority of the United States, shall be the supreme law of the land; and the judges in every state shall be bound thereby; anything in the constitution or laws of any state to the contrary notwithstanding.

It is to be observed that when the people shall adopt the proposed constitution it will be their last and supreme act; it will be adopted not by the people of New Hampshire, Massachusetts, &c., but by the people of the United States; and wherever this constitution, or any part of it, shall be incompatible with the ancient customs, rights, the laws or the constitutions heretofore established in the United States, it will entirely abolish them and do them away: And not only this, but the laws of the United States which shall be; made in pursuance of the federal constitution will be also supreme laws, and wherever they shall be incompatible with those customs, rights, laws or constitutions heretofore established, they will also entirely abolish them and do them away.

By the article before recited, treaties also made under the authority of the United States, shall be the supreme law: It is not said that these treaties shall be made in pursuance of the constitution—nor are there any constitutional bounds set to those who shall make them: The president and two-thirds of the senate will be empowered to make treaties indefinitely, and when these treaties shall be made, they will also abolish all laws and state constitutions incompatible with them. This power in the president and senate is absolute, and the judges will be bound to allow full force to whatever rule, article or thing the president and senate shall establish by treaty, whether it be practicable to set any bounds to those who make treaties, I am not able to say; if not, it proves that this power ought to be more safely lodged.

The federal constitution, the laws of congress made in pursuance of the constitution, and all treaties must have full force and effect in all parts of the United States; and all other laws, rights and constitutions which stand in their way must yield: It is proper the national laws should be supreme, and superior to state or district laws; but then the national laws ought to yield to unalienable or fundamental rights——and national laws, made by a few men, should extend only to a few national objects. This will not be the case with the laws of congress: To have any proper idea of their extent, we must carefully examine the legislative, executive and judicial powers proposed to be lodged in the general government, and consider them in connection with a general clause in art. 1, sect. 8, in these words (after enumerating a number of powers) "To make all laws which shall be necessary and proper for carrying into execution the foregoing powers, and all other powers vested by this constitution in the government of the United States, or in any department or officer thereof."——The powers of this government as has been observed, extend to internal as well as external objects, and to those objects to which all others are subordinate; it is almost impossible to have a just conception of their powers, or of the extent and number of the laws which may be deemed necessary and proper to carry them into effect, till we shall come to exercise those powers and make the laws. In making laws to carry those powers into effect, it is to be expected, that a wise and prudent congress will pay respect to the opinions of a free people, and bottom their laws on those principles which have been considered as essential and fundamental in the British, and in our government: But a congress of a different character will not be bound by the constitution to pay respect to those principles.

It is said that when people make a constitution, and delegate powers, that all powers are not delegated by them to those who govern, is reserved in the people; and that the people, in the present case, have reserved in themselves, and in their state governments, every right and power not expressly given by the federal constitution to those who shall administer the national government. It is said, on the other hand, that the people, when they make a constitution, yield all power not expressly reserved to themselves. The truth is, in either case, it is mere matter of opinion, and men usually take either side of the argument as will best answer their purposes: But the general presumption being, that men who govern, will in doubtful cases, construe laws and constitutions most favourably for increasing their own powers; all wise and prudent people, in forming constitutions, have drawn the line, and carefully described the powers parted with and the powers reserved. By the state constitutions, certain rights have been reserved in the people; or rather, they have been recognized and established in such a manner, that state legislatures are bound to respect them, and to make no laws infringing upon them. The state legislatures are obliged to take notice of the bills of rights of their respective states. The bills of rights, and the state constitutions, are fundamental compacts only between those who govern, and the people of the same state.

In the year 1788 the people of the United States made a federal constitution, which is a fundamental compact between them and their federal rulers; these rulers, in the nature of things, cannot be bound to take notice of any other compact. It would be absurd for them, in making laws, to look over thirteen, fifteen, or twenty state constitutions, to see what rights are established as fundamental, and must not be infringed upon, in making laws in the society. It is true, they would be bound to do it if the people, in their federal compact, should refer to the state constitutions, recognize all parts not inconsistent with the federal constitution, and direct their federal rulers to take notice of them accordingly; but this is not the case, as the plan stands proposed at present; and it is absurd, to suppose so unnatural an idea is intended or implied. I think my opinion is not only founded in reason, but I think it is supported by the report of the convention itself. If there are a number of rights established by the state constitutions, and which will remain sacred, and the general government is bound to take notice of them—it must take notice of one as well as another; and if unnecessary to recognize or establish one by the federal constitution, it would be unnecessary to recognize or establish another by it. If the federal constitution is to be construed so far in connection with the state constitution, as to leave the trial by jury in civil causes, for instance, secured; on the same principles it would have left the trial by jury in criminal causes, the benefits of the writ of habeas corpus, &c. secured; they all stand on the same footing; they are the common rights of Americans, and have been recognized by the state constitutions: But the convention found it necessary to recognize or re-establish the benefits of that writ, and the jury trial in criminal cases. As to *expost facto* laws, the convention has done the same in one case, and gone further in another. It is a part of the compact between the people of each state and their rulers, that no *expost facto* laws shall be made. But the convention, by Art. 1, Sect. 10, have put a sanction upon this part even of the state compacts. In fact, the 9th and 10th Sections in Art. 1, in the proposed constitution, are no more nor less, than a partial bill of rights; they establish certain principles as part of the compact upon which the federal legislators and officers can never infringe. It is here wisely stipulated, that the federal legislature shall never pass a bill of attainder, or *expost facto* law; that no tax shall be laid on articles exported, &c. The establishing of one right implies the necessity of establishing another and similar one.

On the whole, the position appears to me to be undeniable, that this bill of rights ought to be carried farther, and some other principles established, as a part of this fundamental compact between the people of the United States and their federal rulers.

It is true, we are not disposed to differ much, at present, about religion; but when we are making a constitution, it is to be hoped, for ages and millions yet unborn, why not establish the free exercise of religion, as a part of the national compact. There are other essential rights, which we have justly understood to be the rights of freemen; as freedom from hasty and unreasonable search warrants, warrants not founded on oath, and not issued with due caution, for searching and seizing men's papers, property, and persons. The trials by jury in civil causes, it is said, varies so much in the several states, that no words could be found for the uniform establishment of it. If so, the federal legislation will not be able to establish it by any general laws. I confess I am of opinion it may be established, but not in that beneficial manner in which we may enjoy it, for the reasons beforementioned. When I speak of the jury trial of the vicinage, or the trial of the fact in the neighborhood, I do not lay so much stress upon the circumstance of our being tried by our neighbours: in this enlightened country men may be probably impartially tried by those who do not live very near them: but the trial of facts in the neighbourhood is of great importance in other respects. Nothing can be more essential than the cross examining witnesses, and generally before the triers of the facts in question. The common people can establish facts with much more ease with oral than written evidence; when trials of facts are removed to a distance from the homes of the parties and witnesses, oral evidence becomes intolerably expensive, and the parties must depend on written evidence, which to the common people is expensive and almost useless; it must be frequently taken ex porte, and but very seldom leads to the proper discovery of truth.

The trial by jury is very important in another point of view. It is essential in every free country, that common people should have a part and share of influence, in the judicial as well as in the legislative department. To hold open to them the offices of senators, judges, and offices to fill which an expensive education is required, cannot answer any valuable purposes for them; they are not in a situation to be brought forward and to fill those offices; these, and most other offices of any considerable importance, will be occupied by the few. The few, the well born, &c. as Mr. Adams calls them, in judicial decisions as well as in legislation, are generally disposed, and very naturally too, to favour those of their own description.[1]

The trial by jury in the judicial department, and the collection of the people by their representatives in the legislature, are those fortunate inventions which have procured for them, in this country, their true proportion of influence, and the wisest and most fit means of protecting themselves in the community. Their situation, as jurors and representatives, enables them to acquire information and knowledge in the affairs and government of the society; and to come forward, in turn, as the centinels and guardians of each other. I am very sorry that even a few of our countrymen should consider jurors and representatives in a different point of view, as ignorant,

[1] John Adams, who had become increasingly conservative after the beginning of the Revolution, was suspected of an excessive admiration for the English monarchical system.

troublesome bodies, which ought not to have any share in the concerns of government.

I confess I do not see in what cases the congress can, with any pretence of right, make a law to suppress the freedom of the press; though I am not clear, that congress is restrained from laying any duties whatever on printing, and from laying duties particularly heavy on certain pieces printed, and perhaps congress may require large bonds for the payment of these duties. Should the printer say, the freedom of the press was secured by the constitution of the state in which he lived, congress might, and perhaps, with great propriety, answer, that the federal constitution is the only compact existing between them and the people; in this compact the people have named no others, and therefore congress, in exercising the powers assigned them, and in making laws to carry them into execution, are restrained by nothing beside the federal constitution, any more than a state legislature is restrained by a compact between the magistrates and people of a county, city, or town of which the people, in forming the state constitution, have taken no notice.

It is not my object to enumerate rights of inconsiderable importance; but there are others, no doubt, which ought to be established as a fundamental part of the national system.

It is worthy of observation, that all treaties are made by foreign nations with a confederacy of thirteen states—that the western country is attached to thirteen states—thirteen states have jointly and severally engaged to pay the public debts.—Should a new government be formed of nine, ten, eleven, or twelve states, those treaties could not be considered as binding on the foreign nations who made them. However, I believe the probability to be, that if nine states adopt the constitution, the others will.[2]

It may also be worthy our examination; how far the provision for amending this plan, when it shall be adopted, is of any importance. No measures can be taken towards amendments, unless two-thirds of the congress, or two-thirds of the legislature of the several states shall agree.—While power is in the hands of the people, or democratic part of the community, more especially as at present, it is easy, according to the general course of human affairs, for the few influential men in the community, to obtain conventions, alterations in government,

[2] It was necessary for nine of the original thirteen states to ratify the proposed Constitution in order for it to become law. On June 21, 1788, New Hampshire became the ninth state to ratify.

and to persuade the common people that they may change for the better, and to get from them a part of the power: But when power is once transferred from the many to the few, all changes become extremely difficult; the government, in this case, being beneficial to the few, they will be exceedingly artful and adroit in preventing any measures which may lead to a change; and nothing will produce it, but great exertions and severe struggles on the part of the common people. Every man of reflection must see, that the change now proposed, is a transfer of power from the many to the few, and the probability is, the artful and ever active aristocracy, will prevent all peaceful measures for changes, unless when they shall discover some favorable moment to increase their own influence. I am sensible, thousands of men in the United States, are disposed to adopt the proposed constitution, though they perceive it to be essentially defective, under an idea that amendments of it, may be obtained when necessary. This is a pernicious idea, it argues a servility of character totally unfit for the support of free government; it is very repugnant to that perpetual jealousy respecting liberty, so absolutely necessary in all free states, spoken of by Mr. Dickinson.[3]—However, if our countrymen are so soon changed, and the language of 1774, is become odious to them, it will be in vain to use the language of freedom, or to attempt to rouse them to free enquiries: But I shall never believe this is the case with them, whatever present appearances may be, till I shall have very strong evidence indeed of it.

Your's, &c.

THE FEDERAL FARMER.

LETTER V.

OCTOBER 15th, 1787.

DEAR SIR,

Thus I have examined the federal constitution as far as a few days leisure would permit. It opens to my mind a new scene; instead of seeing powers cautiously lodged in the hands of numerous legislators, and many magistrates, we see all important powers collecting in one centre, where a few men will possess them almost at discretion. And instead of checks in the formation of the government, to secure the rights of the people against the usurpations of those they appoint to gov-

[3] John Dickinson had drawn up the "Petition to the King" and the "Address to the People of Canada" for the First Continental Congress.

ern, we are to understand the equal division of lands among our people, and the strong arm furnished them by nature and situation, are to secure them against those usurpations. If there are advantages in the equal division of our lands, and the strong and manly habits of our people, we ought to establish governments calculated to give duration to them, and not governments which never can work naturally, till that equality of property, and those free and manly habits shall be destroyed; these evidently are not the natural basis of the proposed constitution. No man of reflection, and skilled in the science of government, can suppose these will move on harmoniously together for ages, or even for fifty years. As to the little circumstances commented upon, by some writers, with applause—as the age of a representative, of the president, &c. —they have, in my mind, no weight in the general tendency of the system.

There are, however, in my opinion, many good things in the proposed system. It is founded on elective principles, and the deposits of powers in different hands, is essentially right. The guards against those evils we have experienced in some states in legislation are valuable indeed; but the value of every feature in this system is vastly lessened for the want of that one important feature in a free government, a representation of the people. Because we have sometimes abused democracy, I am not among those men who think a democratic branch a nuisance; which branch shall be sufficiently numerous to admit some of the best informed men of each order in the community into the administration of government.

While the radical defects in the proposed system are not so soon discovered, some temptations to each state, and to many classes of men to adopt it, are very visible. It uses the democratic language of several of the state constitutions, particularly that of Massachusetts; the eastern states will receive advantages so far as the regulation of trade, by a bare majority, is committed to it: Connecticut and New Jersey will receive their share of a general impost: The middle states will receive the advantages surrounding the seat of government; The southern states will receive protection, and have their negroes represented in the legislature, and large back countries will soon have a majority in it. This system promises a large field of employment to military gentlemen, and gentlemen of the law; and in case the government shall be executed without convulsions, it will afford security to creditors, to the clergy, salary-men and others depending on money payments. So far as the system promises justice and reasonable advantages, in these respects, it ought to be supported by all honest men: but whenever it promises unequal and improper advantages to any particular states, or orders of men, it ought to be opposed.

I have, in the course of these letters observed, that there are many good things in the proposed constitution, and I have endeavored to point out many important defects in it. I have admitted that we want a federal system—that we have a system presented, which, with several alterations may be made a tolerable good one—I have admitted there is a well founded uneasiness among creditors and mercantile men. In this situation of things, you ask me what I think ought to be done? My opinion in this case is only the opinion of an individual, and so far only as it corresponds with the opinions of the honest and substantial part of the community, is it entitled to consideration. Though I am fully satisfied that the state conventions ought most seriously to direct their exertions to altering and amending the system proposed before they shall adopt it—yet I have not sufficiently examined the subject, or formed an opinion, how far it will be practicable for those conventions to carry their amendments. As to the idea, that it will be in vain for those conventions to attempt amendments, it cannot be admitted; it is impossible to say whether they can or not until the attempt shall be made; and when it shall be determined, by experience, that the conventions cannot agree in amendments, it will then be an important question before the people of the United States, whether they will adopt or not the system proposed in its present form. This subject of consolidating the states is new: and because forty or fifty men have agreed in a system, to suppose the good sense of this country, an enlightened nation, must adopt it without examination, and though in a state of profound peace, without endeavouring to amend those parts they perceive are defective, dangerous to freedom, and destructive of the valuable principles of republican government—is truly humiliating. It is true there may be danger in delay; but there is danger in adopting the system in its present form; and I see the danger in either case will arise principally from the conduct and views of two very unprincipled parties in the United States—two fires, between which the honest and substantial people have long found themselves situated. One party is composed of little insurgents, men in debt, who want no law, and who want a share of the property of others;

these are called levellers, Shayites,[1] &c. The other party is composed of a few, but more dangerous men, with their servile dependents; these avariciously grasp at all power and property; you may discover in all the actions of these men, an evident dislike to free and equal government, and they will go systematically to work to change, essentially, the forms of government in this country; these are called aristocrats, m——ites, &c. &c. Between these two parties is the weight of the community; the men of middling property, men not in debt on the one hand, and men, on the other, content with republican governments, and not aiming at immense fortunes, offices, and power. In 1786, the little insurgents, the levellers, came forth, invaded the rights of others, and attempted to establish governments according to their wills.[2] Their movements evidently gave encouragement to the other party, which, in 1787, has taken the political field, and with its fashionable dependants, and the tongue and the pen, is endeavoring to establish in a great haste, a politer kind of government. These two parties, which will probably be opposed or united as it may suit their interests and views, are really insignificant, compared with the solid, free and independent part of the community. It is not my intention to suggest, that either of these parties, and the real friends of the proposed constitution, are the same men. The fact is, these aristocrats support and hasten the adoption of the proposed constitution, merely because they think it is a stepping stone to their favorite object. I think I am well founded in this idea; I think the general politics of these men support it, as well as the common observation among them, That the proffered plan is the best that can be got at present, it will do for a few years, and lead to something better. The sensible and judicious part of the community will carefully weigh all these circumstances; they will view the late convention as a respectable body of men—America probably never will see an assembly of men, of a like number, more respectable. But the members of the convention met without knowing the sentiments of one man in ten thousand in these states respecting the new ground taken. Their doings are but the first attempts in the most important scene ever opened. Though each individual in the state conventions will not, probably, be so respectable as each individual in the federal convention, yet as the state conventions will probably consist of fifteen hundred or two thousand men

[1] *Shayites,* or *Shaysites,* were followers of Daniel Shays.
[2] Shays' Rebellion occurred in 1786.

of abilities, and versed in the science of government, collected from all parts of the community and from all orders of men, it must be acknowledged that the weight of respectability will be in them—In them will be collected the solid sense and the real political character of the country. Being revisers of the subject, they will possess peculiar advantages. To say that these conventions ought not to attempt, coolly and deliberately, the revision of the system, or that they cannot amend it, is very foolish or very assuming. If these conventions, after examining the system, adopt it, I shall be perfectly satisfied, and wish to see men make the administration of the government an equal blessing to all orders of men. I believe the great body of our people to be virtuous and friendly to good government, to the protection of liberty and property; and it is the duty of all good men, especially of those who are placed as sentinels to guard their rights—it is their duty to examine into the prevailing politics of parties, and to disclose them—while they avoid exciting undue suspicions, to lay facts before the people, which will enable them to form a proper judgment. Men who wish the people of this country to determine for themselves, and deliberately to fit the government to their situation, must feel some degree of indignation at those attempts to hurry the adoption of a system, and to shut the door against examination. The very attempts create suspicions, that those who make them have secret views, or see some defects in the system, which, in the hurry of affairs, they expect will escape the eye of a free people.

What can be the views of those gentlemen in Pennsylvania, who precipitated decisions on this subject? What can be the views of those gentlemen in Boston, who countenanced the Printers in shutting up the press against a fair and free investigation of this important system in the usual way. The members of the convention have done their duty——why should some of them fly to their states—almost forget a propriety of behaviour, and precipitate measures for the adoption of a system of their own making? I confess candidly, when I consider these circumstances in connection with the unguarded parts of the system I have mentioned, I feel disposed to proceed with very great caution, and to pay more attention than usual to the conduct of particular characters. If the constitution presented be a good one, it will stand the test with a well informed people: all are agreed that there shall be state conventions to examine it; and we must believe it will be adopted, unless we suppose it is a bad one, or that those conventions will make false divisions respecting it. I admit improper measures are taken against the adoption of the system as well for it——all who object to the plan proposed ought to point out the defects objected to, and to propose those amendments with which they can accept it, or to propose some other system of government, that the public mind may be known, and that we may be brought to agree in some system of government, to strengthen and execute the present, or to provide a substitute. I consider the field of enquiry just opened, and that we are to look to the state conventions for ultimate decisions on the subject before us; it is not to be presumed, that they will differ about small amendments, and lose a system when they shall have made it substantially good; but touching the essential amendments, it is to be presumed the several conventions will pursue the most rational measures to agree in and obtain them; and such defects as they shall discover and not remove, they will probably notice, keep them in view as the ground work of future amendments, and in the firm and manly language which every free people ought to use, will suggest to those who may hereafter administer the government, that it is their expectation, that the system will be so organized by legislative acts, and the government so administered, as to render those defects as little injurious as possible. Our countrymen are entitled to an honest and faithful government; to a government of laws and not of men; and also to one of their chusing—as a citizen of the country, I wish to see these objects secured, and licentious, assuming, and overbearing men restrained; if the constitution or social compact be vague and unguarded, then we depend wholly upon the prudence, wisdom and moderation of those who manage the affairs of government; or on what, probably, is equally uncertain and precarious, the success of the people oppressed by the abuse of government, in receiving it from the hands of those who abuse it, and placing it in the hands of those who will use it well.

In every point of view, therefore, in which I have been able, as yet, to contemplate this subject, I can discern but one rational mode of proceeding relative to it: and that is to examine it with freedom and candour, to have state conventions some months hence, which shall examine coolly every article, clause, and word in the system proposed, and to adopt it with such amendments as they shall think fit. How far the state conventions ought to pursue the mode prescribed by the federal convention of adopting or rejecting the plan in toto, I leave it to them to determine. Our examination of the subject hitherto has been rather of a general nature. The republican characters in the several states, who wish to make this plan more adequate to security of liberty and property, and to the duration of the principles of a free government, will, no doubt, collect their opinions to certain points, and accurately define those alterations and amendments they wish; if it shall be found they essentially disagree in them, the conventions will then be able to determine whether to adopt the plan as it is, or what will be proper to be done.

Under these impressions, and keeping in view the improper and unadvisable lodgment of powers in the general government, organized as it at present is, touching internal taxes, armies and militia, the elections of its own members, causes between citizens of different states, &c. and the want of a more perfect bill of rights, &c. I drop the subject for the present, and when I shall have leisure to revise and correct my ideas respecting it, and to collect into points the opinions of those who wish to make the system more secure and safe, perhaps I may proceed to point out particularly for your consideration, the amendments which ought to be ingrafted into this system, not only in conformity to my own, but the deliberate opinions of others—you will with me perceive, that the objections to the plan proposed may, by a more leisure examination be set in a stronger point of view, especially the important one, that there is no substantial representation of the people provided for in a government in which the most essential powers, even as to the internal police of the country, is proposed to be lodged.

I think the honest and substantial part of the community will wish to see this system altered, permanency and consistency given to the constitution we shall adopt; and therefore they will be anxious to apportion the powers to the features and organizations of the government, and to see abuse in the exercise of power more effectually guarded against. It is suggested, that state officers, from interested motives will oppose the constitution presented——I see no reason for this, their places in general will not be effected, but new openings to offices and places of profit must evidently be made by the adoption of the constitution in its present form.

Your's, &c.

THE FEDERAL FARMER.

To the REPUBLICAN.

ALEXANDER HAMILTON, JOHN JAY, JAMES MADISON

The didactic nature of so much of the writing of the Founding Fathers is nowhere better illustrated than in the fact that the greatest single work of American political theory was composed as a series of newspaper articles designed to persuade the people of the State of New York to ratify the proposed Constitution. From October 27, 1787, to August 15, 1788, *The Federalist* papers appeared in a number of New York newspapers. The project, originated by Hamilton, was conceived of as an answer to the barrage of articles attacking the proposed Constitution when it was released by Congress for ratification by the states. The home of a number of vigorous opponents to the Constitution, New York was an influential state that had to be won by the Federalists.

Exactly how influential *The Federalist* was in achieving ratification in New York can only be guessed at, but the evidence would seem to indicate that ratification, which was passed in New York by the slim margin of three votes, was due more to the skillful political maneuvering and compromises of its proponents than it was to *The Federalist*. But as inauspicious as its origins seemed to be, *The Federalist* was destined to become a handbook for all who wished to understand what the Framers of the Constitution desired in a government. Hamilton, Jay, and Madison, writing under the pseudonym Publius, were intent on demonstrating that the compromises arrived at in Philadelphia had resulted in the creation of a new Constitution which possessed the virtues of balanced government and that only such a government was capable of synthesizing the "violent contests" among the states. For all three of the authors of *The Federalist,* liberty was that which had to be guarded; they shared a distrust of liberty unregulated by law which was matched by their distrust of power unregulated by law. In "Number Ten," the most famous of *The Federalist* papers, Madison describes the inevitability of conflict among different interests in any society which values liberty. Such conflict, he tells us, is endemic to a society which insists that man is born free. Only by working from within the confines of balanced government can we prevent excessive liberty from destroying the true meaning of liberty, an ordered and stable existence for all. Like the other delegates to the Philadelphia Convention, Madison was looking for a "republican remedy for the diseases most incident to republican government." Such a remedy, he believed, was provided for in the new Constitution.

The entire *Federalist* comprises eighty-five papers, of which almost one-third are reprinted in their entirety here.

Text: Jacob E. Cooke, ed., *The Federalist.* Middletown, Conn., 1961.

The Federalist Papers

THE FEDERALIST NO. 1
ALEXANDER HAMILTON

October 27, 1787

To the People of the State of New York.

After an unequivocal experience of the inefficacy of the subsisting Fœderal Government, you are called upon to deliberate on a new Constitution for the United States of America. The subject speaks its own importance; comprehending in its consequences, nothing less than the existence of the UNION, the safety and welfare of the parts of which it is composed, the fate of an empire, in many respects, the most interesting in the world. It has been frequently remarked, that it seems to have been reserved to the people of this country, by their conduct and example, to decide the important question, whether societies of men are really capable or not, of establishing good government from reflection and choice, or whether they are forever destined to depend, for their political constitutions, on accident and force. If there be any truth in the remark, the crisis, at which we are arrived, may with propriety be regarded as the æra in which that decision is to be made; and a wrong election of the part we shall act, may, in this view, deserve to be considered as the general misfortune of mankind.

This idea will add the inducements of philanthropy to those of patriotism to heighten the solicitude, which all considerate and good men must feel for the event. Happy will it be if our choice should be directed by a judicious estimate of our true interests, unperplexed and unbiassed by considerations not connected with the public good. But this is a thing more ardently to be wished, than seriously to be expected. The plan offered to our deliberations, affects too many particular interests, innovates upon too many local institutions, not to involve in its discussion a variety of objects foreign to its merits, and of views, passions and prejudices little favourable to the discovery of truth.

Among the most formidable of the obstacles which the new Constitution will have to encounter, may readily be distinguished the obvious interest of a certain class of men in every State to resist all changes which may hazard a diminution of the power, emolument and consequence of the offices they hold under the State-establishments—and the perverted ambition of another class of men, who will either hope to aggrandise themselves by the confusions of their country, or will flatter themselves with fairer prospects of elevation from the subdivision of the empire into several partial confederacies, than from its union under one government.

It is not, however, my design to dwell upon observations of this nature. I am well aware that it would be disingenuous to resolve indiscriminately the opposition of any set of men (merely because their situations might subject them to suspicion) into interested or ambitious views: Candour will oblige us to admit, that even such men may be actuated by upright intentions; and it cannot be doubted that much of the opposition which has made its appearance, or may hereafter make its appearance, will spring from sources, blameless at least, if not respectable, the honest errors of minds led astray by preconceived jealousies and fears. So numerous indeed and so powerful are the causes, which serve to give a false bias to the judgment, that we upon many occasions, see wise and good men on the wrong as well as on the right side of questions, of the first magnitude to society. This circumstance, if duly attended to, would furnish a lesson of moderation to those, who are ever so much persuaded of their being in the right, in any controversy. And a further reason for caution, in this respect, might be drawn from the reflection, that we are not always sure, that those who advocate the truth are influenced by purer principles than their antagonists. Ambition, avarice, personal animosity, party opposition, and many other motives, not more laudable than these, are apt to operate as well upon those who support as upon those who oppose the right side of a question. Were there not even these inducements to moderation, nothing could be more illjudged than that intolerant spirit, which has, at all times, characterized political parties. For, in politics as in religion, it is equally absurd to aim at making proselytes by fire and sword. Heresies in either can rarely be cured by persecution.

And yet however just these sentiments will be allowed to be, we have already sufficient indications, that it will happen in this as in all former cases of great national discussion. A torrent of angry and malignant passions will be let loose. To judge from the conduct of the opposite parties, we shall be led to conclude, that they will mutually hope to evince the justness of their opinions, and to increase the number of their converts by the loudness of their declamations, and by the bitterness of their invectives. An enlightened zeal for the energy and efficiency of government will be stigmatized, as the off-spring of a temper fond of despotic power and hostile to the principles of liberty. An overscrupulous jealousy of danger to the rights of the people, which is more commonly the fault of the head than of the heart, will be represented as mere pretence and artifice; the bait for popularity at the expence of public good. It will be forgotten, on the one hand, that jealousy is the usual concomitant of violent love, and that the noble enthusiasm of liberty is too apt to be infected with a spirit of narrow and illiberal distrust. On the other hand, it will be equally forgotten, that the vigour of government is essential to the security of liberty; that, in the contemplation of a sound and well informed judgment, their interest can never be separated; and that a dangerous ambition more often lurks behind the specious mask of zeal for the rights of the people, than under the forbidding appearance of zeal for the firmness and efficiency of government. History will teach us, that the former has been found a much more certain road to the introduction of despotism, than the latter, and that of those men who have overturned the liberties of republics the greatest number have begun their career, by paying an obsequious court to the people, commencing Demagogues and ending Tyrants.

In the course of the preceding observations I have had an eye, my Fellow Citizens, to putting you upon your guard against all attempts, from whatever quarter, to influence your decision in a matter of the utmost moment to your welfare by any impressions other than those which may result from the evidence of truth. You will, no doubt, at the same time, have collected from the general scope of them that they proceed from a source not unfriendly to the new Constitution. Yes, my Countrymen, I own to you, that, after having given it an attentive consideration, I am clearly of opinion, it is your interest to adopt it. I am convinced, that this is the safest course for your liberty, your dignity, and your happiness.[1] I effect not reserves, which I do not feel. I will not amuse you with an appearance of deliberation, when I have decided. I frankly acknowledge to you my convictions, and I will freely lay before you the reasons on which they are founded. The consciousness of good intentions disdains ambiguity. I shall not however multiply professions on this head. My motives must remain in the depository of my own breast: My arguments will be open to all, and may be judged of by all. They shall at least be offered in a spirit, which will not disgrace the cause of truth.

I propose in a series of papers to discuss the following interesting particulars—*The utility of the* UNION *to your political prosperity—The insufficiency of the present Confederation to preserve that Union—The necessity of a government at least equally energetic with the one proposed to the attainment of this object—The conformity of the proposed constitution to the true principles of republican government—Its analogy to your own state constitution*—and lastly, *The additional security, which its adoption will afford to the preservation of that species of government, to liberty and to property.*

In the progress of this discussion I shall endeavour to give a satisfactory answer to all the objections which shall have made their appearance that may seem to have any claim to your attention.

It may perhaps be thought superfluous to offer arguments to prove the utility of the UNION, a point, no doubt, deeply engraved on the hearts of the great body of the people in every state, and one, which it may be imagined has no adversaries. But the fact is, that we already hear it whispered in the private circles of those who oppose the new constitution, that the Thirteen States are of too great extent for any general system, and that we must of necessity resort to separate confederacies of distinct portions of the whole.* This doctrine will, in all probability, be gradually propagated, till it has votaries enough to countenance an open avowal of it. For nothing can be more evident, to those who are able to take an enlarged view of the subject, than the alternative of an adoption of the new Constitution, or a dismemberment of the Union. It will

[1] Hamilton was not as enthusiastic about the proposed Constitution as this paragraph would seem to indicate. He considered it to be much too weak and desired a far more centralized and powerful federal government.

* *The same idea, tracing the arguments to their consequences, is held out in several of the late publications against the New Constitution.*

therefore be of use to begin by examining the advantages of that Union, the certain evils and the probable dangers, to which every State will be exposed from its dissolution. This shall accordingly constitute the subject of my next address.

PUBLIUS.

THE FEDERALIST NO. 2

JOHN JAY

October 31, 1787

To the People of the State of New York.

When the people of America reflect that they are now called upon to decide a question, which, in its consequences, must prove one of the most important, that ever engaged their attention, the propriety of their taking a very comprehensive, as well as a very serious view of it, will be evident.

Nothing is more certain than the indispensable necessity of Government, and it is equally undeniable, that whenever and however it is instituted, the people must cede to it some of their natural rights, in order to vest it with requisite powers. It is well worthy of consideration therefore, whether it would conduce more to the interest of the people of America, that they should, to all general purposes, be one nation, under one fœderal Government, than that they should divide themselves into separate confederacies, and give to the head of each, the same kind of powers which they are advised to place in one national Government.

It has until lately been a received and uncontradicted opinion, that the prosperity of the people of America depended on their continuing firmly united, and the wishes, prayers, and efforts of our best and wisest Citizens have been constantly directed to that object. But Politicians now appear, who insist that this opinion is erroneous, and that instead of looking for safety and happiness in union, we ought to seek it in a division of the States into distinct confederacies or sovereignties. However extraordinary this new doctrine may appear, it nevertheless has its advocates; and certain characters who were much opposed to it formerly, are at present of the number. Whatever may be the arguments or inducements, which have wrought this change in the sentiments and declarations of these Gentlemen, it certainly would not be wise in the people at large to adopt these new political tenets without being fully convinced that they are founded in truth and sound Policy.

It has often given me pleasure to observe, that Independent America was not composed of detached and distant territories, but that one connected, fertile, wide spreading country was the portion of our western sons of liberty. Providence has in a particular manner blessed it with a variety of soils and productions, and watered it with innumerable streams, for the delight and accomodation of its inhabitants. A succession of navigable waters forms a kind of chain round its borders, as if to bind it together; while the most noble rivers in the world, running at convenient distances, present them with highways for the easy communication of friendly aids, and the mutual transportation and exchange of their various commodities.

With equal pleasure I have as often taken notice, that Providence has been pleased to give this one connected country, to one united people, a people descended from the same ancestors, speaking the same language, professing the same religion, attached to the same principles of government, very similar in their manners and customs, and who, by their joint counsels, arms and efforts, fighting side by side throughout a long and bloody war, have nobly established their general Liberty and Independence.

This country and this people seem to have been made for each other, and it appears as if it was the design of Providence, that an inheritance so proper and convenient for a band of brethren, united to each other by the strongest ties, should never be split into a number of unsocial, jealous and alien sovereignties.

Similar sentiments have hitherto prevailed among all orders and denominations of men among us. To all general purposes we have uniformly been one people—each individual citizen every where enjoying the same national rights, privileges, and protection. As a nation we have made peace and war—as a nation we have vanquished our common enemies—as a nation we have formed alliances and made treaties, and entered into various compacts and conventions with foreign States.

A strong sense of the value and blessings of Union induced the people, at a very early period, to institute a Fœderal Government to preserve and perpetuate it. They formed it almost as soon as they had a political existence; nay at a time, when their habitations were in flames, when many of their Citizens were bleeding, and when the progress of hostility and desolation left little room for those calm and mature enquiries and reflections, which must ever precede the formation of a wise and well balanced government for a free people. It is not to be wondered at that a Government instituted in times so inauspicious, should on experiment be found greatly deficient and inadequate to the purpose it was intended to answer.

This intelligent people perceived and regretted these defects. Still continuing no less attached to union, than enamoured of liberty, they observed the danger, which immediately threatened the former and more remotely the latter; and being persuaded that ample security for both, could only be found in a national Government more wisely framed, they, as with one voice, convened the late Convention at Philadelphia, to take that important subject under consideration.

This Convention, composed of men, who possessed the confidence of the people, and many of whom had become highly distinguished by their patriotism, virtue and wisdom, in times which tried the minds and hearts of men, undertook the arduous task. In the mild season of peace, with minds unoccupied by other subjects, they passed many months in cool uninterrupted and daily consultations: and finally, without having been awed by power, or influenced by any passions except love for their Country, they presented and recommended to the people the plan produced by their joint and very unanimous counsels.

Admit, for so is the fact, that this plan is only *recommended,* not imposed, yet let it be remembered, that it is neither recommended to *blind* approbation, nor to *blind* reprobation; but to that sedate and candid consideration, which the magnitude and importance of the subject demand, and which it certainly ought to receive. But this, (as was remarked in the foregoing number of this Paper,) is more to be wished than expected that it may be so considered and examined. Experience on a former occasion teaches us not to be too sanguine in such hopes. It is not yet forgotten, that well grounded apprehensions of imminent danger induced the people of America to form the Memorable Congress of 1774.[1] That Body recommended certain measures to their Constituents, and the event proved their wisdom; yet it is fresh in our memories how soon the Press began to teem with Pamphlets and weekly Papers against those very measures. Not only many of the Officers of Government who obeyed the

[1] Jay is referring to the First Continental Congress, which met at Philadelphia on September 5, 1774. The Congress recommended formation of a Continental Association, an end to imports from Great Britain after December 1, 1774, the discontinuance of the slave trade on that same date, and organized nonconsumption of British products. Extra-legal machinery, consisting of county, city, and town-elected committees, was established for purposes of enforcement.

dictates of personal interest, but others from a mistaken estimate of consequences, or the undue influence of former attachments, or whose ambition aimed at objects which did not correspond with the public good, were indefatigable in their endeavours to persuade the people to reject the advice of that Patriotic Congress. Many indeed were deceived and deluded, but the great majority of the people reasoned and decided judiciously; and happy they are in reflecting that they did so.

They considered that the Congress was composed of many wise and experienced men. That being convened from different parts of the country, they brought with them and communicated to each other a variety of useful information. That in the course of the time they passed together in enquiring into and discussing the true interests of their country, they must have acquired very accurate knowledge on that head. That they were individually interested in the public liberty and prosperity, and therefore that it was not less their inclination, than their duty, to recommend only such measures, as after the most mature deliberation they really thought prudent and adviseable.

These and similar considerations then induced the people to rely greatly on the judgment and integrity of the Congress; and they took their advice, notwithstanding the various arts and endeavours used to deter and disuade them from it. But if the people at large had reason to confide in the men of that Congress, few of whom had then been fully tried or generally known, still greater reason have they now to respect the judgment and advice of the Convention, for it is well known that some of the most distinguished members of that Congress, who have been since tried and just approved for patriotism and abilities, and who have grown old in acquiring political information, were also members of this Convention and carried into it their accumulated knowledge and experience.[2]

It is worthy of remark that not only the first, but every succeeding Congress, as well as the late Convention, have invariably joined with the people in thinking that the prosperity of America depended on its Union. To preserve and perpetuate it, was the great object of the people in forming that Convention, and it is also the great object of the plan which

[2] The Constitutional Convention officially opened on May 25, 1787, in Philadelphia's State House (Independence Hall). Washington and Franklin were the two most famous delegates present, although neither of them played a very important role in framing the new constitution.

the Convention has advised them to adopt. With what propriety therefore, or for what good purposes, are attempts at this particular period, made by some men, to depreciate the importance of the Union? or why is it suggested that three or four confederacies would be better than one? I am persuaded in my own mind, that the people have always thought right on this subject, and that their universal and uniform attachment to the cause of the Union, rests on great and weighty reasons, which I shall endeavour to develope and explain in some ensuing papers. They who promote the idea of substituting a number of distinct confederacies in the room of the plan of the Convention, seems clearly to foresee that the rejection of it would put the continuance of the Union in the utmost jeopardy. That certainly would be the case, and I sincerely wish that it may be as clearly foreseen by every good Citizen, that whenever the dissolution of the Union arrives, America will have reason to exclaim in the words of the Poet, "FAREWELL, A LONG FAREWELL, TO ALL MY GREATNESS."

PUBLIUS.

THE FEDERALIST NO. 6
ALEXANDER HAMILTON

November 14, 1787

To the People of the State of New York.

The three last numbers of this Paper have been dedicated to an enumeration of the dangers to which we should be exposed, in a state of disunion, from the arms and arts of foreign nations.[1] I shall now proceed to delineate dangers of a different, and, perhaps, still more alarming kind, those which will in all probability flow from dissentions between the States themselves, and from domestic factions and convulsions. These have been already in some instances slightly anticipated, but they deserve a more particular and more full investigation.

A man must be far gone in Utopian speculations who can seriously doubt, that if these States should either be wholly disunited, or only united in partial confederacies, the subdivisions into which they might be thrown would have frequent and violent contests with each other. To presume a want of motives for such contests, as an argument against their existence, would be to forget that men are ambitious, vindictive and rapacious. To look for a continuation of harmony

[1] The three previous papers were written by John Jay, who from 1784 to 1790 served as Secretary of Foreign Affairs.

between a number of independent unconnected sovereignties, situated in the same neighbourhood, would be to disregard the uniform course of human events, and to set at defiance the accumulated experience of ages.

The causes of hostility among nations are innumerable. There are some which have a general and almost constant operation upon the collective bodies of society: Of this description are the love of power or the desire of preeminence and dominion—the jealousy of power, or the desire of equality and safety. There are others which have a more circumscribed, though an equally operative influence, within their spheres: Such are the rivalships and competitions of commerce between commercial nations. And there are others, not less numerous than either of the former, which take their origin intirely in private passions; in the attachments, enmities, interests, hopes and fears of leading individuals in the communities of which they are members. Men of this class, whether the favourites of a king or of a people, have in too many instances abused the confidence they possessed; and assuming the pretext of some public motive, have not scrupled to sacrifice the national tranquility to personal advantage, or personal gratification.

The celebrated Pericles, in compliance with the resentments of a prostitute,* at the expence of much of the blood and treasure of his countrymen, attacked, vanquished and destroyed, the city of the *Samnians*. The same man, stimulated by private pique against the *Megarensians,*† another nation of Greece, or to avoid a prosecution with which he was threatened as an accomplice in a supposed theft of the statuary *Phidias,*‡ or to get rid of the accusations prepared to be brought against him for dissipating the funds of the State in the purchase of popularity,§ or from a combination of all these causes, was the primitive author of that famous and fatal war, distinguished in the Grecian annals by the name of the *Pelopponesian* war; which, after various vicissitudes, intermissions and renewals, terminated in the ruin of the Athenian commonwealth.

The ambitious Cardinal, who was Prime Minister to Henry VIIIth. permitting his vanity to aspire to the Tripple-Crown,||

* ASPASIA, vide PLUTARCH's life of Pericles.

† — Idem.

‡ — Idem. Phidias was supposed to have stolen some public gold with the connivance of Pericles for the embelishment of the statue of Minerva.

§ — Idem.

|| Worn by the Popes.

entertained hopes of succeeding in the acquisition of that splendid prize by the influence of the Emperor Charles Vth.[2] To secure the favour and interest of this enterprising and powerful Monarch, he precipitated England into a war with France, contrary to the plainest dictates of Policy, and at the hazard of the safety and independence, as well of the Kingdom over which he presided by his councils, as of Europe in general. For if there ever was a Sovereign who bid fair to realise the project of universal monarchy it was the Emperor Charles Vth, of whose intrigues Wolsey was at once the instrument and the dupe.

The influence which the bigottry of one female,* the petulancies of another,† and the cabals of a third,‡ had in the co[n]temporary policy, ferments and pacifications of a considerable part of Europe are topics that have been too often descanted upon not to be generally known.[3]

To multiply examples of the agency of personal considerations in the production of great national events, either foreign or domestic, according to their direction would be an unnecessary waste of time. Those who have but a superficial acquaintance with the sources from which they are to be drawn will themselves recollect a variety of instances; and those who have a tolerable knowledge of human nature will not stand in need of such lights, to form their opinion either of the reality or extent of that agency. Perhaps however a reference, tending to illustrate the general principle, may with propriety be made to a case which has lately happened among ourselves. If SHAYS had not been a *desperate debtor* it is much to be doubted whether Massachusetts would have been plunged into a civil war.[4]

But notwithstanding the concurring testimony of experience,

[2] Thomas Wolsey (1475?–1530), an English cardinal and statesman, who, at the insistence of Henry VIII, concluded a secret treaty with Charles V of Germany for an alliance against France.

* Madame De Maintenon.

† Dutchess of Marlborough.

‡ Madame De Pompadoure.

[3] Madame de Maintenon was secretly married to Louis XIV of France in 1684. She successfully persuaded Louis to persecute the French Huguenots. The Duchess of Marlborough was a highly influential political and personal confidante of Queen Anne, until her intrigues and arrogance led to a break with the Queen. Madame de Pompadour, mistress to Louis XV of France from 1745 to 1764, helped to choose France's ministers and helped to determine the nation's policies.

[4] The Shays' Rebellion of 1786 in western Massachusetts was a debtors' uprising designed to force the legislature to heed the demands of debt-ridden farmers for paper money and stay laws on farm foreclosures. On February 4, 1787, the uprising was crushed by state troops commanded by General Benjamin Lincoln.

in this particular, there are still to be found visionary, or designing men, who stand ready to advocate the paradox of perpetual peace between the States, though dismembered and alienated from each other. The genius of republics (say they) is pacific; the spirit of commerce has a tendency to soften the manners of men and to extinguish those inflammable humours which have so often kindled into wars. Commercial republics, like ours, will never be disposed to waste themselves in ruinous contentions with each other. They will be governed by mutual interest, and will cultivate a spirit of mutual amity and concord.

Is it not (we may ask these projectors in politics) the true interest of all nations to cultivate the same benevolent and philosophic spirit? If this be their true interest, have they in fact pursued it? Has it not, on the contrary, invariably been found, that momentary passions and immediate interests have a more active and imperious controul over human conduct than general or remote considerations of policy, utility or justice? Have republics in practice been less addicted to war than monarchies? Are not the former administered by *men* as well as the latter? Are there not aversions, predilections, rivalships and desires of unjust acquisition that affect nations as well as kings? Are not popular assemblies frequently subject to the impulses of rage, resentment, jealousy, avarice, and of other irregular and violent propensities? Is it not well known that their determinations are often governed by a few individuals, in whom they place confidence, and are of course liable to be tinctured by the passions and views of those individuals? Has commerce hitherto done any thing more than change the objects of war? Is not the love of wealth as domineering and enterprising a passion as that of power or glory? Have there not been as many wars founded upon commercial motives, since that has become the prevailing system of nations, as were before occasioned b[y] the cupidity of territory or dominion? Has not the spirit of commerce in many instances administered new incentives to the appetite both for the one and for the other? Let experience the least fallible guide of human opinions be appealed to for an answer to these inquiries.

Sparta, Athens, Rome and Carthage were all Republics; two of them, Athens and Carthage, of the commercial kind. Yet were they as often engaged in wars, offensive and defensive, as the neighbouring Monarchies of the same times. Sparta was little better than a well regulated camp; and Rome was never sated of carnage and conquest.

Carthage, though a commercial Republic, was the aggressor in the very war that ended in her destruction. Hannibal had carried her arms into the heart of Italy and to the gates of Rome, before Scipio, in turn, gave him an overthrow in the territories of Carthage and made a conquest of the Commonwealth.

Venice in latter times figured more than once in wars of ambition; 'till becoming an object of terror to the other Italian States, Pope Julius the Second found means to accomplish that formidable league,* which gave a deadly blow to the power and pride of this haughty Republic.

The Provinces of Holland, 'till they were overwhelmed in debts and taxes, took a leading and conspicuous part in the wars of Europe. They had furious contests with England for the dominion of the sea; and were among the most persevering and most implacable of the opponents of Lewis XIV.

In the government of Britain the representatives of the people compose one branch of the national legislature. Commerce has been for ages the predominant pursuit of that country. Few nations, nevertheless, have been more frequently engaged in war; and the wars, in which that kingdom has been engaged, have in numerous instances proceeded from the people.

There have been, if I may so express it, almost as many popular as royal wars. The cries of the nation and the importunities of their representatives have, upon various occasions, dragged their monarchs into war, or continued them in it contrary to their inclinations, and, sometimes, contrary to the real interests of the State. In that memorable struggle for superiority, between the rival Houses of *Austria* and *Bourbon* which so long kept Europe in a flame, it is well known that the antipathies of the English against the French, seconding the ambition, or rather the avarice of a favourite leader,† protracted the war beyond the limits marked out by sound policy and for a considerable time in opposition to the views of the Court.[5]

* The LEAGUE OF CAMBRAY, comprehending the Emperor, the King of France, the King of Arragon, and most of the Italian Princes and States.

† The Duke of Marlborough.

[5] John Churchill (1650–1722), the first Duke of Marlborough, was commander in chief of the combined English and Dutch armies in the War of the Spanish Succession, 1701–1714. In 1709, he refused an offer to conclude the war on reasonable terms, despite the fact that his own party in England, the Tories, was opposed to the war's continuation.

The wars of these two last mentioned nations have in a great measure grown out of commercial considerations—the desire of supplanting and the fear of being supplanted either in particular branches of traffic or in the general advantages of trade and navigation; and sometimes even the more culpable desire of sharing in the commerce of other nations, without their consent.

The last war but two between Britain and Spain sprang from the attempts of the English merchants, to prosecute an illicit trade with the Spanish main.[6] These unjustifiable practices on their part produced severities on the part of the Spaniards, towards the subjects of Great Britain, which were not more justifiable; because they exceeded the bounds of a just retaliation, and were chargeable with inhumanity and cruelty. Many of the English who were taken on the Spanish coasts were sent to dig in the mines of Potosi; and by the usual progress of a spirit of resentment, the innocent were after a while confounded with the guilty in indiscriminate punishment. The complaints of the merchants kindled a violent flame throughout the nation, which soon after broke out in the house of commons, and was communicated from that body to the ministry. Letters of reprisal were granted and a war ensued, which in its consequences overthrew all the alliances that but twenty years before had been formed, with sanguine expectations of the most beneficial fruits.[7]

From this summary of what has taken place in other countries, whose situations have borne the nearest resemblance to our own, what reason can we have to confide in those reveries, which would seduce us into an expectation of peace and cordiality between the members of the present confederacy, in a state of separation? Have we not already seen enough of the fallacy and extravagance of those idle theories which have amused us with promises of an exemption from the imperfections, weaknesses and evils incident to society in every shape? Is it not time to awake from the deceitful dream of a golden age, and to adopt as a practical maxim for the direction of our political conduct, that we, as well as the other inhabitants of the globe, are yet remote from the happy empire of perfect wisdom and perfect virtue?

[6] The War of Jenkins' Ear, 1739–1742, was soon absorbed into the War of the Austrian Succession, 1740–1748. It arose from Spanish mistreatment of English merchant seamen who had defied Spain's strict colonial trading regulations.

[7] The Treaty of Utrecht of 1713 established the continental balance of power system.

Let the point of extreme depression to which our national dignity and credit have sunk—let the inconveniences felt every where from a lax and ill administration of government—let the revolt of a part of the State of North Carolina—the late menacing disturbances in Pennsylvania and the actual insurrections and rebellions in Massachusetts declare![8]

So far is the general sense of mankind from corresponding with the tenets of those, who endeavour to lull asleep our apprehensions of discord and hostility between the States, in the event of disunion, that it has from long observation of the progress of society become a sort of axiom in politics, that vicinity, or nearness of situation, constitutes nations natural enemies. An intelligent writer expresses himself on this subject to this effect—"NEIGHBOURING NATIONS (says he) are naturally ENEMIES of each other, unless their common weakness forces them to league in a CONFEDERATE REPUBLIC, and their constitution prevents the differences that neighbourhood occasions, extinguishing that secret jealousy, which disposes all States to aggrandise themselves at the expence of their neighbours."* This passage, at the same time points out the EVIL and suggests the REMEDY.

PUBLIUS.

THE FEDERALIST NO. 9
ALEXANDER HAMILTON

November 21, 1787

To the People of the State of New York.

A Firm Union will be of the utmost moment to the peace and liberty of the States as a barrier against domestic faction and insurrection. It is impossible to read the history of the petty Republics of Greece and Italy, without feeling sensations of horror and disgust at the distractions with which they were continually agitated, and at the rapid succession of revolutions, by which they were kept in a state of perpetual vibration, between the extremes of tyranny and anarchy. If they exhibit occasional calms, these only serve as short-lived contrasts to the furious storms that are to succeed. If now and then intervals

[8] In 1784, four dissatisfied western counties in North Carolina formed the new state of Franklin. Internal dissension, a lack of recognition from other states, and the opposition of North Carolina forced Franklin to submit to North Carolina in 1787. That same year, the inhabitants of the Wyoming Valley attempted to secede from Pennsylvania and establish a new state, a movement quickly crushed by the Pennsylvania Assembly. For the Shays' Rebellion, see above, Note 4.

* Vide Principes des Negotiations par L'Abbe de Mably.

of felicity open themselves to view, we behold them with a mixture of regret arising from the reflection that the pleasing scenes before us are soon to be overwhelmed by the tempestuous waves of sedition and party-rage. If momentary rays of glory break forth from the gloom, while they dazzle us with a transient and fleeting brilliancy, they at the same time admonish us to lament that the vices of government should pervert the direction and tarnish the lustre of those bright talents and exalted indowments, for which the favoured soils, that produced them, have been so justly celebrated.

From the disorders that disfigure the annals of those republics, the advocates of despotism have drawn arguments, not only against the forms of republican government, but against the very principles of civil liberty. They have decried all free government, as inconsistent with the order of society, and have indulged themselves in malicious exultation over its friends and partizans. Happily for mankind, stupendous fabrics reared on the basis of liberty, which have flourished for ages, have in a few glorious instances refuted their gloomy sophisms. And, I trust, America will be the broad and solid foundation of other edifices not less magnificent, which will be equally permanent monuments of their errors.

But it is not to be denied that the portraits, they have sketched of republican government, were too just copies of the originals from which they were taken. If it had been found impracticable, to have devised models of a more perfect structure, the enlightened friends to liberty would have been obliged to abandon the cause of that species of government as indefensible. The science of politics, however, like most other sciences has received great improvement. The efficacy of various principles is now well understood, which were either not known at all, or imperfectly known to the ancients. The regular distribution of power into distinct departments—the introduction of legislative ballances and checks—the institution of courts composed of judges, holding their offices during good behaviour—the representation of the people in the legislature by deputies of their own election—these are either wholly new discoveries or have made their principal progress towards perfection in modern times. They are means, and powerful means, by which the excellencies of republican government may be retained and its imperfections lessened or avoided. To this catalogue of circumstances, that tend to the amelioration of popular systems of civil government, I shall venture, however novel it may appear to some, to add one more on a principle, which has been made the foundation of an objection to the New Constitution, I mean the ENLARGEMENT of the ORBIT within which such systems are to revolve either in respect to the dimensions of a single State, or to the consolidation of several smaller States into one great confederacy. The latter is that which immediately concerns the object under consideration. It will however be of use to examine the principle in its application to a single State which shall be attended to in another place.

The utility of a confederacy, as well to suppress faction and to guard the internal tranquillity of States, as to increase their external force and security, is in reality not a new idea. It has been practiced upon in different countries and ages, and has received the sanction of the most applauded writers, on the subjects of politics. The opponents of the PLAN proposed have with great assiduity cited and circulated the observations of Montesquieu on the necessity of a contracted territory for a republican government. But they seem not to have been apprised of the sentiments of that great man expressed in another part of his work, nor to have adverted to the consequences of the principle to which they subscribe, with such ready acquiescence.

When Montesquieu recommends a small extent for republics, the standards he had in view were of dimensions, far short of the limits of almost every one of these States. Neither Virginia, Massachusetts, Pennsylvania, New-York, North-Carolina, nor Georgia, can by any means be compared with the models, from which he reasoned and to which the terms of his description apply. If we therefore take his ideas on this point, as the criterion of truth, we shall be driven to the alternative, either of taking refuge at once in the arms of monarchy, or of spliting ourselves into an infinity of little jealous, clashing, tumultuous commonwealths, the wretched nurseries of unceasing discord and the miserable objects of universal pity or contempt. Some of the writers, who have come forward on the other side of the question, seem to have been aware of the dilemma; and have even been bold enough to hint at the division of the larger States, as a desirable thing. Such an infatuated policy, such a desperate expedient, might, by the multiplication of petty offices, answer the views of men, who possess not qualifications to extend their influence beyond the narrow circles of personal intrigue, but it could never promote the greatness or happiness of the people of America.

Referring the examination of the principle itself to another place, as has been already mentioned, it will be sufficient to remark here, that in the sense of the author who has been most emphatically quoted upon the occasion, it would only dictate a reduction of the SIZE of the more considerable MEMBERS of the Union; but would not militate against their being all comprehended in one Confederate Government. And this is the true question, in the discussion of which we are at present interested.

So far are the suggestions of Montesquieu from standing in opposition to a general Union of the States, that he explicitly treats of a CONFEDERATE REPUBLIC as the expedient for extending the sphere of popular government and reconciling the advantages of monarchy with those of republicanism.

"It is very probable (says he*) that mankind would have been obliged, at length, to live constantly under the government of a SINGLE PERSON, had they not contrived a kind of constitution, that has all the internal advantages of a republican, together with the external force of a monarchial government. I mean a CONFEDERATE REPUBLIC.

"This form of Government is a Convention, by which several smaller *States* agree to become members of a larger *one,* which they intend to form. It is a kind of assemblage of societies, that constitute a new one, capable of encreasing by means of new associations, till they arrive to such a degree of power as to be able to provide for the security of the united body.

"A republic of this kind, able to withstand an external force, may support itself without any internal corruption. The form of this society prevents all manner of inconveniencies.

"If a single member should attempt to usurp the supreme authority, he could not be supposed to have an equal authority and credit, in all the confederate states. Were he to have too great influence over one, this would alarm the rest. Were he to subdue a part, that which would still remain free might oppose him with forces, independent of those which he had usurped, and overpower him before he could be settled in his usurpation.

"Should a popular insurrection happen, in one of the confederate States, the others are able to quell it. Should abuses creep into one part, they are reformed by those that remain sound. The State may be destroyed on one side, and not on the

* *Spirit of Laws, Vol. I. Book IX. Chap. I.*

other; the confederacy may be dissolved, and the confederates preserve their sovereignty.

"As this government is composed of small republics it enjoys the internal happiness of each, and with respect to its external situation it is possessed, by means of the association of all the advantages of large monarchies."

I have thought it proper to quote at length these interesting passages, because they contain a luminous abrigement of the principal arguments in favour of the Union, and must effectually remove the false impressions, which a misapplication of other parts of the work was calculated to produce. They have at the same time an intimate connection with the more immediate design of this Paper; which is to illustrate the tendency of the Union to repress domestic faction and insurrection.

A distinction, more subtle than accurate has been raised between a *confederacy* and a *consolidation* of the States. The essential characteristic of the first is said to be, the restriction of its authority to the members in their collective capacities, without reaching to the individuals of whom they are composed. It is contended that the national council ought to have no concern with any object of internal administration. An exact equality of suffrage between the members has also been insisted upon as a leading feature of a Confederate Government. These positions are in the main arbitrary; they are supported neither by principle nor precedent. It has indeed happened that governments of this kind have generally operated in the manner, which the distinction, taken notice of, supposes to be inherent in their nature—but there have been in most of them extensive exceptions to the practice, which serve to prove as far as example will go, that there is no absolute rule on the subject. And it will be clearly shewn, in the course of this investigation, that as far as the principle contended for has prevailed, it has been the cause of incurable disorder and imbecility in the government.

The definition of a *Confederate Republic* seems simply to be, an "assemblage of societies" or an association of two or more States into one State. The extent, modifications and objects of the Fœderal authority are mere matters of discretion. So long as the separate organisation of the members be not abolished, so long as it exists by a constitutional necessity for local purposes, though it should be in perfect subordination to the general authority of the Union, it would still be, in fact and in theory, an association of States, or a confederacy. The proposed Constitution, so far from implying an abolition of the State Governments, makes them constituent parts of the national sovereignty by allowing them a direct representation in the Senate, and leaves in their possession certain exclusive and very important portions of sovereign power. This fully corresponds, in every rational import of the terms, with the idea of a Fœderal Government.

In the Lycian confederacy, which consisted of twenty three CITIES or republics, the largest were intitled to *three* votes in the COMMON COUNCIL, those of the middle class to *two* and the smallest to *one*. The COMMON COUNCIL had the appointment of all the judges and magistrates of the respective CITIES. This was certainly the most delicate species of interference in their internal administration; for if there be any thing, that seems exclusively appropriated to the local jurisdictions, it is the appointment of their own officers. Yet Montesquieu, speaking of this association, says "Were I to give a model of an excellent confederate republic, it would be that of Lycia." Thus we perceive that the distinctions insisted upon were not within the contemplation of this enlightened civilian, and we shall be led to conclude that they are the novel refinements of an erroneous theory.

PUBLIUS.

THE FEDERALIST NO. 10

JAMES MADISON

November 22, 1787

To the People of the State of New York.

Among the numerous advantages promised by a well constructed Union, none deserves to be more accurately developed than its tendency to break and control the violence of faction. The friend of popular governments, never finds himself so much alarmed for their character and fate, as when he contemplates their propensity to this dangerous vice. He will not fail therefore to set a due value on any plan which, without violating the principles to which he is attached, provides a proper cure for it. The instability, injustice and confusion introduced into the public councils, have in truth been the mortal diseases under which popular governments have every where perished; as they continue to be the favorite and fruitful topics from which the adversaries to liberty derive their most specious declamations. The valuable improvements made by the American Constitutions on the popular models, both ancient and modern, cannot certainly be too much admired;

but it would be an unwarrantable partiality, to contend that they have as effectually obviated the danger on this side as was wished and expected. Complaints are every where heard from our most considerate and virtuous citizens, equally the friends of public and private faith, and of public and personal liberty; that our governments are too unstable; that the public good is disregarded in the conflicts of rival parties; and that measures are too often decided, not according to the rules of justice, and the rights of the minor party; but by the superior force of an interested and over-bearing majority. However anxiously we may wish that these complaints had no foundation, the evidence of known facts will not permit us to deny that they are in some degree true. It will be found indeed, on a candid review of our situation, that some of the distresses under which we labor, have been erroneously charged on the operation of our governments; but it will be found, at the same time, that other causes will not alone account for many of our heaviest misfortunes; and particularly, for that prevailing and increasing distrust of public engagements, and alarm for private rights, which are echoed from one end of the continent to the other. These must be chiefly, if not wholly, effects of the unsteadiness and injustice, with which a factious spirit has tainted our public administrations.

By a faction I understand a number of citizens, whether amounting to a majority or minority of the whole, who are united and actuated by some common impulse of passion, or of interest, adverse to the rights of other citizens, or to the permanent and aggregate interests of the community.

There are two methods of curing the mischiefs of faction: the one, by removing its causes; the other, by controling its effects.

There are again two methods of removing the causes of faction: the one by destroying the liberty which is essential to its existence; the other, by giving to every citizen the same opinions, the same passions, and the same interests.

It could never be more truly said than of the first remedy, that it is worse than the disease. Liberty is to faction, what air is to fire, an aliment without which it instantly expires. But it could not be a less folly to abolish liberty, which is essential to political life, because it nourishes faction, than it would be to wish the annihilation of air, which is essential to animal life, because it imparts to fire its destructive agency.

The second expedient is as impracticable, as the first would be unwise. As long as the reason of man continues fallible, and he is at liberty to exercise it, different opinions will be formed. As long as the connection subsists between his reason and his self-love, his opinions and his passions will have a reciprocal influence on each other; and the former will be objects to which the latter will attach themselves. The diversity in the faculties of men from which the rights of property originate, is not less an insuperable obstacle to a uniformity of interests. The protection of these faculties is the first object of Government. From the protection of different and unequal faculties of acquiring property, the possession of different degrees and kinds of property immediately results: and from the influence of these on the sentiments and views of the respective proprietors, ensues a division of the society into different interests and parties.

The latent causes of faction are thus sown in the nature of man; and we see them every where brought into different degrees of activity, according to the different circumstances of civil society. A zeal for different opinions concerning religion, concerning Government and many other points, as well of speculation as of practice; an attachment to different leaders ambitiously contending for pre-eminence and power; or to persons of other descriptions whose fortunes have been interesting to the human passions, have in turn divided mankind into parties, inflamed them with mutual animosity, and rendered them much more disposed to vex and oppress each other, than to co-operate for their common good. So strong is this propensity of mankind to fall into mutual animosities, that where no substantial occasion presents itself, the most frivolous and fanciful distinctions have been sufficient to kindle their unfriendly passions, and excite their most violent conflicts. But the most common and durable source of factions, has been the various and unequal distribution of property. Those who hold, and those who are without property, have ever formed distinct interests in society. Those who are creditors, and those who are debtors, fall under a like discrimination. A landed interest, a manufacturing interest, a mercantile interest, a monied interest, with many lesser interests, grow up of necessity in civilized nations, and divide them into different classes, actuated by different sentiments and views. The regulation of these various and interfering interests forms the principal task of modern Legislation, and involves the spirit of party and faction in the necessary and ordinary operations of Government.

No man is allowed to be a judge in his own cause; because

his interest would certainly bias his judgment, and, not improbably, corrupt his integrity. With equal, nay with greater reason, a body of men, are unfit to be both judges and parties, at the same time; yet, what are many of the most important acts of legislation, but so many judicial determinations, not indeed concerning the rights of single persons, but concerning the rights of large bodies of citizens; and what are the different classes of legislators, but advocates and parties to the causes which they determine? Is a law proposed concerning private debts? It is a question to which the creditors are parties on one side, and the debtors on the other. Justice ought to hold the balance between them. Yet the parties are and must be themselves the judges; and the most numerous party, or, in other words, the most powerful faction must be expected to prevail. Shall domestic manufactures be encouraged, and in what degree, by restrictions on foreign manufactures? are questions which would be differently decided by the landed and the manufacturing classes; and probably by neither, with a sole regard to justice and the public good. The apportionment of taxes on the various descriptions of property, is an act which seems to require the most exact impartiality; yet, there is perhaps no legislative act in which greater opportunity and temptation are given to a predominant party, to trample on the rules of justice. Every shilling with which they over-burden the inferior number, is a shilling saved to their own pockets.

It is in vain to say, that enlightened statesmen will be able to adjust these clashing interests, and render them all subservient to the public good. Enlightened statesmen will not always be at the helm: Nor, in many cases, can such an adjustment be made at all, without taking into view indirect and remote considerations, which will rarely prevail over the immediate interest which one party may find in disregarding the rights of another, or the good of the whole.

The inference to which we are brought, is, that the *causes* of faction cannot be removed; and that relief is only to be sought in the means of controling its *effects*.

If a faction consists of less than a majority, relief is supplied by the republican principle, which enables the majority to defeat its sinister views by regular vote: It may clog the administration, it may convulse the society; but it will be unable to execute and mask its violence under the forms of the Constitution. When a majority is included in a faction, the form of popular government on the other hand enables it to sacrifice to its ruling passion or interest, both the public good and the rights of other citizens. To secure the public good, and private rights, against the danger of such a faction, and at the same time to preserve the spirit and the form of popular government, is then the great object to which our enquiries are directed: Let me add that it is the great desideratum, by which alone this form of government can be rescued from the opprobrium under which it has so long labored, and be recommended to the esteem and adoption of mankind.

By what means is this object attainable? Evidently by one of two only. Either the existence of the same passion or interest in a majority at the same time, must be prevented; or the majority, having such co-existent passion or interest, must be rendered, by their number and local situation, unable to concert and carry into effect schemes of oppression. If the impulse and the opportunity be suffered to coincide, we well know that neither moral nor religious motives can be relied on as an adequate control. They are not found to be such on the injustice and violence of individuals, and lose their efficacy in proportion to the number combined together; that is, in proportion as their efficacy becomes needful.

From this view of the subject, it may be concluded, that a pure Democracy, by which I mean, a Society, consisting of a small number of citizens, who assemble and administer the Government in person, can admit of no cure for the mischiefs of faction. A common passion or interest will, in almost every case, be felt by a majority of the whole; a communication and concert results from the form of Government itself; and there is nothing to check the inducements to sacrifice the weaker party, or an obnoxious individual. Hence it is, that such Democracies have ever been spectacles of turbulence and contention; have ever been found incompatible with personal security, or the rights of property; and have in general been as short in their lives, as they have been violent in their deaths. Theoretic politicians, who have patronized this species of Government, have erroneously supposed, that by reducing mankind to a perfect equality in their political rights, they would, at the same time, be perfectly equalized and assimilated in their possessions, their opinions, and their passions.

A Republic, by which I mean a Government in which the scheme of representation takes place, opens a different prospect, and promises the cure for which we are seeking. Let us examine the points in which it varies from pure Democracy, and we shall comprehend both the nature of the cure, and the efficacy which it must derive from the Union.

The two great points of difference between a Democracy and a Republic are, first, the delegation of the Government, in the latter, to a small number of citizens elected by the rest: secondly, the greater number of citizens, and greater sphere of country, over which the latter may be extended.

The effect of the first difference is, on the one hand to refine and enlarge the public views, by passing them through the medium of a chosen body of citizens, whose wisdom may best discern the true interest of their country, and whose patriotism and love of justice, will be least likely to sacrifice it to temporary or partial considerations. Under such a regulation, it may well happen that the public voice pronounced by the representatives of the people, will be more consonant to the public good, than if pronounced by the people themselves convened for the purpose. On the other hand, the effect may be inverted. Men of factious tempers, of local prejudices, or of sinister designs, may by intrigue, by corruption or by other means, first obtain the suffrages, and then betray the interests of the people. The question resulting is, whether small or extensive Republics are most favorable to the election of proper guardians of the public weal: and it is clearly decided in favor of the latter by two obvious considerations.

In the first place it is to be remarked that however small the Republic may be, the Representatives must be raised to a certain number, in order to guard against the cabals of a few; and that however large it may be, they must be limited to a certain number, in order to guard against the confusion of a multitude. Hence the number of Representatives in the two cases, not being in proportion to that of the Constituents, and being proportionally greatest in the small Republic, it follows, that if the proportion of fit characters, be not less, in the large than in the small Republic, the former will present a greater option, and consequently a greater probability of a fit choice.

In the next place, as each Representative will be chosen by a greater number of citizens in the large than in the small Republic, it will be more difficult for unworthy candidates to practise with success the vicious arts, by which elections are too often carried; and the suffrages of the people being more free, will be more likely to centre on men who possess the most attractive merit, and the most diffusive and established characters.

It must be confessed, that in this, as in most other cases,

there is a mean, on both sides of which inconveniencies will be found to lie. By enlarging too much the number of electors, you render the representative too little acquainted with all their local circumstances and lesser interests; as by reducing it too much, you render him unduly attached to these, and too little fit to comprehend and pursue great and national objects. The Federal Constitution forms a happy combination in this respect; the great and aggregate interests being referred to the national, the local and particular, to the state legislatures.

The other point of difference is, the greater number of citizens and extent of territory which may be brought within the compass of Republican, than of Democratic Government; and it is this circumstance principally which renders factious combinations less to be dreaded in the former, than in the latter. The smaller the society, the fewer probably will be the distinct parties and interests composing it; the fewer the distinct parties and interests, the more frequently will a majority be found of the same party; and the smaller the number of individuals composing a majority, and the smaller the compass within which they are placed, the more easily will they concert and execute their plans of oppression. Extend the sphere, and you take in a greater variety of parties and interests; you make it less probable that a majority of the whole will have a common motive to invade the rights of other citizens; or if such a common motive exists, it will be more difficult for all who feel it to discover their own strength, and to act in unison with each other. Besides other impediments, it may be remarked, that where there is a consciousness of unjust or dishonorable purposes, communication is always checked by distrust, in proportion to the number whose concurrence is necessary.

Hence it clearly appears, that the same advantage, which a Republic has over a Democracy, in controling the effects of faction, is enjoyed by a large over a small Republic—is enjoyed by the Union over the States composing it. Does this advantage consist in the substitution of Representatives, whose enlightened views and virtuous sentiments render them superior to local prejudices, and to schemes of injustice? It will not be denied, that the Representation of the Union will be most likely to possess these requisite endowments. Does it consist in the greater security afforded by a greater variety of parties, against the event of any one party being able to outnumber and oppress the rest? In an equal degree does the encreased variety of parties, comprised within the Union, encrease this security. Does it, in fine, consist in the greater obstacles opposed to the concert and accomplishment of the secret wishes of an unjust and interested majority? Here, again, the extent of the Union gives it the most palpable advantage.

The influence of factious leaders may kindle a flame within their particular States, but will be unable to spread a general conflagration through the other States: a religious sect, may degenerate into a political faction in a part of the Confederacy; but the variety of sects dispersed over the entire face of it, must secure the national Councils against any danger from that source: a rage for paper money, for an abolition of debts, for an equal division of property, or for any other improper or wicked project, will be less apt to pervade the whole body of the Union, than a particular member of it; in the same proportion as such a malady is more likely to taint a particular county or district, than an entire State.

In the extent and proper structure of the Union, therefore, we behold a Republican remedy for the diseases most incident to Republican Government. And according to the degree of pleasure and pride, we feel in being Republicans, ought to be our zeal in cherishing the spirit, and supporting the character of Federalists.

PUBLIUS.

THE FEDERALIST NO. 14
JAMES MADISON

November 30, 1787

To the People of the State of New York.

We have seen the necessity of the union as our bulwark against foreign danger, as the conservator of peace among ourselves, as the guardian of our commerce and other common interests, as the only substitute for those military establishments which have subverted the liberties of the old world; and as the proper antidote for the diseases of faction, which have proved fatal to other popular governments, and of which alarming symptoms have been betrayed by our own. All that remains, within this branch of our enquiries, is to take notice of an objection, that may be drawn from the great extent of country which the union embraces. A few observations on this subject will be the more proper, as it is perceived that the adversaries of the new constitution are availing themselves of a prevailing prejudice, with regard to the practicable sphere of republican administration, in order to supply by imaginary difficulties, the want of those solid objections, which they endeavor in vain to find.

The error which limits Republican Government to a narrow district, has been unfolded and refuted in preceding papers. I remark here only, that it seems to owe its rise and prevalence, chiefly to the confounding of a republic with a democracy: And applying to the former reasonings drawn from the nature of the latter. The true distinction between these forms was also adverted to on a former occasion. It is, that in a democracy, the people meet and exercise the government in person; in a republic they assemble and administer it by their representatives and agents. A democracy consequently will be confined to a small spot. A republic may be extended over a large region.

To this accidental source of the error may be added the artifice of some celebrated authors, whose writings have had a great share in forming the modern standard of political opinions. Being subjects either of an absolute, or limited monarchy, they have endeavored to heighten the advantages or palliate the evils of those forms; by placing in comparison with them, the vices and defects of the republican, and by citing as specimens of the latter, the turbulent democracies of ancient Greece, and modern Italy. Under the confusion of names, it has been an easy task to transfer to a republic, observations applicable to a democracy only, and among others, the observation that it can never be established but among a small number of people, living within a small compass of territory.

Such a fallacy may have been the less perceived as most of the governments of antiquity were of the democratic species; and even in modern Europe, to which we owe the great principle of representation, no example is seen of a government wholly popular, and founded at the same time wholly on that principle. If Europe has the merit of discovering this great mechanical power in government, by the simple agency of which, the will of the largest political body may be concentred, and its force directed to any object, which the public good requires; America can claim the merit of making the discovery the basis of unmixed and extensive republics. It is only to be lamented, that any of her citizens should wish to deprive her of the additional merit of displaying its full efficacy on the establishment of the comprehensive system now under her consideration.

As the natural limit of a democracy is that distance from the central point, which will just permit the most remote citizens to assemble as often as their public functions demand; and will include no greater number than can join in those functions; so the natural limit of a republic is that distance from the center, which will barely allow the representatives of the people to meet as often as may be necessary for the administration of public affairs. Can it be said, that the limits of the United States exceed this distance? It will not be said by those who recollect that the Atlantic coast is the longest side of the union; that during the term of thirteen years, the representatives of the States have been almost continually assembled; and that the members from the most distant States are not chargeable with greater intermissions of attendance, than those from the States in the neighbourhood of Congress.

That we may form a juster estimate with regard to this interesting subject, let us resort to the actual dimensions of the union. The limits as fixed by the treaty of peace are on the east the Atlantic, on the south the latitude of thirty-one degrees, on the west the Mississippi, and on the north an irregular line running in some instances beyond the forty-fifth degree, in others falling as low as the forty-second. The southern shore of Lake Erie lies below that latitude. Computing the distance between the thirty-one and forty-five degrees, it amounts to nine hundred and seventy-three common miles; computing it from thirty-one to forty-two degrees to seven hundred, sixty-four miles and an half. Taking the mean for the distance, the amount will be eight hundred, sixty-eight miles and three-fourths. The mean distance from the Atlantic to the Mississippi does not probably exceed seven hundred and fifty miles. On a comparison of this extent, with that of several countries in Europe, the practicability of rendering our system commensurate to it, appears to be demonstrable. It is not a great deal larger than Germany, where a Diet representing the whole empire is continually assembled; or than Poland before the late dismemberment, where another national Diet was the depository of the supreme power. Passing by France and Spain, we find that in Great Britain, inferior as it may be in size, the representatives of the northern extremity of the island, have as far to travel to the national Council, as will be required of those of the most remote parts of the union.

Favorable as this view of the subject may be, some observations remain which will place it in a light still more satisfactory.

In the first place it is to be remembered, that the general government is not to be charged with the whole power of making and administering laws. Its jurisdiction is limited to certain enumerated objects, which concern all the members of the republic, but which are not to be attained by the separate provisions of any. The subordinate governments which can extend their care to all those other objects, which can be separately provided for, will retain their due authority and activity. Were it proposed by the plan of the Convention to abolish the governments of the particular States, its adversaries would have some ground for their objection, though it would not be difficult to shew that if they were abolished, the general government would be compelled by the principle of self-preservation, to reinstate them in their proper jurisdiction.

A second observation to be made is, that the immediate object of the Fœderal Constitution is to secure the union of the Thirteen Primitive States, which we know to be practicable; and to add to them such other States, as may arise in their own bosoms or in their neighbourhoods, which we cannot doubt to be equally practicable. The arrangements that may be necessary for those angles and fractions of our territory, which lie on our north western frontier, must be left to those whom further discoveries and experience will render more equal to the task.

Let it be remarked in the third place, that the intercourse throughout the union will be daily facilitated by new improvements. Roads will every where be shortened, and kept in better order; accommodations for travellers will be multiplied and meliorated; and interior navigation on our eastern side will be opened throughout, or nearly throughout the whole extent of the Thirteen States. The communication between the western and Atlantic districts, and between different parts of each, will be rendered more and more easy by those numerous canals with which the beneficence of nature has intersected our country, and which art finds it so little difficult to connect and complete.

A fourth and still more important consideration is, that as almost every State will on one side or other, be a frontier, and will thus find in a regard to its safety, an inducement to make some sacrifices for the sake of the general protection;

so the States which lie at the greatest distance from the heart of the union, and which of course may partake least of the ordinary circulation of its benefits, will be at the same time immediately contiguous to foreign nations, and will consequently stand on particular occasions, in greatest need of its strength and resources. It may be inconvenient for Georgia or the States forming our western or north eastern borders to send their representatives to the seat of government, but they would find it more so to struggle alone against an invading enemy, or even to support alone the whole expence of those precautions, which may be dictated by the neighbourhood of continual danger. If they should derive less benefit therefore from the union in some respects, than the less distant States, they will derive greater benefit from it in other respects, and thus the proper equilibrium will be maintained throughout.

I submit to you my fellow citizens, these considerations, in full confidence that the good sense which has so often marked your decisions, will allow them their due weight and effect; and that you will never suffer difficulties, however formidable in appearance or however fashionable the error on which they may be founded, to drive you into the gloomy and perilous scene into which the advocates for disunion would conduct you. Hearken not to the unnatural voice which tells you that the people of America, knit together as they are by so many chords of affection, can no longer live together as members of the same family; can no longer continue the mutual guardians of their mutual happiness; can no longer be fellow citizens of one great respectable and flourishing empire. Hearken not to the voice which petulantly tells you that the form of government recommended for your adoption is a novelty in the political world; that it has never yet had a place in the theories of the wildest projectors; that it rashly attempts what it is impossible to accomplish. No my countrymen, shut your ears against this unhallowed language. Shut your hearts against the poison which it conveys; the kindred blood which flows in the veins of American citizens, the mingled blood which they have shed in defence of their sacred rights, consecrate their union, and excite horror at the idea of their becoming aliens, rivals, enemies. And if novelties are to be shunned, believe me the most alarming of all novelties, the most wild of all projects, the most rash of all attempts, is that of rending us in pieces, in order to preserve our liberties and promote our happiness. But why is the experiment of an extended republic to be rejected merely because it may comprise what is new?

Is it not the glory of the people of America, that whilst they have paid a decent regard to the opinions of former times and other nations, they have not suffered a blind veneration for antiquity, for custom, or for names, to overrule the suggestions of their own good sense, the knowledge of their own situation, and the lessons of their own experience? To this manly spirit, posterity will be indebted for the possession, and the world for the example of the numerous innovations displayed on the American theatre, in favor of private rights and public happiness. Had no important step been taken by the leaders of the revolution for which a precedent could not be discovered, no government established of which an exact model did not present itself, the people of the United States might, at this moment, have been numbered among the melancholy victims of misguided councils, must at best have been labouring under the weight of some of those forms which have crushed the liberties of the rest of mankind. Happily for America, happily we trust for the whole human race, they pursued a new and more noble course. They accomplished a revolution which has no parallel in the annals of human society: They reared the fabrics of governments which have no model on the face of the globe. They formed the design of a great confederacy, which it is incumbent on their successors to improve and perpetuate. If their works betray imperfections, we wonder at the fewness of them. If they erred most in the structure of the union; this was the work most difficult to be executed; this is the work which has been new modelled by the act of your Convention, and it is that act on which you are now to deliberate and to decide.

PUBLIUS.

THE FEDERALIST NO. 15
ALEXANDER HAMILTON

December 1, 1787

To the People of the State of New York.

In the course of the preceding papers, I have endeavoured, my Fellow Citizens, to place before you in a clear and convincing light, the importance of Union to your political safety and happiness. I have unfolded to you a complication of dangers to which you would be exposed should you permit that sacred knot which binds the people of America together to be severed or dissolved by ambition or by avarice, by jealousy or by misrepresentation. In the sequel of the inquiry, through which I propose to accompany you, the truths intended to be inculcated will receive further confirmation from facts and arguments hitherto unnoticed. If the road, over which you will still have to pass, should in some places appear to you tedious or irksome, you will recollect, that you are in quest of information on a subject the most momentous which can engage the attention of a free people: that the field through which you have to travel is in itself spacious, and that the difficulties of the journey have been unnecessarily increased by the mazes with which sophistry has beset the way. It will be my aim to remove the obstacles to your progress in as compendious a manner, as it can be done, without sacrificing utility to dispatch.

In pursuance of the plan, which I have laid down, for the discussion of the subject, the point next in order to be examined is the "insufficiency of the present confederation to the preservation of the Union." It may perhaps be asked, what need is there of reasoning or proof to illustrate a position, which is not either controverted or doubted; to which the understandings and feelings of all classes of men assent; and which in substance is admitted by the opponents as well as by the friends of the New Constitution? It must in truth be acknowledged that however these may differ in other respects, they in general appear to harmonise in this sentiment at least, that there are material imperfections in our national system, and that something is necessary to be done to rescue us from impending anarchy. The facts that support this opinion are no longer objects of speculation. They have forced themselves upon the sensibility of the people at large, and have at length extorted from those, whose mistaken policy has had the principal share in precipitating the extremity, at which we are arrived, a reluctant confession of the reality of those defects in the scheme of our Fœderal Government, which have been long pointed out and regretted by the intelligent friends of the Union.

We may indeed with propriety be said to have reached almost the last stage of national humiliation. There is scarcely any thing that can wound the pride, or degrade the character of an independent nation, which we do not experience. Are there engagements to the performance of which we are held by every tie respectable among men? These are the subjects of constant and unblushing violation. Do we owe debts to foreigners and to our own citizens contracted in a time of imminent peril, for the preservation of our political existence?

These remain without any proper or satisfactory provision for their discharge. Have we valuable territories and important posts in the possession of a foreign power, which by express stipulations ought long since to have been surrendered. These are still retained, to the prejudice of our interests not less than of our rights.[1] Are we in a condition to resent, or to repel the aggression? We have neither troops nor treasury nor government.* Are we even in a condition to remonstrate with dignity? The just imputations on our own faith, in respect to the same treaty, ought first to be removed. Are we entitled by nature and compact to a free participation in the navigation of the Mississippi? Spain excludes us from it.[2] Is public credit an indispensable resource in time of public danger? We seem to have abandoned its cause as desperate and irretrievable. Is commerce of importance to national wealth? Ours is at the lowest point of declension. Is respectability in the eyes of foreign powers a safeguard against foreign encroachments? The imbecility of our Government even forbids them to treat with us: Our ambassadors abroad are the mere pageants of mimic sovereignty. Is a violent and unnatural decrease in the value of land a symptom of national distress? The price of improved land in most parts of the country is much lower than can be accounted for by the quantity of waste land at market, and can only be fully explained by that want of private and public confidence, which are so alarmingly prevalent among all ranks and which have a direct tendency to depreciate property of every kind. Is private credit the friend and patron of industry? That most useful kind which relates to borrowing and lending is reduced within the narrowest limits, and this still more from an opinion of insecurity than from the scarcity of money. To shorten an enumeration of particulars which can afford neither pleasure nor instruction it may in general be demanded, what indication is there of national disorder, poverty and insignificance that could befal a community so peculiarly blessed with natural advantages as we are, which

[1] Because the government under the Articles of Confederation was unable to force the states to honor certain articles of the peace treaty with Great Britain, notably those on the treatment of Loyalists and the collection of debts by English creditors, Great Britain refused to evacuate certain western posts which were still occupied at the war's end.

* *I mean for the Union.*

[2] After the Jay-Gardoqui Treaty fell through in 1786, Spain did not accede to American demands for recognition of the boundary claims of the Treaty of Paris in 1783 (the Mississippi to the west, the 31st parallel to the south) or to demands for navigational rights on the Mississippi and the right of deposit in New Orleans until Thomas Pinckney obtained them in the Treaty of San Lorenzo in 1795.

does not form a part of the dark catalogue of our public misfortunes?

This is the melancholy situation, to which we have been brought by those very maxims and councils, which would now deter us from adopting the proposed constitution; and which not content with having conducted us to the brink of a precipice, seem resolved to plunge us into the abyss, that awaits us below. Here, my Countrymen, impelled by every motive that ought to influence an enlightened people, let us make a firm stand for our safety, our tranquillity, our dignity, our reputation. Let us at last break the fatal charm which has too long seduced us from the paths of felicity and prosperity.

It is true, as has been before observed, that facts too stubborn to be resisted have produced a species of general assent to the abstract proposition that there exist material defects in our national system; but the usefulness of the concession, on the part of the old adversaries of fœderal measures, is destroyed by a strenuous opposition to a remedy, upon the only principles, that can give it a chance of success. While they admit that the Government of the United States is destitute of energy; they contend against conferring upon it those powers which are requisite to supply that energy: They seem still to aim at things repugnant and irreconcilable—at an augmentation of Fœderal authority without a diminution of State authority—at sovereignty in the Union and complete independence in the members. They still in fine seem to cherish with blind devotion the political monster of an *imperium in imperio*. This renders a full display of the principal defects of the confederation necessary, in order to shew, that the evils we experience do not proceed from minute or partial imperfections, but from fundamental errors in the structure of the building which cannot be amended otherwise than by an alteration in the first principles and main pillars of the fabric.

The great and radical vice in the construction of the existing Confederation is in the principle of LEGISLATION for STATES OF GOVERNMENTS, in their CORPORATE or COLLECTIVE CAPACITIES and as contradistinguished from the INDIVIDUALS of whom they consist. Though this principle does not run through all the powers delegated to the Union; yet it pervades and governs those, on which the efficacy of the rest depends. Except as to the rule of apportionment, the United States have an indefinite discretion to make requisitions for men and money; but they have no authority to raise either by regulations extending to the individual citizens of America. The consequence of this is, that though in theory their resolutions concerning those objects are laws, constitutionally binding on the members of the Union, yet in practice they are mere recommendations, which the States observe or disregard at their option.

It is a singular instance of the capriciousness of the human mind, that after all the admonitions we have had from experience on this head, there should still be found men, who object to the New Constitution for deviating from a principle which has been found the bane of the old; and which is in itself evidently incompatible with the idea of GOVERNMENT; a principle in short which if it is to be executed at all must substitute the violent and sanguinary agency of the sword to the mild influence of the Magistracy.

There is nothing absurd or impracticable in the idea of a league or alliance between independent nations, for certain defined purposes precisely stated in a treaty; regulating all the details of time, place, circumstance and quantity; leaving nothing to future discretion; and depending for its execution on the good faith of the parties. Compacts of this kind exist among all civilized nations subject to the usual vicissitudes of peace and war, of observance and non observance, as the interests or passions of the contracting powers dictate. In the early part of the present century, there was an epidemical rage in Europe for this species of compacts; from which the politicians of the times fondly hoped for benefits which were never realised. With a view to establishing the equilibrium of power and the peace of that part of the world, all the resources of negotiation were exhausted, and triple and quadruple alliances were formed; but they were scarcely formed before they were broken, giving an instructive but afflicting lesson to mankind how little dependence is to be placed on treaties which have no other sanction than the obligations of good faith; and which oppose general considerations of peace and justice to the impulse of any immediate interest and passion.

If the particular States in this country are disposed to stand in a similar relation to each other, and to drop the project of a general DISCRETIONARY SUPERINTENDENCE, the scheme would indeed be pernicious, and would entail upon us all the mischiefs that have been enumerated under the first head; but it would have the merit of being at least consistent and practicable. Abandoning all views towards a confederate Government, this would bring us to a simple alliance offensive and defensive; and would place us in a situation to be alternately friends and enemies of each other as our mutual jealousies and rivalships nourished by the intrigues of foreign nations should prescribe to us.

But if we are unwilling to be placed in this perilous situation; if we will still adhere to the design of a national government, or which is the same thing of a superintending power under the direction of a common Council, we must resolve to incorporate into our plan those ingredients which may be considered as forming the characteristic difference between a league and a government; we must extend the authority of the union to the persons of the citizens,—the only proper objects of government.

Government implies the power of making laws. It is essential to the idea of a law, that it be attended with a sanction; or, in other words, a penalty or punishment for disobedience. If there be no penalty annexed to disobedience, the resolutions or commands which pretend to be laws will in fact amount to nothing more than advice or recommendation. This penalty, whatever it may be, can only be inflicted in two ways; by the agency of the Courts and Ministers of Justice, or by military force; by the COERTION of the magistracy, or by the COERTION of arms. The first kind can evidently apply only to men—the last kind must of necessity be employed against bodies politic, or communities or States. It is evident, that there is no process of a court by which their observance of the laws can in the last resort be enforced. Sentences may be denounced against them for violations of their duty; but these sentences can only be carried into execution by the sword. In an association where the general authority is confined to the collective bodies of the communities that compose it, every breach of the laws must involve a state of war, and military execution must become the only instrument of civil obedience. Such a state of things can certainly not deserve the name of government, nor would any prudent man choose to commit his happiness to it.

There was a time when we were told that breaches, by the States, of the regulations of the fœderal authority were not to be expected—that a sense of common interest would preside over the conduct of the respective members, and would beget a full compliance with all the constitutional requisitions of the Union. This language at the present day would appear as wild as a great part of what we now hear from the same quarter will be thought, when we shall have received further lessons from that best oracle of wisdom, experience. It at all times betrayed an ignorance of the true springs by which human conduct is actuated, and belied the original inducements to the establishment of civil power. Why has government been instituted at all? Because the passions of men will not conform to the dictates of reason and justice, without constraint. Has it been found that bodies of men act with more rectitude or greater disinterestedness than individuals? The contrary of this has been inferred by all accurate observers of the conduct of mankind; and the inference is founded upon obvious reasons. Regard to reputation has a less active influence, when the infamy of a bad action is to be divided among a number, than when it is to fall singly upon one. A spirit of faction which is apt to mingle its poison in the deliberations of all bodies of men, will often hurry the persons of whom they are composed into improprieties and excesses, for which they would blush in a private capacity.

In addition to all this, there is in the nature of sovereign power an impatience of controul, that disposes those who are invested with the exercise of it, to look with an evil eye upon all external attempts to restrain or direct its operations. From this spirit it happens that in every political association which is formed upon the principle of uniting in a common interest a number of lesser sovereignties, there will be found a kind of excentric tendency in the subordinate or inferior orbs, by the operation of which there will be a perpetual effort in each to fly off from the common center. This tendency is not difficult to be accounted for. It has its origin in the love of power. Power controuled or abridged is almost always the rival and enemy of that power by which it is controuled or abriged. This simple proposition will teach us how little reason there is to expect, that the persons, entrusted with the administration of the affairs of the particular members of a confederacy, will at all times be ready, with perfect good humour, and an unbiassed regard to the public weal, to execute the resolutions or decrees of the general authority. The reverse of this results from the constitution of human nature.

If therefore the measures of the confederacy cannot be executed, without the intervention of the particular administrations, there will be little prospect of their being executed at all. The rulers of the respective members, whether they have a constitutional right to do it or not, will undertake to judge of the propriety of the measures themselves. They will consider the conformity of the thing proposed or required to their immediate interests or aims, the momentary conveniences or inconveniences that would attend its adoption. All this will be done, and in a spirit of interested and suspicious scrutiny, without that knowledge of national circumstances and reasons of state, which is essential to a right judgment, and with that strong predilection in favour of local objects, which can hardly fail to mislead the decision. The same process must be repeated in every member of which the body is constituted; and the execution of the plans, framed by the councils of the whole, will always fluctuate on the discretion of the ill-informed and prejudiced opinion of every part. Those who have been conversant in the proceedings of popular assemblies; who have seen how difficult it often is, when there is no exterior pressure of circumstances, to bring them to harmonious resolutions on important points, will readily conceive how impossible it must be to induce a number of such assemblies, deliberating at a distance from each other, at different times, and under different impressions, long to cooperate in the same views and pursuits.

In our case, the concurrence of thirteen distinct sovereign wills is requisite under the confederation to the complete execution of every important measure, that proceeds from the Union. It has happened as was to have been foreseen. The measures of the Union have not been executed; and the delinquencies of the States have step by step matured themselves to an extreme; which has at length arrested all the wheels of the national government, and brought them to an awful stand. Congress at this time scarcely possess the means of keeping up the forms of administration; 'till the States can have time to agree upon a more substantial substitute for the present shadow of a fœderal government. Things did not come to this desperate extremity at once. The causes which have been specified produced at first only unequal and disproportionate degrees of compliance with the requisitions of the Union. The greater deficiencies of some States furnished the pretext of example and the temptation of interest to the complying, or to the least delinquent States. Why should we do more in proportion than those who are embarked with us in the same political voyage? Why should we consent to bear more than our proper share of the common burthen? These were suggestions which human selfishness could not withstand, and which even speculative men, who looked forward to remote consequences, could not, without hesitation, combat. Each State yielding to the persuasive voice of immediate interest and convenience has successively withdrawn its support, 'till the frail and tottering edifice seems ready to fall upon our heads and to crush us beneath its ruins.

PUBLIUS.

THE FEDERALIST NO. 16
ALEXANDER HAMILTON

December 4, 1787

To the People of the State of New York.

The tendency of the principle of legislation for States, or communities, in their political capacities, as it has been exemplified by the experiment we have made of it, is equally attested by the events which have befallen all other governments of the confederate kind, of which we have any account, in exact proportion to its prevalence in those systems. The confirmations of this fact will be worthy of a distinct and particular examination. I shall content myself with barely observing here, that of all the confederacies of antiquity, which history has handed down to us, the Lycian and Achæan leagues, as far as there remain vestiges of them, appear to have been most free from the fetters of that mistaken principle, and were accordingly those which have best deserved, and have most liberally received the applauding suffrages of political writers.

This exceptionable principle may as truly as emphatically be stiled the parent of anarchy: It has been seen that delinquencies in the members of the Union are its natural and necessary offspring; and that whenever they happen, the only constitutional remedy is force, and the immediate effect of the use of it, civil war.

It remains to enquire how far so odious an engine of government, in its application to us, would even be capable of answering its end. If there should not be a large army, constantly at the disposal of the national government, it would either not be able to employ force at all, or when this could be done, it would amount to a war between different parts of the confederacy, concerning the infractions of a league; in which the strongest combination would be most likely to prevail, whether it consisted of those who supported, or of those who resisted the general authority. It would rarely happen that the delinquency to be redressed would be confined to a single member, and if there were more than one, who had neglected their duty, similarity of situation would induce them to unite for common defence. Independent of this motive of sympathy, if a large and influential State should happen to be the aggressing member, it would commonly have weight enough with its neighbours, to win over some of them as associates to its cause. Specious arguments of danger to the common liberty could easily be contrived; plausible excuses for the deficiencies of the party, could, without difficulty be invented, to alarm the apprehensions, inflame the passions, and conciliate the good will even of those States which were not chargeable with any violation, or omission of duty. This would be the more likely to take place, as the delinquencies of the larger members might be expected sometimes to proceed from an ambitious premeditation in their rulers, with a view to getting rid of all external controul upon their designs of personal aggrandizement; the better to effect which, it is presumable they would tamper beforehand with leading individuals in the adjacent States. If associates could not be found at home, recourse would be had to the aid of foreign powers, who would seldom be disinclined to encouraging the dissentions of a confederacy, from the firm Union of which they had so much to fear. When the sword is once drawn, the passions of men observe no bounds of moderation. The suggestions of wounded pride, the instigations of irritated resentment, would be apt to carry the States, against which the arms of the Union were exerted to any extremes necessary to revenge the affront, or to avoid the disgrace of submission. The first war of this kind would probably terminate in a dissolution of the Union.

This may be considered as the violent death of the confederacy. Its more natural death is what we now seem to be on the point of experiencing, if the fœderal system be not speedily renovated in a more substantial form. It is not probable, considering the genius of this country, that the complying States would often be inclined to support the authority of the Union by engaging in a war against the non-complying States. They would always be more ready to pursue the milder course of putting themselves upon an equal footing with the delinquent members, by an imitation of their example. And the guilt of all would thus become the security of all. Our past experience has exhibited the operation of this spirit in its full light. There would in fact be an insuperable difficulty in ascertaining when force could with propriety be employed. In the article of pecuniary contribution, which would be the most usual source of delinquency, it would often be impossible to decide whether it had proceded from disinclination, or inability. The pretence of the latter would always be at hand. And the case must be very flagrant in which its fallacy could be detected with sufficient certainty to justify the harsh expedient of compulsion. It is easy to see that this problem alone, as often as it should occur, would open a wide field for the exercise of factious views, of partiality and of oppression, in the majority that happened to prevail in the national council.

It seems to require no pains to prove that the States ought not to prefer a national constitution, which could only be kept in motion by the instrumentality of a large army, continually on foot to execute the ordinary requisitions or decrees of the government. And yet this is the plain alternative involved by those who wish to deny it the power of extending its operations to individuals. Such a scheme, if practicable at all, would instantly degenerate into a military despotism; but it will be found in every light impracticable. The resources of the Union would not be equal to the maintenance of an army considerable enough to confine the larger States within the limits of their duty; nor would the means ever be furnished of forming such an army in the first instance. Whoever considers the populousness and strength of several of these States singly at the present juncture, and looks forward to what they will become, even at the distance of half a century, will at once dismiss as idle and visionary any scheme, which aims at regulating their movements by laws, to operate upon them in their collective capacities, and to be executed by a coertion applicable to them in the same capacities. A project of this kind is little less romantic than that monster-taming spirit, which is attributed to the fabulous heroes and demi-gods of antiquity.

Even in those confederacies, which have been composed of members smaller than many of our counties, the principle of legislation for sovereign States, supported by military coertion, has never been found effectual. It has rarely been attempted to be employed, but against the weaker members: And in most instances attempts to coerce the refractory and disobedient, have been the signals of bloody wars; in which one half of the confederacy has displayed its banners against the other half.

The result of these observations to an intelligent mind must be clearly this, that if it be possible at any rate to construct a Fœderal Government capable of regulating the common concerns and preserving the general tranquility, it must be founded, as to the objects committed to its care, upon the reverse of the principle contended for by the opponents of the proposed constitution. It must carry its agency to the persons of the citizens. It must stand in need of no intermediate legislations; but must itself be empowered to employ the arm of the ordinary magistrate to execute its own resolutions. The majesty of the national authority must be manifested through the medium of the Courts of Justice. The government of the Union, like that of each State, must be able to address itself immediately to the hopes and fears of individuals; and to attract to its support, those passions, which have the strongest influence upon the human heart. It must in short, possess all the means and have a right to resort to all the methods of executing the powers, with which it is entrusted, that are possessed and exercised by the governments of the particular States.

To this reasoning it may perhaps be objected, that if any State should be disaffected to the authority of the Union, it could at any time obstruct the execution of its laws, and bring the matter to the same issue of force, with the necessity of which the opposite scheme is reproached.

The plausibility of this objection will vanish the moment we advert to the essential difference between a mere NON COMPLIANCE and a DIRECT and ACTIVE RESISTANCE. If the interposition of the State-Legislatures be necessary to give effect to a measure of the Union, they have only NOT TO ACT or TO ACT EVASIVELY, and the measure is defeated. This neglect of duty may be disguised under affected but unsubstantial provisions, so as not to appear, and of course not to excite any alarm in the people for the safety of the constitution. The State leaders may even make a merit of their surreptitious invasions of it, on the ground of some temporary convenience, exemption, or advantage.

But if the execution of the laws of the national government, should not require the intervention of the State Legislatures; if they were to pass into immediate operation upon the citizens themselves, the particular governments could not interrupt their progress without an open and violent exertion of an unconstitutional power. No omissions, nor evasions would answer the end. They would be obliged to act, and in such a manner, as would leave no doubt that they had encroached on the national rights. An experiment of this nature would always be hazardous—in the face of a constitution in any degree competent to its own defence, and of a people enlightened enough to distinguish between a legal exercise and an illegal usurpation of authority. The success of it would require not merely a factious majority in the Legislature, but the concurrence of the courts of justice, and of the body of the people. If the Judges were not embarked in a conspiracy with the Legislature they would pronounce the resolutions of such a majority to be contrary to the supreme law of the land, unconstitutional and void. If the people were not tainted with the spirit of their State representatives, they, as the natural guardians of the constitution, would throw their weight into the national scale, and give it a decided preponderancy in the contest. Attempts of this kind would not often be made with levity or rashness; because they could seldom be made without danger to the authors; unless in cases of a tyrannical exercise of the Fœderal authority.

If opposition to the national government should arise from the disorderly conduct of refractory, or seditious individuals, it could be overcome by the same means which are daily employed against the same evil, under the State governments. The Magistracy, being equally the Ministers of the law of the land, from whatever source it might emanate, would doubtless be as ready to guard the national as the local regulations from the inroads of private licentiousness. As to those partial commotions and insurrections which sometimes disquiet society, from the intrigues of an inconsiderable faction, or from sudden or occasional ill humours that do not infect the great body of the community, the general government could command more extensive resources for the suppression of disturbances of that kind, than would be in the power of any single member. And as to those mortal feuds, which in certain conjunctures spread a conflagration through a whole nation, or through a very large proportion of it, proceeding either from weighty causes of discontent given by the government, or from the contagion of some violent popular paroxism, they do not fall within any ordinary rules of calculation. When they happen, they commonly amount to revolutions and dismemberments of empire. No form of government can always either avoid or controul them. It is in vain to hope to guard against events too mighty for human foresight or precaution, and it would be idle to object to a government because it could not perform impossibilities.

PUBLIUS.

THE FEDERALIST NO. 23
ALEXANDER HAMILTON

December 18, 1787

To the People of the State of New York.

The necessity of a Constitution, at least equally energetic with the one proposed, to the preservation of the Union, is the point, at the examination of which we are now arrived.

This enquiry will naturally divide itself into three branches—the objects to be provided for by a Fœderal Government—the quantity of power necessary to the accomplishment of those objects—the persons upon whom that power ought to operate. Its distribution and organization will more properly claim our attention under the succeeding head.

The principal purposes to be answered by Union are these—The common defence of the members—the preservation of the public peace as well against internal convulsions as external attacks—the regulation of commerce with other nations and between the States—the superintendence of our intercourse, political and commercial, with foreign countries.

The authorities essential to the care of the common defence are these—to raise armies—to build and equip fleets—to prescribe rules for the government of both—to direct their operations—to provide for their support. These powers ought to exist without limitation: *Because it is impossible to foresee or define the extent and variety of national exigencies, or the correspondent extent & variety of the means which may be necessary to satisfy them.* The circumstances that endanger the safety of nations are infinite; and for this reason no constitutional shackles can wisely be imposed on the power to which the care of it is committed. This power ought to be co-extensive with all the possible combinations of such circumstances; and ought to be under the direction of the same councils, which are appointed to preside over the common defence.

This is one of those truths, which to a correct and unprejudiced mind, carries its own evidence along with it; and may be obscured, but cannot be made plainer by argument or reasoning. It rests upon axioms as simple as they are universal. The *means* ought to be proportioned to the *end;* the persons, from whose agency the attainment of any *end* is expected, ought to possess the *means* by which it is to be attained.

Whether there ought to be a Fœderal Government intrusted with the care of the common defence, is a question in the first instance open to discussion; but the moment it is decided in the affirmative, it will follow, that that government ought to be cloathed with all the powers requisite to the complete execution of its trust. And unless it can be shewn, that the circumstances which may affect the public safety are reducible within certain determinate limits; unless the contrary of this position can be fairly and rationally disputed, it must be admitted, as a necessary consequence, that there can be no limitation of that authority, which is to provide for the defence and protection of the community, in any matter essential to its efficacy; that is, in any matter essential to the *formation, direction* or *support* of the NATIONAL FORCES.

Defective as the present Confederation has been proved to bc, this principle appears to have been fully recognized by the framers of it; though they have not made proper or adequate provision for its exercise. Congress have an unlimited discretion to make requisitions of men and money—to govern the army and navy—to direct their operations. As their requisitions were made constitutionally binding upon the States, who are in fact under the most solemn obligations to furnish the supplies required of them, the intention evidently was, that the United States should command whatever resources were by them judged requisite to "the common defence and general welfare." It was presumed that a sense of their true interests, and a regard to the dictates of good faith, would be found sufficient pledges for the punctual performance of the duty of the members to the Fœderal Head.

The experiment has, however demonstrated, that this expectation was ill founded and illusory; and the observations made under the last head, will, I imagine, have sufficed to convince the impartial and discerning, that there is an absolute necessity for an entire change in the first principles of the system: That if we are in earnest about giving the Union energy and duration, we must abandon the vain project of legislating upon the States in their collective capacities: We must extend the laws of the Fœderal Government to the individual citizens of America: We must discard the fallacious scheme of quotas and requisitions, as equally impracticable and unjust. The result from all this is, that the Union ought to be invested with full power to levy troops; to build and equip fleets, and to raise the revenues, which will be required for the formation and support of an army and navy, in the customary and ordinary modes practiced in other governments.

If the circumstances of our country are such, as to demand a compound instead of a simple, a confederate instead of a sole government, the essential point which will remain to be adjusted, will be to discriminate the OBJECTS, as far as it can be done, which shall appertain to the different provinces or departments of power; allowing to each the most ample authority for fulfilling the objects committed to its charge. Shall the Union be constituted the guardian of the common safety? Are fleets and armies and revenues necessary to this purpose? The government of the Union must be empowered to pass all laws, and to make all regulations which have relation to them. The same must be the case, in respect to commerce, and to every other matter to which its jurisdiction is permitted to extend. Is the administration of justice between the citizens of the same State, the proper department of the local governments? These must possess all the authorities which are connected with this object, and with every other that may be allotted to their particular cognizance and direction. Not to confer in each case a degree of power, commensurate to the end, would be to violate the most obvious rules of prudence and propriety, and improvidently to trust the great interests of the nation to hands, which are disabled from managing them with vigour and success.

Who so likely to make suitable provisions for the public defence, as that body to which the guardianship of the public safety is confided—which, as the center of information, will best understand the extent and urgency of the dangers that threaten—as the representative of the WHOLE will feel itself most deeply interested in the preservation of every part—which, from the responsibility implied in the duty assigned to it, will be most sensibly impressed with the necessity of proper exertions—and which, by the extension of its authority throughout the States, can alone establish uniformity and concert in the plans and measures, by which the common safety is to be secured? Is there not a manifest inconsistency in devolving upon the Fœderal Government the care of the general defence, and leaving in the State governments the *effective* powers, by which it is to be provided for? Is not a want of co-operation the infallible consequence of such a system? And will not weakness, disorder, an undue distribution of the burthens and calamities of war, an unnecessary and intolerable increase of expence, be its natural and inevitable concomitants? Have we not had unequivocal experience of its effects in the course of the revolution, which we have just accomplished?

Every view we may take of the subject, as candid enquirers after truth, will serve to convince us, that it is both unwise and dangerous to deny the Fœderal Government an unconfined authority, as to all those objects which are intrusted to its management. It will indeed deserve the most vigilant and careful attention of the people, to see that it be modelled in such a manner, as to admit of its being safely vested with the requisite powers. If any plan which has been, or may be offered to our consideration, should not, upon a dispassionate inspection, be found to answer this description, it ought to be rejected. A government, the Constitution of which renders it unfit to be trusted with all the powers, which a free people *ought to delegate to any government,* would be an unsafe and improper depository of the NATIONAL INTERESTS, wherever THESE can with propriety be confided, the co-incident powers may safely accompany them. This is the true result of all just reasoning upon the subject. And the adversaries of the plan, promulgated by the Convention, ought to have confined themselves to showing that the internal structure of the proposed government, was such as to render it unworthy of the confidence of the people. They ought not to have wandered into inflammatory declamations, and unmeaning cavils about the extent of the powers. The POWERS are not too extensive for the OBJECTS of Fœderal administration, or in other words, for the management of our NATIONAL INTERESTS; nor can any satisfactory argument be framed to shew that they are chargeable with such an excess. If it be true, as has been insinuated by some of the writers on the other side, that the difficulty arises from the nature of the thing, and that the extent of the country will not permit us to form a government, in which such ample powers can safely be reposed, it would prove that we ought to contract our views, and resort to the expedient of separate Confederacies, which will move within more practicable spheres. For the absurdity must continually stare us in the face of confiding to a government, the direction of the most essential national interests, without daring to trust it with the authorities which are indispensable to their proper and efficient management. Let us not attempt to reconcile contradictions, but firmly embrace a rational alternative.

I trust, however, that the impracticability of one general system cannot be shewn. I am greatly mistaken, if any thing of weight, has yet been advanced of this tendency; and I flatter myself, that the observations which have been made in the course of these papers, have sufficed to place the reverse of that position in as clear a light as any matter still in the womb of time and experience can be susceptible of. This at all events must be evident, that the very difficulty itself drawn from the extent of the country, is the strongest argument in favour of an energetic government; for any other can certainly never preserve the Union of so large an empire. If we embrace the tenets of those, who oppose the adoption of the proposed Constitution, as the standard of our political creed, we cannot fail to verify the gloomy doctrines, which predict the impracticability of a national system, pervading the entire limits of the present Confederacy.

PUBLIUS.

THE FEDERALIST NO. 37
JAMES MADISON

January 11, 1788

To the People of the State of New York.

In reviewing the defects of the existing Confederation, and shewing that they cannot be supplied by a Government of less energy than that before the public, several of the most important principles of the latter fell of course under consideration. But as the ultimate object of these papers is to determine clearly and fully the merits of this Constitution, and the expediency of adopting it, our plan cannot be compleated without taking a more critical and thorough survey of the work of the Convention; without examining it on all its sides; comparing it in all its parts, and calculating its probable effects. That this remaining task may be executed under impressions conducive to a just and fair result, some reflections must in this place be indulged, which candor previously suggests. It is a misfortune, inseparable from human affairs, that public measures are rarely investigated with that spirit of moderation which is essential to a just estimate of their real tendency to advance or obstruct the public good; and that this spirit is more apt to be diminished than prompted, by those occasions which require an unusual exercise of it. To those who have been led by experience to attend to this consideration, it could not appear surprising, that the act of the Convention which recommends so many important changes and innovations, which may be viewed in so many lights and relations, and which touches the springs of so many passions and interests, should find or excite dispositions unfriendly both on one side, and on the other, to a fair discussion and accurate judgment of its merits. In some, it has been too evident from their own publications, that they have scanned the proposed Constitution, not only with a predisposition to censure; but with a predetermination to condemn: as the language held by others betrays an opposite predetermination or bias, which must render their opinions also of little moment in the question. In placing however, these different characters on a level, with respect to the weight of their opinions, I wish not to insinuate that there may not be a material difference in the purity of their intentions. It is but just to remark in favor of the latter description, that as our situation is universally admitted to be peculiarly critical, and to require indispensibly, that something should be done for our relief, the predetermined patron of what has been actually done, may have taken his bias from the weight of these considerations, as well as from considerations of a sinister nature. The predetermined adversary on the other hand, can have been governed by no venial motive whatever. The intentions of the first may be upright, as they may on the contrary be culpable. The views of the last cannot be upright, and must be culpable. But the truth is, that these papers are not addressed to persons falling under either of these characters. They solicit the attention of those only, who add to a sincere zeal for the happiness of their country, a temper favorable to a just estimate of the means of promoting it.

Persons of this character will proceed to an examination of the plan submitted by the Convention, not only without a disposition to find or to magnify faults; but will see the propriety of reflecting that a faultless plan was not to be expected. Nor will they barely make allowances for the errors which may be chargeable on the fallibility to which the Convention, as a body of men, were liable; but will keep in mind that they themselves also are but men, and ought not to assume an infallibility in rejudging the fallible opinions of others.

With equal readiness will it be perceived, that besides these inducements to candor, many allowances ought to be made for the difficulties inherent in the very nature of the undertaking referred to the Convention.

The novelty of the undertaking immediately strikes us. It has been shewn in the course of these papers, that the existing Confederation is founded on principles which are fallacious; that we must consequently change this first foundation, and with it, the superstructure resting upon it. It has been shewn, that the other confederacies which could be consulted as precedents, have been viciated by the same erroneous principles, and can therefore furnish no other light than that of beacons, which gave warning of the course to be shunned, without pointing out that which ought to be pursued. The most that the Convention could do in such a situation, was to avoid the errors suggested by the past experience of other countries, as well as of our own; and to provide a convenient mode of rectifying their own errors, as future experience may unfold them.

Among the difficulties encountered by the Convention, a very important one must have lain, in combining the requisite stability and energy in Government, with the inviolable attention due to liberty, and to the Republican form. Without substantially accomplishing this part of their undertaking, they would have very imperfectly fulfilled the object of their appointment, or the expectation of the public: Yet, that it could not be easily accomplished, will be denied by no one, who is unwilling to betray his ignorance of the subject. Energy in Government is essential to that security against external and internal danger, and to that prompt and salutary execution of the laws, which enter into the very definition of good Government. Stability in Government, is essential to national character, and to the advantages annexed to it, as well as to that repose and confidence in the minds of the people, which are among the chief blessings of civil society. An irregular and mutable legislation, is not more an evil in itself, than it is odious to the people; and it may be pronounced with assurance, that the people of this country, enlightened as they are, with regard to the nature, and interested, as the great body of them are, in the effects of good Government, will never be satisfied, till some remedy be applied to the vicissitudes and uncertainties, which characterize the State administrations. On comparing, however, these valuable ingredients with the vital principles of liberty, we must perceive at once, the difficulty of mingling them together in their due proportions. The genius of Republican liberty, seems to demand on one side, not only that all power should be derived from the people; but, that those entrusted with it should be kept in dependence on the people, by a short duration of their appointments; and, that, even during this short period, the trust should be placed not in a few, but in a number of hands. Stability, on the contrary, requires, that the hands, in which power is lodged, should continue for a length of time, the same. A frequent change of men will result from a frequent return of electors, and a frequent change of measures, from a frequent change of men: whilst energy in Government requires not only a certain duration of power, but the execution of it by a single hand. How far the Convention may have succeeded in this part of their work, will better appear on a more accurate view of it. From the cursory view, here taken, it must clearly appear to have been an arduous part.

Not less arduous must have been the task of marking the proper line of partition, between the authority of the general, and that of the State Governments. Every man will be sensible of this difficulty, in proportion, as he has been accustomed to contemplate and discriminate objects, extensive and complicated in their nature. The faculties of the mind itself have never yet been distinguished and defined, with satisfactory precision, by all the efforts of the most acute and metaphysical Philosophers. Sense, perception, judgment, desire, volition, memory, imagination, are found to be separated by such delicate shades, and minute gradations, that their boundaries have eluded the most subtle investigations, and remain a pregnant source of ingenious disquisition and controversy. The boundaries between the great kingdoms of nature, and still more, between the various provinces, and lesser portions, into which they are subdivided, afford another illustration of the same important truth. The most sagacious and laborious naturalists have never yet succeeded, in tracing with certainty, the line which separates the district of vegetable life from the neighboring region of unorganized matter, or which marks the termination of the former and the commencement of the animal empire. A still greater obscurity lies in the distinctive characters, by which the objects in each of these great departments of nature, have been arranged and assorted. When we pass from the works of nature, in which all the delineations are perfectly accurate, and appear to be otherwise only from the imperfection of the eye which surveys them, to the institutions of man, in which the obscurity arises as well from the object itself, as from the organ by which it is contemplated; we must perceive the necessity of moderating still farther our expectations and hopes from the efforts of human sagacity. Experience has instructed us that no skill in the science of Government has yet been able to discriminate and define, with sufficient certainty, its three great provinces, the Legislative, Executive and Judiciary; or even the privileges and powers of the different Legislative branches. Questions daily occur in the course of practice, which prove the obscurity which reigns in these subjects, and which puzzle the greatest adepts in political science. The experience of ages, with the continued and combined labors of the most enlightened Legislators and jurists, have been equally unsuccessful in delineating the several objects and limits of different codes of laws and different tribunals of justice. The precise extent of the common law, the statute law, the maritime law, the ecclesiastical law, the law of corporations and other local laws and customs, remain still to be clearly and finally established in Great-Britain, where accuracy in such subjects has been more industriously pursued than in any other part of the world. The jurisdiction of her several courts, general and local, of law, of equity, of admiralty, &c. is not less a source of frequent and intricate discussions, sufficiently denoting the indeterminate limits by which they are respectively circumscribed. All new laws, though penned with the greatest technical skill, and passed on the fullest and most mature deliberation, are considered as more or less obscure and equivocal, until their meaning be liquidated and ascertained by a series of particular discussions and adjudications. Besides the obscurity arising from the complexity of objects, and the imperfection of the human faculties, the medium through which the conceptions of men are conveyed to each other, adds a fresh embarrassment. The use of words is to express ideas. Perspicuity therefore requires not only that the ideas should be distinctly formed, but that they should be expressed by words distinctly and exclusively appropriated to them. But no language is so copious as to supply words and phrases for every complex idea, or so correct as not to include many equivocally denoting different ideas. Hence, it must happen, that however accurately objects may be discriminated in themselves, and however accurately the discrimination may be considered, the definition of them may be rendered inaccurate by the inaccuracy of the terms in which it is delivered. And this unavoidable inaccuracy must be greater or less, according to the complexity and novelty of the objects defined. When the Almighty himself condescends to address mankind in their own language, his meaning, luminous as it must be, is rendered dim and doubtful, by the cloudy medium through which it is communicated. Here then are three sources of vague and incorrect definitions; indistinctness of the object, imperfection of the organ of conception, inadequateness of the vehicle of ideas. Any one of these must produce a certain degree of obscurity. The Convention, in delineating the boundary between the Federal and State jurisdictions, must have experienced the full effect of them all.

To the difficulties already mentioned, may be added the interfering pretensions of the larger and smaller States. We cannot err in supposing that the former would contend for a participation in the Government, fully proportioned to their superior wealth and importance; and that the latter would not be less tenacious of the equality at present enjoyed by them. We may well suppose that neither side would entirely yield to the other, and consequently that the struggle could be terminated only by compromise. It is extremely probable also, that after the ratio of representation had been adjusted, this very compromise must have produced a fresh struggle between the same parties, to give such a turn to the organization of the Government, and to the distribution of its powers, as would encrease the importance of the branches, in forming which they had respectively obtained the greatest share of influence. There are features in the Constitution which warrant each of these suppositions; and as far as either of them is well founded, it shews that the Convention must have been compelled to sacrifice theoretical propriety to the force of extraneous considerations.

Nor could it have been the large and small States only which would marshal themselves in opposition to each other on various points. Other combinations, resulting from a difference of local position and policy, must have created additional difficulties. As every State may be divided into different districts, and its citizens into different classes, which give birth to contending interests and local jealousies; so the different parts of the United States are distinguished from each other, by a variety of circumstances, which produce a like effect on a larger scale. And although this variety of interests, for reasons sufficiently explained in a former paper, may have a salutary influence on the administration of the Government when formed; yet every one must be sensible of the contrary influence which must have been experienced in the task of forming it.

Would it be wonderful if under the pressure of all these difficulties, the Convention should have been forced into some deviations from that artificial structure and regular symmetry, which an abstract view of the subject might lead an ingenious theorist to bestow on a Constitution planned in his closet or in his imagination? The real wonder is, that so many difficulties should have been surmounted; and surmounted with a unanimity almost as unprecedented as it must have been unexpected. It is impossible for any man of candor to reflect on this circumstance, without partaking of the astonishment. It is impossible for the man of pious reflection not to perceive in it, a finger of that Almighty hand which has been so frequently and signally extended to our relief in the critical stages of the revolution. We had occasion in a former paper, to take notice of the repeated trials which have been unsuccessfully made in the United Netherlands, for reforming the baneful and notorious vices of their Constitution. The history of almost all the great councils and consultations, held among mankind for reconciling their discordant opinions, assuaging their mutual jealousies, and adjusting their respective interests, is a history of factions, contentions, and disappointments; and may be classed among the most dark and degrading pictures which display the infirmities and depravities of the human character. If, in a few scattered instances, a brighter aspect is presented, they serve only as exceptions to admonish us of the general truth; and by their lustre to darken the gloom of the adverse prospect to which they are contrasted. In revolving the causes from which these exceptions result, and applying them to the particular instance before us, we are necessarily led to two important conclusions. The first is, that the Convention must have enjoyed in a very singular degree, an exemption from the pestilential influence of party animosities; the diseases most incident to deliberative bodies, and most apt to contaminate their proceedings. The second conclusion is, that all the deputations composing the Convention, were either satisfactorily accommodated by the final act; or were induced to accede to it, by a deep conviction of the necessity of sacrificing private opinions and partial interests to the public good, and by a despair of seeing this necessity diminished by delays or by new experiments.

PUBLIUS.

THE FEDERALIST NO. 38
JAMES MADISON

January 12, 1788

To the People of the State of New York.

It is not a little remarkable that in every case reported by antient history, in which government has been established with deliberation and consent, the task of framing it has not been committed to an assembly of men; but has been performed by some individual citizen of pre-eminent wisdom and approved integrity. Minos, we learn, was the primitive founder of the government of Crete; as Zaleucus was of that of the Locrians. Theseus first, and after him Draco and Solon, instituted the government of Athens. Lycurgus was the Lawgiver of Sparta. The foundation of the original government of Rome was laid by Romulus; and the work compleated by two of his elective successors, Numa, and Tullus Hostilius. On the abolition of Royalty, the Consular administration was substituted by Brutus, who stepped forward with a project for such a reform, which he alledged had been prepared by Servius Tullius, and to which his address obtained the assent and ratification of the Senate and people. This remark is applicable to confederate governments also. Amphyction, we are told, was the author of that which bore his name. The Achæan League received its first birth from Achæus and its second from Aratus. What degree of agency these reputed Lawgivers might have in their respective establishments, or how far they might be cloathed with the legitimate authority of the people, cannot in every instance be ascertained. In some however, the proceeding was strictly regular. Draco appears to have been entrusted by the people of Athens, with indefinite powers to reform its government and laws. And Solon, according to Plutarch, was in a manner compelled by the universal suffrage of his fellow citizens, to take upon him the sole and absolute power of new modelling the Constitution. The proceedings under Lycurgus were less regular; but as far as the advocates for a regular reform could prevail, they all turned their eyes towards the single efforts of that celebrated patriot and sage, instead of seeking to bring about a revolution, by the intervention of a deliberative body of citizens. Whence could it have proceeded that a people jealous as the Greeks were of their liberty, should so far abandon the rules of caution, as to place their destiny in the hands of a single citizen? Whence could it have proceeded, that the Atheniens, a people who would not suffer an army to be commanded by fewer than ten Generals, and who required no other proof of danger to their liberties than the illustrious merit of a fellow citizen should consider one illustrious citizen as a more eligible depository of the fortunes of themselves and their posterity, than a select body of citizens, from whose common deliberations more wisdom, as well as more safety, might have been expected? These questions cannot be fully answered without supposing that the fears of discord and disunion among a number of Counsellors, exceeded the apprehension of treachery or incapacity in a single individual. History informs us likewise of the difficulties with which these celebrated reformers had to contend; as well as of the expedients which they were obliged to employ, in order to carry their reforms into effect. Solon, who seems to have indulged a more temporising policy, confessed that he had not given to his countrymen the government best suited to their happiness, but most tolerable to their prejudices. And Lycurgus, more true to his object, was under the necessity of mixing a portion of violence with the authority of superstition; and of securing his final success, by a voluntary renunciation, first of his country, and then of his life. If these lessons teach us, on one hand, to admire the improvement made by America on the ancient mode of preparing and establishing regular plans of government; they serve not less on the other, to admonish us of the hazards and difficulties incident to such experiments, and of the great imprudence of unnecessarily multiplying them.

Is it an unreasonable conjecture that the errors which may be contained in the plan of the Convention are such as have resulted rather from the defect of antecedent experience on this complicated and difficult subject, than from a want of accuracy or care in the investigation of it; and consequently such as will not be ascertained until an actual trial shall have pointed them out? This conjecture is rendered probable not only by many considerations of a general nature, but by the particular case of the articles of confederation. It is observable that among the numerous objections and amendments suggested by the several States, when these articles were submitted for their ratification, not one is found which alludes to the great and radical error, which on actual trial has discovered itself. And if we except the observations which New-Jersey was led to make rather by her local situation than by her peculiar foresight, it may be questioned whether a single suggestion was of sufficient moment to justify a revision of the system.[1] There is abundant reason nevertheless to suppose that immaterial as these objections were they would have been adhered to with a very dangerous inflexibility in some States, had not a zeal for their opinions and supposed interests, been

[1] New Jersey delegates had objected to certain weaknesses of the Articles of Confederation as early as June 23, 1778. New Jersey demanded that Congress be given exclusive power to regulate foreign trade and that all lands formerly belonging to the crown be taken over by the United States.

stifled by the more powerful sentiment of self-preservation. One State, we may remember, persisted for several years in refusing her concurrence, although the enemy remained the whole period at our gates, or rather in the very bowels of our country. Nor was her pliancy in the end effected by a less motive than the fear of being chargeable with protracting the public calamities, and endangering the event of the contest.[2] Every candid reader will make the proper reflections on these important facts.

A patient who finds his disorder daily growing worse; and that an efficacious remedy can no longer be delayed without extreme danger; after cooly revolving his situation, and the characters of different physicians, selects and calls in such of them as he judges most capable of administering relief, and best entitled to his confidence. Thc physicians attend: The case of the patient is carefully examined: a consultation held. They are unanimously agreed that the symptoms are critical, but that the case, with proper and timely relief, is so far from being desperate, that it may be made to issue in an improvement of his constitution. They are equally unanimous in prescribing the remedy by which this happy effect is to be produced. The prescription is no sooner made known however, than a number of persons interpose, and without denying the reality or danger of the disorder, assure the patient that the prescription will be poison to his constitution, and forbid him under pain of certain death to make use of it. Might not the patient reasonably demand before he ventured to follow this advice, that the authors of it should at least agree among themselves, on some other remedy to be substituted? and if he found them differing as much from one another, as from his first counsellors, would he not act prudently, in trying the experiment unanimously recommended by the latter, rather than in hearkening to those who could neither deny the necessity of a speedy remedy, nor agree in proposing one?

Such a patient, and in such a situation is America at this moment. She has been sensible of her malady. She has obtained a regular and unanimous advice from men of her own deliberate choice. And she is warned by others against following this advice, under pain of the most fatal consequences. Do the monitors deny the reality of her danger? No. Do they deny

[2] Maryland did not ratify the Articles of Confederation until March 1, 1781. Her refusal was ostensibly based on the fact that not all of the states had ceded their western lands to the United States; in actuality, Maryland was acting in the interests of certain land speculators.

the necessity of some speedy and powerful remedy? No. Are they agreed, are any two of them agreed in their objections to the remedy proposed, or in the proper one to be substituted? Let them speak for themselves. This one tells us that the proposed constitution ought to be rejected, because it is not a confederation of the States, but a Government over individuals. Another admits that it ought to be a government over individuals, to a certain extent, but by no means to the extent proposed. A third does not object to the Government over individuals, or to the extent proposed, but to the want of a bill of rights. A fourth concurs in the absolute necessity of a bill of rights, but contends that it ought to be declaratory not of the personal rights of individuals, but of the rights reserved to the States in their political capacity. A fifth is of opinion that a bill of rights of any sort would be superfluous and misplaced, and that the plan would be unexceptionable, but for the fatal power of regulating the times and places of election. An objector in a large State exclaims loudly against the unreasonable equality of representation in the Senate. An objector in a small State is equally loud against the dangerous inequality in the house of representatives. From this quarter we are alarmed with the amazing expence from the number of persons who are to administer the new Government. From another quarter, and sometimes from the same quarter, on another occasion, the cry is that the Congress will be but the shadow of a representation, and that the Government would be far less objectionable, if the number and the expence were doubled. A patriot in a State that does not import or export, discerns insuperable objections against the power of direct taxation. The patriotic adversary in a State of great exports and imports, is not less dissatisfied that the whole burden of taxes may be thrown on consumption. This Politician discovers in the constitution a direct and irresistible tendency to monarchy. That is equally sure, it will end in aristocracy. Another is puzzled to say which of these shapes it will ultimately assume, but sees clearly it must be one or other of them. Whilst a fourth is not wanting who with no less confidence affirms that the constitution is so far from having a bias towards either of these dangers, that the weight on that side will not be sufficient to keep it upright and firm against its opposite propensities. With another class of adversaries to the constitution, the language is that the legislative executive and judiciary departments are intermixed in such a manner as to contradict all the ideas of regular government, and all the requisite precautions in favour of liberty. Whilst this objection circulates in vague and general expressions, there are not a few who lend their sanction to it. Let each one come forward with his particular explanation and scarce any two are exactly agreed on the subject. In the eyes of one the junction of the Senate with the President in the responsible function of appointing to offices, instead of vesting this executive power in the executive, alone, is the vicious part of the organization. To another, the exclusion of the house of representatives whose numbers alone could be a due security against corruption and partiality in the exercise of such a power, is equally obnoxious. With another, the admission of the President into any share of power which must ever be a dangerous engine in the hands of the executive magistrate, is an unpardonable violation of the maxims of republican jealousy. No part of the arrangement according to some is more inadmissible than the trial of impeachments by the Senate, which is alternately a member both of the legislative and executive departments, when this power so evidently belonged to the judiciary department. We concur fully, reply others, in the objection to this part of the plan, but we can never agree that a reference of impeachments to the judiciary authority would be an amendment of the error. Our principal dislike to the organisation arises from the extensive powers already lodged in that department. Even among the zealous patrons of a council of State, the most irreconcilable variance is discovered concerning the mode in which it ought to be constituted. The demand of one gentleman is that the council should consist of a small number, to be appointed by the most numerous branch of the Legislature. Another would prefer a larger number, and considers it as a fundamental condition that the appointment should be made by the President himself.

As it can give no umbrage to the writers against the plan of the Fœderal Constitution, let us suppose that as they are the most zealous, so they are also the most sagacious of those who think the late Convention were unequal to the task assigned them, and that a wiser and better plan might and ought to be substituted. Let us further suppose that their country should concur both in this favorable opinion of their merits, and in their unfavorable opinion of the Convention, and should accordingly proceed to form them into a second Convention, with full powers and for the express purpose of revising and remoulding the work of the first. Were the experiment to be seriously made, though it requires some effort to view it seriously even in fiction, I leave it to be decided by the sample of opinions just exhibited, whether with all their enmity to their predecessors, they would in any one point depart so widely from their example, as in the discord and ferment that would mark their own deliberations; and whether the Constitution, now before the public, would not stand as fair a chance for immortality, as Lycurgus gave to that of Sparta, by making its change to depend on his own return from exile and death, if it were to be immediately adopted, and were to continue in force, not until a BETTER, but until ANOTHER should be agreed upon by this new assembly of Lawgivers.

It is a matter both of wonder and regret, that those who raise so many objections against the new Constitution, should never call to mind the defects of that which is to be exchanged for it. It is not necessary that the former should be perfect; it is sufficient that the latter is more imperfect. No man would refuse to give brass for silver or gold, because the latter had some alloy in it. No man would refuse to quit a shattered and tottering habitation, for a firm and commodious building, because the latter had not a porch to it; or because some of the rooms might be a little larger or smaller, or the ceiling a little higher or lower than his fancy would have planned them. But waving illustrations of this sort, is it not manifest that most of the capital objections urged against the new system, lie with tenfold weight against the existing Confederation? Is an indefinite power to raise money dangerous in the hands of a fœderal government? The present Congress can make requisitions to any amount they please; and the States are constitutionally bound to furnish them; they can emit bills of credit as long as they will pay for the paper; they can borrow both abroad and at home, as long as a shilling will be lent. Is an indefinite power to raise troops dangerous? The Confederation gives to Congress that power also; and they have already begun to make use of it. Is it improper and unsafe to intermix the different powers of government in the same body of men? Congress, a single body of men, are the sole depository of all the fœderal powers. Is it particularly dangerous to give the keys of the treasury, and the command of the army, into the same hands? The Confederation places them both in the hands of Congress. Is a Bill of Rights essential to liberty? The Confederation has no Bill of Rights. Is it an objection against the new Constitution, that it empowers the Senate with the concurrence of the Executive to make treaties which are to be the laws of the land? The existing Congress, without any such controul, can make treaties which they themselves have declared, and most of the States have recognized, to be the supreme law of the land. Is the importation of slaves permitted by the new Constitution for twenty years? By the old, it is permitted for ever.

I shall be told that however dangerous this mixture of powers may be in theory, it is rendered harmless by the dependence of Congress on the States for the means of carrying them into practice: That however large the mass of powers may be, it is in fact a lifeless mass. Then say I in the first place, that the Confederation is chargeable with the still greater folly of declaring certain powers in the fœderal government to be absolutely necessary, and at the same time rendering them absolutely nugatory: And in the next place, that if the Union is to continue, and no better government be substituted, effective powers must either be granted to or assumed by the existing Congress, in either of which events the contrast just stated will hold good. But this is not all. Out of this lifeless mass has already grown an excrescent power, which tends to realize all the dangers that can be apprehended from a defective construction of the supreme government of the Union. It is now no longer a point of speculation and hope that the Western territory is a mine of vast wealth to the United States, and although it is not of such a nature as to extricate them from their present distresses, or for some time to come, to yield any regular supplies for the public expences, yet must it hereafter be able under proper management both to effect a gradual discharge of the domestic debt, and to furnish for a certain period, liberal tributes to the Federal Treasury. A very large proportion of this fund has been already surrendered by individual States; and it may with reason be expected, that the remaining States will not persist in withholding similar proofs of their equity and generosity. We may calculate therefore that a rich and fertile country, of an area equal to the inhabitated extent of the United States, will soon become a national stock. Congress have assumed the administration of this stock. They have begun to render it productive. Congress have undertaken to do more; they have proceeded to form new States; to erect temporary Governments; to appoint officers for them; and to prescribe the conditions on which such States shall be admitted into the confederacy. All this has been done; and done without the least colour of constitutional authority. Yet no blame has been whispered; no alarm has been sounded. A GREAT and INDE-

PENDENT fund of revenue is passing into the hands of a SINGLE BODY of men, who can RAISE TROOPS to an INDEFINITE NUMBER, and appropriate money to their support for an INDEFINITE PERIOD OF TIME. And yet there are men who have not only been silent spectators of this prospect; but who are advocates for the system which exhibits it; and at the same time urge against the new system the objections which we have heard. Would they not act with more consistency in urging the establishment of the latter, as no less necessary to guard the Union against the future powers and resources of a body constructed like the existing Congress, than to save it from the dangers threatened by the present impotency of that assembly?

I mean not by any thing here said to throw censure on the measures which have been pursued by Congress. I am sensible they could not have done otherwise. The public interest, the necessity of the case, imposed upon them the task of overleaping their constitutional limits. But is not the fact an alarming proof of the danger resulting from a government which does not possess regular powers commensurate to its objects? A dissolution or usurpation is the dreadful dilemma to which it is continually exposed.

PUBLIUS.

THE FEDERALIST NO. 39
JAMES MADISON

January 16, 1788

To the People of the State of New York.

The last paper having concluded the observations which were meant to introduce a candid survey of the plan of government reported by the Convention, we now proceed to the execution of that part of our undertaking. The first question that offers itself is, whether the general form and aspect of the government be strictly republican? It is evident that no other form would be reconcileable with the genius of the people of America; with the fundamental principles of the revolution; or with that honorable determination, which animates every votary of freedom, to rest all our political experiments on the capacity of mankind for self-government. If the plan of the Convention therefore be found to depart from the republican character, its advocates must abandon it as no longer defensible.

What then are the distinctive characters of the republican form? Were an answer to this question to be sought, not by recurring to principles, but in the application of the term by political writers, to the constitutions of different States, no satisfactory one would ever be found. Holland, in which no particle of the supreme authority is derived from the people, has passed almost universally under the denomination of a republic. The same title has been bestowed on Venice, where absolute power over the great body of the people, is exercised in the most absolute manner, by a small body of hereditary nobles. Poland, which is a mixture of aristocracy and of monarchy in their worst forms, has been dignified with the same appellation. The government of England, which has one republican branch only, combined with a hereditary aristocracy and monarchy, has with equal impropriety been frequently placed on the list of republics. These examples, which are nearly as dissimilar to each other as to a genuine republic, shew the extreme inaccuracy with which the term has been used in political disquisitions.

If we resort for a criterion, to the different principles on which different forms of government are established, we may define a republic to be, or at least may bestow that name on, a government which derives all its powers directly or indirectly from the great body of the people; and is administered by persons holding their offices during pleasure, for a limited period, or during good behaviour. It is *essential* to such a government, that it be derived from the great body of the society, not from an inconsiderable proportion, or a favored class of it; otherwise a handful of tyrannical nobles, exercising their oppressions by a delegation of their powers, might aspire to the rank of republicans, and claim for their government the honorable title of republic. It is *sufficient* for such a government, that the persons administering it be appointed, either directly or indirectly, by the people; and that they hold their appointments by either of the tenures just specified; otherwise every government in the United States, as well as every other popular government that has been or can be well organized or well executed, would be degraded from the republican character. According to the Constitution of every State in the Union, some or other of the officers of government are appointed indirectly only by the people. According to most of them the chief magistrate himself is so appointed. And according to one, this mode of appointment is extended to one of the coordinate branches of the legislature. According to all the Constitutions also, the tenure of the highest offices is extended to a definite period, and in many instances, both within the legislative and executive departments, to a period of years. According to the provisions of most of the constitutions, again, as well as according to the most respectable and received opinions on the subject, the members of the judiciary department are to retain their offices by the firm tenure of good behaviour.

On comparing the Constitution planned by the Convention, with the standard here fixed, we perceive at once that it is in the most rigid sense conformable to it. The House of Representatives, like that of one branch at least of all the State Legislatures, is elected immediately by the great body of the people. The Senate, like the present Congress, and the Senate of Maryland, derives its appointment indirectly from the people. The President is indirectly derived from the choice of the people, according to the example in most of the States. Even the judges, with all other officers of the Union, will, as in the several States, be the choice, though a remote choice, of the people themselves. The duration of the appointments is equally conformable to the republican standard, and to the model of the State Constitutions. The House of Representatives is periodically elective as in all the States: and for the period of two years as in the State of South-Carolina. The Senate is elective for the period of six years; which is but one year more than the period of the Senate of Maryland; and but two more than that of the Senates of New-York and Virginia. The President is to continue in office for the period of four years; as in New-York and Delaware, the chief magistrate is elected for three years, and in South-Carolina for two years. In the other States the election is annual. In several of the States however, no constitutional provision is made for the impeachment of the Chief Magistrate. And in Delaware and Virginia, he is not impeachable till out of office. The President of the United States is impeachable at any time during his continuance in office. The tenure by which the Judges are to hold their places, is, as it unquestionably ought to be, that of good behaviour. The tenure of the ministerial offices generally will be a subject of legal regulation, conformably to the reason of the case, and the example of the State Constitutions.

Could any further proof be required of the republican complextion of this system, the most decisive one might be found in its absolute prohibition of titles of nobility, both under the Federal and the State Governments; and in its express guarantee of the republican form to each of the latter.

But it was not sufficient, say the adversaries of the proposed Constitution, for the Convention to adhere to the republican form. They ought, with equal care, to have preserved the *federal* form, which regards the union as a *confederacy* of sovereign States; instead of which, they have framed a *national* government, which regards the union as a *consolidation* of the States. And it is asked by what authority this bold and radical innovation was undertaken. The handle which has been made of this objection requires, that it should be examined with some precision.

Without enquiring into the accuracy of the distinction on which the objection is founded, it will be necessary to a just estimate of its force, first to ascertain the real character of the government in question; secondly, to enquire how far the Convention were authorised to propose such a government; and thirdly, how far the duty they owed to their country, could supply any defect of regular authority.

First. In order to ascertain the real character of the government it may be considered in relation to the foundation on which it is to be established; to the sources from which its ordinary powers are to be drawn; to the operation of those powers; to the extent of them; and to the authority by which future changes in the government are to be introduced.

On examining the first relation, it appears on one hand that the Constitution is to be founded on the assent and ratification of the people of America, given by deputies elected for the special purpose; but on the other, that this assent and ratification is to be given by the people, not as individuals composing one entire nation; but as composing the distinct and independent States to which they respectively belong. It is to be the assent and ratification of the several States, derived from the supreme authority in each State, the authority of the people themselves. The act therefore establishing the Constitution, will not be a *national* but a *federal* act.

That it will be a federal and not a national act, as these terms are understood by the objectors, the act of the people as forming so many independent States, not as forming one aggregate nation, is obvious from this single consideration that it is to result neither from the decision of a *majority* of the people of the Union, nor from that of a *majority* of the States. It must result from the *unanimous* assent of the several States that are parties to it, differing no other wise from their ordinary assent than in its being expressed, not by the legislative authority, but by that of the people themselves. Were the people regarded in this transaction as forming one nation, the will of the majority of the whole people of the United States, would bind the minority; in the same manner as the majority must be determined either by a comparison of the individual votes; or by considering the will of a majority of the States, as evidence of the will of a majority of the people of the United States. Neither of these rules has been adopted. Each State in ratifying the Constitution, is considered as a sovereign body independent of all others, and only to be bound by its own voluntary act. In this relation then the new Constitution will, if established, be a *federal* and not a *national* Constitution.

The next relation is to the sources from which the ordinary powers of government are to be derived. The house of representatives will derive its powers from the people of America, and the people will be represented in the same proportion, and on the same principle, as they are in the Legislature of a particular State. So far the Government is *national* not *federal.* The Senate on the other hand will derive its powers from the States, as political and co-equal societies; and these will be represented on the principle of equality in the Senate, as they now are in the existing Congress. So far the government is *federal,* not *national.* The executive power will be derived from a very compound source. The immediate election of the President is to be made by the States in their political characters. The votes allotted to them, are in a compound ratio, which considers them partly as distinct and co-equal societies; partly as unequal members of the same society. The eventual election, again is to be made by that branch of the Legislature which consists of the national representatives; but in this particular act, they are to be thrown into the form of individual delegations from so many distinct and co-equal bodies politic. From this aspect of the Government, it appears to be of a mixed character presenting at least as many *federal* as *national* features.

The difference between a federal and national Government as it relates to the *operation of the Government* is supposed to consist in this, that in the former, the powers operate on the political bodies composing the confederacy, in their political capacities: In the latter, on the individual citizens, composing the nation, in their individual capacities. On trying the Constitution by this criterion, it falls under the *national,* not the *federal* character; though perhaps not so compleatly, as has been understood. In several cases and particularly in the trial of controversies to which States may be parties, they must be viewed and proceeded against in their collective and political capacities only. So far the national countenance of the Government on this side seems to be disfigured by a few federal features. But this blemish is perhaps unavoidable in any plan; and the operation of the Government on the people in their individual capacities, in its ordinary and most essential proceedings, may on the whole designate it in this relation a *national* Government.

But if the Government be national with regard to the *operation* of its powers, it changes its aspect again when we contemplate it in relation to the *extent* of its powers. The idea of a national Government involves in it, not only an authority over the individual citizens; but an indefinite supremacy over all persons and things, so far as they are objects of lawful Government. Among a people consolidated into one nation, this supremacy is compleatly vested in the national Legislature. Among communities united for particular purposes, it is vested partly in the general, and partly in the municipal Legislatures. In the former case, all local authorities are subordinate to the supreme; and may be controuled, directed or abolished by it at pleasure. In the latter the local or municipal authorities form distinct and independent portions of the supremacy, no more subject within their respective spheres to the general authority, than the general authority is subject to them, within its own sphere. In this relation then the proposed Government cannot be deemed a *national* one; since its jurisdiction extends to certain enumerated objects only, and leaves to the several States a residuary and inviolable sovereignty over all other objects. It is true that in controversies relating to the boundary between the two jurisdictions, the tribunal which is ultimately to decide, is to be established under the general Government. But this does not change the principle of the case. The decision is to be impartially made, according to the rules of the Constitution; and all the usual and most effectual precautions are taken to secure this impartiality. Some such tribunal is clearly essential to prevent an appeal to the sword, and a dissolution of the compact; and that it ought to be established under the general, rather than under the local Governments; or to speak more properly, that it could be safely established under the first alone, is a position not likely to be combated.

If we try the Constitution by its last relation, to the authority by which amendments are to be made, we find it neither wholly *national,* nor wholly *federal.* Were it wholly national, the supreme and ultimate authority would reside in the *majority* of the people of the Union; and this authority would be competent at all times, like that of a majority of every national society, to alter or abolish its established Government. Were it wholly federal on the other hand, the concurrence of each State in the Union would be essential to every alteration that would be binding on all. The mode provided by the plan of the Convention is not founded on either of these principles. In requiring more than a majority, and particularly, in computing the proportion by *States,* not by *citizens,* it departs from the *national,* and advances towards the *federal* character: In rendering the concurrence of less than the whole number of States sufficient, it loses again the *federal,* and partakes of the *national* character.

The proposed Constitution therefore is in strictness neither a national nor a federal constitution; but a composition of both. In its foundation, it is federal, not national; in the sources from which the ordinary powers of the Government are drawn, it is partly federal, and partly national: in the operation of these powers, it is national, not federal: In the extent of them again, it is federal, not national: And finally, in the authoritative mode of introducing amendments, it is neither wholly federal, nor wholly national.

PUBLIUS.

THE FEDERALIST NO. 40
JAMES MADISON

January 18, 1788

To the People of the State of New York.

The *second* point to be examined is, whether the Convention were authorised to frame and propose this mixed Constitution.

The powers of the Convention ought in strictness to be determined, by an inspection of the commissions given to the members by their respective constituents. As all of these however had reference, either to the recommendation from the meeting at Annapolis in September, 1786, or to that from Congress in February, 1787, it will be sufficient to recur to these particular acts.[1]

[1] The Annapolis Convention, which lasted from September 11 to September 14, 1786, was called as a commercial convention by Virginia. It passed an address to the states calling for a future convention in Philadelphia "to render the constitution of the Federal Government adequate to the exigencies of the Union." On February 21, 1787, Congress endorsed the resolution.

The act from Annapolis recommends the "appointment of commissioners to take into consideration, the situation of the United States, to devise *such further provisions* as shall appear to them necessary to render the Constitution of the Fœderal Government *adequate to the exigencies of the Union;* and to report such an act for that purpose, to the United States in Congress assembled, as when agreed to by them, and afterwards confirmed by the Legislature of every State, will effectually provide for the same."

The recommendatory act of Congress is in the words following: "Whereas there is provision in the articles of confederation and perpetual Union, for making alterations therein, by the assent of a Congress of the United States, and of the Legislatures of the several States: And whereas experience hath evinced, that there are defects in the present confederation, as a mean to remedy which, several of the States, and *particularly the State of New-York,* by express instructions to their delegates in Congress, have suggested a Convention for the purposes expressed in the following resolution; and such Convention appearing to be the most probable mean of establishing in these States, a *firm national government.*

"Resolved, That in the opinion of Congress, it is expedient, that on the 2d Monday in May next, a Convention of delegates, who shall have been appointed by the several States, be held at Philadelphia for the sole and express purpose *of revising the articles of confederation,* and reporting to Congress and the several Legislatures, such *alterations and provisions therein,* as shall, when agreed to in Congress, and confirmed by the States, render the Fœderal Constitution *adequate to the exigencies of government and the preservation of the Union.*"

From these two acts it appears, 1st. that the object of the Convention was to establish in these States, *a firm national government*; 2d. that this Government was to be such as would be *adequate to the exigencies of government* and *the preservation of the Union;* 3d. that these purposes were to be effected by *alterations and provisions in the articles of confederation,* as it is expressed in the act of Congress, or by *such further provisions as should appear necessary,* as it stands in the recommendatory act from Annapolis; 4th. that the alterations and provisions were to be reported to Congress, and to the States, in order to be agreed to by the former, and confirmed by the latter.

From a comparison and fair construction of these several

modes of expression, is to be deduced the authority, under which the Convention acted. They were to frame a *national government,* adequate to the *exigencies of government* and *of the Union,* and to reduce the articles of confederation into such form as to accomplish these purposes.

There are two rules of construction dictated by plain reason, as well as founded on legal axioms. The one is, that every part of the expression ought, if possible, to be allowed some meaning, and be made to conspire to some common end. The other is, that where the several parts cannot be made to coincide, the less important should give way to the more important part; the means should be sacrificed to the end, rather than the end to the means.

Suppose then that the expressions defining the authority of the Convention, were irreconcileably at variance with each other; that a *national* and *adequate government* could not possibly, in the judgment of the Convention, be effected by *alterations* and *provisions* in the *articles of confederation,* which part of the definition ought to have been embraced, and which rejected? Which was the more important, which the less important part? Which the end, which the means? Let the most scrupulous expositors of delegated powers: Let the most inveterate objectors against those exercised by the Convention, answer these questions. Let them declare, whether it was of most importance to the happiness of the people of America, that the articles of confederation should be disregarded, and an adequate government be provided, and the Union preserved; or that an adequate government should be omitted, and the articles of confederation preserved. Let them declare, whether the preservation of these articles was the end for securing which a reform of the government was to be introduced as the means; or whether the establishment of a government, adequate to the national happiness, was the end at which these articles themselves originally aimed, and to which they ought, as insufficient means, to have been sacrificed.

But is it necessary to suppose that these expressions are absolutely irreconcileable to each other; that no *alterations* or *provisions* in *the articles of the confederation,* could possibly mould them into a national and adequate government; into such a government as has been proposed by the Convention?

No stress it is presumed will in this case be laid on the *title,* a change of that could never be deemed an exercise of ungranted power. *Alterations* in the body of the instrument, are expressly authorised. *New provisions* therein are also expressly authorised. Here then is a power to change the title; to insert new articles; to alter old ones. Must it of necessity be admitted that this power is infringed, so long as a part of the old articles remain? Those who maintain the affirmative, ought at least to mark the boundary between authorised and usurped innovations, between that degree of change, which lies within the compass of *alterations and further provisions;* and that which amounts to a *transmutation* of the government. Will it be said that the alterations ought not to have touched the substance of the confederation? The States would never have appointed a Convention with so much solemnity, nor described its objects with so much latitude, if some *substantial* reform had not been in contemplation. Will it be said that the *fundamental principles* of the confederation were not within the purview of the Convention, and ought not to have been varied? I ask what are these principles? do they require that in the establishment of the Constitution, the States should be regarded as distinct and independent sovereigns? They are so regarded by the Constitution proposed. Do they require that the members of the government should derive their appointment from the Legislatures, not from the people of the State? One branch of the new government is to be appointed by these Legislatures; and under the confederation the delegates to Congress *may all* be appointed immediately by the people, and in two States* are actually so appointed. Do they require that the powers of the Government should act on the States, and not immediately on individuals? In some instances, as has been shewn, the powers of the new Government will act on the States in their collective characters. In some instances also those of the existing Government act immediately on individuals. In cases of capture, of piracy, of the post-office, of coins, weights and measures, of trade with the Indians, of claims under grants of land by different States, and above all, in the case of trials by Courts-martial in the army and navy, by which death may be inflicted without the intervention of a jury, or even of a civil Magistrate; in all these cases the powers of the confederation operate immediately on the persons and interests of individual citizens. Do these fundamental principles require particularly, that no tax should be levied without the intermediate agency of the States! The confederation itself authorises a direct tax to a

* *Connecticut and Rhode-island.*

certain extent on the post-office. The power of coinage has been so construed by Congress, as to levy a tribute immediately from that source also. But pretermitting these instances, was it not an acknowledged object of the Convention, and the universal expectation of the people, that the regulation of trade should be submitted to the general government in such a form as would render it an immediate source of general revenue? Had not Congress repeatedly recommended this measure as not inconsistent with the fundamental principles of the confederation? Had not every State but one, had not New-York herself, so far complied with the plan of Congress, as to recognize the *principle* of the innovation? Do these principles in fine require that the powers of the general government should be limited, and that beyond this limit, the States should be left in possession of their sovereignty and independence? We have seen that in the new government as in the old, the general powers are limited, and that the States in all unenumerated cases, are left in the enjoyment of their sovereign and independent jurisdiction.

The truth is, that the great principles of the Constitution proposed by the Convention, may be considered less as absolutely new, than as the expansion of principles which are found in the articles of Confederation. The misfortune under the latter system has been, that these principles are so feeble and confined as to justify all the charges of inefficiency which have been urged against it; and to require a degree of enlargement which gives to the new system, the aspect of an entire transformation of the old.

In one particular it is admitted that the Convention have departed from the tenor of their commission. Instead of reporting a plan requiring the confirmation *of the Legislatures of all the States,* they have reported a plan which is to be confirmed by the *people,* and may be carried into effect by *nine States only*. It is worthy of remark, that this objection, though the most plausible, has been the least urged in the publications which have swarmed against the Convention. The forbearance can only have proceeded from an irresistible conviction of the absurdity of subjecting the fate of 12 States, to the perverseness or corruption of a thirteenth; from the example of inflexible opposition given by *a majority* of 1-60th of the people of America to a measure approved and called for by the voice of twelve States comprising 59-60ths of the people; an example still fresh in the memory and indignation of every citizen who has felt for the wounded honor and prosperity of his country.[2] As this objection, therefore, has been in a manner waved by those who have criticised the powers of the Convention, I dismiss it without further observation.

The *third* point to be enquired into is, how far considerations of duty arising out of the case itself, could have supplied any defect of regular authority.

In the preceding enquiries, the powers of the Convention have been analised and tried with the same rigour, and by the same rules, as if they had been real and final powers, for the establishment of a Constitution for the United States. We have seen, in what manner they have borne the trial, even on that supposition. It is time now to recollect, that the powers were merely advisory and recommendatory; that they were so meant by the States, and so understood by the Convention; and that the latter have accordingly planned and proposed a Constitution, which is to be of no more consequence than the paper on which it is written, unless it be stamped with the approbation of those to whom it is addressed. This reflection places the subject in a point of view altogether different, and will enable us to judge with propriety of the course taken by the Convention.

Let us view the ground on which the Convention stood. It may be collected from their proceedings, that they were deeply and unanimously impressed with the crisis which had led their country almost with one voice to make so singular and solemn an experiment, for correcting the errors of a system by which this crisis had been produced; that they were no less deeply and unanimously convinced, that such a reform as they have proposed, was absolutely necessary to effect the purposes of their appointment. It could not be unknown to them, that the hopes and expectations of the great body of citizens, throughout this great empire, were turned with the keenest anxiety, to the event of their deliberations. They had every reason to believe that the contrary sentiments agitated the minds and bosoms of every external and internal foe to the liberty and prosperity of the United States. They had seen in the origin and progress of the experiment, the alacrity with which the *proposition* made by a single State (Virginia) towards a partial amendment of the confederation, had been attended to and promoted. They had seen the *liberty assumed* by a *very few* deputies, from a *very few* States, convened at Annapolis, of recommending a great and critical object,

[2] Rhode Island, the smallest state in the Union, refused to send a delegation to the Constitutional Convention.

wholly foreign to their commission, not only justified by the public opinion, but actually carried into effect, by twelve out of the thirteen States. They had seen in a variety of instances, assumptions by Congress, not only of recommendatory, but of operative powers, warranted in the public estimation, by occasions and objects infinitely less urgent than those by which their conduct was to be governed. They must have reflected, that in all great changes of established governments, forms ought to give way to substance; that a rigid adherence in such cases to the former, would render nominal and nugatory, the transcendent and precious right of the people to 'abolish or alter their governments as to them shall seem most likely to effect their safety and happiness;'* since it is impossible for the people spontaneously and universally, to move in concert towards their object; and it is therefore essential, that such changes be instituted by some *informal and unauthorised propositions,* made by some patriotic and respectable citizen or number of citizens. They must have recollected that it was by this irregular and assumed privilege of proposing to the people plans for their safety and happiness, that the States were first united against the danger with which they were threatened by their antient government; that Committees and Congresses, were formed for concentrating their efforts, and defending their rights; and that *Conventions* were *elected in the several States,* for establishing the constitutions under which they are now governed; nor could it have been forgotten that no little ill-timed scruples, no zeal for adhering to ordinary forms, were any where seen, except in those who wished to indulge under these masks, their secret enmity to the substance contended for. They must have borne in mind, that as the plan to be framed and proposed, was to be submitted *to the people themselves,* the disapprobation of this supreme authority would destroy it for ever; its approbation blot out all antecedent errors and irregularities. It might even have occurred to them, that where a disposition to cavil prevailed, their neglect to execute the degree of power vested in them, and still more their recommendation of any measure whatever not warranted by their commission, would not less excite animadversion, than a recommendation at once of a measure fully commensurate to the national exigencies.

Had the Convention under all these impressions, and in the midst of all these considerations, instead of exercising a manly

* *Declaration of Independence.*

confidence in their country, by whose confidence they had been so peculiarly distinguished, and of pointing out a system capable in their judgment of securing its happiness, taken the cold and sullen resolution of disappointing its ardent hopes of sacrificing substance to forms, of committing the dearest interests of their country to the uncertainties of delay, and the hazard of events; let me ask the man, who can raise his mind to one elevated conception; who can awaken in his bosom, one patriotic emotion, what judgment ought to have been pronounced by the impartial world, by the friends of mankind, by every virtuous citizen, on the conduct and character of this assembly, or if there be a man whose propensity to condemn, is susceptible of no controul, let me then ask what sentence he has in reserve for the twelve States, who *usurped the power* of sending deputies to the Convention, a body utterly unknown to their constitutions; for Congress, who recommended the appointment of this body, equally unknown to the confederation; and for the State of New-York in particular, who first urged and then complied with this unauthorised interposition.[3]

But that the objectors may be disarmed of every pretext, it shall be granted for a moment, that the Convention were neither authorised by their commission, nor justified by circumstances, in proposing a Constitution for their country: Does it follow that the Constitution ought for that reason alone to be rejected? If according to the noble precept it be lawful to accept good advice even from an enemy, shall we set the ignoble example of refusing such advice even when it is offered by our friends? The prudent enquiry in all cases, ought surely to be not so much *from whom* the advice comes, as whether the advice be *good*.

The sum of what has been here advanced and proved, is that the charge against the Convention of exceeding their powers, except in one instance little urged by the objectors, has no foundation to support it; that if they had exceeded their powers, they were not only warranted but required, as the confidential servants of their country, by the circumstances in which they were placed, to exercise the liberty which they assumed, and that finally, if they had violated both their powers, and their obligations in proposing a Constitution, this ought nevertheless to be embraced, if it be calculated to accomplish

[3] As early as July, 1782, New York had requested that the Congress call a convention to consider amendments to the Articles of Confederation.

the views and happiness of the people of America. How far this character is due to the Constitution, is the subject under investigation.

PUBLIUS.

THE FEDERALIST NO. 47
JAMES MADISON

January 30, 1788

To the People of the State of New York.

Having reviewed the general form of the proposed government, and the general mass of power allotted to it: I proceed to examine the particular structure of this government, and the distribution of this mass of power among its constituent parts.

One of the principal objections inculcated by the more respectable adversaries to the constitution, is its supposed violation of the political maxim, that the legislative, executive and judiciary departments ought to be separate and distinct. In the structure of the federal government, no regard, it is said, seems to have been paid to this essential precaution in favor of liberty. The several departments of power are distributed and blended in such a manner, as at once to destroy all symmetry and beauty of form; and to expose some of the essential parts of the edifice to the danger of being crushed by the disproportionate weight of other parts.

No political truth is certainly of greater intrinsic value or is stamped with the authority of more enlightened patrons of liberty than that on which the objection is founded. The accumulation of all powers legislative, executive and judiciary in the same hands, whether of one, a few or many, and whether hereditary, self appointed, or elective, may justly be pronounced the very definition of tyranny. Were the federal constitution therefore really chargeable with this accumulation of power or with a mixture of powers having a dangerous tendency to such an accumulation, no further arguments would be necessary to inspire a universal reprobation of the system. I persuade myself however, that it will be made apparent to every one, that the charge cannot be supported, and that the maxim on which it relies, has been totally misconceived and misapplied. In order to form correct ideas on this important subject, it will be proper to investigate the sense, in which the preservation of liberty requires, that the three great departments of power should be separate and distinct.

The oracle who is always consulted and cited on this subject, is the celebrated Montesquieu. If he be not the author of this invaluable precept in the science of politics, he has the merit at least of displaying, and recommending it most effectually to the attention of mankind. Let us endeavour in the first place to ascertain his meaning on this point.

The British constitution was to Montesquieu, what Homer has been to the didactic writers on epic poetry. As the latter have considered the work of the immortal Bard, as the perfect model from which the principles and rules of the epic art were to be drawn, and by which all similar works were to be judged; so this great political critic appears to have viewed the constitution of England, as the standard, or to use his own expression, as the mirrour of political liberty; and to have delivered in the form of elementary truths, the several characteristic principles of that particular system. That we may be sure then not to mistake his meaning in this case, let us recur to the source from which the maxim was drawn.

On the slightest view of the British constitution we must perceive, that the legislative, executive and judiciary departments are by no means totally separate and distinct from each other. The executive magistrate forms an integral part of the legislative authority. He alone has the prerogative of making treaties with foreign sovereigns, which when made have, under certain limitations, the force of legislative acts. All the members of the judiciary department are appointed by him; can be removed by him on the address of the two Houses of Parliament, and form, when he pleases to consult them, one of his constitutional councils. One branch of the legislative department forms also, a great constitutional council to the executive chief; as on another hand, it is the sole depositary of judicial power in cases of impeachment, and is invested with the supreme appellate jurisdiction, in all other cases. The judges again are so far connected with the legislative department, as often to attend and participate in its deliberations, though not admitted to a legislative vote.

From these facts by which Montesquieu was guided it may clearly be inferred, that in saying "there can be no liberty where the legislative and executive powers are united in the same person, or body of magistrates," or "if the power of judging be not separated from the legislative and executive powers," he did not mean that these departments ought to have no *partial agency* in, or no *controul* over the acts of each other. His meaning, as his own words import, and still more conclusively as illustrated by the example in his eye, can amount to no more than this, that where the *whole* power of one department is exercised by the same hands which possess the *whole* power of another department, the fundamental principles of a free constitution, are subverted. This would have been the case in the constitution examined by him, if the King who is the sole executive magistrate, had possessed also the compleat legislative power, or the supreme administration of justice; or if the entire legislative body, had possessed the supreme judiciary, or the supreme executive authority. This however is not among the vices of that constitution. The magistrate in whom the whole executive power resides cannot of himself make a law, though he can put a negative on every law, nor administer justice in person, though he has the appointment of those who do administer it. The judges can exercise no executive prerogative, though they are shoots from the executive stock, nor any legislative function, though they may be advised with by the legislative councils. The entire legislature, can perform no judiciary act, though by the joint act of two of its branches, the judges may be removed from their offices; and though one of its branches is possessed of the judicial power in the last resort. The entire legislature again can exercise no executive prerogative, though one of its branches constitutes the supreme executive magistracy; and another, on the empeachment of a third, can try and condemn all the subordinate officers in the executive department.

The reasons on which Montesquieu grounds his maxim are a further demonstration of his meaning. "When the legislative and executive powers are united in the same person or body" says he, "there can be no liberty, because apprehensions may arise lest *the same* monarch or senate should *enact* tyrannical laws, to *execute* them in a tyrannical manner." Again "Were the power of judging joined with the legislative, the life and liberty of the subject would be exposed to arbitrary controul, for *the judge* would then be *the legislator*. Were it joined to the executive power, *the judge* might behave with all the violence of *an oppressor*." Some of these reasons are more fully explained in other passages; but briefly stated as they are here, they sufficiently establish the meaning which we have put on this celebrated maxim of this celebrated author.

If we look into the constitutions of the several states we find that notwithstanding the emphatical, and in some instances, the unqualified terms in which this axiom has been laid down, there is not a single instance in which the several departments of power have been kept absolutely separate and distinct. New-Hampshire, whose constitution was the last formed, seems to have been fully aware of the impossibility and inexpediency of avoiding any mixture whatever of these departments; and has qualified the doctrine by declaring "that the legislative, executive and judiciary powers ought to be kept as separate from, and independent of each other *as the nature of a free government will admit; or as is consistent with that chain of connection, that binds the whole fabric of the constitution in one indissoluble bond of unity and amity.*" Her constitution accordingly mixes these departments in several respects. The senate which is a branch of the legislative department is also a judicial tribunal for the trial of empeachments. The president who is the head of the executive department, is the presiding member also of the senate; and besides an equal vote in all cases, has a casting vote in case of a tie. The executive head is himself eventually elective every year by the legislative department; and his council is every year chosen by and from the members of the same department. Several of the officers of state are also appointed by the legislature. And the members of the judiciary department are appointed by the executive department.

The constitution of Massachusetts has observed a sufficient though less pointed caution in expressing this fundamental article of liberty. It declares "that the legislative department shall never exercise the executive and judicial powers, or either of them: The executive shall never exercise the legislative and judicial powers, or either of them: The judicial shall never exercise the legislative and executive powers, or either of them." This declaration corresponds precisely with the doctrine of Montesquieu as it has been explained, and is not in a single point violated by the plan of the Convention. It goes no farther than to prohibit any one of the entire departments from exercising the powers of another department. In the very constitution to which it is prefixed, a partial mixture of powers has been admitted. The Executive Magistrate has a qualified negative on the Legislative body; and the Senate, which is a part of the Legislature, is a court of impeachment for members both of the executive and judiciary departments. The members of the judiciary department again are appointable by the executive department, and removeable by the same authority, on the address of the two legislative branches. Lastly, a number of the officers of government are annually appointed by the legislative department. As the appointment to offices, particularly executive offices, is in its nature an executive function, the compilers of the Constitution have in this last point at least, violated the rule established by themselves.

I pass over the constitutions of Rhode-Island and Connecticut, because they were formed prior to the revolution; and even before the principle under examination had become an object of political attention.

The constitution of New-York contains no declaration on this subject; but appears very clearly to have been framed with an eye to the danger of improperly blending the different departments. It gives nevertheless to the executive magistrate a partial controul over the legislative department; and what is more, gives a like controul to the judiciary department, and even blends the executive and judiciary departments in the exercise of this controul. In its council of appointment, members of the legislative are associated with the executive authority in the appointment of officers both executive and judiciary. And its court for the trial of impeachments and correction of errors, is to consist of one branch of the legislature and the principal members of the judiciary department.

The constitution of New-Jersey has blended the different powers of government more than any of the preceding. The governor, who is the executive magistrate, is appointed by the legislature; is chancellor and ordinary or surrogate of the state; is a member of the supreme court of appeals, and president with a casting vote, of one of the legislative branches. The same legislative branch acts again as executive council to the governor, and with him constitutes the court of appeals. The members of the judiciary department are appointed by the legislative department, and removeable by one branch of it, on the impeachment of the other.

According to the constitution of Pennsylvania, the president, who is head of the executive department, is annually elected by a vote in which the legislative department predominates. In conjunction with an executive council, he appoints the members of the judiciary department, and forms a court of impeachments for trial of all officers, judiciary as well as executive. The judges of the supreme court, and justices of the peace, seem also to be removeable by the legislature; and the executive power of pardoning in certain cases to be referred to the same department. The members of the executive council are made EX OFFICIO justices of peace throughout the state.

In Delaware, the chief executive magistrate is annually elected by the legislative department. The speakers of the two legislative branches are vice-presidents in the executive department. The executive chief, with six others, appointed three by each of the legislative branches, constitute the supreme court of appeals: He is joined with the legislative department in the appointment of the other judges. Throughout the states it appears that the members of thc legislature may at the same time be justices of the peace. In this state, the members of one branch of it are EX OFFICIO justices of peace; as are also the members of the executive council. The principal officers of the executive department are appointed by the legislative; and one branch of the latter forms a court of impeachments. All officers may be removed on address of the legislature.

Maryland has adopted the maxim in the most unqualified terms; declaring that the legislative, executive and judicial powers of government, ought to be forever separate and distinct from each other. Her constitution, notwithstanding makes the executive magistrate appointable by the legislative department; and the members of the judiciary, by the executive department.

The language of Virginia is still more pointed on this subject. Her constitution declares, "that the legislative, executive and judiciary departments, shall be separate and distinct; so that neither exercise the powers properly belonging to the other; nor shall any person exercise the powers of more than one of them at the same time; except that the justices of the county courts shall be eligible to either house of assembly." Yet we find not only this express exception, with respect to the members of the inferior courts; but that the chief magistrate with his executive council are appointable by the legislature; that two members of the latter are triennially displaced at the pleasure of the legislature; and that all the principal offices, both executive and judiciary, are filled by the same department. The executive prerogative of pardon, also is in one case vested in the legislative department.

The constitution of North-Carolina, which declares, "that the legislative, executive and supreme judicial powers of government, ought to be forever separate and distinct from each other," refers at the same time to the legislative department, the appointment not only of the executive chief, but all the principal officers within both that and the judiciary department.

In South-Carolina, the constitution makes the executive

magistracy eligible by the legislative department. It gives to the latter also the appointment of the members of the judiciary department, including even justices of the peace and sheriffs; and the appointment of officers in the executive department, down to captains in the army and navy of the state.

In the constitution of Georgia, where it is declared, "that the legislative, executive and judiciary departments shall be separate and distinct, so that neither exercise the powers properly belonging to the other." We find that the executive department is to be filled by appointments of the legislature; and the executive prerogative of pardon, to be finally exercised by the same authority. Even justices of the peace are to be appointed by the legislature.

In citing these cases in which the legislative, executive and judiciary departments, have not been kept totally separate and distinct, I wish not to be regarded as an advocate for the particular organizations of the several state governments. I am fully aware that among the many excellent principles which they exemplify, they carry strong marks of the haste, and still stronger of the inexperience, under which they were framed. It is but too obvious that in some instances, the fundamental principle under consideration has been violated by too great a mixture, and even an actual consolidation of the different powers; and that in no instance has a competent provision been made for maintaining in practice the separation delineated on paper. What I have wished to evince is, that the charge brought against the proposed constitution, of violating a sacred maxim of free government, is warranted neither by the real meaning annexed to that maxim by its author; nor by the sense in which it has hitherto been understood in America. This interesting subject will be resumed in the ensuing paper.

PUBLIUS.

THE FEDERALIST NO. 48
JAMES MADISON

February 1, 1788

To the People of the State of New York.

It was shewn in the last paper, that the political apothegm there examined, does not require that the legislative, executive and judiciary departments should be wholly unconnected with each other. I shall undertake in the next place, to shew that unless these departments be so far connected and blended, as to give to each a constitutional controul over the others, the degree of separation which the maxim requires as essential to a free government, can never in practice, be duly maintained.

It is agreed on all sides, that the powers properly belonging to one of the departments, ought not to be directly and compleatly administered by either of the other departments. It is equally evident, that neither of them ought to possess directly or indirectly, an overruling influence over the others in the administration of their respective powers. It will not be denied, that power is of an encroaching nature, and that it ought to be effectually restrained from passing the limits assigned to it. After discriminating therefore in theory, the several classes of power, as they may in their nature be legislative, executive, or judiciary; the next and most difficult task, is to provide some practical security for each against the invasion of the others. What this security ought to be, is the great problem to be solved.

Will it be sufficient to mark with precision the boundaries of these departments in the Constitution of the government, and to trust to these parchment barriers against the encroaching spirit of power? This is the security which appears to have been principally relied on by the compilers of most of the American Constitutions.[1] But experience assures us, that the efficacy of the provision has been greatly over-rated; and that some more adequate defence is indispensibly necessary for the more feeble, against the more powerful members of the government. The legislative department is every where extending the sphere of its activity, and drawing all power into its impetuous vortex.

The founders of our republics have so much merit for the wisdom which they have displayed, that no task can be less pleasing than that of pointing out the errors into which they have fallen. A respect for truth however obliges us to remark, that they seem never for a moment to have turned their eyes from the danger to liberty from the overgrown and all-grasping prerogative of an hereditary magistrate, supported and fortified by an hereditary branch of the legislative authority. They seem never to have recollected the danger from legislative usurpations; which by assembling all power in the same hands, must lead to the same tyranny as is threatened by executive usurpations.

In a government, where numerous and extensive prerogatives are placed in the hands of a hereditary monarch, the

[1] Madison is speaking of the state constitutions.

executive department is very justly regarded as the source of danger, and watched with all the jealousy which a zeal for liberty ought to inspire. In a democracy, where a multitude of people exercise in person the legislative functions, and are continually exposed by their incapacity for regular deliberation and concerted measures, to the ambitious intrigues of their executive magistrates, tyranny may well be apprehended on some favorable emergency, to start up in the same quarter. But in a representative republic, where the executive magistracy is carefully limited both in the extent and the duration of its power; and where the legislative power is exercised by an assembly, which is inspired by a supposed influence over the people with an intrepid confidence in its own strength; which is sufficiently numerous to feel all the passions which actuate a multitude; yet not so numerous as to be incapable of pursuing the objects of its passions, by means which reason prescribes; it is against the enterprising ambition of this department, that the people ought to indulge all their jealousy and exhaust all their precautions.

The legislative department derives a superiority in our governments from other circumstances. Its constitutional powers being at once more extensive and less susceptible of precise limits, it can with the greater facility, mask under complicated and indirect measures, the encroachments which it makes on the co-ordinate departments. It is not unfrequently a question of real-nicety in legislative bodies, whether the operation of a particular measure, will, or will not extend beyond the legislative sphere. On the other side, the executive power being restrained within a narrower compass, and being more simple in its nature; and the judiciary being described by land marks, still less uncertain, projects of usurpation by either of these departments, would immediately betray and defeat themselves. Nor is this all: As the legislative department alone has access to the pockets of the people, and has in some Constitutions full discretion, and in all, a prevailing influence over the pecuniary rewards of those who fill the other departments, a dependence is thus created in the latter, which gives still greater facility to encroachments of the former.

I have appealed to our own experience for the truth of what I advance on this subject. Were it necessary to verify this experience by particular proofs, they might be multiplied without end. I might find a witness in every citizen who has shared in, or been attentive to, the course of public administrations. I might collect vouchers in abundance from the records and archieves of every State in the Union. But as a more concise and at the same time, equally satisfactory evidence, I will refer to the example of two States, attested by two unexceptionable authorities.

The first example is that of Virginia, a State which, as we have seen, has expressly declared in its Constitution, that the three great departments ought not to be intermixed. The authority in support of it is Mr. Jefferson, who, besides his other advantages for remarking the operation of the government, was himself the chief magistrate of it. In order to convey fully the ideas with which his experience had impressed him on this subject, it will be necessary to quote a passage of some length from his very interesting "Notes on the State of Virginia."(P. 195.) "All the powers of government, legislative, executive and judiciary, result to the legislative body. The concentrating these in the same hands is precisely the definition of despotic government. It will be no alleviation that these powers will be exercised by a plurality of hands, and not by a single one, 173 despots would surely be as oppressive as one. Let those who doubt it turn their eyes on the republic of Venice. As little will it avail us that they are chosen by ourselves. An *elective despotism,* was not the government we fought for; but one which should not only be founded on free principles, but in which the powers of government should be so divided and balanced among several bodies of magistracy, as that no one could transcend their legal limits, without being effectually checked and restrained by the others. For this reason that Convention which passed the ordinance of government, laid its foundation on this basis, that the legislative, executive and judiciary departments should be separate and distinct, so that no person should exercise the powers of more than one of them at the same time. *But no barrier was provided between these several powers.* The judiciary and executive members were left dependent on the legislative for their subsistence in office, and some of them for their continuance in it. If therefore the Legislature assumes executive and judiciary powers, no opposition is likely to be made; nor if made can it be effectual; because in that case, they may put their proceeding into the form of an act of Assembly, which will render them obligatory on the other branches. They have accordingly *in many* instances *decided rights* which should have been left to *judiciary controversy;* and *the direction of the executive during the whole time of their session, is becoming habitual and familiar.*"

The other State which I shall take for an example, is Pennsylvania; and the other authority the council of censors which assembled in the years 1783 and 1784.[2] A part of the duty of this body, as marked out by the Constitution was "to enquire whether the Constitution had been preserved inviolate in every part; and whether the legislative and executive branches of government had performed their duty as guardians of the people, or assumed to themselves, or exercised other or greater powers than they are entitled to by the Constitution." In the execution of this trust, the council were necessarily led to a comparison, of both the legislative and executive proceedings, with the constitutional powers of these departments; and from the facts enumerated, and to the truth of most of which, both sides in the council subscribed, it appears that the Constitution had been flagrantly violated by the Legislature in a variety of important instances.

A great number of laws had been passed violating without any apparent necessity, the rule requiring that all bills of a public nature, shall be previously printed for the consideration of the people; altho' this is one of the precautions chiefly relied on by the Constitution, against improper acts of the Legislature.

The constitutional trial by jury had been violated; and powers assumed, which had not been delegated by the Constitution.

Executive powers had been usurped.

The salaries of the Judges, which the Constitution expressly requires to be fixed, had been occasionally varied; and cases belonging to the judiciary department, frequently drawn within legislative cognizance and determination.

Those who wish to see the several particulars falling under each of these heads, may consult the Journals of the council which are in print. Some of them, it will be found may be imputable to peculiar circumstances connected with the war: But the greater part of them may be considered as the spontaneous shoots of an ill-constituted government.

It appears also, that the executive department had not been innocent of frequent breaches of the Constitution. There are three observations however, which ought to be made on this head. *First*. A great proportion of the instances, were either immediately produced by the necessities of the war, or recom-

[2] The Pennsylvania Constitution of 1776 provided for a council composed of two members from each county to meet every seven years. In the winter of 1783–84, and again in the summer of 1784, the council met.

mended by Congress or the Commander in Chief. *Secondly.* In most of the other instances, they conformed either to the declared or the known sentiments of the legislative department. *Thirdly.* The executive department of Pennsylvania is distinguished from that of the other States, by the number of members composing it.[3] In this respect it has as much affinity to a legislative assembly, as to an executive council. And being at once exempt from the restraint of an individual responsibility for the acts of the body, and deriving confidence from mutual example and joint influence; unauthorized measures would of course be more freely hazarded, than where the executive department is administered by a single hand or by a few hands.

The conclusion which I am warranted in drawing from these observations is, that a mere demarkation on parchment of the constitutional limits of the several departments, is not a sufficient guard against those encroachments which lead to a tyrannical concentration of all the powers of government in the same hands.

PUBLIUS.

THE FEDERALIST NO. 49
JAMES MADISON

February 2, 1788

To the People of the State of New York.

The author of the "Notes on the state of Virginia," quoted in the last paper, has subjoined to that valuable work, the draught of a constitution which had been prepared in order to be laid before a convention expected to be called in 1783 by the legislature, for the establishment of a constitution for that commonwealth. The plan, like every thing from the same pen, marks a turn of thinking original, comprehensive and accurate; and is the more worthy of attention, as it equally displays a fervent attachment to republican government, and an enlightened view of the dangerous propensities against which it ought to be guarded. One of the precautions which he proposes, and on which he appears ultimately to rely as a palladium to the weaker departments of power, against the invasions of the stronger, is perhaps altogether his own, and as it immediately relates to the subject of our present enquiry, ought not to be overlooked.

[3] The Pennsylvania Constitution of 1776 provided for a Supreme Executive Council, consisting of one member from the City of Philadelphia and one from each county in the state.

His proposition is, "that whenever any two of the three branches of government shall concur in opinion, each by the voices of two thirds of their whole number, that a convention is necessary for altering the constitution or *correcting breaches of it,* a convention shall be called for the purpose."

As the people are the only legitimate fountain of power, and it is from them that the constitutional charter, under which the several branches of government hold their power, is derived; it seems strictly consonant to the republican theory, to recur to the same original authority, not only whenever it may be necessary to enlarge, diminish, or new-model the powers of government; but also whenever any one of the departments may commit encroachments on the chartered authorities of the others. The several departments being perfectly co-ordinate by the terms of their common commission, neither of them, it is evident, can pretend to an exclusive or superior right of settling the boundaries between their respective powers; and how are the encroachments of the stronger to be prevented, or the wrongs of the weaker to be redressed, without an appeal to the people themselves; who, as the grantors of the commission, can alone declare its true meaning and enforce its observance?

There is certainly great force in this reasoning, and it must be allowed to prove, that a constitutional road to the decision of the people, ought to be marked out, and kept open, for certain great and extraordinary occasions. But there appear to be insuperable objections against the proposed recurrence to the people, as a provision in all cases for keeping the several departments of power within their constitutional limits.

In the first place, the provision does not reach the case of a combination of two of the departments against a third. If the legislative authority, which possesses so many means of operating on the motives of the other departments, should be able to gain to its interest either of the others, or even one-third of its members, the remaining department could derive no advantage from this remedial provision. I do not dwell however on this objection, because it may be thought to lie rather against the modification of the principle, than against the principle itself.

In the next place, it may be considered as an objection inherent in the principle, that as every appeal to the people would carry an implication of some defect in the government, frequent appeals would in great measure deprive the government of that veneration, which time bestows on every thing, and without which perhaps the wisest and freest governments would not possess the requisite stability. If it be true that all governments rest on opinion, it is no less true that the strength of opinion in each individual, and its practical influence on his conduct, depend much on the number which he supposes to have entertained the same opinion. The reason of man, like man himself is timid and cautious, when left alone; and acquires firmness and confidence, in proportion to the number with which it is associated. When the examples, which fortify opinion, are *antient* as well as *numerous*, they are known to have a double effect. In a nation of philosophers, this consideration ought to be disregarded. A reverence for the laws, would be sufficiently inculcated by the voice of an enlightened reason. But a nation of philosophers is as little to be expected as the philosophical race of kings wished for by Plato. And in every other nation, the most rational government will not find it a superfluous advantage, to have the prejudices of the community on its side.

The danger of disturbing the public tranquility by interesting too strongly the public passions, is a still more serious objection against a frequent reference of constitutional questions, to the decision of the whole society. Notwithstanding the success which has attended the revisions of our established forms of government, and which does so much honour to the virtue and intelligence of the people of America, it must be confessed, that the experiments are of too ticklish a nature to be unnecessarily multiplied. We are to recollect that all the existing constitutions were formed in the midst of a danger which repressed the passions most unfriendly to order and concord; of an enthusiastic confidence of the people in their patriotic leaders, which stifled the ordinary diversity of opinions on great national questions; of a universal ardor for new and opposite forms, produced by a universal resentment and indignation against the antient government; and whilst no spirit of party, connected with the changes to be made, or the abuses to be reformed, could mingle its leven in the operation. The future situations in which we must expect to be usually placed, do not present any equivalent security against the danger which is apprehended.

But the greatest objection of all is, that the decisions which would probably result from such appeals, would not answer the purpose of maintaining the constitutional equilibrium of the government. We have seen that the tendency of republican governments is to an aggrandizement of the legislative, at the expence of the other departments. The appeals to the people therefore would usually be made by the executive and judiciary departments. But whether made by one side or the other, would each side enjoy equal advantages on the trial? Let us view their different situations. The members of the executive and judiciary departments, are few in number, and can be personally known to a small part only by the people. The latter by the mode of their appointment, as well as, by the nature and permanency of it, are too far removed from the people to share much in their prepossessions. The former are generally the objects of jealousy: And their administration is always liable to be discoloured and rendered unpopular. The members of the legislative department, on the other hand, are numerous. They are distributed and dwell among the people at large. Their connections of blood, of friendship and of acquaintance, embrace a great proportion of the most influencial part of the society. The nature of their public trust implies a personal influence among the people, and that they are more immediately the confidential guardians of the rights and liberties of the people. With these advantages, it can hardly be supposed that the adverse party would have an equal chance for a favorable issue.

But the legislative party would not only be able to plead their cause most successfully with the people. They would probably be constituted themselves the judges. The same influence which had gained them an election into the legislature, would gain them a seat in the convention. If this should not be the case with all, it would probably be the case with many, and pretty certainly with those leading characters, on whom every thing depends in such bodies. The convention in short would be composed chiefly of men, who had been, who actually were, or who expected to be, members of the department whose conduct was arraigned. They would consequently be parties to the very question to be decided by them.

It might however sometimes happen, that appeals would be made under circumstances less adverse to the executive and judiciary departments. The usurpations of the legislature might be so flagrant and so sudden, as to admit of no specious colouring. A strong party among themselves might take side with the other branches. The executive power might be in the hands of a peculiar favorite of the people. In such a posture of things, the public decision might be less swayed by prepossessions in favor of the legislative party. But still it could never be expected to turn on the true merits of the question. It would inevitably be connected with the spirit of pre-existing parties, or of parties springing out of the question itself. It would be connected with persons of distinguished character and extensive influence in the community. It would be pronounced by the very men who had been agents in, or opponents of the measures, to which the decision would relate. The *passions* therefore not *the reason,* of the public, would sit in judgment. But it is the reason of the public alone that ought to controul and regulate the government. The passions ought to be controuled and regulated by the government.

We found in the last paper that mere declarations in the written constitution, are not sufficient to restrain the several departments within their legal limits. It appears in this, that occasional appeals to the people would be neither a proper nor an effectual provision, for that purpose. How far the provisions of a different nature contained in the plan above quoted, might be adequate, I do not examine. Some of them are unquestionably founded on sound political principles, and all of them are framed with singular ingenuity and precision.

PUBLIUS.

THE FEDERALIST NO. 50
JAMES MADISON[1]

February 5, 1788

To the People of the State of New York.

It may be contended perhaps, that instead of *occasional* appeals to the people, which are liable to the objections urged against them, *periodical* appeals are the proper and adequate means *of preventing and correcting infractions of the Constitution.*

It will be attended to, that in the examination of these expedients, I confine myself to their aptitude for *enforcing* the Constitution by keeping the several departments of power within their due bounds, without particularly considering them, as provisions for *altering* the Constitution itself. In the first view, appeals to the people at fixed periods, appear to be nearly as ineligible, as appeals on particular occasions as they emerge. If the periods be separated by short intervals, the measures to be reviewed and rectified, will have been of recent date, and will be connected with all the circumstances

[1] Both Hamilton and Madison claimed to have written Nos. 50 and 51. In both instances, Madison's is the claim substantiated by most scholarly opinion.

which tend to viciate and pervert the result of occasional revisions. If the periods be distant from each other, the same remark will be applicable to all recent measures, and in proportion as the remoteness of the others may favor a dispassionate review of them, this advantage is inseparable from inconveniences which seem to counterbalance it. In the first place, a distant prospect of public censure would be a very feeble restraint on power from those excesses, to which it might be urged by the force of present motives. Is it to be imagined, that a legislative assembly, consisting of a hundred or two hundred members, eagerly bent on some favorite object, and breaking through the restraints of the Constitution in pursuit of it, would be arrested in their career, by considerations drawn from a censorial revision of their conduct at the future distance of ten, fifteen or twenty years? In the next place, the abuses would often have compleated their mischievous effects, before the remedial provision would be applied. And in the last place, where this might not be the case, they would be of long standing, would have taken deep root, and would not easily be extirpated.

The scheme of revising the Constitution in order to correct recent breaches of it, as well as for other purposes, has been actually tried in one of the States. One of the objects of the council of censors, which met in Pennsylvania, in 1783 and 1784, was, as we have seen to enquire "whether the Constitution had been violated, and whether the legislative and executive departments had encroached on each other." This important and novel experiment in politics, merits in several points of view, very particular attention. In some of them it may perhaps, as a single experiment, made under circumstances somewhat peculiar, be thought to be not absolutely conclusive. But as applied to the case under consideration, it involves some facts which I venture to remark, as a compleat and satisfactory illustration of the reasoning which I have employed.

First. It appears from the names of the gentlemen, who composed the council, that some at least of its most active and leading members, had also been active and leading characters in the parties which pre-existed in the State.

Secondly. It appears that the same active and leading members of the council, had been active and influential members of the legislative and executive branches, within the period to be reviewed; and even patrons or opponents of the very measures to be thus brought to the test of the Constitution.

Two of the members had been Vice-Presidents of the State, and several others, members of the executive council, within the seven preceding years. One of them had been Speaker, and a number of others distinguished members of the legislative assembly, within the same period.

Thirdly. Every page of their proceedings witnesses the effect of all these circumstances on the temper of their deliberations. Throughout the continuance of the council, it was split into two fixed and violent parties. The fact is acknowledged and lamented by themselves. Had this not been the case, the face of their proceedings exhibit a proof equally satisfactory. In all questions, however unimportant in themselves, or unconnected with each other, the same names, stand invariably contrasted on the opposite columns. Every unbiassed observer, may infer without danger of mistake, and at the same time, without meaning to reflect on either party, or any individuals of either party, that unfortunately *passion,* not *reason,* must have presided over their decisions. When men exercise their reason coolly and freely, on a variety of distinct questions, they inevitably fall into different opinions, on some of them. When they are governed by a common passion, their opinions if they are so to be called, will be the same.

Fourthly. It is at least problematical, whether the decisions of this body, do not, in several instances, misconstrue the limits prescribed for the legislative and executive departments, instead of reducing and limiting them within their constitutional places.

Fifthly. I have never understood that the decisions of the council on constitutional questions, whether rightly or erroneously formed, have had any effect in varying the practice founded on legislative constructions. It even appears, if I mistake not, that in one instance, the cotemporary Legislature denied the constructions of the council, and actually prevailed in the contest.

This censorial body therefore, proves at the same time, by its researches, the existence of the disease; and by its example, the inefficacy of the remedy.

This conclusion cannot be invalidated by alledging that the State in which the experiment was made, was at that crisis, and had been for a long time before, violently heated and distracted by the rage of party. Is it to be presumed, that at any future septennial epoch, the same State will be free from parties? Is it to be presumed that any other State, at the same or any other given period, will be exempt from them? Such an event ought to be neither presumed nor desired; because an extinction of parties necessarily implies either a universal alarm for the public safety, or an absolute extinction of liberty.

Were the precaution taken of excluding from the assemblies elected by the people to revise the preceding administration of the government, all persons who should have been concerned in the government within the given period, the difficulties would not be obviated. The important task would probably devolve on men, who with inferior capacities, would in other respects, be little better qualified. Although they might not have been personally concerned in the administration, and therefore not immediately agents in the measures to be examined; they would probably have been involved in the parties connected with these measures, and have been elected under their auspices.

PUBLIUS.

THE FEDERALIST NO. 51

JAMES MADISON

February 6, 1788

To the People of the State of New York.

To what expedient then shall we finally resort for maintaining in practice the necessary partition of power among the several departments, as laid down in the constitution? The only answer that can be given is, that as all these exterior provisions are found to be inadequate, the defect must be supplied, by so contriving the interior structure of the government, as that its several constituent parts may, by their mutual relations, be the means of keeping each other in their proper places. Without presuming to undertake a full development of this important idea, I will hazard a few general observations, which may perhaps place it in a clearer light, and enable us to form a more correct judgment of the principles and structure of the government planned by the convention.

In order to lay a due foundation for that separate and distinct exercise of the different powers of government, which to a certain extent, is admitted on all hands to be essential to the preservation of liberty, it is evident that each department should have a will of its own; and consequently should be so constituted, that the members of each should have as little agency as possible in the appointment of the members of the others. Were this principle rigorously adhered to, it would require that all the appointments for the supreme executive, legislative, and judiciary magistracies, should be drawn from the same fountain of authority, the people, through channels, having no communication whatever with one another. Perhaps such a plan of constructing the several departments would be less difficult in practice than it may in contemplation appear. Some difficulties however, and some additional expence, would attend the execution of it. Some deviations therefore from the principle must be admitted. In the constitution of the judiciary department in particular, it might be inexpedient to insist rigorously on the principle; first, because peculiar qualifications being essential in the members, the primary consideration ought to be to select that mode of choice, which best secures these qualifications; secondly, because the permanent tenure by which the appointments are held in that department, must soon destroy all sense of dependence on the authority conferring them.

It is equally evident that the members of each department should be as little dependent as possible on those of the others, for the emoluments annexed to their offices. Were the executive magistrate, or the judges, not independent of the legislature in this particular, their independence in every other would be merely nominal.

But the great security against a gradual concentration of the several powers in the same department, consists in giving to those who administer each department, the necessary constitutional means, and personal motives, to resist encroachments of the others. The provision for defence must in this, as in all other cases, be made commensurate to the danger of attack. Ambition must be made to counteract ambition. The interest of the man must be connected with the constitutional rights of the place. It may be a reflection on human nature, that such devices should be necessary to controul the abuses of government. But what is government itself but the greatest of all reflections on human nature? If men were angels, no government would be necessary. If angels were to govern men, neither external nor internal controuls on government would be necessary. In framing a government which is to be administered by men over men, the great difficulty lies in this: You must first enable the government to controul the governed; and in the next place, oblige it to controul itself. A dependence on the people is no doubt the primary controul on the government; but experience has taught mankind the necessity of auxiliary precautions.

This policy of supplying by opposite and rival interests, the defect of better motives, might be traced through the whole system of human affairs, private as well as public. We see it particularly displayed in all the subordinate distributions of power; where the constant aim is to divide and arrange the several offices in such a manner as that each may be a check on the other; that the private interest of every individual, may be a centinel over the public rights. These inventions of prudence cannot be less requisite in the distribution of the supreme powers of the state.

But it is not possible to give to each department an equal power of self defence. In republican government the legislative authority, necessarily, predominates. The remedy for this inconveniency is, to divide the legislature into different branches; and to render them by different modes of election, and different principles of action, as little connected with each other, as the nature of their common functions, and their common dependence on the society, will admit. It may even be necessary to guard against dangerous encroachments by still further precautions. As the weight of the legislative authority requires that it should be thus divided, the weakness of the executive may require, on the other hand, that it should be fortified. An absolute negative, on the legislature, appears at first view to be the natural defence with which the executive magistrate should be armed. But perhaps it would be neither altogether safe, nor alone sufficient. On ordinary occasions, it might not be exerted with the requisite firmness; and on extraordinary occasions, it might be perfidiously abused. May not this defect of an absolute negative be supplied, by some qualified connection between this weaker department, and the weaker branch of the stronger department, by which the latter may be led to support the constitutional rights of the former, without being too much detached from the rights of its own department?

If the principles on which these observations are founded be just, as I persuade myself they are, and they be applied as a criterion, to the several state constitutions, and to the federal constitution, it will be found, that if the latter does not perfectly correspond with them, the former are infinitely less able to bear such a test.

There are moreover two considerations particularly applicable to the federal system of America, which place that system in a very interesting point of view.

First. In a single republic, all the power surrendered by the people, is submitted to the administration of a single government; and usurpations are guarded against by a division of the government into distinct and separate departments. In the compound republic of America, the power surrendered by the people, is first divided between two distinct governments, and then the portion allotted to each, subdivided among distinct and separate departments. Hence a double security arises to the rights of the people. The different governments will controul each other; at the same time that each will be controuled by itself.

Second. It is of great importance in a republic, not only to guard the society against the oppression of its rulers; but to guard one part of the society against the injustice of the other part. Different interests necessarily exist in different classes of citizens. If a majority be united by a common interest, the rights of the minority will be insecure. There are but two methods of providing against this evil: The one by creating a will in the community independent of the majority, that is, of the society itself; the other by comprehending in the society so many separate descriptions of citizens, as will render an unjust combination of a majority of the whole, very improbable, if not impracticable. The first method prevails in all governments possessing an hereditary or self appointed authority. This at best is but a precarious security; because a power independent of the society may as well espouse the unjust views of the major, as the rightful interests, of the minor party, and may possibly be turned against both parties. The second method will be exemplified in the federal republic of the United States. Whilst all authority in it will be derived from and dependent on the society, the society itself will be broken into so many parts, interests and classes of citizens, that the rights of individuals or of the minority, will be in little danger from interested combinations of the majority. In a free government, the security for civil rights must be the same as for religious rights. It consists in the one case in the multiplicity of interests, and in the other, in the multiplicity of sects. The degree of security in both cases will depend on the number of interests and sects; and this may be presumed to depend on the extent of country and number of people comprehended under the same government. This view of the subject must particularly recommend a proper federal system to all the sincere and considerate friends of republican government: Since it shews that in exact proportion as the territory of the union may be formed into more circumscribed confederacies or states, oppressive combinations of a majority will be facilitated, the best security under the republican form, for the rights of every class of citizens, will be diminished; and consequently, the stability and independence of some member of the government, the only other security, must be proportionally increased. Justice is the end of government. It is the end of civil society. It ever has been, and ever will be pursued, until it be obtained, or until liberty be lost in the pursuit. In a society under the forms of which the stronger faction can readily unite and oppress the weaker, anarchy may as truly be said to reign, as in a state of nature where the weaker individual is not secured against the violence of the stronger: And as in the latter state even the stronger individuals are prompted by the uncertainty of their condition, to submit to a government which may protect the weak as well as themselves: So in the former state, will the more powerful factions or parties be gradually induced by a like motive, to wish for a government which will protect all parties, the weaker as well as the more powerful. It can be little doubted, that if the state of Rhode Island was separated from the confederacy, and left to itself, the insecurity of rights under the popular form of government within such narrow limits, would be displayed by such reiterated oppressions of factious majorities, that some power altogether independent of the people would soon be called for by the voice of the very factions whose misrule had proved the necessity of it. In the extended republic of the United States, and among the great variety of interests, parties and sects which it embraces, a coalition of a majority of the whole society could seldom take place on any other principles than those of justice and the general good; and there being thus less danger to a minor from the will of the major party, there must be less pretext also, to provide for the security of the former, by introducing into the government a will not dependent on the latter; or in other words, a will independent of the society itself. It is no less certain than it is important, notwithstanding the contrary opinions which have been entertained, that the larger the society, provided it lie within a practicable sphere, the more duly capable it will be of self government. And happily for the *republican cause*, the practicable sphere may be carried to a very great extent, by a judicious modification and mixture of the *federal principle*.

PUBLIUS.

THE FEDERALIST NO. 62
JAMES MADISON[1]

February 27, 1788

To the People of the State of New York.

Having examined the constitution of the house of representatives, and answered such of the objections against it as seemed to merit notice, I enter next on the examination of the senate. The heads into which this member of the government may be considered, are I. the qualifications of senators. II. the appointment of them by the state legislatures. III. the equality of representation in the senate. IV. the number of senators, and the term for which they are to be elected. V. the powers vested in the senate.

I. The qualifications proposed for senators, as distinguished from those of representatives, consist in a more advanced age, and a longer period of citizenship. A senator must be thirty years of age at least; as a representative, must be twenty-five. And the former must have been a citizen nine years; as seven years are required for the latter. The propriety of these distinctions is explained by the nature of the senatorial trust; which requiring greater extent of information and stability of character, requires at the same time that the senator should have reached a period of life most likely to supply these advantages; and which participating immediately in transactions with foreign nations, ought to be exercised by none who are not thoroughly weaned from the prepossessions and habits incident to foreign birth and education. The term of nine years appears to be a prudent mediocrity between a total exclusion of adopted citizens, whose merit and talents may claim a share in the public confidence; and an indiscriminate and hasty admission of them, which might create a channel for foreign influence on the national councils.

II. It is equally unnecessary to dilate on the appointment of senators by the state legislatures. Among the various modes which might have been devised for constituting this branch of the government, that which has been proposed by the convention is probably the most congenial with the public opinion. It is recommended by the double advantage of favouring a select appointment, and of giving to the state governments such an agency in the formation of the federal government,

[1] Nos. 62 and 63 were claimed by both Hamilton and Madison. Madison's claim is the accepted one.

as must secure the authority of the former; and may form a convenient link between the two systems.

III. The equality of representation in the senate is another point, which, being evidently the result of compromise between the opposite pretensions of the large and the small states, does not call for much discussion. If indeed it be right that among a people thoroughly incorporated into one nation, every district ought to have a *proportional* share in the government; and that among independent and sovereign states bound together by a simple league, the parties however unequal in size, ought to have an *equal* share in the common councils, it does not appear to be without some reason, that in a compound republic partaking both of the national and federal character, the government ought to be founded on a mixture of the principles of proportional and equal representation. But it is superfluous to try by the standards of theory, a part of the constitution which is allowed on all hands to be the result not of theory, but "of a spirit of amity, and that mutual deference and concession which the peculiarity of our political situation rendered indispensable." A common government with powers equal to its objects, is called for by the voice, and still more loudly by the political situation of America. A government founded on principles more consonant to the wishes of the larger states, is not likely to be obtained from the smaller states. The only option then for the former lies between the proposed government and a government still more objectionable. Under this alternative the advice of prudence must be, to embrace the lesser evil; and instead of indulging a fruitless anticipation of the possible mischiefs which may ensue, to contemplate rather the advantageous consequences which may qualify the sacrifice.

In this spirit it may be remarked, that the equal vote allowed to each state, is at once a constitutional recognition of the portion of sovereignty remaining in the individual states, and an instrument for preserving that residuary sovereignty. So far the equality ought to be no less acceptable to the large than to the small states; since they are not less solicitous to guard by every possible expedient against an improper consolidation of the states into one simple republic.

Another advantage accruing from this ingredient in the constitution of the senate, is the additional impediment it must prove against improper acts of legislation. No law or resolution can now be passed without the concurrence first of a majority of the people, and then of a majority of the states. It must be acknowledged that this complicated check on legislation may in some instances be injurious as well as beneficial; and that the peculiar defence which it involves in favour of the smaller states would be more rational, if any interests common to them, and distinct from those of the other states, would otherwise be exposed to peculiar danger. But as the larger states will always be able by their power over the supplies to defeat unreasonable exertions of this prerogative of the lesser states; and as the facility and excess of law-making seem to be the diseases to which our governments are most liable, it is not impossible that this part of the constitution may be more convenient in practice than it appears to many in contemplation.

IV. The number of senators and the duration of their appointment come next to be considered. In order to form an accurate judgment on both these points, it will be proper to enquire into the purposes which are to be answered by a senate; and in order to ascertain these it will be necessary to review the inconveniencies which a republic must suffer from the want of such an institution.

First. It is a misfortune incident to republican government, though in a less degree than to other governments, that those who administer it, may forget their obligations to their constituents, and prove unfaithful to their important trust. In this point of view, a senate, as a second branch of the legislative assembly, distinct from, and dividing the power with, a first, must be in all cases a salutary check on the government. It doubles the security to the people, by requiring the concurrence of two distinct bodies in schemes of usurpation or perfidy, where the ambition or corruption of one, would otherwise be sufficient. This is a precaution founded on such clear principles, and now so well understood in the United States, that it would be more than superfluous to enlarge on it. I will barely remark that as the improbability of sinister combinations will be in proportion to the dissimilarity in the genius of the two bodies; it must be politic to distinguish them from each other by every circumstance which will consist with a due harmony in all proper measures, and with the genuine principles of republican government.

Secondly. The necessity of a senate is not less indicated by the propensity of all single and numerous assemblies, to yield to the impulse of sudden and violent passions, and to be seduced by factious leaders, into intemperate and pernicious resolutions. Examples on this subject might be cited without number; and from proceedings within the United States, as well as from the history of other nations. But a position that will not be contradicted need not be proved. All that need be remarked is that a body which is to correct this infirmity ought itself be free from it, and consequently ought to be less numerous. It ought moreover to possess great firmness, and consequently ought to hold its authority by a tenure of considerable duration.

Thirdly. Another defect to be supplied by a senate lies in a want of due acquaintance with the objects and principles of legislation. It is not possible that an assembly of men called for the most part from pursuits of a private nature, continued in appointment for a short time, and led by no permanent motive to devote the intervals of public occupation to a study of the laws, the affairs and the comprehensive interests of their country, should, if left wholly to themselves, escape a variety of important errors in the exercise of their legislative trust. It may be affirmed, on the best grounds, that no small share of the present embarrassments of America is to be charged on the blunders of our governments; and that these have proceeded from the heads rather than the hearts of most of the authors of them. What indeed are all the repealing, explaining and amending laws, which fill and disgrace our voluminous codes, but so many monuments of deficient wisdom; so many impeachments exhibited by each succeeding, against each preceding session; so many admonitions to the people of the value of those aids which may be expected from a well constituted senate?

A good government implies two things; first, fidelity to the object of government, which is the happiness of the people; secondly, a knowledge of the means by which that object can be best attained. Some governments are deficient in both these qualities: Most governments are deficient in the first. I scruple not to assert that in the American governments, too little attention has been paid to the last. The federal constitution avoids this error; and what merits particular notice, it provides for the last in a mode which increases the security for the first.

Fourthly. The mutability in the public councils, arising from a rapid succession of new members, however qualified they may be, points out in the strongest manner, the necessity of some stable institution in the government. Every new election in the states, is found to change one half of the representatives. From this change of men must proceed a change of opinions; and from a change of opinions, a change of measures. But a continual change even of good measures is inconsistent with every rule of prudence, and every prospect of success. The remark is verified in private life, and becomes more just as well as more important, in national transactions.

To trace the mischievous effects of a mutable government would fill a volume. I will hint a few only, each of which will be perceived to be a source of innumerable others.

In the first place it forfeits the respect and confidence of other nations, and all the advantages connected with national character. An individual who is observed to be inconstant to his plans, or perhaps to carry on his affairs without any plan at all, is marked at once by all prudent people as a speedy victim to his own unsteadiness and folly. His more friendly neighbours may pity him; but all will decline to connect their fortunes with his; and not a few will seize the opportunity of making their fortunes out of his. One nation is to another what one individual is to another; with this melancholy distinction perhaps, that the former with fewer of the benevolent emotions than the latter, are under fewer restraints also from taking undue advantage of the indiscretions of each other. Every nation consequently whose affairs betray a want of wisdom and stability, may calculate on every loss which can be sustained from the more systematic policy of its wiser neighbours. But the best instruction on this subject is unhappily conveyed to America by the example of her own situation. She finds that she is held in no respect by her friends; that she is the derision of her enemies; and that she is a prey to every nation which has an interest in speculating on her fluctuating councils and embarrassed affairs.

The internal effects of a mutable policy are still more calamitous. It poisons the blessings of liberty itself. It will be of little avail to the people that the laws are made by men of their own choice, if the laws be so voluminous that they cannot be read, or so incoherent that they cannot be understood; if they be repealed or revised before they are promulgated, or undergo such incessant changes that no man who knows what the law is to-day can guess what it will be to-morrow. Law is defined to be a rule of action; but how can that be a rule, which is little known and less fixed?

Another effect of public instability is the unreasonable advantage it gives to the sagacious, the enterprising and the moneyed few, over the industrious and uninformed mass of the people. Every new regulation concerning commerce or revenue, or in any manner affecting the value of the different species of property, presents a new harvest to those who watch the change, and can trace its consequences; a harvest reared not by themselves but by the toils and cares of the great body of their fellow citizens. This is a state of things in which it may be said with some truth that laws are made for the *few* not for the *many*.

In another point of view great injury results from an unstable government. The want of confidence in the public councils damps every useful undertaking; the success and profit of which may depend on a continuance of existing arrangements. What prudent merchant will hazard his fortunes in any new branch of commerce, when he knows not but that his plans may be rendered unlawful before they can be executed? What farmer or manufacturer will lay himself out for the encouragement given to any particular cultivation or establishment, when he can have no assurance that his preparatory labors and advances will not render him a victim to an inconstant government? In a word no great improvement or laudable enterprise, can go forward, which requires the auspices of a steady system of national policy.

But the most deplorable effect of all is that diminution of attachment and reverence which steals into the hearts of the people, towards a political system which betrays so many marks of infirmity, and disappoints so many of their flattering hopes. No government any more than an individual will long be respected, without being truly respectable, nor be truly respectable without possessing a certain portion of order and stability.

PUBLIUS.

THE FEDERALIST NO. 63
JAMES MADISON

March 1, 1788

To the People of the State of New York.

A fifth desideratum illustrating the utility of a Senate, is the want of a due sense of national character. Without a select and stable member of the government, the esteem of foreign powers will not only be forfeited by an unenlightened and variable policy, proceeding from the causes already mentioned; but the national councils will not possess that sensibility to the opinion of the world, which is perhaps not less necessary in order to merit, than it is to obtain, its respect and confidence.

An attention to the judgment of other nations is important

to every government for two reasons: The one is, that independently of the merits of any particular plan or measure, it is desireable on various accounts, that it should appear to other nations as the offspring of a wise and honorable policy: The second is, that in doubtful cases, particularly where the national councils may be warped by some strong passion, or momentary interest, the presumed or known opinion of the impartial world, may be the best guide that can be followed. What has not America lost by her want of character with foreign nations? And how many errors and follies would she not have avoided, if the justice and propriety of her measures had in every instance been previously tried by the light in which they would probably appear to the unbiassed part of mankind?

Yet however requisite a sense of national character may be, it is evident that it can never be sufficiently possessed by a numerous and changeable body. It can only be found in a number so small, that a sensible degree of the praise and blame of public measures may be the portion of each individual; or in an assembly so durably invested with public trust, that the pride and consequence of its members may be sensibly incorporated with the reputation and prosperity of the community. The half-yearly representatives of Rhode-Island, would probably have been little affected in their deliberations on the iniquitous measures of that state, by arguments drawn from the light in which such measures would be viewed by foreign nations, or even by the sister states; whilst it can scarcely be doubted, that if the concurrence of a select and stable body had been necessary, a regard to national character alone, would have prevented the calamities under which that misguided people is now labouring.

I add as a *sixth* defect, the want in some important cases of a due responsibility in the government to the people, arising from that frequency of elections, which in other cases produces this responsibility. This remark will perhaps appear not only new but paradoxical. It must nevertheless be acknowledged, when explained, to be as undeniable as it is important.

Responsibility in order to be reasonable must be limited to objects within the power of the responsible party; and in order to be effectual, must relate to operations of that power, of which a ready and proper judgment can be formed by the constituents. The objects of government may be divided into two general classes; the one depending on measures which have singly an immediate and sensible operation; the other depending on a succession of well chosen and well connected measures, which have a gradual and perhaps unobserved operation. The importance of the latter description to the collective and permanent welfare of every country needs no explanation. And yet it is evident, that an assembly elected for so short a term as to be unable to provide more than one or two links in a chain of measures, on which the general welfare may essentially depend, ought not to be answerable for the final result, any more than a steward or tenant, engaged for one year, could be justly made to answer for places or improvements, which could not be accomplished in less than half a dozen years. Nor is it possible for the people to estimate the *share* of influence which their annual assemblies may respectively have on events resulting from the mixed transactions of several years. It is sufficiently difficult at any rate to preserve a personal responsibility in the members of a *numerous* body, for such acts of the body as have an immediate, detached and palpable operation on its constituents.

The proper remedy for this defect must be an additional body in the legislative department, which, having sufficient permanency to provide for such objects as require a continued attention, and a train of measures, may be justly and effectually answerable for the attainment of those objects.

Thus far I have considered the circumstances which point out the necessity of a well constructed senate, only as they relate to the representatives of the people. To a people as little blinded by prejudice, or corrupted by flattery, as those whom I address, I shall not scruple to add, that such an institution may be sometimes necessary, as a defence to the people against their own temporary errors and delusions. As the cool and deliberate sense of the community ought in all governments, and actually will in all free governments ultimately prevail over the views of its rulers; so there are particular moments in public affairs, when the people stimulated by some irregular passion, or some illicit advantage, or misled by the artful misrepresentations of interested men, may call for measures which they themselves will afterwards be the most ready to lament and condemn. In these critical moments, how salutary will be the interference of some temperate and respectable body of citizens, in order to check the misguided career, and to suspend the blow meditated by the people against themselves, until reason, justice and truth, can regain their authority over the public mind? What bitter anguish would not the people of Athens have often escaped, if their government had contained so provident a safeguard against the tyranny of their own passions? Popular liberty might then have escaped the indelible reproach of decreeing to the same citizens, the hemlock on one day, and statues on the next.

It may be suggested that a people spread over an extensive region, cannot like the crouded inhabitants of a small district, be subject to the infection of violent passions; or to the danger of combining in the pursuit of unjust measures. I am far from denying that this is a distinction of peculiar importance. I have on the contrary endeavoured in a former paper, to shew that it is one of the principal recommendations of a confederated republic. At the same time this advantage ought not to be considered as superseding the use of auxiliary precautions. It may even be remarked that the same extended situation which will exempt the people of America from some of the dangers incident to lesser republics, will expose them to the inconveniency of remaining for a longer time, under the influence of those misrepresentations which the combined industry of interested men may succeed in distributing among them.

It adds no small weight to all these considerations, to recollect, that history informs us of no long lived republic which had not a senate. Sparta, Rome and Carthage are in fact the only states to whom that character can be applied. In each of the two first there was a senate for life. The constitution of the senate in the last, is less known. Circumstantial evidence makes it probable that it was not different in this particular from the two others. It is at least certain that it had some quality or other which rendered it an anchor against popular fluctuations; and that a smaller council drawn out of the senate was appointed not only for life; but filled up vacancies itself. These examples, though as unfit for the imitation, as they are repugnant to the genius of America, are notwithstanding, when compared with the fugitive and turbulent existence of other antient republics, very instructive proofs of the necessity of some institution that will blend stability with liberty. I am not unaware of the circumstances which distinguish the American from other popular governments, as well antient as modern; and which render extreme circumspection necessary in reasoning from the one case to the other. But after allowing due weight to this consideration, it may still be maintained that there are many points of similitude which render these examples not unworthy of our attention. Many of the defects as we have seen, which can only be supplied by a senatorial institution, are common to a numerous assembly frequently elected by the people, and to the people themselves. There are others peculiar to the former, which require the controul of such an institution. The people can never wilfully betray their own interests: But they may possibly be betrayed by the representatives of the people; and the danger will be evidently greater where the whole legislative trust is lodged in the hands of one body of men, than where the concurrence of separate and dissimilar bodies is required in every public act.

The difference most relied on between the American and other republics, consists in the principle of representation, which is the pivot on which the former move, and which is supposed to have been unknown to the latter, or at least to the antient part of them. The use which has been made of this difference, in reasonings contained in former papers, will have shewn that I am disposed neither to deny its existence nor to undervalue its importance. I feel the less restraint therefore in observing that the position concerning the ignorance of the antient government on the subject of representation is by no means precisely true in the latitude commonly given to it. Without entering into a disquisition which here would be misplaced, I will refer to a few known facts in support of what I advance.

In the most pure democracies of Greece, many of the executive functions were performed not by the people themselves, but by officers elected by the people, and *representing* the people in their *executive* capacity.

Prior to the reform of Solon, Athens was governed by nine Archons, annually *elected by the people at large*. The degree of power delegated to them seems to be left in great obscurity. Subsequent to that period, we find an assembly first of four and afterwards of six hundred members, annually *elected by the people;* and *partially* representing them in their *legislative* capacity; since they were not only associated with the people in the function of making laws; but had the exclusive right of originating legislative propositions to the people. The senate of Carthage also, whatever might be its power or the duration of its appointment, appears to have been *elective* by the suffrages of the people. Similar instances might be traced in most if not all the popular governments of antiquity.

Lastly in Sparta, we meet with the Ephori, and in Rome with the Tribunes; two bodies, small indeed in number, but annually *elected by the whole body of the people,* and considered as the *representatives* of the people, almost in their *plenipotentiary* capacity. The Cosmi of Crete were also annually *elected by the people;* and have been considered by some authors as an institution analogous to those of Sparta and Rome; with this difference only that in the election of that representative body, the right of suffrage was communicated to a part only of the people.

From these facts, to which many others might be added, it is clear that the principle of representation was neither unknown to the antients, nor wholly overlooked in their political constitutions. The true distinction between these and the American Governments lies *in the total exclusion of the people in their collective capacity* from any share in the *latter,* and not in the *total exclusion of representatives of the people,* from the administration of the *former.* The distinction however thus qualified must be admitted to leave a most advantageous superiority in favor of the United States. But to ensure to this advantage its full effect, we must be careful not to separate it from the other advantage, of an extensive territory. For it cannot be believed that any form of representative government, could have succeeded within the narrow limits occupied by the democracies of Greece.

In answer to all these arguments, suggested by reason, illustrated by examples, and enforced by our own experience, the jealous adversary of the constitution will probably content himself with repeating, that a senate appointed not immediately by the people, and for the term of six years, must gradually acquire a dangerous prominence in the government, and finally transform it into a tyrannical aristocracy.

To this general answer the general reply ought to be sufficient; that liberty may be endangered by the abuses of liberty, as well as by the abuses of power; that there are numerous instances of the former as well as of the latter; and that the former rather than the latter is apparently most to be apprehended by the United States. But a more particular reply may be given.

Before such a revolution can be effected, the senate, it is to be observed, must in the first place corrupt itself; must next corrupt the state legislatures, must then corrupt the house of representatives and must finally corrupt the people at large. It is evident that the senate must be first corrupted, before it can attempt an establishment of tyranny. Without corrupting the state legislatures, it cannot prosecute the attempt, because the periodical change of members would otherwise regenerate the whole body. Without exerting the means of corruption with equal success on the house of representatives, the opposition of that co-equal branch of the government would inevitably defeat the attempt; and without corrupting the people themselves, a succession of new representatives would speedily restore all things to their pristine order. Is there any man who can seriously persuade himself, that the proposed senate can, by any possible means within the compass of human address, arrive at the object of a lawless ambition, through all these obstructions?

If reason condemns the suspicion, the same sentence is pronounced by experience. The constitution of Maryland furnishes the most apposite example. The senate of that state is elected, as the federal senate will be, indirectly by the people; and for a term less by one year, than the federal senate. It is distinguished also by the remarkable prerogative of filling up its own vacancies within the term of its appointment: and at the same time, is not under the controul of any such rotation, as is provided for the federal senate. There are some other lesser distinctions, which would expose the former to colorable objections that do not lie against the latter. If the federal senate therefore really contained the danger which has been so loudly proclaimed, some symptoms at least of a like danger ought by this time to have been betrayed by the senate of Maryland; but no such symptoms have appeared. On the contrary the jealousies at first entertained by men of the same description with those who view with terror the correspondent part of the federal constitution, have been gradually extinguished by the progress of the experiment; and the Maryland constitution is daily deriving from the salutary operations of this part of it, a reputation in which it will probably not be rivalled by that of any state in the union.

But if any thing could silence the jealousies on this subject, it ought to be the British example. The senate there, instead of being elected for a term of six years, and of being unconfined to particular families or fortunes, is an hereditary assembly of opulent nobles. The house of representatives, instead of being elected for two years and by the whole body of the people, is elected for seven years; and in very great proportion, by a very small proportion of the people. Here unquestionably ought to be seen in full display, the aristocratic usurpations and tyranny, which are at some future period to be exemplified in the United States. Unfortunately however for the antifederal argument the British history informs us, that this hereditary assembly has not even been able to defend itself against the continual encroachments of the house of representatives; and that it no sooner lost the support of the monarch, than it was actually crushed by the weight of the popular branch.

As far as antiquity can instruct us on this subject, its examples support the reasoning which we have employed. In Sparta the Ephori, the annual representatives of the people, were found an overmatch for the senate for life, continually gained on its authority, and finally drew all power into their own hands. The tribunes of Rome, who were the representatives of the people, prevailed, it is well known, in almost every contest with the senate for life, and in the end gained the most complete triumph over it. This fact is the more remarkable, as unanimity was required in every act of the tribunes, even after their number was augmented to ten. It proves the irresistable force possessed by that branch of a free government, which has the people on its side. To these examples might be added that of Carthage, whose senate, according to the testimony of Polybius, instead of drawing all power into its vortex, had at the commencement of the second punic war, lost almost the whole of its original portion.

Besides the conclusive evidence resulting from this assemblage of facts, that the federal senate will never be able to transform itself, by gradual usurpations, into an independent and aristocratic body; we are warranted in believing that if such a revolution should ever happen from causes which the foresight of man cannot guard against, the house of representatives with the people on their side will at all times be able to bring back the constitution to its primitive form and principles. Against the force of the immediate representatives of the people, nothing will be able to maintain even the constitutional authority of the senate, but such a display of enlightened policy, and attachment to the public good, as will divide with that branch of the legislature, the affections and support of the entire body of the people themselves.

PUBLIUS.

THE FEDERALIST NO. 70
ALEXANDER HAMILTON

March 15, 1788

To the People of the State of New York.

There is an idea, which is not without its advocates, that a vigorous executive is inconsistent with the genius of republican government. The enlightened well wishers to this species of government must at least hope that the supposition is destitute of foundation; since they can never admit its truth, without at the same time admitting the condemnation of their own principles. Energy in the executive is a leading character in the definition of good government. It is essential to the protection of the community against foreign attacks: It is not less essential to the steady administration of the laws, to the protection of property against those irregular and high handed combinations, which sometimes interrupt the ordinary course of justice, to the security of liberty against the enterprises and assaults of ambition, of faction and of anarchy. Every man the least conversant in Roman story knows how often that republic was obliged to take refuge in the absolute power of a single man, under the formidable title of dictator, as well against the intrigues of ambitious individuals, who aspired to the tyranny, and the seditions of whole classes of the community, whose conduct threatened the existence of all government, as against the invasions of external enemies, who menaced the conquest and destruction of Rome.

There can be no need however to multiply arguments or examples on this head. A feeble executive implies a feeble execution of the government. A feeble execution is but another phrase for a bad execution: And a government ill executed, whatever it may be in theory, must be in practice a bad government.

Taking it for granted, therefore, that all men of sense will agree in the necessity of an energetic executive; it will only remain to inquire, what are the ingredients which constitute this energy—how far can they be combined with those other ingredients which constitute safety in the republican sense? And how far does this combination characterise the plan, which has been reported by the convention?

The ingredients, which constitute energy in the executive, are first unity, secondly duration, thirdly an adequate provision for its support, fourthly competent powers.

The circumstances which constitute safety in the republican sense are, Ist. a due dependence on the people, secondly a due responsibility.

Those politicians and statesmen, who have been the most celebrated for the soundness of their principles, and for the justness of their views, have declared in favor of a single executive and a numerous legislature. They have with great propriety considered energy as the most necessary qualification of the former, and have regarded this as most applicable to power in a single hand; while they have with equal propriety considered the latter as best adapted to deliberation and wisdom, and best calculated to conciliate the confidence of the people and to secure their privileges and interests.

That unity is conducive to energy will not be disputed. Decision, activity, secrecy, and dispatch will generally characterise the proceedings of one man, in a much more eminent degree, than the proceedings of any greater number; and in proportion as the number is increased, these qualities will be diminished.

This unity may be destroyed in two ways; either by vesting the power in two or more magistrates of equal dignity and authority; or by vesting it ostensibly in one man, subject in whole or in part to the controul and co-operation of others, in the capacity of counsellors to him. Of the first the two consuls of Rome may serve as an example; of the last we shall find examples in the constitutions of several of the states. New-York and New-Jersey, if I recollect right, are the only states, which have entrusted the executive authority wholly to single men.* Both these methods of destroying the unity of the executive have their partisans; but the votaries of an executive council are the most numerous. They are both liable, if not to equal, to similar objections; and may in most lights be examined in conjunction.

The experience of other nations will afford little instruction on this head. As far however as it teaches any thing, it teaches us not to be inamoured of plurality in the executive. We have seen that the Achæans on an experiment of two Prætors, were induced to abolish one. The Roman history records many instances of mischiefs to the republic from the dissentions between the consuls, and between the military tribunes, who were at times substituted to the consuls. But it gives us no specimens of any peculiar advantages derived to the state, from the circumstance of the plurality of those magistrates. That the dissentions between them were not more frequent, or more fatal, is matter of astonishment; until we advert to the singular position in which the republic was almost continually placed and to the prudent policy pointed out by the circumstances of the state, and pursued by the consuls, of making a division of the government between them. The Patricians en-

** New-York has no council except for the single purpose of appointing to offices; New-Jersey has a council, whom the governor may consult. But I think from the terms of the constitution their resolutions do not bind him.*

gaged in a perpetual struggle with the Plebians for the preservation of their antient authorities and dignities; the consuls, who were generally chosen out of the former body, were commonly united by the personal interest they had in the defence of the privileges of their order. In addition to this motive of union, after the arms of the republic had considerably expanded the bounds of its empire, it became an established custom with the consuls to divide the administration between themselves by lot; one of them remaining at Rome to govern the city and its environs; the other taking the command in the more distant provinces. This expedient must no doubt have had great influence in preventing those collisions and rivalships, which might otherwise have embroiled the peace of the republic.

But quitting the dim light of historical research, and attaching ourselves purely to the dictates of reason and good sense, we shall discover much greater cause to reject than to approve the idea of plurality in the executive, under any modification whatever.

Wherever two or more persons are engaged in any common enterprize or pursuit, there is always danger of difference of opinion. If it be a public trust or office in which they are cloathed with equal dignity and authority, there is peculiar danger of personal emulation and even animosity. From either and especially from all these causes, the most bitter dissentions are apt to spring. Whenever these happen, they lessen the respectability, weaken the authority, and distract the plans and operations of those whom they divide. If they should unfortunately assail the supreme executive magistracy of a country, consisting of a plurality of persons, they might impede or frustrate the most important measures of the government, in the most critical emergencies of the state. And what is still worse, they might split the community into the most violent and irreconcilable factions, adhering differently to the different individuals who composed the magistracy.

Men often oppose a thing merely because they have had no agency in planning it, or because it may have been planned by those whom they dislike. But if they have been consulted and have happened to disapprove, opposition then becomes in their estimation an indispensable duty of self love. They seem to think themselves bound in honor, and by all the motives of personal infallibility to defeat the success of what has been resolved upon, contrary to their sentiments. Men of upright, benevolent tempers have too many opportunities of remarking with horror, to what desperate lengths this disposition is sometimes carried, and how often the great interests of society are sacrificed to the vanity, to the conceit and to the obstinacy of individuals, who have credit enough to make their passions and their caprices interesting to mankind. Perhaps the question now before the public may in its consequences afford melancholy proofs of the effects of this despicable frailty, or rather detestable vice in the human character.

Upon the principles of a free government, inconveniences from the source just mentioned must necessarily be submitted to in the formation of the legislature; but it is unnecessary and therefore unwise to introduce them into the constitution of the executive. It is here too that they may be most pernicious. In the legislature, promptitude of decision is oftener an evil than a benefit. The differences of opinion, and the jarrings of parties in that department of the government, though they may sometimes obstruct salutary plans, yet often promote deliberation and circumspection; and serve to check excess in the majority. When a resolution too is once taken, the opposition must be at an end. That resolution is a law, and resistance to it punishable. But no favourable circumstances palliate or atone for the disadvantages of dissention in the executive department. Here they are pure and unmixed. There is no point at which they cease to operate. They serve to embarrass and weaken the execution of the plan or measure, to which they relate, from the first step to the final conclusion of it. They constantly counteract those qualities in the executive, which are the most necessary ingredients in its composition, vigour and expedition, and this without any counterballancing good. In the conduct of war, in which the energy of the executive is the bulwark of the national security, every thing would be to be apprehended from its plurality.

It must be confessed that these observations apply with principal weight to the first case supposed, that is to a plurality of magistrates of equal dignity and authority; a scheme the advocates for which are not likely to form a numerous sect: But they apply, though not with equal, yet with considerable weight, to the project of a council, whose concurrence is made constitutionally necessary to the operations of the ostensible executive. An artful cabal in that council would be able to distract and to enervate the whole system of administration. If no such cabal should exist, the mere diversity of views and opinions would alone be sufficient to tincture the exercise of the executive authority with a spirit of habitual feebleness and dilatoriness.

But one of the weightiest objections to a plurality in the executive, and which lies as much against the last as the first plan, is that it tends to conceal faults, and destroy responsibility. Responsibility is of two kinds, to censure and to punishment. The first is the most important of the two; especially in an elective office. Man, in public trust, will much oftener act in such a manner as to render him unworthy of being any longer trusted, than in such a manner as to make him obnoxious to legal punishment. But the multiplication of the executive adds to the difficulty of detection in either case. It often becomes impossible, amidst mutual accusations, to determine on whom the blame or the punishment of a pernicious measure, or series of pernicious measures ought really to fall. It is shifted from one to another with so much dexterity, and under such plausible appearances, that the public opinion is left in suspense about the real author. The circumstances which may have led to any national miscarriage or misfortune are sometimes so complicated, that where there are a number of actors who may have had different degrees and kinds of agency, though we may clearly see upon the whole that there has been mismanagement, yet it may be impracticable to pronounce to whose account the evil which may have been incurred is truly chargeable.

"I was overruled by my council. The council were so divided in their opinions, that it was impossible to obtain any better resolution on the point." These and similar pretexts are constantly at hand, whether true or false. And who is there that will either take the trouble or incur the odium of a strict scrutiny into the secret springs of the transaction? Should there be found a citizen zealous enough to undertake the unpromising task, if there happen to be a collusion between the parties concerned, how easy is it to cloath the circumstances with so much ambiguity, as to render it uncertain what was the precise conduct of any of those parties?

In the single instance in which the governor of this state is coupled with a council, that is in the appointment to offices, we have seen the mischiefs of it in the view now under consideration. Scandalous appointments to important offices have been made. Some cases indeed have been so flagrant, that ALL PARTIES have agreed in the impropriety of the thing. When enquiry has been made, the blame has been laid by the governor on the members of the council; who on their part have charged it upon his nomination: While the people remain altogether at a loss to determine by whose influence their interests have been committed to hands so unqualified, and so manifestly improper. In tenderness to individuals, I forbear to descend to particulars.

It is evident from these considerations, that the plurality of the executive tends to deprive the people of the two greatest securities they can have for the faithful exercise of any delegated power; first, the restraints of public opinion, which lose their efficacy as well on account of the division of the censure attendant on bad measures among a number, as on account of the uncertainty on whom it ought to fall; and secondly, the opportunity of discovering with facility and clearness the misconduct of the persons they trust, in order either to their removal from office, or to their actual punishment, in cases which admit of it.

In England the king is a perpetual magistrate; and it is a maxim, which has obtained for the sake of the public peace, that he is unaccountable for his administration, and his person sacred. Nothing therefore can be wiser in that kingdom than to annex to the king a constitutional council, who may be responsible to the nation for the advice they give. Without this there would be no responsibility whatever in the executive department; an idea inadmissible in a free government. But even there the king is not bound by the resolutions of his council, though they are answerable for the advice they give. He is the absolute master of his own conduct, in the exercise of his office; and may observe or disregard the council given to him at his sole discretion.

But in a republic, where every magistrate ought to be personally responsible for his behaviour in office, the reason which in the British constitution dictates the propriety of a council not only ceases to apply, but turns against the institution. In the monarchy of Great-Britain, it furnishes a substitute for the prohibited responsibility of the chief magistrate; which serves in some degree as a hostage to the national justice for his good behaviour. In the American republic it would serve to destroy, or would greatly diminish the intended and necessary responsibility of the chief magistrate himself.

The idea of a council to the executive, which has so generally obtained in the state constitutions, has been derived from that maxim of republican jealousy, which considers power as safer in the hands of a number of men than of a single man. If the maxim should be admitted to be applicable to the case, I should contend that the advantage on that side would not counterballance the numerous disadvantages on the opposite side. But I do not think the rule at all applicable to the executive power. I clearly concur in opinion in this particular with a writer whom the celebrated Junius pronounces to be "deep, solid and ingenious," that, "the executive power is more easily confined when it is one":* That it is far more safe there should be a single object for the jealousy and watchfulness of the people; and in a word that all multiplication of the executive is rather dangerous than friendly to liberty.

A little consideration will satisfy us, that the species of security sought for in the multiplication of the executive is unattainable. Numbers must be so great as to render combination difficult; or they are rather a source of danger than of security. The united credit and influence of several individuals must be more formidable to liberty than the credit and influence of either of them separately. When power therefore is placed in the hands of so small a number of men, as to admit of their interests and views being easily combined in a common enterprise, by an artful leader, it becomes more liable to abuse and more dangerous when abused, than if it be lodged in the hands of one man; who from the very circumstance of his being alone will be more narrowly watched and more readily suspected, and who cannot unite so great a mass of influence as when he is associated with others. The Decemvirs of Rome, whose name denotes their number,† were more to be dreaded in their usurpation than any ONE of them would have been. No person would think of proposing an executive much more numerous than that body, from six to a dozen have been suggested for the number of the council. The extreme of these numbers is not too great for an easy combination; and from such a combination America would have more to fear, than from the ambition of any single individual. A council to a magistrate, who is himself responsible for what he does, are generally nothing better than a clog upon his good intentions; are often the instruments and accomplices of his bad, and are almost always a cloak to his faults.

I forbear to dwell upon the subject of expence; though it be evident that if the council should be numerous enough to answer the principal end, aimed at by the institution, the

* De Lome.
† *Ten.*

salaries of the members, who must be drawn from their homes to reside at the seat of government, would form an item in the catalogue of public expenditures, too serious to be incurred for an object of equivocal utility.

I will only add, that prior to the appearance of the constitution, I rarely met with an intelligent man from any of the states, who did not admit as the result of experience, that the UNITY of the Executive of this state was one of the best of the distinguishing features of our constitution.

PUBLIUS.

THE FEDERALIST NO. 71
ALEXANDER HAMILTON

March 18, 1788

To the People of the State of New York.

Duration in office has been mentioned as the second requisite to the energy of the executive authority. This has relation to two objects: To the personal firmness of the Executive Magistrate in the employment of his constitutional powers; and to the stability of the system of administration which may have been adopted under his auspices. With regard to the first, it must be evident, that the longer the duration in office, the greater will be the probability of obtaining so important an advantage. It is a general principle of human nature, that a man will be interested in whatever he possesses, in proportion to the firmness or precariousness of the tenure, by which he holds it; will be less attached to what he holds by a momentary or uncertain title, than to what he enjoys by a durable or certain title; and of course will be willing to risk more for the sake of the one, than for the sake of the other. This remark is not less applicable to a political privilege, or honor, or trust, than to any article of ordinary property. The inference from it is, that a man acting in the capacity of Chief Magistrate, under a consciousness, that in a very short time he *must* lay down his office, will be apt to feel himself too little interested in it, to hazard any material censure or perplexity, from the independent exertion of his powers, or from encountering the ill-humors, however transient, which may happen to prevail either in a considerable part of the society itself, or even in a predominant faction in the legislative body. If the case should only be, that he *might* lay it down, unless continued by a new choice; and if he should be desirous of being continued, his wishes conspiring with his fears would tend still more powerfully to corrupt his integrity, or debase his fortitude. In either case feebleness and irresolution must be the characteristics of the station.

There are some, who would be inclined to regard the servile pliancy of the executive to a prevailing current, either in the community, or in the Legislature, as its best recommendation. But such men entertain very crude notions, as well of the purposes for which government was instituted, as of the true means by which the public happiness may be promoted. The republican principle demands, that the deliberate sense of the community should govern the conduct of those to whom they entrust the management of their affairs; but it does not require an unqualified complaisance to every sudden breese of passion, or to every transient impulse which the people may receive from the arts of men, who flatter their prejudices to betray their interests. It is a just observation, that the people commonly *intend* the PUBLIC GOOD. This often applies to their very errors. But their good sense would despise the adulator, who should pretend that they always *reason right* about the *means* of promoting it. They know from experience, that they sometimes err; and the wonder is, that they so seldom err as they do; beset as they continually are by the wiles of parasites and sycophants, by the snares of the ambitious, the avaricious, the desperate; by the artifices of men, who possess their confidence more than they deserve it, and of those who seek to possess, rather than to deserve it. When occasions present themselves in which the interests of the people are at variance with their inclinations, it is the duty of the persons whom they have appointed to be the guardians of those interests, to withstand the temporary delusion, in order to give them time and opportunity for more cool and sedate reflection. Instances might be cited, in which a conduct of this kind has saved the people from very fatal consequences of their own mistakes, and has procured lasting monuments of their gratitude to the men, who had courage and magnanimity enough to serve them at the peril of their displeasure.

But however inclined we might be to insist upon an unbounded complaisance in the executive to the inclinations of the people, we can with no propriety contend for a like complaisance to the humors of the Legislature. The latter may sometimes stand in opposition to the former; and at other times the people may be entirely neutral. In either supposition, it is certainly desirable that the executive should be in a situation to dare to act his own opinion with vigor and decision.

The same rule, which teaches the propriety of a partition between the various branches of power, teaches us likewise that this partition ought to be so contrived as to render the one independent of the other. To what purpose separate the executive, or the judiciary, from the legislative, if both the executive and the judiciary are so constituted as to be at the absolute devotion of the legislative? Such a separation must be merely nominal and incapable of producing the ends for which it was established. It is one thing to be subordinate to the laws, and another to be dependent on the legislative body. The first comports with, the last violates, the fundamental principles of good government; and whatever may be the forms of the Constitution, unites all power in the same hands. The tendency of the legislative authority to absorb every other, has been fully displayed and illustrated by examples, in some preceding numbers. In governments purely republican, this tendency is almost irresistible. The representatives of the people, in a popular assembly, seem sometimes to fancy that they are the people themselves; and betray strong symptoms of impatience and disgust at the least sign of opposition from any other quarter; as if the exercise of its rights by either the executive or judiciary, were a breach of their privilege and an outrage to their dignity. They often appear disposed to exert an imperious controul over the other departments; and as they commonly have the people on their side, they always act with such momentum as to make it very difficult for the other members of the government to maintain the balance of the Constitution.

It may perhaps be asked how the shortness of the duration in office can affect the independence of the executive on the legislature, unless the one were possessed of the power of appointing or displacing the other? One answer to this enquiry may be drawn from the principle already remarked, that is from the slender interest a man is apt to take in a short lived advantage, and the little inducement it affords him to expose himself on account of it to any considerable inconvenience or hazard. Another answer, perhaps more obvious, though not more conclusive, will result from the consideration of the influence of the legislative body over the people, which might be employed to prevent the re-election of a man, who by an upright resistance to any sinister project of that body, should have made himself obnoxious to its resentment.

It may be asked also whether a duration of four years

would answer the end proposed, and if it would not, whether a less period which would at least be recommended by greater security against ambitious designs, would not for that reason be preferable to a longer period, which was at the same time too short for the purpose of inspiring the desired firmness and independence of the magistrate?

It cannot be affirmed, that a duration of four years or any other limited duration would completely answer the end proposed; but it would contribute towards it in a degree which would have a material influence upon the spirit and character of the government. Between the commencement and termination of such a period there would always be a considerable interval, in which the prospect of annihilation would be sufficiently remote not to have an improper effect upon the conduct of a man endued with a tolerable portion of fortitude; and in which he might reasonably promise himself, that there would be time enough, before it arrived, to make the community sensible of the propriety of the measures he might incline to pursue. Though it be probable, that as he approached the moment when the public were by a new election to signify their sense of his conduct, his confidence and with it, his firmness would decline; yet both the one and the other would derive support from the opportunities, which his previous continuance in the station had afforded him of establishing himself in the esteem and good will of his constituents. He might then hazard with safety, in proportion to the proofs he had given of his wisdom and integrity, and to the title he had acquired to the respect and attachment of his fellow citizens. As on the one hand, a duration of four years will contribute to the firmness of the executive in a sufficient degree to render it a very valuable ingredient in the composition; so on the other, it is not long enough to justify any alarm for the public liberty. If a British House of Commons, from the most feeble beginnings, *from the mere power of assenting or disagreeing to the imposition of a new tax,* have by rapid strides, reduced the prerogatives of the crown and the privileges of the nobility within the limits they conceived to be compatible with the principles of a free government; while they raised themselves to the rank and consequence of a coequal branch of the Legislature; if they have been able in one instance to abolish both the royalty and the aristocracy, and to overturn all the ancient establishments as well in the church as State; if they have been able on a recent occasion to make the monarch tremble at the prospect of an innovation* attempted by them; what would be to be feared from an elective magistrate of four years duration, with the confined authorities of a President of the United States? What but that he might be unequal to the task which the Constitution assigns him? I shall only add that if his duration be such as to leave a doubt of his firmness, that doubt is inconsistent with a jealousy of his encroachments.

PUBLIUS.

THE FEDERALIST NO. 78
ALEXANDER HAMILTON

May 28, 1788

We proceed now to an examination of the judiciary department of the proposed government.

In unfolding the defects of the existing confederation, the utility and necessity of a federal judicature have been clearly pointed out. It is the less necessary to recapitulate the considerations there urged; as the propriety of the institution in the abstract is not disputed: The only questions which have been raised being relative to the manner of constituting it, and to its extent. To these points therefore our observations shall be confined.

The manner of constituting it seems to embrace these several objects—1st. The mode of appointing the judges. 2d. The tenure by which they are to hold their places. 3d. The partition of the judiciary authority between different courts, and their relations to each other.

First. As to the mode of appointing the judges: This is the same with that of appointing the officers of the union in general, and has been so fully discussed in the two last numbers, that nothing can be said here which would not be useless repetition.

Second. As to the tenure by which the judges are to hold their places: This chiefly concerns their duration in office; the provisions for their support; and the precautions for their responsibility.

According to the plan of the convention, all the judges who may be appointed by the United States are to hold their offices *during good behaviour,* which is conformable to the most

* *This was the case with respect to Mr. Fox's India bill which was carried in the House of Commons, and rejected in the House of Lords, to the entire satisfaction, as it is said, of the people.*

approved of the state constitutions; and among the rest, to that of this state. Its propriety having been drawn into question by the adversaries of that plan, is no light symptom of the rage for objection which disorders their imaginations and judgments. The standard of good behaviour for the continuance in office of the judicial magistracy is certainly one of the most valuable of the modern improvements in the practice of government. In a monarchy it is an excellent barrier to the despotism of the prince: In a republic it is a no less excellent barrier to the encroachments and oppressions of the representative body. And it is the best expedient which can be devised in any government, to secure a steady, upright and impartial administration of the laws.

Whoever attentively considers the different departments of power must perceive, that in a government in which they are separated from each other, the judiciary, from the nature of its functions, will always be the least dangerous to the political rights of the constitution; because it will be least in a capacity to annoy or injure them. The executive not only dispenses the honors, but holds the sword of the community. The legislature not only commands the purse, but prescribes the rules by which the duties and rights of every citizen are to be regulated. The judiciary on the contrary has no influence over either the sword or the purse, no direction either of the strength or of the wealth of the society, and can take no active resolution whatever. It may truly be said to have neither Force nor Will, but merely judgment; and must ultimately depend upon the aid of the executive arm even for the efficacy of its judgments.

This simple view of the matter suggests several important consequences. It proves incontestibly that the judiciary is beyond comparison the weakest of the three departments of power;* that it can never attack with success either of the other two; and that all possible care is requisite to enable it to defend itself against their attacks. It equally proves, that though individual oppression may now and then proceed from the courts of justice, the general liberty of the people can never be endangered from that quarter: I mean, so long as the judiciary remains truly distinct from both the legislative and executive. For I agree that "there is no liberty, if the power of judging be not separated from the legislative and executive

* The celebrated Montesquieu speaking of them says, "of the three powers above mentioned, the JUDICIARY is next to nothing." Spirit of Laws, vol. 1, page 186.

powers."* And it proves, in the last place, that as liberty can have nothing to fear from the judiciary alone, but would have every thing to fear from its union with either of the other departments; that as all the effects of such an union must ensue from a dependence of the former on the latter, notwithstanding a nominal and apparent separation; that as from the natural feebleness of the judiciary, it is in continual jeopardy of being overpowered, awed or influenced by its coordinate branches; and that as nothing can contribute so much to its firmness and independence, as permanency in office, this quality may therefore be justly regarded as an indispensable ingredient in its constitution; and in a great measure as the citadel of the public justice and the public security.

The complete independence of the courts of justice is peculiarly essential in a limited constitution. By a limited constitution I understand one which contains certain specified exceptions to the legislative authority; such for instance as that it shall pass no bills of attainder, no *ex post facto* laws, and the like. Limitations of this kind can be preserved in practice no other way than through the medium of the courts of justice; whose duty it must be to declare all acts contrary to the manifest tenor of the constitution void. Without this, all the reservations of particular rights or privileges would amount to nothing.

Some perplexity respecting the right of the courts to pronounce legislative acts void, because contrary to the constitution, has arisen from an imagination that the doctrine would imply a superiority of the judiciary to the legislative power. It is urged that the authority which can declare the acts of another void, must necessarily be superior to the one whose acts may be declared void. As this doctrine is of great importance in all the American constitutions, a brief discussion of the grounds on which it rests cannot be unacceptable.

There is no position which depends on clearer principles, than that every act of a delegated authority, contrary to the tenor of the commission under which it is exercised, is void. No legislative act therefore contrary to the constitution can be valid. To deny this would be to affirm that the deputy is greater than his principal; that the servant is above his master; that the representatives of the people are superior to the people themselves; that men acting by virtue of powers may do not only what their powers do not authorise, but what they forbid.

* Idem. page 181.

If it be said that the legislative body are themselves the constitutional judges of their own powers, and that the construction they put upon them is conclusive upon the other departments, it may be answered, that this cannot be the natural presumption, where it is not to be collected from any particular provisions in the constitution. It is not otherwise to be supposed that the constitution could intend to enable the representatives of the people to substitute their *will* to that of their constituents. It is far more rational to suppose that the courts were designed to be an intermediate body between the people and the legislature, in order, among other things, to keep the latter within the limits assigned to their authority. The interpretation of the laws is the proper and peculiar province of the courts. A constitution is in fact, and must be, regarded by the judges as a fundamental law. It therefore belongs to them to ascertain its meaning as well as the meaning of any particular act proceeding from the legislative body. If there should happen to be an irreconcileable variance between the two, that which has the superior obligation and validity ought of course to be preferred; or in other words, the constitution ought to be preferred to the statute, the intention of the people to the intention of their agents.

Nor does this conclusion by any means suppose a superiority of the judicial to the legislative power. It only supposes that the power of the people is superior to both; and that where the will of the legislature declared in its statutes, stands in opposition to that of the people declared in the constitution, the judges ought to be governed by the latter, rather than the former. They ought to regulate their decisions by the fundamental laws, rather than by those which are not fundamental.

The exercise of judicial discretion in determining between two contradictory laws, is exemplified in a familiar instance. It not uncommonly happens, that there are two statutes existing at one time, clashing in whole or in part with each other, and neither of them containing any repealing clause or expression. In such a case, it is the province of the courts to liquidate and fix their meaning and operation: So far as they can by any fair construction be reconciled to each other; reason and law conspire to dictate that this should be done. Where this is impracticable, it becomes a matter of necessity to give effect to one, in exclusion of the other. The rule which has obtained in the courts for determining their relative validity is that the last in order of time shall be preferred to the first. But this is mere rule of construction, not derived from any positive law, but from the nature and reason of the thing. It is a rule not enjoined upon the courts by legislative provision, but adopted by themselves, as consonant to truth and propriety, for the direction of their conduct as interpreters of the law. They thought it reasonable, that between the interfering acts of an *equal* authority, that which was the last indication of its will, should have the preference.

But in regard to the interfering acts of a superior and subordinate authority, of an original and derivative power, the nature and reason of the thing indicate the converse of that rule as proper to be followed. They teach us that the prior act of a superior ought to be preferred to the subsequent act of an inferior and subordinate authority; and that, accordingly, whenever a particular statute contravenes the constitution, it will be the duty of the judicial tribunals to adhere to the latter, and disregard the former.

It can be of no weight to say, that the courts on the pretence of a repugnancy, may substitute their own pleasure to the constitutional intentions of the legislature. This might as well happen in the case of two contradictory statutes; or it might as well happen in every adjudication upon any single statute. The courts must declare the sense of the law; and if they should be disposed to exercise WILL instead of JUDGMENT, the consequence would equally be the substitution of their pleasure to that of the legislative body. The observation, if it proved any thing, would prove that three ought to be no judges distinct from that body.

If then the courts of justice are to be considered as the bulwarks of a limited constitution against legislative encroachments, this consideration will afford a strong argument for the permanent tenure of judicial offices, since nothing will contribute so much as this to that independent spirit in the judges, which must be essential to the faithful performance of so arduous a duty.

This independence of the judges is equally requisite to guard the constitution and the rights of individuals from the effects of those ill humours which the arts of designing men, or the influence of particular conjunctures, sometimes disseminate among the people themselves, and which, though they speedily give place to better information and more deliberate reflection, have a tendency in the mean time to occasion dangerous innovations in the government, and serious oppressions of the minor party in the community. Though I trust the friends of the proposed constitution will never concur with its enemies* in questioning that fundamental principle of republican government, which admits the right of the people to alter or abolish the established constitution whenever they find it inconsistent with their happiness; yet it is not to be inferred from this principle, that the representatives of the people, whenever a momentary inclination happens to lay hold of a majority of their constituents incompatible with the provisions in the existing constitution, would on that account be justifiable in a violation of those provisions; or that the courts would be under a greater obligation to connive at infractions in this shape, than when they had proceeded wholly from the cabals of the representative body. Until the people have by some solemn and authoritative act annulled or changed the established form, it is binding upon themselves collectively, as well as individually; and no presumption, or even knowledge of their sentiments, can warrant their representatives in a departure from it, prior to such an act. But it is easy to see that it would require an uncommon portion of fortitude in the judges to do their duty as faithful guardians of the constitution, where legislative invasions of it had been instigated by the major voice of the community.

But it is not with a view to infractions of the constitution only that the independence of the judges may be an essential safeguard against the effects of occasional ill humours in the society. These sometimes extend no farther than to the injury of the private rights of particular classes of citizens, by unjust and partial laws. Here also the firmness of the judicial magistracy is of vast importance in mitigating the severity, and confining the operation of such laws. It not only serves to moderate the immediate mischiefs of those which may have been passed, but it operates as a check upon the legislative body in passing them; who, perceiving that obstacles to the success of an iniquitous intention are to be expected from the scruples of the courts, are in a manner compelled by the very motives of the injustice they meditate, to qualify their attempts. This is a circumstance calculated to have more influence upon the character of our governments, than but few may be aware of. The benefits of the integrity and moderation of the judiciary have already been felt in more states than one; and though they may have displeased those whose sinister expectations they may have disappointed, they must have commanded

* Vide Protest of the minority of the convention of Pennsylvania, Martin's speech, &c.

the esteem and applause of all the virtuous and disinterested. Considerate men of every description ought to prize whatever will tend to beget or fortify that temper in the courts; as no man can be sure that he may not be tomorrow the victim of a spirit of injustice, by which he may be a gainer to-day. And every man must now feel that the inevitable tendency of such a spirit is to sap the foundations of public and private confidence, and to introduce in its stead, universal distrust and distress.

That inflexible and uniform adherence to the rights of the constitution and of individuals, which we perceive to be indispensable in the courts of justice, can certainly not be expected from judges who hold their offices by a temporary commission. Periodical appointments, however regulated, or by whomsoever made, would in some way or other be fatal to their necessary independence. If the power of making them was committed either to the executive or legislature, there would be danger of an improper complaisance to the branch which possessed it; if to both, there would be an unwillingness to hazard the displeasure of either; if to the people, or to persons chosen by them for the special purpose, there would be too great a disposition to consult popularity, to justify a reliance that nothing would be consulted but the constitution and the laws.

There is yet a further and a weighty reason for the permanency of the judicial offices; which is deducible from the nature of the qualifications they require. It has been frequently remarked with great propriety, that a voluminous code of laws is one of the inconveniences necessarily connected with the advantages of a free government. To avoid an arbitrary discretion in the courts, it is indispensable that they should be bound down by strict rules and precedents, which serve to define and point out their duty in every particular case that comes before them; and it will readily be conceived from the variety of controversies which grow out of the folly and wickedness of mankind, that the records of those precedents must unavoidably swell to a very considerable bulk, and must demand long and laborious study to acquire a competent knowledge of them. Hence it is that there can be but few men in the society, who will have sufficient skill in the laws to qualify them for the stations of judges. And making the proper deductions for the ordinary depravity of human nature, the number must be still smaller of those who unite the requisite integrity with the requisite knowledge. These considerations apprise us, that the government can have no great option between fit characters; and that a temporary duration in office, which would naturally discourage such characters from quitting a lucrative line of practice to accept a seat on the bench, would have a tendency to throw the administration of justice into hands less able, and less well qualified to conduct it with utility and dignity. In the present circumstances of this country, and in those in which it is likely to be for a long time to come, the disadvantages on this score would be greater than they may at first sight appear; but it must be confessed that they are far inferior to those which present themselves under the other aspects of the subject.

Upon the whole there can be no room to doubt that the convention acted wisely in copying from the models of those constitutions which have established *good behaviour* as the tenure of their judicial offices in point of duration; and that so far from being blameable on this account, their plan would have been inexcuseably defective if it had wanted this important feature of good government. The experience of Great Britain affords an illustrious comment on the excellence of the institution.

PUBLIUS.

THE FEDERALIST NO. 84
ALEXANDER HAMILTON

May 28, 1788

In the course of the foregoing review of the constitution I have taken notice of, and endeavoured to answer, most of the objections which have appeared against it. There however remain a few which either did not fall naturally under any particular head, or were forgotten in their proper places. These shall now be discussed; but as the subject has been drawn into great length, I shall so far consult brevity as to comprise all my observations on these miscellaneous points in a single paper.

The most considerable of these remaining objections is, that the plan of the convention contains no bill of rights. Among other answers given to this, it has been upon different occasions remarked, that the constitutions of several of the states are in a similar predicament. I add, that New-York is of this number. And yet the opposers of the new system in this state, who profess an unlimited admiration for its constitution, are among the most intemperate partizans of a bill of rights.

To justify their zeal in this matter, they alledge two things; one is, that though the constitution of New-York has no bill of rights prefixed to it, yet it contains in the body of it various provisions in favour of particular privileges and rights, which in substance amount to the same thing; the other is, that the constitution adopts in their full extent the common and statute law of Great-Britain, by which many other rights not expressed in it are equally secured.

To the first I answer, that the constitution proposed by the convention contains, as well as the constitution of this state, a number of such provisions.

Independent of those, which relate to the structure of the government, we find the following: Article I. section 3. clause 7. "Judgment in cases of impeachment shall not extend further than to removal from office, and disqualification to hold and enjoy any office of honour, trust or profit under the United States; but the party convicted shall nevertheless be liable and subject to indictment, trial, judgment and punishment, according to law." Section 9. of the same article, clause 2. "The privilege of the writ of *habeas corpus* shall not be suspended, unless when in cases of rebellion or invasion the public safety may require it." Clause 3. "No bill of attainder or *ex post facto* law shall be passed." Clause 7. "No title of nobility shall be granted by the United States: And no person holding any office of profit or trust under them, shall, without the consent of the congress, accept of any present, emolument, office or title, of any kind whatever, from any king, prince or foreign state." Article III. section 2. clause 3. "The trial of all crimes, except in cases of impeachment, shall be by jury; and such trial shall be held in the state where the said crimes shall have been committed; but when not committed within any state, the trial shall be at such place or places as the congress may by law have directed." Section 3, of the same article, "Treason against the United States shall consist only in levying war against them, or in adhering to their enemies, giving them aid and comfort. No person shall be convicted of treason unless on the testimony of two witnesses to the same overt act, or on confession in open court." And clause 3, of the same section. "The congress shall have power to declare the punishment of treason, but no attainder of treason shall work corruption of blood, or forfeiture, except during the life of the person attainted."

It may well be a question whether these are not upon the whole, of equal importance with any which are to be found in the constitution of this state. The establishment of the writ of *habeas corpus,* the prohibition of *ex post facto* laws, and of TITLES OF NOBILITY, *to which we have no corresponding provisions in our constitution,* are perhaps greater securities to liberty and republicanism than any it contains. The creation of crimes after the commission of the fact, or in other words, the subjecting of men to punishment for things which, when they were done, were breaches of no law, and the practice of arbitrary imprisonments have been in all ages the favourite and most formidable instruments of tyranny. The observations of the judicious Blackstone* in reference to the latter, are well worthy of recital. "To bereave a man of life (says he) or by violence to confiscate his estate, without accusation or trial, would be so gross and notorious an act of despotism, as must at once convey the alarm of tyranny throughout the whole nation; but confinement of the person by secretly hurrying him to gaol, where his sufferings are unknown or forgotten, is a less public, a less striking, and therefore *a more dangerous engine* of arbitrary government." And as a remedy for this fatal evil, he is every where peculiarly emphatical in his encomiums on the *habeas corpus* act, which in one place he calls "the BULWARK of the British constitution."†

Nothing need be said to illustrate the importance of the prohibition of titles of nobility. This may truly be denominated the corner stone of republican government; for so long as they are excluded, there can never be serious danger that the government will be any other than that of the people.

To the second, that is, to the pretended establishment of the common and statute law by the constitution, I answer, that they are expressly made subject "to such alterations and provisions as the legislature shall from time to time make concerning the same." They are therefore at any moment liable to repeal by the ordinary legislative power, and of course have no constitutional sanction. The only use of the declaration was to recognize the ancient law, and to remove doubts which might have been occasioned by the revolution. This consequently can be considered as no part of a declaration of rights, which under our constitutions must be intended as limitations of the power of the government itself.

It has been several times truly remarked, that bills of rights are in their origin, stipulations between kings and their subjects, abridgments of prerogative in favor of privilege, reserva-

* Vide Blackstone's Commentaries, vol. 1, page 136.
† Idem, vol. 4, page 438.

tions of rights not surrendered to the prince. Such was MAGNA CHARTA, obtained by the Barons, sword in hand, from king John. Such were the subsequent confirmations of that charter by subsequent princes. Such was the *petition of right* assented to by Charles the First, in the beginning of his reign. Such also was the declaration of right presented by the lords and commons to the prince of Orange in 1688, and afterwards thrown into the form of an act of parliament, called the bill of rights. It is evident, therefore, that according to their primitive signification, they have no application to constitutions professedly founded upon the power of the people, and executed by their immediate representatives and servants. Here, in strictness, the people surrender nothing, and as they retain every thing, they have no need of particular reservations. "WE THE PEOPLE of the United States, to secure the blessings of liberty to ourselves and our posterity, do *ordain* and *establish* this constitution for the United States of America." Here is a better recognition of popular rights than volumes of those aphorisms which make the principal figure in several of our state bills of rights, and which would sound much better in a treatise of ethics than in a constitution of government.

But a minute detail of particular rights is certainly far less applicable to a constitution like that under consideration, which is merely intended to regulate the general political interests of the nation, than to a constitution which has the regulation of every species of personal and private concerns. If therefore the loud clamours against the plan of the convention on this score, are well founded, no epithets of reprobation will be too strong for the constitution of this state. But the truth is, that both of them contain all, which in relation to their objects, is reasonably to be desired.

I go further, and affirm that bills of rights, in the sense and in the extent in which they are contended for, are not only unnecessary in the proposed constitution, but would even be dangerous. They would contain various exceptions to powers which are not granted; and on this very account, would afford a colourable pretext to claim more than were granted. For why declare that things shall not be done which there is no power to do? Why for instance, should it be said, that the liberty of the press shall not be restrained, when no power is given by which restrictions may be imposed? I will not contend that such a provision would confer a regulating power; but it is evident that it would furnish, to men disposed to usurp, a plausible pretence for claiming that power. They might urge with a semblance of reason, that the constitution ought not to be charged with the absurdity of providing against the abuse of an authority, which was not given, and that the provision against restraining the liberty of the press afforded a clear implication, that a power to prescribe proper regulations concerning it, was intended to be vested in the national government. This may serve as a specimen of the numerous handles which would be given to the doctrine of constructive powers, by the indulgence of an injudicious zeal for bills of rights.

On the subject of the liberty of the press, as much has been said, I cannot forbear adding a remark or two: In the first place, I observe that there is not a syllable concerning it in the constitution of this state, and in the next, I contend that whatever has been said about it in that of any other state, amounts to nothing. What signifies a declaration that "the liberty of the press shall be inviolably preserved?" What is the liberty of the press? Who can give it any definition which would not leave the utmost latitude for evasion? I hold it to be impracticable; and from this, I infer, that its security, whatever fine declarations may be inserted in any constitution respecting it, must altogether depend on public opinion, and on the general spirit of the people and of the government.* And here, after all, as intimated upon another occasion, must we seek for the only solid basis of all our rights.

There remains but one other view of this matter to conclude the point. The truth is, after all the declamation we have heard, that the constitution is itself in every rational sense, and to every useful purpose, A BILL OF RIGHTS. The several bills of rights, in Great-Britain, form its constitution, and conversely

* To show that there is a power in the constitution by which the liberty of the press may be affected, recourse has been had to the power of taxation. It is said that duties may be laid upon publications so high as to amount to a prohibition. I know not by what logic it could be maintained that the declarations in the state constitutions, in favour of the freedom of the press, would be a constitutional impediment to the imposition of duties upon publications by the state legislatures. It cannot certainly be pretended that any degree of duties, however low, would be an abrigement of the liberty of the press. We know that newspapers are taxed in Great-Britain, and yet it is notorious that the press no where enjoys greater liberty than in that country. And if duties of any kind may be laid without a violation of that liberty, it is evident that the extent must depend on legislative discretion, regulated by public opinion; so that after all, general declarations respecting the liberty of the press will give it no greater security than it will have without them. The same invasions of it may be effected under the state constitutions which contain those declarations through the means of taxation, as under the proposed constitution which has nothing of the kind. It would be quite as significant to declare that government ought to be free, that taxes ought not to be excessive, &c., as that the liberty of the press ought to be restrained.

the constitution of each state is its bill of rights. And the proposed constitution, if adopted, will be the bill of rights of the union. Is it one object of a bill of rights to declare and specify the political privileges of the citizens in the structure and administration of the government? This is done in the most ample and precise manner in the plan of the convention, comprehending various precautions for the public security, which are not to be found in any of the state constitutions. Is another object of a bill of rights to define certain immunities and modes of proceeding, which are relative to personal and private concerns? This we have seen has also been attended to, in a variety of cases, in the same plan. Adverting therefore to the substantial meaning of a bill of rights, it is absurd to allege that it is not to be found in the work of the convention. It may be said that it does not go far enough, though it will not be easy to make this appear; but it can with no propriety be contended that there is no such thing. It certainly must be immaterial what mode is observed as to the order of declaring the rights of the citizens, if they are to be found in any part of the instrument which establishes the government. And hence it must be apparent that much of what has been said on this subject rests merely on verbal and nominal distinctions, which are entirely foreign from the substance of the thing.

Another objection, which has been made, and which from the frequency of its repetition it is to be presumed is relied on, is of this nature:—It is improper (say the objectors) to confer such large powers, as are proposed, upon the national government; because the seat of that government must of necessity be too remote from many of the states to admit of a proper knowledge on the part of the constituent, of the conduct of the representative body. This argument, if it proves any thing, proves that there ought to be no general government whatever. For the powers which it seems to be agreed on all hands, ought to be vested in the union, cannot be safely intrusted to a body which is not under every requisite controul. But there are satisfactory reasons to shew that the objection is in reality not well founded. There is in most of the arguments which relate to distance a palpable illusion of the imagination. What are the sources of information by which the people in Montgomery county must regulate their judgment of the conduct of their representatives in the state legislature? Of personal observation they can have no benefit. This is confined to the citizens on the spot. They must therefore depend on the information of intelligent men, in whom they confide—and how must these men obtain their information? Evidently from the complection of public measures, from the public prints, from correspondences with their representatives, and with other persons who reside at the place of their deliberation. This does not apply to Montgomery county only, but to all the counties, at any considerable distance from the seat of government.

It is equally evident that the same sources of information would be open to the people, in relation to the conduct of their representatives in the general government; and the impediments to a prompt communication which distance may be supposed to create, will be overballanced by the effects of the vigilance of the state governments. The executive and legislative bodies of each state will be so many centinels over the persons employed in every department of the national administration; and as it will be in their power to adopt and pursue a regular and effectual system of intelligence, they can never be at a loss to know the behaviour of those who represent their constituents in the national councils, and can readily communicate the same knowledge to the people. Their disposition to apprise the community of whatever may prejudice its interests from another quarter, may be relied upon, if it were only from the rivalship of power. And we may conclude with the fullest assurance, that the people, through that channel, will be better informed of the conduct of their national representatives, than they can be by any means they now possess of that of their state representatives.

It ought also to be remembered, that the citizens who inhabit the country at and near the seat of government, will in all questions that affect the general liberty and prosperity, have the same interest with those who are at a distance; and that they will stand ready to sound the alarm when necessary, and to point out the actors in any pernicious project. The public papers will be expeditious messengers of intelligence to the most remote inhabitants of the union.

Among the many extraordinary objections which have appeared against the proposed constitution, the most extraordinary and the least colourable one, is derived from the want of some provision respecting the debts due *to* the United States. This has been represented as a tacit relinquishment of those debts, and as a wicked contrivance to screen public defaulters. The newspapers have teemed with the most inflammatory railings on this head; and yet there is nothing clearer than that the suggestion is entirely void of foundation, and is the offspring of extreme ignorance or extreme dishonesty. In addition to the remarks I have made upon the subject in another place, I shall only observe, that as it is a plain dictate of common sense, so it is also an established doctrine of political law, that "*States neither lose any of their rights, nor are discharged from any of their obligations by a change in the form of their civil government.*"*

The last objection of any consequence which I at present recollect, turns upon the article of expence. If it were even true that the adoption of the proposed government would occasion a considerable increase of expence, it would be an objection that ought to have no weight against the plan. The great bulk of the citizens of America, are with reason convinced that union is the basis of their political happiness. Men of sense of all parties now, with few exceptions, agree that it cannot be preserved under the present system, nor without radical alterations; that new and extensive powers ought to be granted to the national head, and that these require a different organization of the federal government, a single body being an unsafe depository of such ample authorities. In conceding all this, the question of expence must be given up, for it is impossible, with any degree of safety, to narrow the foundation upon which the system is to stand. The two branches of the legislature are in the first instance, to consist of only sixty-five persons, which is the same number of which congress, under the existing confederation, may be composed. It is true that this number is intended to be increased; but this is to keep pace with the increase of the population and resources of the country. It is evident, that a less number would, even in the first instance, have been unsafe; and that a continuance of the present number would, in a more advanced stage of population, be a very inadequate representation of the people.

Whence is the dreaded augmentation of expence to spring? One source pointed out, is the multiplication of offices under the new government. Let us examine this a little.

It is evident that the principal departments of the administration under the present government, are the same which will be required under the new. There are now a secretary at war, a secretary for foreign affairs, a secretary for domestic affairs, a board of treasury consisting of three persons, a treasurer,

* Vide Rutherford's Institutes, vol. 2. book II, chap. x. sect. xiv, and xv.—Vide also Grotius, book II, chap. ix, sect. viii, and ix.

assistants, clerks, &c. These offices are indispensable under any system, and will suffice under the new as well as under the old. As to ambassadors and other ministers and agents in foreign countries, the proposed constitution can make no other difference, than to render their characters, where they reside, more respectable, and their services more useful. As to persons to be employed in the collection of the revenues, it is unquestionably true that these will form a very considerable addition to the number of federal officers; but it will not follow, that this will occasion an increase of public expence. It will be in most cases nothing more than an exchange of state officers for national officers. In the collection of all duties, for instance, the persons employed will be wholly of the latter description. The states individually will stand in no need of any for this purpose. What difference can it make in point of expence, to pay officers of the customs appointed by the state, or those appointed by the United States? There is no good reason to suppose, that either the number or the salaries of the latter, will be greater than those of the former.

Where then are we to seek for those additional articles of expence which are to swell the account to the enormous size that has been represented to us? The chief item which occurs to me, respects the support of the judges of the United States. I do not add the president, because there is now a president of congress, whose expences may not be far, if any thing, short of those which will be incurred on account of the president of the United States. The support of the judges will clearly be an extra expence, but to what extent will depend on the particular plan which may be adopted in practice in regard to this matter. But it can upon no reasonable plan amount to a sum which will be an object of material consequence.

Let us now see what there is to counterballance any extra expences that may attend the establishment of the proposed government. The first thing that presents itself is, that a great part of the business, which now keeps congress sitting through the year, will be transacted by the president. Even the management of foreign negociations will naturally devolve upon him according to general principles concerted with the senate, and subject to their final concurrence. Hence it is evident, that a portion of the year will suffice for the session of both the senate and the house of representatives: We may suppose about a fourth for the latter, and a third or perhaps a half for the former. The extra business of treaties and appointments may give this extra occupation to the senate. From this circumstance we may infer, that until the house of representatives shall be increased greatly beyond its present number, there will be a considerable saving of expence from the difference between the constant session of the present, and the temporary session of the future congress.

But there is another circumstance, of great importance in the view of economy. The business of the United States has hitherto occupied the state legislatures as well as congress. The latter has made requisitions which the former have had to provide for. Hence it has happened that the sessions of the state legislatures have been protracted greatly beyond what was necessary for the execution of the mere local business of the states. More than half their time has been frequently employed in matters which related to the United States. Now the members who compose the legislatures of the several states amount to two thousand and upwards; which number has hitherto performed what under the new system will be done in the first instance by sixty-five persons, and probably at no future period by above a fourth or a fifth of that number. The congress under the proposed government will do all the business of the United States themselves, without the intervention of the state legislatures, who thenceforth will have only to attend to the affairs of their particular states, and will not have to sit in any proportion as long as they have heretofore done. This difference, in the time of the sessions of the state legislatures, will be all clear gain, and will alone form an article of saving, which may be regarded as an equivalent for any additional objects of expence that may be occasioned by the adoption of the new system.

The result from these observations is, that the sources of additional expence from the establishment of the proposed constitution are much fewer than may have been imagined, that they are counterbalanced by considerable objects of saving, and that while it is questionable on which side the scale will preponderate, it is certain that a government less expensive would be incompetent to the purposes of the union.

PUBLIUS.

THE FEDERALIST NO. 85
ALEXANDER HAMILTON

May 28, 1788

According to the formal division of the subject of these papers, announced in my first number, there would appear still to remain for discussion, two points, "the analogy of the proposed government to your own state constitution," and "the additional security, which its adoption will afford to republican government, to liberty and to property." But these heads have been so fully anticipated and exhausted in the progress of the work, that it would now scarcely be possible to do any thing more than repeat, in a more dilated form, what has been heretofore said; which the advanced stage of the question, and the time already spent upon it conspire to forbid.

It is remarkable, that the resemblance of the plan of the convention to the act which organizes the government of this state holds, not less with regard to many of the supposed defects, than to the real excellencies of the former. Among the pretended defects, are the re-eligibility of the executive, the want of a council, the omission of a formal bill of rights, the omission of a provision respecting the liberty of the press: These and several others, which have been noted in the course of our inquiries, are as much chargeable on the existing constitution of this state, as on the one proposed for the Union. And a man must have slender pretensions to consistency, who can rail at the latter for imperfections which he finds no difficulty in excusing in the former. Nor indeed can there be a better proof of the insincerity and affectation of some of the zealous adversaries of the plan of the convention among us, who profess to be the devoted admirers of the government under which they live, than the fury with which they have attacked that plan, for matters in regard to which our own constitution is equally, or perhaps more vulnerable.

The additional securities to republican government, to liberty and to property, to be derived from the adoption of the plan under consideration, consist chiefly in the restraints which the preservation of the union will impose on local factions and insurrections, and on the ambition of powerful individuals in single states, who might acquire credit and influence enough, from leaders and favorites, to become the despots of the people; in the diminution of the opportunities to foreign intrigue, which the dissolution of the confederacy would invite and facilitate; in the prevention of extensive military establishments, which could not fail to grow out of wars between the states in a disunited situation; in the express guarantee of a republican form of government to each; in the absolute and universal exclusion of titles of nobility; and in the precautions against the repetition of those practices on the part of the state governments, which have undermined the foundations of property and credit, have planted mutual distrust in the breasts of all classes of citizens, and have occasioned an almost universal prostration of morals.

Thus have I, my fellow citizens, executed the task I had assigned to myself; with what success, your conduct must determine. I trust at least you will admit, that I have not failed in the assurance I gave you respecting the spirit with which my endeavours should be conducted. I have addressed myself purely to your judgments, and have studiously avoided those asperities which are too apt to disgrace political disputants of all parties, and which have been not a little provoked by the language and conduct of the opponents of the constitution. The charge of a conspiracy against the liberties of the people, which has been indiscriminately brought against the advocates of the plan, has something in it too wanton and too malignant not to excite the indignation of every man who feels in his own bosom a refutation of the calumny. The perpetual charges which have been rung upon the wealthy, the well-born and the great, have been such as to inspire the disgust of all sensible men. And the unwarrantable concealments and misrepresentations which have been in various ways practiced to keep the truth from the public eye, have been of a nature to demand the reprobation of all honest men. It is not impossible that these circumstances may have occasionally betrayed me into intemperances of expression which I did not intend: It is certain that I have frequently felt a struggle between sensibility and moderation, and if the former has in some instances prevailed, it must be my excuse that it has been neither often nor much.

Let us now pause and ask ourselves whether, in the course of these papers, the proposed constitution has not been satisfactorily vindicated from the aspersions thrown upon it, and whether it has not been shewn to be worthy of the public approbation, and necessary to the public safety and prosperity. Every man is bound to answer these questions to himself, according to the best of his conscience and understanding, and to act agreeably to the genuine and sober dictates of his judgment. This is a duty, from which nothing can give him a dispensation. 'Tis one that he is called upon, nay, constrained by all the obligations that form the bands of society, to discharge sincerely and honestly. No partial motive, no particular interest, no pride of opinion, no temporary passion or prejudice, will justify to himself, to his country or to his posterity, an improper election of the part he is to act. Let him beware of an obstinate adherence to party. Let him reflect that the object upon which he is to decide is not a particular interest of the community, but the very existence of the nation. And let him remember that a majority of America has already given its sanction to the plan, which he is to approve or reject.

I shall not dissemble, that I feel an intire confidence in the arguments, which recommend the proposed system to your adoption; and that I am unable to discern any real force in those by which it has been opposed. I am persuaded, that it is the best which our political situation, habits and opinions will admit, and superior to any the revolution has produced.

Concessions on the part of the friends of the plan, that it has not a claim to absolute perfection, has afforded matter of no small triumph to its enemies. Why, say they, should we adopt an imperfect thing? Why not amend it, and make it perfect before it is irrevocably established? This may be plausible enough, but it is only plausible. In the first place I remark, that the extent of these concessions has been greatly exaggerated. They have been stated as amounting to an admission, that the plan is radically defective; and that, without material alterations, the rights and the interests of the community cannot be safely confided to it. This, as far as I have understood the meaning of those who make the concessions, is an intire perversion of their sense. No advocate of the measure can be found who will not declare as his sentiment, that the system, though it may not be perfect in every part, is upon the whole a good one, is the best that the present views and circumstances of the country will permit, and is such an one as promises every species of security which a reasonable people can desire.

I answer in the next place, that I should esteem it the extreme of imprudence to prolong the precarious state of our national affairs, and to expose the union to the jeopardy of successive experiments, in the chimerical pursuit of a perfect plan. I never expect to see a perfect work from imperfect man. The result of the deliberations of all collective bodies must necessarily be a compound as well of the errors and prejudices, as of the good sense and wisdom of the individuals of whom they are composed. The compacts which are to embrace thirteen distinct states, in a common bond of amity and union, must as necessarily be a compromise of as many dissimilar interests and inclinations. How can perfection spring from such materials?

The reasons assigned in an excellent little pamphlet lately published in this city* are unanswerable to shew the utter improbability of assembling a new convention, under circumstances in any degree so favourable to a happy issue, as those in which the late convention met, deliberated and concluded. I will not repeat the arguments there used, as I presume the production itself has had an extensive circulation. It is certainly well worthy the perusal of every friend to his country. There is however one point of light in which the subject of amendments still remains to be considered; and in which it has not yet been exhibited to public view. I cannot resolve to conclude, without first taking a survey of it in this aspect.

It appears to me susceptible of absolute demonstration, that it will be far more easy to obtain subsequent than previous amendments to the constitution. The moment an alteration is made in the present plan, it becomes, to the purpose of adoption, a new one, and must undergo a new decision of each state. To its complete establishment throughout the union, it will therefore require the concurrence of thirteen states. If, on the contrary, the constitution proposed should once be ratified by all the states as it stands, alterations in it may at any time be effected by nine states. Here then the chances are as thirteen to nine† in favour of subsequent amendments, rather than of the original adoption of an intire system.

This is not all. Every constitution for the United States must inevitably consist of a great variety of particulars, in which thirteen independent states are to be accommodated in their interests or opinions of interest. We may of course expect to see, in any body of men charged with its original formation, very different combinations of the parts upon different points. Many of those who form the majority on one question may become the minority on a second, and an association dissimilar to either may constitute the majority on a third. Hence the necessity of moulding and arranging all the particulars which are to compose the whole in such a manner as to satisfy all the parties to the compact; and hence also an immense multiplication of difficulties and casualties in obtaining the collective assent to a final act. The degree of that multiplication

* Intitled "An Address to the people of the state of New-York."

† It may rather be said TEN, for though two-thirds may set on foot the measure, three-fourths must ratify.

must evidently be in a ratio to the number of particulars and the number of parties.

But every amendment to the constitution, if once established, would be a single proposition, and might be brought forward singly. There would then be no necessity for management or compromise, in relation to any other point, no giving nor taking. The will of the requisite number would at once bring the matter to a decisive issue. And consequently whenever nine* or rather ten states, were united in the desire of a particular amendment, that amendment must infallibly take place. There can therefore be no comparison between the facility of effecting an amendment, and that of establishing in the first instance a complete constitution.

In opposition to the probability of subsequent amendments it has been urged, that the persons delegated to the administration of the national government, will always be disinclined to yield up any portion of the authority of which they were once possessed. For my own part I acknowledge a thorough conviction that any amendments which may, upon mature consideration, be thought useful, will be applicable to the organization of the government, not to the mass of its powers; and on this account alone, I think there is no weight in the observation just stated. I also think there is little weight in it on another account. The intrinsic difficulty of governing THIRTEEN STATES at any rate, independent of calculations upon an ordinary degree of public spirit and integrity, will, in my opinion, constantly *impose* on the national rulers the *necessity* of a spirit of accommodation to the reasonable expectations of their constituents. But there is yet a further consideration, which proves beyond the possibility of doubt, that the observation is futile. It is this, that the national rulers, whenever nine states concur, will have no option upon the subject. By the fifth article of the plan the congress will be *obliged,* "on the application of the legislatures of two-thirds of the states, (which at present amounts to nine) to call a convention for proposing amendments, which *shall be valid* to all intents and purposes, as part of the constitution, when ratified by the legislatures of three-fourths of the states, or by conventions in three-fourths thereof." The words of this article are peremptory. The congress "*shall* call a convention." Nothing in this particular is left to the discretion of that body. And of consequence all the declamation about their disinclina-

* It may rather be said TEN, for though two-thirds may set on foot the measure, three-fourths must ratify.

tion to a change, vanishes in air. Nor however difficult it may be supposed to unite two-thirds or three-fourths of the state legislatures, in amendments which may affect local interests, can there be any room to apprehend any such difficulty in a union on points which are merely relative to the general liberty or security of the people. We may safely rely on the disposition of the state legislatures to erect barriers against the encroachments of the national authority.

If the foregoing argument is a fallacy, certain it is that I am myself deceived by it; for it is, in my conception, one of those rare instances in which a political truth can be brought to the test of mathematical demonstration. Those who see the matter in the same light with me, however zealous they may be for amendments, must agree in the propriety of a previous adoption, as the most direct road to their own object.

The zeal for attempts to amend, prior to the establishment of the constitution, must abate in every man, who, is ready to accede to the truth of the following observations of a writer, equally solid and ingenious: "To balance a large state or society (says he) whether monarchial or republican, on general laws, is a work of so great difficulty, that no human genius, however comprehensive, is able by the mere dint of reason and reflection, to effect it. The judgments of many must unite in the work: EXPERIENCE must guide their labour: TIME must bring it to perfection: And the FEELING of inconveniences must correct the mistakes which they *inevitably* fall into, in their first trials and experiments."* These judicious reflections contain a lesson of moderation to all the sincere lovers of the union, and ought to put them upon their guard against hazarding anarchy, civil war, a perpetual alienation of the states from each other, and perhaps the military despotism of a victorious demagogue, in the pursuit of what they are not likely to obtain, but from TIME and EXPERIENCE. It may be in me a defect of political fortitude, but I acknowledge, that I cannot entertain an equal tranquillity with those who affect to treat the dangers of a longer continuance in our present situation as imaginary. A NATION without a NATIONAL GOVERNMENT is, in my view, an awful spectacle. The establishment of a constitution, in time of profound peace, by the voluntary consent of a whole people, is a PRODIGY, to the completion of which I look forward with trembling anxiety. I can reconcile it to no rules of prudence to let go the hold we now have, in so ardu-

* Hume's Essays, vol. I, page 128.—The rise of arts and sciences.

ous an enterprise, upon seven out of the thirteen states; and after having passed over so considerable a part of the ground to recommence the course. I dread the more the consequences of new attempts, because I KNOW that POWERFUL INDIVIDUALS, in this and in other states, are enemies to a general national government, in every possible shape.

PUBLIUS.

THE CONSTITUTION As far as its effect upon the nature of American society is concerned, the Constitution was undoubtedly the most important document to emerge from the era of the American Revolution. If it has too often been characterized as God-given and God-endowed, this is no more than an indication of its immense success; its original purpose was to provide the cement which would bind the Union together, and in this it has succeeded remarkably well. The "more perfect Union" that it established was not to be challenged until eighty-three years had passed. Since that time, it has not been challenged at all.

But the Constitution created in Philadelphia in 1787 is not the Constitution under which we live today. On December 15, 1791, the First Ten Amendments, known as the Bill of Rights, were added. Subsequent amendments made further changes in the original document. And perhaps even more important in changing the Constitution has been the continuous process of judicial interpretation, which has forced the nation to periodically re-examine what the Founding Fathers agreed upon at Philadelphia. It remains, however, a document with an air of permanence, and the system of representative government that it molded is as good a testimony to its effectiveness as anything else. For, no matter how severely threatened, that system has endured until today.

The Constitution of The United States of America

WE THE PEOPLE of the United States, in Order to form a more perfect Union, establish Justice, insure domestic Tranquility, provide for the common defence, promote the general Welfare, and secure the Blessings of Liberty to ourselves and our Posterity, do ordain and establish this CONSTITUTION for the United States of America.

ARTICLE I.

SECTION 1. All legislative Powers herein granted shall be vested in a Congress of the United States which shall consist of a Senate and House of Representatives.

SECTION 2. The House of Representatives shall be composed of Members chosen every second Year by the People of the several States, and the Electors in each State shall have the Qualifications requisite for Electors of the most numerous Branch of the State Legislature.

No Person shall be a Representative who shall not have attained to the Age of twenty-five Years, and been seven Years a Citizen of the United States, and who shall not, when elected, be an Inhabitant of that State in which he shall be chosen.

Representatives and direct Taxes shall be apportioned among the several States which may be included within this Union, according to their respective Numbers, which shall be determined by adding to the whole Number of free Persons, including those bound to Service for a Term of Years, and excluding Indians not taxed, three fifths of all other Persons. The actual Enumeration shall be made within three Years after the first Meeting of the Congress of the United States, and within every subsequent Term of ten Years, in such Manner as they shall by Law direct. The Number of Representatives shall not exceed one for every thirty Thousand, but each State shall have at Least one Representative; and until such enumeration shall be made, the State of New Hampshire shall be entitled to chuse three, Massachusetts eight, Rhode-Island and Providence Plantations one, Connecticut five, New-York six, New Jersey four, Pennsylvania eight, Delaware one, Maryland six, Virginia ten, North Carolina five, South Carolina five, and Georgia three.

When vacancies happen in the Representation from any State, the Executive Authority thereof shall issue Writs of Election to fill such Vacancies.

The House of Representatives shall chuse their Speaker and other Officers; and shall have the sole Power of Impeachment.

SECTION 3. The Senate of United States shall be composed of two Senators from each State, chosen by the Legislature thereof, for six Years; and each Senator shall have one Vote.

Immediately after they shall be assembled in Consequence of the first Election, they shall be divided as equally as may be into three Classes. The Seats of the Senators of the first Class shall be vacated at the Expiration of the second Year, of the second Class at the Expiration of the fourth Year, and of the third Class at the Expiration of the sixth Year, so that one-third may be chosen every second Year; and if Vacancies happen by Resignation, or otherwise, during the

Recess of the Legislature of any State, the Executive thereof may make temporary Appointments until the next Meeting of the Legislature, which shall then fill such Vacancies.

No Person shall be a Senator who shall not have attained to the Age of thirty Years, and been nine Years a Citizen of the United States, and who shall not, when elected, be an Inhabitant of that State for which he shall be chosen.

The Vice President of the United States shall be President of the Senate, but shall have no Vote, unless they be equally divided.

The Senate shall chuse their other Officers, and also a President pro tempore, in the absence of the Vice President, or when he shall exercise the Office of President of the United States.

The Senate shall have the sole Power to try all Impeachments. When sitting for that Purpose, they shall be on Oath or Affirmative. When the President of the United States is tried, the Chief Justice shall preside: And no Person shall be convicted without the Concurrence of two thirds of the Members present.

Judgment in Cases of Impeachment shall not extend further than to removal from Office, and disqualification to hold and enjoy any Office of honor, Trust or Profit under the United States; but the Party convicted shall nevertheless be liable and subject to Indictment, Trial, Judgment and Punishment, according to Law.

SECTION 4. The Times, Places and Manner of holding Elections for Senators and Representatives, shall be prescribed in each State by the Legislature thereof; but the Congress may at any time by Law make or alter such Regulations, except as to the Place of Chusing Senators.

The Congress shall assemble at least once in every Year, and such Meeting shall be on the first Monday in December, unless they shall by Law appoint a different Day.

SECTION 5. Each House shall be the Judge of the Elections, Returns and Qualifications of its own Members, and a Majority of each shall constitute a Quorum to do Business; but a smaller number may adjourn from day to day, and may be authorized to compel the Attendance of absent Members, in such Manner, and under such Penalties as each House may provide.

Each House may determine the Rules of its Proceedings, punish its Members for disorderly Behavior, and, with the Concurrence of two thirds, expel a Member.

Each House shall keep a Journal of its Proceedings, and from time to time publish the same, excepting such Parts as may in their Judgment require Secrecy; and the Yeas and Nays of the Members of either House on any question shall, at the Desire of one fifth of those Present, be entered on the Journal.

Neither House, during the Session of Congress, shall, without the Consent of the other, adjourn for more than three days, nor to any other Place than that in which the two Houses shall be sitting.

SECTION 6. The Senators and Representatives shall receive a Compensation for their Services, to be ascertained by Law, and paid out of the Treasury of the United States. They shall in all Cases, except Treason, Felony and Breach of the Peace, be privileged from Arrest during their Attendance at the Session of their respective Houses, and in going to and returning from the same; and for any Speech or Debate in either House, they shall not be questioned in any other Place.

No Senator or Representative shall, during the Time for which he was elected, be appointed to any civil Office under the Authority of the United States, which shall have been created, or the Emoluments whereof shall have been encreased during such time; and no Person holding any Office under the United States, shall be a Member of either House during his Continuance in Office.

SECTION 7. All Bills for raising Revenue shall originate in the House of Representatives; but the Senate may propose or concur with Amendments as on other Bills.

Every Bill which shall have passed the House of Representatives and the Senate, shall, before it becomes a Law, be presented to the President of the United States; If he approve he shall sign it, but if not he shall return it, with his Objections to that House in which it shall have originated, who shall enter the Objections at large on their Journal, and proceed to reconsider it. If after such Reconsideration two thirds of that House shall agree to pass the Bill, it shall be sent, together with the Objections, to the other House, by which it shall likewise be reconsidered, and if approved by two thirds of that House, it shall become a Law. But in all such Cases the Votes of both Houses shall be determined by Yeas and Nays, and the Names of the Persons voting for and against the Bill shall be entered on the Journal of each House respectively. If any Bill shall not be returned by the President within ten Days (Sundays excepted) after it shall have been presented to him, the Same shall be a Law, in like Manner as if he had signed it, unless the Congress by their Adjournment prevent its Return, in which Case it shall not be a Law.

Every Order, Resolution, or Vote to which the Concurrence of the Senate and House of Representatives may be necessary (except on a question of Adjournment) shall be presented to the President of the United States; and before the Same shall take Effect, shall be approved by him, or being disapproved by him, shall be repassed by two thirds of the Senate and House of Representatives, according to the Rules and Limitations prescribed in the Case of a Bill.

SECTION 8. The Congress shall have Power to lay and collect Taxes, Duties, Imposts and Excises, to pay the Debts and provide for the common Defence and general Welfare of the United States; but all Duties, Imposts and Excises shall be uniform throughout the United States;

To borrow money on the credit of the United States;

To regulate Commerce with foreign Nations, and among the several States, and with the Indian Tribes;

To establish an uniform Rule of Naturalization, and uniform Laws on the subject of Bankruptcies throughout the United States;

To coin Money, regulate the Value thereof, and of foreign Coin, and fix the Standard of Weights and Measures;

To provide for the Punishment of counterfeiting the Securities and current Coin of the United States;

To establish Post Offices and post Roads;

To promote the Progress of Science and useful Arts, by securing for limited Times to Authors and Inventors the exclusive Right to their respective Writings and Discoveries;

To constitute Tribunals inferior to the supreme Court;

To define and punish Piracies and Felonies committed on the high Seas, and Offenses against the Law of Nations;

To declare War, grant Letters of Marque and Reprisal, and make Rules concerning Captures on Land and Water;

To raise and support Armies, but no Appropriation of Money to that Use shall be for a longer Term than two Years;

To provide and maintain a Navy;

To make Rules for the Government and Regulation of the land and naval Forces;

To provide for calling forth the Militia to execute the Laws of the Union, suppress Insurrections and repel Invasions;

To provide for organizing, arming, and disciplining the Militia, and for governing such Part of them as may be employed in the Service of the United States, reserving to the States respectively, the Appointment of the Officers, and the Authority of training the Militia according to the discipline prescribed by Congress;

To exercise exclusive Legislation in all Cases whatsoever, over such District (not exceeding ten Miles square) as may, by Cession of particular States, and the acceptance of Congress, become the Seat of the Government of the United States, and to exercise like Authority over all Places purchased by the Consent of the Legislature of the State in which the Same shall be, for the Erection of Forts, Magazines, Arsenals, dock-Yards, and other needful Buildings;—And

To make all Laws which shall be necessary and proper for carrying into Execution the foregoing Powers, and all other Powers vested by this Constitution in the Government of the United States, or in any Department or Officer thereof.

SECTION 9. The Migration or Importation of such Persons as any of the States now existing shall think proper to admit, shall not be prohibited by the Congress prior to the Year one thousand eight hundred and eight, but a tax or duty may be imposed on such Importation, not exceeding ten dollars for each Person.

The privilege of the Writ of Habeas Corpus shall not be suspended, unless when in Cases of Rebellion or Invasion the public Safety may require it.

No Bill of Attainder or ex post facto Law shall be passed.

No capitation, or other direct, Tax shall be laid, unless in Proportion to the Census or Enumeration herein before directed to be taken.

No Tax or Duty shall be laid on Articles exported from any State.

No Preference shall be given by any Regulation of Commerce or Revenue to the Ports of one State over those of another: nor shall Vessels bound to, or from, one State, be obliged to enter, clear, or pay Duties in another.

No Money shall be drawn from the Treasury, but in Consequence of Appropriations made by Law; and a regular Statement and Account of the Receipts and Expenditures of all public Money shall be published from time to time.

No Title of Nobility shall be granted by the United States: And no Person holding any Office of Profit or Trust under them, shall, without the Consent of the Congress, accept of any present, Emolument, Office, or Title, of any kind whatever, from any King, Prince, or foreign State.

SECTION 10. No State shall enter into any Treaty, Alliance, or Confederation; grant Letters of Marque and Reprisal; coin Money; emit Bills of Credit; make any Thing but gold and silver Coin a Tender in Payment of Debts; pass any Bill of Attainder, ex post facto Law, or Law impairing the Obligation of Contracts, or grant any Title of Nobility.

No State shall, without the Consent of the Congress, lay any Imposts or Duties on Imports or Exports, except what may be absolutely necessary for executing it's inspection Laws: and the net Produce of all Duties and Imposts, laid by any State on Imports or Exports, shall be for the Use of the Treasury of the United States; and all such Laws shall be subject to the Revision and Controul of the Congress.

No State shall, without the Consent of Congress, lay any duty of Tonnage, keep Troops, or Ships of War in time of Peace, enter into any Agreement or Compact with another State, or with a foreign Power, or engage in War, unless actually invaded, or in such imminent Danger as will not admit of delay.

ARTICLE II.

SECTION 1. The executive Power shall be vested in a President of the United States of America. He shall hold his Office during the Term of four Years, and, together with the Vice-President, chosen for the same Term, be elected, as follows

Each State shall appoint, in such Manner as the Legislature thereof may direct, a Number of Electors, equal to the whole Number of Senators and Representatives to which the State may be entitled in the Congress: but no Senator or Representative, or Person holding an Office of Trust or Profit under the United States, shall be appointed an Elector.

The Electors shall meet in their respective States, and vote by Ballot for two persons, of whom one at least shall not be an Inhabitant of the same State with themselves. And they shall make a List of all the Persons voted for, and of the Number of Votes for each; which List they shall sign and certify, and transmit sealed to the Seat of the Government of the United States, directed to the President of the Senate. The President of the Senate shall, in the Presence of the Senate and House of Representatives, open all the Certificates, and the Votes shall then be counted. The Person having the greatest Number of Votes shall be the President, if such Number be a Majority of the whole Number of Electors appointed; and if there be more than one who have such Majority, and have an equal Number of Votes, then the House of Representatives shall immediately chuse by Ballot one of them for President; and if no Person have a Majority, then from the five highest on the List the said House shall in like Manner chuse the President. But in chusing the President, the Votes shall be taken by States, the Representation from each State having one Vote; A quorum for this Purpose shall consist of a Member or Members from two-thirds of the States, and a Majority of all the States shall be necessary to a Choice. In every Case, after the Choice of the President, the Person having the greatest Number of Votes of the Electors shall be the Vice President. But if there should remain two or more who have equal Votes, the Senate shall chuse from them by Ballot the Vice-President.

The Congress may determine the Time of chusing the Electors, and the Day on which they shall give their Votes; which Day shall be the same throughout the United States.

No person except a natural born Citizen, or a Citizen of the United States, at the time of the Adoption of this Constitution, shall be eligible to the Office of President; neither shall any Person be eligible to that Office who shall not have attained to the Age of thirty-five Years, and been fourteen Years a Resident within the United States.

In Case of the Removal of the President from Office, or of his Death, Resignation, or Inability to discharge the Powers and Duties of the said Office, the same shall devolve on the Vice President, and the Congress may by Law provide for the Case of Removal, Death, Resignation or Inability, both of the President and Vice President, declaring what Officer shall then act as President, and such Officer shall act accordingly, until the Disability be removed, or a President shall be elected.

The President shall, at stated Times, receive for his Services, a Compensation, which shall neither be encreased nor diminished during the Period for which he shall have been elected, and he shall not receive within that Period any other Emolument from the United States, or any of them.

Before he enter on the Execution of his Office, he shall take the following Oath or Affirmation:—"I do solemnly swear (or affirm) that I will faithfully execute the Office of President of the United States, and will to the best of my Ability, preserve, protect and defend the Constitution of the United States."

SECTION 2. The President shall be Commander in Chief

of the Army and Navy of the United States, and of the Militia of the several States, when called into the actual Service of the United States; he may require the Opinion in writing, of the principal Officer in each of the executive Departments, upon any subject relating to the Duties of their respective Offices, and he shall have Power to Grant Reprieves and Pardons for Offenses against the United States, except in Cases of Impeachment.

He shall have Power, by and with the Advice and Consent of the Senate, to make Treaties, provided two-thirds of the Senators present concur; and he shall nominate, and by and with the Advice and Consent of the Senate, shall appoint Ambassadors, other public Ministers and Consuls, Judges of the supreme Court, and all other Officers of the United States, whose Appointments are not herein otherwise provided for, and which shall be established by Law: but the Congress may by Law vest the Appointment of such inferior Officers, as they think proper, in the President alone, in the Courts of Law, or in the Heads of Departments.

The President shall have Power to fill up all Vacancies that may happen during the Recess of the Senate, by granting Commissions which shall expire at the End of their next Session.

SECTION 3. He shall from time to time give to the Congress Information of the State of the Union, and recommend to their Consideration such Measures as he shall judge necessary and expedient; he may, on extraordinary Occasions, convene both Houses, or either of them, and in Case of Disagreement between them, with Respect to the Time of Adjournment, he may adjourn them to such Time as he shall think proper; he shall receive Ambassadors and other public Ministers; he shall take Care that the Laws be faithfully executed, and shall Commission all the Officers of the United States.

SECTION 4. The President, Vice President and all civil Officers of the United States, shall be removed from Office on Impeachment for, and Conviction of, Treason, Bribery, or other high Crimes and Misdemeanors.

ARTICLE III.

SECTION 1. The judicial Power of the United States, shall be vested in one supreme Court, and in such inferior Courts as the Congress may from time to time ordain and establish.

The Judges, both of the supreme and inferior Courts, shall hold their Offices during good Behaviour, and shall, at stated Times, receive for their Services a Compensation which shall not be diminished during their Continuance in Office.

SECTION 2. The judicial Power shall extend to all Cases, in Law and Equity, arising under this Constitution, the Laws of the United States, and Treaties made, or which shall be made, under their Authority;—to all Cases affecting Ambassadors, other public Ministers and Consuls;—to all Cases of admiralty and maritime Jurisdiction;—to Controversies to which the United States shall be a Party;—to Controversies between two or more States;—between a State and Citizens of another State;—between Citizens of different States;—between Citizens of the same State claiming Lands under Grants of different States, and between a State, or the Citizens thereof, and foreign States, Citizens or Subjects.

In all Cases affecting Ambassadors, other public Ministers and Consuls, and those in which a State shall be Party, the supreme Court shall have original Jurisdiction. In all the other Cases before mentioned, the supreme Court shall have appellate Jurisdiction, both as to Law and Fact, with such Exceptions, and under such Regulations as the Congress shall make.

The trial of all Crimes, except in Cases of Impeachment, shall be by Jury; and such Trial shall be held in the State where the said Crimes shall have been committed; but when not committed within any State, the Trial shall be at such Place or Places as the Congress may by Law have directed.

SECTION 3. Treason against the United States, shall consist only in levying War against them, or in adhering to their Enemies, giving them Aid and Comfort. No Person shall be convicted of Treason unless on the Testimony of two Witnesses to the same overt Act, or on Confession in open Court.

The Congress shall have power to declare the Punishment of Treason, but no Attainder of Treason shall work Corruption of Blood, or Forfeiture except during the Life of the Person attainted.

ARTICLE IV.

SECTION 1. Full Faith and Credit shall be given in each State to the public Acts, Records, and judicial Proceedings of every other State. And the Congress may by general Laws prescribe the Manner in which such Acts, Records and Proceedings shall be proved, and the Effect thereof.

SECTION 2. The Citizens of each State shall be entitled to all Privileges and Immunities of Citizens in the several States.

A Person charged in any State with Treason, Felony, or other Crime, who shall flee from Justice, and be found in another State, shall on demand of the executive Authority of the State from which he fled, be delivered up, to be removed to the State having Jurisdiction of the Crime.

No Person held to Service or Labour in one State, under the Laws thereof, escaping into another, shall, in Consequence of any Law or Regulation therein, be discharged from such Service or Labour, but shall be delivered up on Claim of the Party to whom such Service or Labour may be due.

SECTION 3. New States may be admitted by the Congress into this Union; but no new State shall be formed or erected within the Jurisdiction of any other State; nor any State be formed by the Junction of two or more States, or parts of States, without the Consent of the Legislatures of the States concerned as well as of the Congress.

The Congress shall have Power to dispose of and make all needful Rules and Regulations respecting the Territory or other Property belonging to the United States; and nothing in this Constitution shall be so construed as to Prejudice any Claims of the United States, or of any particular State.

SECTION 4. The United States shall guarantee to every State in this Union a Republican Form of Government, and shall protect each of them against Invasion; and on Application of the Legislature, or of the Executive (when the Legislature cannot be convened) against domestic Violence.

ARTICLE V.

The Congress, whenever two-thirds of both Houses shall deem it necessary, shall propose Amendments to this Constitution, or, on the Application of the Legislatures of two-thirds of the several States, shall call a Convention for proposing Amendments, which, in either Case, shall be valid to all Intents and Purposes, as part of this Constitution, when ratified by the Legislatures of three-fourths of the several States, or by Conventions in three-fourths thereof, as the one or the other Mode of Ratification may be proposed by the Congress; Provided that no Amendment which may be made prior to the Year One thousand eight hundred and eight shall in any Manner affect the first and fourth Clauses in the Ninth

Section of the first Article; and that no State, without its Consent, shall be deprived of its equal Suffrage in the Senate.

ARTICLE VI.

All Debts contracted and Engagements entered into, before the Adoption of this Constitution, shall be as valid against the United States under this Constitution, as under the Confederation.

This Constitution, and the Laws of the United States which shall be made in Pursuance thereof; and all Treaties made, or which shall be made, under the Authority of the United States, shall be the supreme Law of the Land; and the Judges in every State shall be bound thereby, any Thing in the Constitution or Laws of any State to the Contrary notwithstanding.

The Senators and Representatives before mentioned, and the Members of the several State Legislatures, and all executive and judicial Officers, both of the United States and of the several States, shall be bound by Oath or Affirmation, to support this Constitution; but no religious Test shall ever be required as a Qualification to any Office or public Trust under the United States.

ARTICLE VII.

The Ratification of the Conventions of nine States shall be sufficient for the Establishment of this Constitution between the States so ratifying the Same.

DONE in Convention by the Unanimous Consent of the States present the Seventeenth Day of September in the Year of our Lord one thousand seven hundred and Eighty seven and of the Independence of the United States of America the Twelfth. In Witness whereof We have hereunto subscribed our Names.

Go WASHINGTON
Presidt and deputy from Virginia

New Hampshire.
JOHN LANGDON
NICHOLAS GILMAN

Massachusetts.
NATHANIEL GORHAM
RUFUS KING

Connecticut.
WM SAML JOHNSON
ROGER SHERMAN

New York.
ALEXANDER HAMILTON

New Jersey.
WIL: LIVINGSTON
DAVID BREARLEY
WM PATTERSON
JONA: DAYTON

Pennsylvania.
B. FRANKLIN
ROBT. MORRIS
THOS FITZSIMONS
JAMES WILSON
THOMAS MIFFLIN
GEO. CLYMER
JARED INGERSOLL
GOUV MORRIS

Delaware.
GEO: READ
JOHN DICKINSON
JACO: BROOM
GUNNING BEDFORD jun
RICHARD BASSETT

Maryland.
JAMES McHENRY
DANL CARROLL
DAN: of ST THOS JENIFER

Virginia.
JOHN BLAIR—
JAMES MADISON Jr.

North Carolina.
WM BLOUNT
HU WILLIAMSON

South Carolina.
J. RUTLEDGE
CHARLES PINCKNEY
CHARLES COTESWORTH PINCKNEY
PIERCE BUTLER.

Georgia.
WILLIAM FEW
ABR BALDWIN

Attest:

WILLIAM JACKSON, *Secretary.*

ARTICLES IN ADDITION TO, AND AMENDMENT OF, THE CONSTITUTION OF THE UNITED STATES OF AMERICA, PROPOSED BY CONGRESS, AND RATIFIED BY THE LEGISLATURES OF THE SEVERAL STATES, PURSUANT TO THE FIFTH ARTICLE OF THE ORIGINAL CONSTITUTION.

[ARTICLE I.]

Congress shall make no law respecting an establishment of religion, or prohibiting the free exericse thereof; or abridging the freedom of speech, or of the press; or the right of the people peaceably to assemble, and to petition the Government for a redress of grievances.

[ARTICLE II.]

A well regulated Militia, being necessary to the security of a free State, the right of the people to keep and bear Arms, shall not be infringed.

[ARTICLE III.]

No Soldier shall, in time of peace be quartered in any house, without the consent of the Owner, nor in time of war, but in a manner to be prescribed by law.

[ARTICLE IV.]

The right of the people to be secure in their persons, houses, papers, and effects, against unreasonable searches and seizures, shall not be violated, and no Warrants shall issue, but upon probable cause, supported by Oath or affirmation, and particularly describing the place to be searched, and the persons or things to be seized.

[ARTICLE V.]

No person shall be held to answer for a capital, or otherwise infamous crime, unless on a presentment or indictment of a Grand Jury, except in cases arising in the land or naval forces, or in the Militia, when in actual service in time of War or public danger; nor shall any person be subject for the same offence to be twice put in jeopardy of life or limb; nor shall be compelled in any criminal case to be a witness against himself, nor be deprived of life, liberty, or property, without due process of law; nor shall private property be taken for public use, without just compensation.

[ARTICLE VI.]

In all criminal prosecutions, the accused shall enjoy the right to a speedy and public trial, by an impartial jury of the State and district wherein the crime shall have been committed, which district shall have been previously ascertained by law, and to be informed of the nature and cause of the accusation; to be confronted with the witnesses against him; to have compulsory process for obtaining witnesses in his favor, and to have the Assistance of Counsel for his defence.

[ARTICLE VII.]

In suits at common law, where the value in controversy shall exceed twenty dollars, the right of trial by jury shall be preserved, and no fact tried by a jury, shall be otherwise re-examined in any Court of the United States, than according to the rules of the common law.

[ARTICLE VIII.]

Excessive bail shall not be required, nor excessive fines imposed, nor cruel and unusual punishments inflicted.

[ARTICLE IX.]

The enumeration in the Constitution, of certain rights, shall not be construed to deny or disparage others retained by the people.

[ARTICLE X.]

The powers not delegated to the United States by the Constitution, nor prohibited by it to the States, are reserved to the States respectively, or to the people.

ARTICLE XI.

The Judicial power of the United States shall not be construed to extend to any suit in law or equity, commenced or prosecuted against one of the United States by Citizens of any Foreign State.

ARTICLE XII.

The Electors shall meet in their respective states and vote by ballot for President and Vice-President, one of whom, at least, shall not be an inhabitant of the same state with themselves; they shall name in their ballots the person voted for as President, and in distinct ballots the person voted for as Vice-President, and they shall make distinct lists of all persons voted for as President, and of all persons voted for as Vice-President, and of the number of votes for each, which lists they shall sign and certify, and transmit sealed to the seat of the government of the United States, directed to the President of the Senate;—The President of the Senate shall, in presence of the Senate and House of Representatives, open all the certificates and the votes shall then be counted;—The person having the greatest number of votes for President, shall be the President, if such number be a majority of the whole number of Electors appointed; and if no person have such majority, then from the persons having the highest numbers not exceeding three on the list of those voted for as President, the House of Representatives shall choose immediately, by ballot, the President. But in choosing the President, the votes shall be taken by states, the representation from each state having one vote; a quorum for this purpose shall consist of a member or members from two-thirds of the states, and a majority of all the states shall be necessary to a choice. And if the House of Representatives shall not choose a President whenever the right of choice shall devolve upon them, before the fourth day of March next following, then the Vice-President shall act as President, as in the case of the death or other constitutional disability of the President.—The person having the greatest number of votes as Vice-President, shall be the Vice-President, if such number be a majority of the whole number of Electors appointed, and if no person have a majority, then from the two highest numbers on the list, the Senate shall choose the Vice-President; a quorum for the purpose shall consist of two-thirds of the whole number of Senators, and a majority of the whole number shall be necessary to a choice. But no person constitutionally ineligible to the office of President shall be eligible to that of Vice-President of the United States.

ARTICLE XIII.

SECTION 1. Neither slavery nor involuntary servitude, except as a punishment for crime whereof the party shall have been duly convicted, shall exist within the United States, or any place subject to their jurisdiction.

SECTION 2. Congress shall have power to enforce this article by appropriate legislation.

ARTICLE XIV.

SECTION 1. All persons born or naturalized in the United States, and subject to the jurisdiction thereof, are citizens of the United States and of the State wherein they reside. No State shall make or enforce any law which shall abridge the privileges or immunities of citizens of the United States; nor shall any State deprive any person of life, liberty, or property, without due process of law; nor deny to any person within its jurisdiction the equal protection of the laws.

SECTION 2. Representatives shall be apportioned among the several States according to their respective numbers, counting the whole number of persons in each State, excluding Indians not taxed. But when the right to vote at any election for the choice of electors for President and Vice-President of the United States, Representatives in Congress, the Executive and Judicial officers of a State, or the members of the Legislature thereof, is denied to any of the male inhabitants of such State, being twenty-one years of age, and citizens of the United States, or in any way abridged, except for participation in rebellion, or other crime, the basis of representation therein shall be reduced in the proportion which the number of such male citizens shall bear to the whole number of male citizens twenty-one years of age in such State.

SECTION 3. No person shall be a Senator or Representative in Congress, or elector of President and Vice-President, or hold any office, civil or military, under the United States, or under any State, who, having previously taken an oath, as a member of Congress, or as an officer of the United States, or as a member of any State legislature, or as an executive or judicial officer of any State, to support the Constitution of the United States, shall have engaged in insurrection or rebellion against the same, or given aid or comfort to the enemies thereof. But Congress may by a vote of two-thirds of each House, remove such disability.

SECTION 4. The validity of the public debt of the United States, authorized by law, including debts incurred for payment of pensions and bounties for services in suppressing insurrection or rebellion, shall not be questioned. But neither the United States nor any State shall assume or pay any debt or obligation incurred in aid of insurrection or rebellion against the United States, or any claim for the loss of emancipation of any slave; but all such debts, obligations and claims shall be held illegal and void.

SECTION 5. The Congress shall have power to enforce, by appropriate legislation, the provisions of this article.

ARTICLE XV.

SECTION 1. The right of citizens of the United States to vote shall not be denied or abridged by the United States or by any State on account of race, color, or previous conditions of servitude—

SECTION 2. The Congress shall have power to enforce this article by appropriate legislation.

ARTICLE XVI.

The Congress shall have power to lay and collect taxes on incomes, from whatever source derived, without apportionment among the several States, and without regard to any census or enumeration.

ARTICLE XVII.

The Senate of the United States shall be composed of two Senators from each State, elected by the people thereof, for six years; and each Senator shall have one vote. The electors in each State shall have the qualifications requisite for electors of the most numerous branch of the State legislatures.

When vacancies happen in the representation of any State in the Senate, the executive authority of such State shall issue writs of election to fill such vacancies: *Provided,* That the legislature of any State may empower the executive thereof to make temporary appointments until the people fill the vacancies by election as the legislature may direct.

This amendment shall not be so construed as to affect the election or term of any Senator chosen before it becomes valid as part of the Constitution.

ARTICLE XVIII.

SECTION 1. After one year from the ratification of this article the manufacture, sale, or transportation of intoxicating liquors therein, the importation thereof into, or the exportation thereof from the United States and all territory subject to the jurisdiction thereof for beverage purposes is hereby prohibited.

SECTION 2. The Congress and the several States shall have concurrent power to enforce this article by appropriate legislation.

SECTION 3. This article shall be inoperative unless it shall have been ratified as an amendment to the Constitution by the legislatures of the several States, as provided in the Constitution, within seven years from the date of the submission hereof to the States by the Congress.

ARTICLE XIX.

The right of citizens of the United States to vote shall not be denied or abridged by the United States or by any State on account of sex.

Congress shall have power to enforce this article by appropriate legislation.

ARTICLE XX.

SECTION 1. The terms of the President and Vice President shall end at noon on the 20th day of January, and the terms of Senators and Representatives at noon on the 3d day of January, of the years in which such terms would have ended if this article had not been ratified; and the terms of their successors shall then begin.

SECTION 2. The Congress shall assemble at least once in every year, and such meeting shall begin at noon on the 3d day of January, unless they shall by law appoint a different day.

SECTION 3. If, at the time fixed for the beginning of the

term of the President, the President elect shall have died, the Vice President elect shall become President. If a President shall not have been chosen before the time fixed for the beginning of his term, or if the President elect shall have failed to qualify, then the Vice President elect shall act as President until a President shall have qualified; and the Congress may by law provide for the case wherein neither a President elect nor a Vice President elect shall have qualified, declaring who shall then act as President, or the manner in which one who is to act shall be selected, and such person shall act accordingly until a President or Vice President shall have qualified.

SECTION 4. The Congress may by law provide for the case of the death of any of the persons from whom the House of Representatives may choose a President whenever the right of choice shall have devolved upon them, and for the case of the death of any of the persons from whom the Senate may choose a Vice President whenever the right of choice shall have devolved upon them.

SECTION 5. Sections 1 and 2 shall take effect on the 15th day of October following the ratification of this article.

SECTION 6. This article shall be inoperative unless it shall have been ratified as an amendment to the Constitution by the legislatures of three-fourths of the several States within seven years from the date of its submission.

ARTICLE XXI.

SECTION 1. The eighteenth article of amendment to the Constitution of the United States is hereby repealed.

SECTION 2. The transportation or importation into any State, Territory, or possession of the United States for delivery or use therein of intoxicating liquors, in violation of the laws thereof, is hereby prohibited.

SECTION 3. The article shall be inoperative unless it shall have been ratified as an amendment to the Constitution by conventions in the several States, as provided in the Constitution, within seven years from the date of the submission hereof to the States by the Congress.

ARTICLE XXII.

SECTION 1. No person shall be elected to the office of the President more than twice, and no person who has held the office of President, or acted as President, for more than two years of a term to which some other person was elected President shall be elected to the office of the President more than once. But this Article shall not apply to any person holding the office of President when this Article was proposed by the Congress, and shall not prevent any person who may be holding the office of President, or acting as President, during the term within which this Article becomes operative from holding the office of President or acting as President during the remainder of such term.

SECTION 2. This article shall be inoperative unless it shall have been ratified as an amendment to the Constitution by the legislatures of three-fourths of the several States within seven years from the date of its submission to the States by the Congress.